THE DIFFICULT FLOWERING OF SURINAM

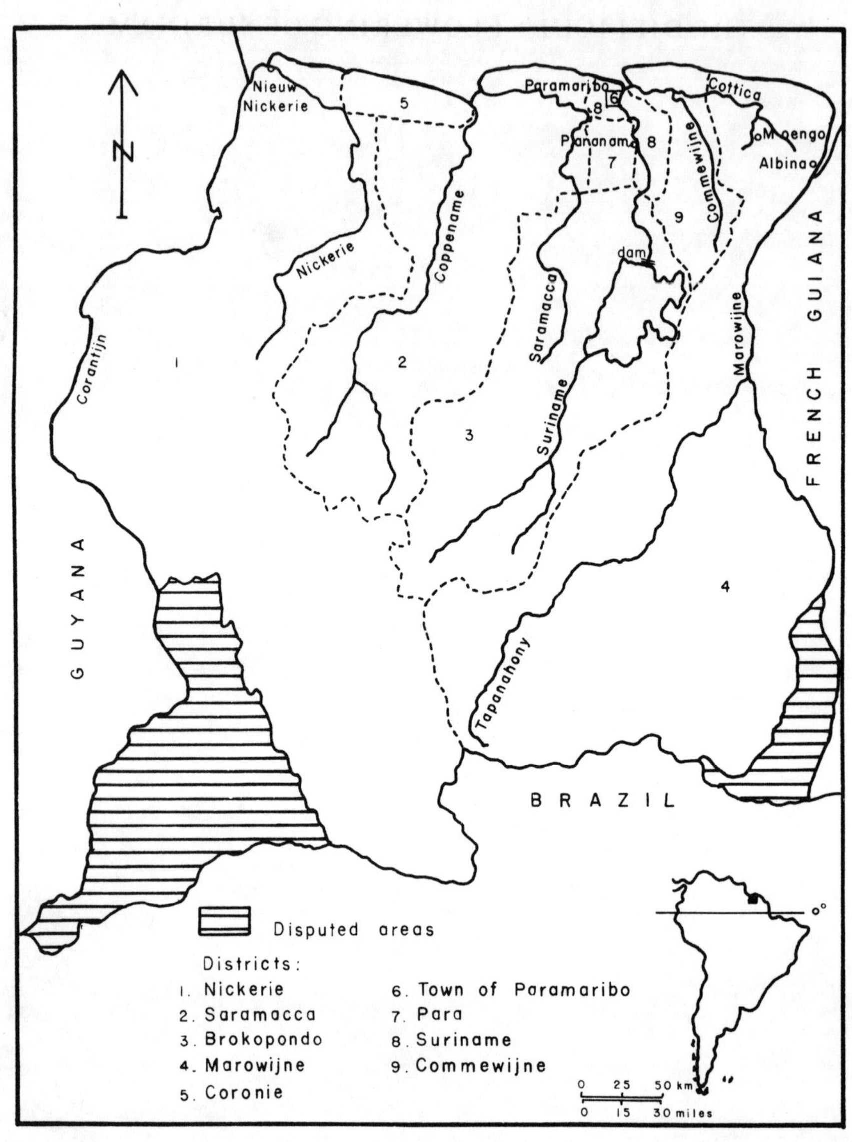
N
Nieuw Nickerie
Paramaribo
Paranam
Cottica
Moengo
Albina
Coppename
Nickerie
Saramacca
Commewijne
dam
Corantijn
Suriname
Marowijne
FRENCH GUIANA
GUYANA
Tapanahony
BRAZIL
1
2
3
4
5
6
7
8
9
Disputed areas
Districts:
1. Nickerie
2. Saramacca
3. Brokopondo
4. Marowijne
5. Coronie
6. Town of Paramaribo
7. Para
8. Suriname
9. Commewijne
0 25 50 km
0 15 30 miles
0°

SURINAM

THE DIFFICULT FLOWERING OF SURINAM

ETHNICITY AND POLITICS IN A PLURAL SOCIETY

by

EDWARD DEW

MARTINUS NIJHOFF/THE HAGUE/1978

FOR MAC and IAN

ISBN 90 247 2057 5

Published with a grant from the Netherlands Organization for the
Advancement of Pure Research

PRINTED IN THE NETHERLANDS

TABLE OF CONTENTS

Foreword vii

Acknowledgements ix

1. INTRODUCTION 1

I. Geography and Economic Conditions 1
II. Ethnic Groups 4
III. Other Sources of Social Differentiation 8

2. THE ROOTS OF ABRASA 21

I. The First Transplants 21
II. The Later Transplants 25
III. Color-Line Conflict Among the Creoles 32
IV. Kielstra and the Change in Cultural Policy 42

3. NATIONALISM, CULTURAL MOBILIZATION, AND THE EMERGENCE OF POLITICAL PARTIES (1942-1948) 49

I. The Socio-Economic Effects of the War 50
II. *Unie Suriname* and the Bos Verschuur Incident 53
III. Defining the Terms of Autonomy 56
IV. Cultural Mobilization and the Rise of Parties 59
V. Delays and *Staten* Impatience 64
VI. Universal Suffrage and the First Roundtable Conference 68

4. THE STRUGGLE FOR POWER IN THE NEW REGIME (1949-1954) 74

I. The 1949 Elections 74
II. The Interim Orders and the Crisis of 1950-51 82
III. The 1951 Elections 93
IV. The Last Roundtable Conferences and the Kingdom Statute 97

5. Verbroedering: Rejection and Approval (1955-1967) 102

I. Trouble in the NPS 103
II. The 1955 Elections 109
III. The *Eenheidsfront* Government 114
IV. The 1958 Elections 117
V. *Verbroedering* in Power 122
VI. The 1963 Elections 133
VII. The Second *Verbroedering* Government 136
VIII. Pengel, Lachmon, and the Politics of *Verbroedering* 138

6. Flying with a Clipped Wing (1967-1973) 142

I. The 1966 Election Law Debate 143
II. The 1967 Elections 145
III. The NPS-VHP Break-up 151
IV. The Strikes of February 1969 and Pengel's Fall 154
V. The 1969 Elections 157
VI. The VHP-PNP Government and Death of Pengel 160
VII. Escalation of Strikes 163
VIII. The 1973 Elections 168

7. The Struggle for Independence (1973-1975) 175

I. The New Government 176
II. Independence by 1975 177
III. Migration and the Double Nationality Problem 179
IV. Tensions in the NPK 180
V. Economic Self-Sufficiency 181
VI. New VHP Demands 181
VII. The Talks, and Fires, of May 184
VIII. New NPK Divisions 185
IX. Strains in the VHP 186
X. The Dutch Parliamentary Debates 188
XI. The "Showdown" 190

8. Conclusion 197

I. The Plural Society and Ethnic Mobilization 197
II. Multipolarity and Consociational Democracy 201
III. The "Outbidding Phenomenon" 206

Bibliography 210

Index 224

FOREWORD

In the months immediately preceding Surinam's independence, November 25, 1975, warning signals went up on both sides of the Atlantic. This small, ethnically plural society was torn by severe political conflict. Elections in November 1973 had brought an end to political collaboration between Creoles and Hindustanis, the country's two largest ethnic groups; and the Creoles, now in control of the government, were resolutely pushing (over Hindustani opposition) to sever their colonial ties with the Netherlands. But defections from the Creole benches during the summer of 1975 had produced a virtual stalemate in the legislature, heightening fears that the government would act unilaterally. The failure of Creole and Hindustani leaders to resolve their differences led many observers in both the Netherlands and Surinam to predict a collapse of democracy and/or violent conflict once independence was proclaimed.

Ironically, the dramatic, last-minute resolution of the struggle precipitated not only general jubilation and relief, but also self-congratulation, as the leaders of Surinam's multiethnic society, long priding themselves on achievements in harmonious understanding, pulled out all stops in their independence day oratory. No-one could forget the nightmare of the preceding few years. But neither could anyone familiar with Surinam's historical development flatly reject the rhetoric as being without some foundation. In fact, Surinam, while severely tested by the most complex multi-ethnic population in the Caribbean, *does* have a record of which she can be proud and which deserves to be more widely known. Far from the beaten (tourist) path, Surinam offers countless pleasant surprises to its visitors, not the least of which is its picture of peaceful cross-ethnic interpersonal relations. A careful study of the development of these relations, from colonial times to the present, should reveal some of the techniques developed (and lessons learned) by Surinamers for grappling with this world-wide social problem.

In particular, Surinam's ethnic politics, for most of its experiment with democratic self-rule, has been guided by what political scientists designate as "consociational" principles involving cross-ethnic resource and power sharing. While it is difficult to conceive of a more effective means to quiet the conflict potential in a multi-ethnic society, the problems in applying these principles need to be pinpointed more clearly. Surinam's apparent abandonment of "consociationalism" in the 1970s is, in many ways, an indication of the model's inherent frailty. Moreover, the ability of the system to survive the independence struggle without bloodshed requires that consociationalism be assessed in a broader perspective.

The theoretical considerations mentioned here will be taken up again in the conclusion. It is the purpose of this study, however, to introduce the general reader to Surinam's ethnic politics, and Chapters One through Seven are organized to tell a story more than to make a point. Chapter One describes the society – its setting, resources, demographic features, and ethnic forces. Chapter Two chronicles Surinam's history from colonial settlement to the outbreak of World War Two, depicting the conditions under which the society's population was assembled and socialized. The next five chapters describe Surinam's modern political development, moving from the formation of ethnic political parties and their struggle over universal suffrage (Three), to intra-ethnic conflict over the consolidation of power (Four), to the development of consociationalism as a technique for achieving ethnic harmony (Five), to that model's breakdown (Six) and the ensuing independence struggle (Seven).

ACKNOWLEDGEMENTS

This study was the result of three periods of research in Surinam (June-August 1971, August 1973-February 1974, and January-February 1976), plus a year's work in the Netherlands (August 1975-August 1976). The funds that made this study possible were provided by the Fairfield University Faculty Research Committee, the Ford and Rockefeller Foundations Program in Support of Social Science and Legal Research on Population Policy, and the Netherlands Institute for Advanced Study in the Humanities and Social Sciences (NIAS).

There are countless Surinamers to be thanked for their assistance in my fieldwork. In particular, I want to single out Fred Ormskirk, Irma Gomes-Tjon, and Earl Glaanen-Weijgel on the staff of Surinam's *Staten*, T.L. Waaldijk, A.J.A. Quintus Bosz, F.E.M. Mitrasing, S.E. Werners, Hans Lim A Po, and Evert Azimullah of the Law School at the University of Surinam, and B.W.H. Bos Verschuur, G.J.C. van der Schroeff, S.F. Helstone, and J. Lemmer. The members of the *Staten*, government officials, and party members that I interviewed were uniformly cooperative and helpful. I am also indebted to H.L. de Vries, C.R. Biswamitre, R.J.A. van Lier, J. Einaar, W.E. Juglall, A.L. Smit, J. Sedney, H.E. Lamur, S. Wolf, A.A. Biswamitre, and J.P. Kaulesar Sukul for their assistance to me in the Netherlands. Fred Ormskirk, B.W.H. Bos Verschuur, and F.E.M. Mitrasing each read the main body of the manuscript and made many valuable comments.

Others who helped this project at various stages were Arend Lijphart, Hans Speckmann, Raymond Buve, Bert Gastmann, James and Dorothy Guyot, Annemarie de Waal Malefijt, John Lenoir, Richard Price, France Olivieira, Frank Bovenkerk, J. van de Walle, Parsudi Suparlan, Edward Shils, and Albert Trouwborst. At *all* stages, my wife, Anke, stood by with pencil in hand. If I have failed to remove, or improve, those passages that gave any of my readers concern, the responsibility is my own.

I am also grateful to Professor H.A.J.F. Misset, J.E. Glastra van Loon-Boon, and the staff of NIAS for their many services. Finally, in facilitating the publication of this study, I am indebted to the Netherlands Organization for the Advancement of Pure Scientific Research in the Hague.

There are, of course, still others. It's possible that this book might have gotten more deeply into its subject were it not for the diverting comradeship of the many acquaintances our trips to Surinam gave us. But since you made my work all the more enjoyable, you're forgiven! Special, very special, thanks are also due my sister-in-law, Jaike van Dijk, for her limitless hospitality and patience. Finally, my sons, Mac and Ian, made their own "heavy" investments: learning Dutch, tolerating long Sunday drives in search of political rallies, xeroxing and collating beyond the call of duty, and eagerly sharing our growing appreciation of all that is Surinam. It is because of my hope that they'll once again return to this fascinating land that I dedicate this book to them.

CHAPTER ONE

INTRODUCTION

Wan bon
someni wiwiri
wan bon

Dobru (1973)*

I. GEOGRAPHY AND ECONOMIC CONDITIONS

Surinam is a tropical country located on the northern coast of South America, bordered on the West by Guyana and on the East by French Guiana. With a territory of 163,265 square kilometers,[1] it is somewhat smaller than Guyana (210,000 km^2) and almost twice the size of French Guiana (91,000 km^2). In comparison to lands on other continents, it is roughly the size of Bangladesh, or the American State of Wisconsin, and about four times the size of the Netherlands. Although Surinam is bordered on the South by Brazil, it has had little contact with this neighbor, as the vast majority of its population is settled along a thin strip of land bordering the Atlantic Ocean.

Surinam's land-surface may be divided into three distinctive areas. The populated coastal strip consists of rich, sea-level clays, washed from the Amazon and Surinam's own rivers, and protected from the ocean by natural ridges along the coast. Agricultural development was made possible by Dutch dike-building and poldering technology which drained and protected lands bordering the country's numerous rivers. This technique was applied initially along the Suriname, Commewijne, Saramacca, and Cottica Rivers in the central region, and later was extended to the Nickerie River in the West. Once

* One tree/so many leaves/one tree. From R. Dobru (Robin Ravales), *Flowers Must Not Grow Today* (Paramaribo: "Afi-Kofi," 1973), p. 7.

[1] This figure includes two disputed areas in the interior – one on the border with Guyana and the other bordering French Guiana.

the drainage networks and sluice gates were installed along the rivers, new lands further inland were opened and linked to the older drainage systems.

The coastal zone is protected on the South by a narrow savanna belt. Higher, and geologically older, than the coastal plain, this region's economic value is its vast bauxite reserves, that extend somewhat diagonally (like the savanna, itself,) from near to the coast in the East to the north-central interior in the West. Also located in this region is the large Zanderij airfield and the Afobaka Dam (Surinam's major hydro-electric project, south of Zanderij). Beyond the savanna, the landscape becomes hilly and occasionally mountainous. This interior region, of dense tropical rainforest, comprises over three-fourths of Surinam's land-surface. Rivers rising in this region (from West to East: the Corantijn, Nickerie, Coppename, Saramacca, Suriname and the tributaries of the Marowijne) are generally navigable only between the many rapids along their course. The resource potential here has still to be explored, although lumbering and some gold placer mining exist.

Surinam's economic development and diversification have been slow and spasmodic. With the gradual collapse of the sugar economy, upon which Surinam's growth in the plantation era had rested, some agricultural diversification took place. Impoldered lands were used by ex-slaves for planting cotton and then, increasingly, by ex-contract-laborers of Asian background for rice production. Efforts to grow cacao, coffee, and bananas were important in the nineteenth and early twentieth centuries, but only banana production remains significant today. Citrus fruits have become increasingly important, and efforts are being made to safeguard and develop the coconut industry. Surinam is reasonably self-sufficient in her food supply: livestook, poultry, dairy goods, vegetables, cooking oils, etc. But only rice, and to a smaller extent, bananas, citrus fruits, and sugar, are of potential importance as exports – along with fish, timber and related wood products. Together, the value of the agricultural and forestry sectors of Surinam's economy is only about 1/13 of the total gross domestic product.[2]

By far the most productive sector of the economy is mining, particularly the mining of bauxite, the principal source of aluminum. During the First World War, geologists from the Aluminum Company of America (Alcoa) discovered large deposits of high-grade bauxite ore close to the surface, along the Cottica River near the Indian village of Moengo.[3] Alcoa quickly signed a 75-

[2] In 1973, the value of these two sectors was Sf 48 million ($ 26.6 million) in contrast to mining's Sf 198 million ($ 110 million), and the total Gross Domestic Product of Sf 618 million ($ 343.9 million) (Economic Information Service, *A Statistic Survey of Surinam* (Paramaribo: Department of Economic Affairs, September 1975), p. 18).

[3] *Surinaams Bauxiet: Een Beschrijving van de Samenwerking in de Ontwikkeling van een Bodemrijkdom* (Paramaribo: N.V. Surinaamsche Bauxiet Mij., 1955), p. 106.

year leasehold to the area, and established a subsidiary, the *Surinaamsche Bauxiet Maatschappij*, in December 1916.[4] The first shipments of bauxite to the United States took place in 1922, and by 1929, it had become Surinam's leading export product.[5] During the Second World War, the smaller Dutch *Billiton Maatschappij* (now a subsidiary of Shell) joined with Alcoa to develop new bauxite operations along the Suriname River at Paranam and Onverdacht. After the opening of alumina and aluminum smelters in 1965 (the first to be built in the Third World), Surinam's export of these two products has become a major source of governmental revenue and foreign exchange.[6]

Table 1.1. Employment in Surinam, by Sector, January 1974.

	Number	*Percent*
Agriculture, cattle-breeding and fishing	37,500	28.8
Forestry and processing	1,900	1.5
Mining, quarrying and processing	7,350	5.6
Manufacturing	7,300	5.6
Electricity, Gas and Water	1,050	0.8
Construction	2,200	1.7
Trade, restaurants and hotels	14,500	11.2
Transport, storage and communication	2,400	1.8
Financial, insurance and business services	1,400	1.1
Government	30,000	23.1
Other community, social and personal services	7,400	5.7
Total	113,000	86.9
Correction for additional offices	-13,000	-10.0
Total of working population	100,000	76.9
Unemployed	30,000	23.1
Total of labor force	130,000	100.0

Source: Algemeen Bureau voor de Statistiek, *National Accounts* cited in Economic Information Service, *A Statistic Survey of Surinam* (Paramaribo: Department of Economic Affairs, 1975), p. 19.

Nevertheless, as Table 1.1 reveals, only about six percent of the economically active population was employed in the mining sector in 1974, as compared to 29 percent in agriculture and 23 percent in government. Roughly 23

[4] *Ibid.*, p. 107.

[5] *Ibid.*, pp. 108, 117; and Willem F.L. Buschkens, *The Family System of the Paramaribo Creoles* (The Hague: Martinus Nijhoff, 1974), pp. 118-20.

[6] Together, the export of bauxite, alumina and aluminum accounted for Sf 277.5 in 1972 and 273.4 million in 1973, or between 85 and 90 percent of the value of Surinam's total exports in those years (Economic Information Service, *op. cit.*, p. 29).

percent were unemployed, although many feel this figure may actually be much higher.[7]

In comparison with most Third World countries, Surinam has a reasonably high *per capita* national income: Sf 1,300 (or about $ 722) in 1973.[8] However, it is badly distributed. The high index of unemployment (and underemployment), the barely self-sufficient nature of many farmers, and the low wages paid in many occupations (leading to Table 1.1's double counting of jobs for 13,000 workers) reveal, as G.J. Kruijer and others point out, serious problems of poverty and hardship among the Surinam population.[9] Housing and living conditions for large segments of the population (including large segments of each ethnic group) are primitive,[10] and while extended family networks and cooperative mutual aid organizations (along with a very limited amount of public welfare assistance) all serve to keep the poorest groups fed and clothed,[11] there remains a great deal that must be done.

II. ETHNIC GROUPS

Despite its location over 500 miles to the East of the Caribbean Sea, Surinam is considered a Caribbean country because of the composition of its population and its history as a plantation society under European domination. Its population, for the most part, has its origins in slavery or contract labor, organized by the colony's European settlers over the centuries in which the plantation economy flourished.

In 1971, the population of Surinam was 384,903. Table 1.2 shows the ethnic breakdown among Surinam's seven major population groups in the 1964 and 1971 censuses.

A. Amerindians. The original inhabitants of the land, the Amerindian peoples, are now vastly outnumbered by the transplanted "newcomers." Peter Kloos

[7] Andries de Jong estimates the figure at 29 percent, while, adding the estimated disguised unemployment in Surinam, the figure may go as high as 50 percent (*Suriname Onafhankelijk* (Amsterdam: Nieuw Schrift, 1974), pp. 10-13).

[8] Economic Information Service, *op. cit.*, p. 18. *Time Magazine* places Surinam's *per capita* G.N.P. at $ 880, above all other South American countries except Argentina ($ 1,250) and Venezuela ($ 1,360) (December 22, 1975, pp. 22-23).

[9] G.J. Kruijer, *Suriname, Neokolonie in Rijksverband* (Meppel: Boom, 1973), pp. 27, 56-57, 164ff.

[10] See, for example, Gerard van Westerloo, *Frimangron: Reportages uit een Zuidamerikaanse Republiek* (Amsterdam: Arbeiderspers, 1975), pp. 57-73; and Buschkens, *op. cit.*, pp. 137-43.

[11] Van Westerloo, *op. cit.*, pp. 5-40. Robin Ravales (Dobru) provides an autobiographical example of extended family mutual assistance in *Wan Monki Fri: Bevrijding en Strijd* (Paramaribo: Eldorado, 1969), pp. 15-24. See also, Buschkens, *op. cit.*, pp. 144-63.

Table 1.2. Surinam Population by Ethnic Groups, 1964 and 1971.

Ethnic Group	*1964 (000)*	*1971 (000)*
Creole	115.0	118.5
Hindustani	112.6	142.3
Javanese	48.5	58.9
Chinese	5.3	6.4
Amerindian	7.3	10.2
European	4.3	4.0
Bush Negro	27.7	39.5
Other and Unknown	3.5	5.1
Total	324.2	384.9

Source: Algemeen Bureau voor de Statistiek, *Derde Algemene Volkstelling, Suriname in Cijfers*, No. 33 (Paramaribo: 1967), Table 1A, n.p., and A.B.S., *Voorlopig Resultaat Vierde Algemene Volkstelling, Suriname in Cijfers*, No. 60 (Paramaribo: 1973), p. 4.

estimates the tribal Amerindian population as being 43 percent Carib, 39 percent Arawak, and 18 percent others (Waiyana, Trio, Wayarikule, Wama, and Akuliyo – all of these located far in the interior).[12] In addition, the 1964 Census identified another 2,979 Amerindians as no longer living under tribal organization.[13] The Carib and Arawak peoples live, for the most part, in the coastal and savanna regions of Surinam, on the fringes of the more settled areas.

Agriculture, for the larger tribes, is still of the slash-and-burn variety. But trading contacts (involving handicrafts, fish, lumber, etc.) have provided a continuing link to the urban areas, while missionary activities (especially by the Roman Catholics) have provided medical services and education to the more populous settlements. A number of informants described the Amerindians as a languishing element in Surinam's society, facing extinction in a matter of decades. Nevertheless, the election of an Amerindian candidate to the national legislature in 1973 for the first time in Surinam's history, was accompanied by a large inter-tribal parade and celebration, involving hundreds of people and revealing great pride and hope for this group's continued role in the society.

B. Bush Negroes. Among the descendants of slaves, one finds two distinct ethnic groups: Creoles, the partly or wholly Negroid descendants of plantation slaves, who remained in the settled region of the colony; and Bush

[12] Peter Kloos, *The Maroni River Caribs of Surinam* (Assen: Van Gorcum, 1971), pp. 1, 11.

[13] Algemeen Bureau voor de Statistiek *Suriname in Cijfers No. 33* (Paramaribo: 1967), Table 1A, n.p.

Negroes, Negroid descendants of the escaped slaves, who established a tribal way of life in the colony's interior. Their freedom was finally recognized in peace treaties with the Dutch in the 1700s. The Bush Negroes in the 1964 Census were divided into the following tribes: Saramaccaners – 8,872 (32 percent), Aukaners or Djukas – 14,597 (53 percent), Matuariërs – 1,391 (5 percent), Paramaccaners – 1,632 (6 percent), Bonnis or Alukus – 279 (1 percent), Kwintis – 107 (0.4 percent), and unknown – 820 (3 percent).[14] The 1964 Census did not distinguish Bush Negroes living under tribal authority from those living outside it. But the residential breakdown (Table 1.7, below) reveals about 2,400 Bush Negroes (or about 9 percent of the total) living in areas clearly outside the Bush Negro domain in the interior. As some of this may be a temporary phenomenon, reflecting a condition of migrant work, one cannot conclude that the authority of the tribal chiefs is no longer accepted. But one may assume that a measure of Western acculturation has accompanied this out-migration, making this sub-group somewhat distinct and behaviorally independent of the tribal members in the interior.[15]

As with the Amerindians, Bush Negro agriculture is slash-and-burn. Nevertheless, their settlements along the Saramacca, Suriname and Marowijne Rivers (and their tributaries), are usually permanent. Christian missionary posts are located throughout the interior, providing health care and some education to tribal members. But trade with the coastal settlements is extensive, involving lumber, dug-out canoes, and fine wood-carvings. Since the mid-1960s, a number of Bush Negroes have been elected to the national legislature, and their role will become increasingly important as Surinam begins to develop its resources in the interior.

C. Creoles. Those descendants of plantation slaves who remained on the plantations, receiving their freedom with Abolition (1863) or before, acquired many of the cultural values of the Europeans and became fully distinct, if not, on occasion, antagonistic, to the Bush Negroes. Because of miscegenation over the years, the Creole group is far from homogeneous. Besides the racially significant color gradations produced by centuries of cross-breeding between Blacks, Europeans and Mulattos, there are many "Creoles" with still other origins. Although figures are not available, I would estimate that perhaps as many as ten percent of the Creoles derive partly (in descending order of frequency) from Amerindian, Chinese, Hindustani, Javanese, or other ethnic origins. Relations between these "Creoles" and their non-Creole "brethren"

[14] *Ibid.*, p. 18.

[15] Lou Lichtveld, "De Bosnegers," in Albert Helman (Lou Lichtveld), ed., *Cultureel Mozaïek van Suriname* (Zutphen: De Walburg Pers, 1977), pp. 187-88.

vary. While it is possible for Creole-Javanese and Creole-Amerindians to be considered Javanese or Amerindian if they retain the cultural practices of these groups, the Creole-Chinese and *Doglas* (Creole-Hindustanis) are ascriptively considered Creoles, and the *Doglas* are generally ostracized by Hindustanis.

D. Hindustanis. The largest of Surinam's many population groups are the Hindustanis, mostly descendants of contract laborers who arrived in Surinam between 1873 and 1917. Elsewhere in the Caribbean called "East Indians," the Hindustanis came from the North-Eastern Provinces of India, bringing with them distinctive cultural and religious practices that have increased the complexity of Surinam's plural society.

Still heavily dependent upon agriculture for their livelihood, the Hindustanis acquired small land-holdings from the faltering plantations after their contracts had run out, planting rice where once sugar had grown. Their strong joint-family organization and thrift made it possible for many to educate their children and achieve considerable occupational and social mobility.

E. Javanese. Also introduced as contract laborers to Surinam between 1890 and 1939 were the Javanese. Brought from the Dutch East Indies to supplement and later replace the Hindustanis on the remaining sugar plantations, the Javanese add a distinct element to the population that is not found anywhere else in the Caribbean.

Unlike the Hindustanis, they have been slower to make the transition from agriculture to other occupations in the society. Although no longer bound by contract labor, many Javanese are still engaged in plantation work on the remaining sugar plantation at Marienburg in the Commewijne District. Others have followed the example of the Hindustanis, acquiring small parcels of land to cultivate rice. Of the several ethnic groups in the settled area of the coastal lowlands, this is the most impoverished and least educated. Despite the existence of political parties that have been organized to represent the interests of the Javanese, they have been consistently out-maneuvered by and dependent upon collaboration with their stronger Hindustani and Creole counterparts.

F. Others. In addition to the above groups, Surinam's society includes a large Chinese community – many of whom are descendants of contract laborers brought to Surinam in the 1850s and 1860s. Others have arrived more recently from Hong Kong and elsewhere in the Chinese diaspora around the world. In addition, there are fairly significant numbers of Europeans, Lebanese,

German and Portuguese Jews, as well as some Latin and North Americans, West Indians, Koreans and Japanese. Most of these, like the Chinese, are involved in business, mining or industry.

G. Differential Patterns of Growth. The growth patterns between the 1964 and 1971 censuses (Table 1.2) are striking. Hindustanis have grown at a rate of 3.1 percent per year, overtaking the Creoles to become the largest population group in Surinam. The Javanese growth rate has been somewhat lower (2.6 percent), but still remains above that of the Creoles (0.5 percent).[16] This latter figure may be partly attributed to a high rate of Creole emigration in these years, but it also represents a lower birth-rate, as Humphrey Lamur's research has indicated.[17] In terms of population 16 years and older, the ratio between Creoles and Hindustanis was somewhat more balanced in 1971: 64,595 to 68,623.[18] But it was clear that, if political organization remained based upon ethnicity and/or cultural affiliations, the Hindustani group would eventually have the potential to dominate the society, unless the other groups could form effective alliances to prevent it.

III. OTHER SOURCES OF SOCIAL DIFFERENTIATION

Although an examination of Surinam's politics reveals the overriding importance of ethnicity, fragmentation *within* ethnic blocs has occurred so frequently that it becomes essential to identify the underlying divisions within each ethnic group that impede, at least to some extent, the easy translation of ethnic strength into cohesive political action.

A. Religion. Because more detailed data from the 1971 Census were not yet available, I have made use of the 1964 Census to sketch a more complete picture of the degree of diversity which characterizes Surinam's society. In terms of religion, the population has been broken down into six categories: Protestant, Catholic, Hindu, Mohammedan, Heathen and Other (including Unknown). Table 1.3 shows these divisions, by ethnic group, for the year 1964.

[16] A.B.S., *Voorlopig Resultaat Vierde Algemene Volkstelling. Suriname in Cijfers No. 60* (Paramaribo: 1973), p. 5.

[17] H.E. Lamur, "Fertility Decline in Suriname, 1964-1970," *Boletín de Estudios Latinoamericanos y del Caribe* 16 (June 1974), pp. 29-30. See also his *The Demographic Evolution of Surinam, 1920-1970* (The Hague: Martinus Nijhoff, 1973), Ch. Two, and p. 145.

[18] A.B.S., *Voorlopig Resultaat...*, p. 8.

Table 1.3. Population by Cultural Origin and Religion, 1964.

Group	*Total*	*Percent*	*Protestant*	*Catholic*	*Hindu*	*Mohammedan*	*Heathen*	*Other & Unknown*
Creoles	114,961	35.4	59,630	47,658	272	443		6,958
Hindustanis	112,633	34.7	1,136	4,021	86,911	19,157		1,408
Javanese	48,463	14.9	1,319	1,668	162	43,933		1,381
Chinese	5,339	1.7	804	3,456	4	28		1,047
European	4,322	1.4	1,544	1,666	2	11		1,099
Bush Negro	27,698	8.5	5,548	5,275			16,875	
Amerindians	7,287	2.3	284	5,889	8	16	960	130
Other & Unknown	3,508	1.1	802	1,533	216	221		736
Total	324,211	100.0	71,067	71,166	87,575	63,809	17,835	12,759
Percent	100.0		21.9	21.9	27.1	19.7	5.5	3.9

Source: Algemeen Bureau voor de Statistiek, *Derde Algemene Volkstelling. Suriname in Cijfers*, No. 33 (Paramaribo, 1967), Table 7, n.p.

As can be seen, the Creole group is almost evenly divided between Protestant and Catholic adherents, while a not inconsiderable number of the three Asian groups has also been "won over" to Christian religions. The Protestant group may be further subdivided into a series of denominations ranging from the largest – the Moravian "*Herrnhutters*" (or *Evangelische Broeder Gemeenschap*) – through smaller groups of Lutherans, Dutch Reformed Calvinists, African Methodists, Seventh Day Adventists, etc.

Although the 1964 Census indicates that 4/5 of the Hindustanis are of the Hindu religion, this group may be further subdivided into adherents of the orthodox Hindu religion (represented by the *Sanatan Dharm*) and two smaller reformist Hindu sects (the *Arya Pratinidhi Sabha* and *Arya Dewaker*). J.D. Speckmann estimated in 1965 that the two Aryan groups together formed about 16 percent of the total Hindustani population (or about 21 percent of the Hindus).[19] Moreover, the retention of some caste differentiation among orthodox Hindus is important. Though strict differentiation of the higher castes has been greatly attenuated, the attitude of these towards the "Untouchables" group (in Surinam, called the *chamars*, or leatherworking caste in India) has remained somewhat aloof.[20] Although marriage may be parentally approved between a high caste member and a *chamar* of wealthy origins,[21] the continued discrimination by some Hindus against *chamars* may have helped to increase the following of the Aryan reformers who reject the notion of caste altogether.

Like the Hindus, the Mohammedans are similarly divided. Hindustani Moslems are divided between traditionalist *Sunnis* and the reformist *Ahmadiya*.[22] Conflict over religious issues and leadership, both between and within these two groups, appears to be considerable, and Hindustani Moslems are generally considered one of the most fractionated groups in Surinam. But conflicts are also severe among Javanese Moslems. Here, too, the conflict is between reformists (the *Sahabatul Islam)* and traditionalists (ironically calling themselves the *Ahmadiyah*).[23] The principal issue dividing them is the proper direction of prayer (West for the traditionalists – since this was the practice in Java, and East for the reformers – as this is the closest direction to

[19] J.D. Speckmann, *Marriage and Kinship Among the Indians in Surinam* (Assen: Van Gorcum, 1965), p. 49.

[20] *Ibid.*, pp. 107-08; and Anke van Dijk Dew, *Fertility and Culture Among Hindus in Surinam* (New Haven: Yale University Department of Epidemiology and Public Health, Master's Thesis, 1975), pp. 76-77.

[21] Speckmann, *op. cit.*, p. 109.

[22] *Ibid.*, pp. 49-50.

[23] The term is associated with the reform movement in Islam, but somehow was taken by the traditionalists out of ignorance.

Mecca), but other issues, involving the *slametan*, *tajub* and other ceremonies, the use of Arabic in religious rituals, etc., have been divisive. The traditionalists appear to be in the majority among the Javanese.[24]

The category "Heathen" represents the practice among Bush Negroes of *Winti*, a traditional set of beliefs of African origin,[25] and among Amerindians of their several ancestral religious practices. That so many Bush Negroes and Amerindians are classified under the Christian religious headings is somewhat misleading, as their actual religious practice and belief systems are generally syncretic.[26] The same may be said for large segments of the Creole lower class.[27]

B. Language. According to the 1964 Census, there are four widely spoken languages in Surinam: Dutch, *Sranantongo* (a Creole admixture of African, English, Dutch, and Portuguese roots),[28] *Sarnami Hindostans* (of Hindi and

Table 1.4. Surinam Population, Age Six and Above, by Best Spoken Language, and Ethnic Group, 1964.

Ethnic Group	*Dutch*	*Sranan-tongo*	*Sarnami Hindostans*	*Javanese*	*Other*	*Total*
Creole	61,389	27,939	195	90	1,318	90,931
Hindustani	11,250	1,496	71,505	23	443	84,717
Javanese	2,724	561	22	34,766	35	38,108
Amerindian[a]	980	944	1	–	447	2,372
Chinese	2,581	237	1	5	1,663	4,487
European	3,455	15	1	4	144	3,619
Other	1,558	156	2	37	528	2,281
Total	83,937	31,348	71,727	34,925	4,578	226,515
%	37.1	13.8	31.7	15.4	2.0	100.0

[a]Not living in tribal groups.
Source: A.B.S., *Derde Algemene Volkstelling, Suriname in Cijfers*, No. 33 (Paramaribo: 1967), Table 36, n.p.

[24] G.D. van Wengen, *De Javanen in de Surinaamse Samenleving* (Leiden: manuscript, 1972), pp. 92ff; and Parsudi Suparlan, *The Javanese in Surinam: Ethnicity in an Ethnically Plural Society* (Doctoral Dissertation, University of Illinois, 1976), pp. 195, 204ff, and 337.

[25] C.J. Wooding, *Winti: Een Afro-Amerikaanse Godsdienst in Suriname* (Meppel: Boom, 1972).

[26] *Ibid.*, p. 204; Kloos, *op. cit.*, pp. 234-37; and J.D. Lenoir, "Surinam National Development and Maroon Cultural Autonomy," paper presented to the Caribbean Studies Association meeting, San Juan, Puerto Rico, January 8-11, 1975, pp. 14-18.

[27] Buschkens, *op. cit.*, pp. 158-59; Rudolf van Lier, *Samenleving in een Grensgebied: Een Sociaal-Historische Studie van Suriname* (Deventer: Van Loghum Slaterus, 1971), pp. 11, 300.

[28] For a historic and literary analysis of this language's development, combined with representative writings, see Jan Voorhoeve and Ursy M. Lichtveld, eds., *Creole Drum: An Anthology of Creole Literature in Surinam* (New Haven: Yale University Press, 1975).

Urdu origins with Dutch and *Sranantongo* additions), and Javanese. Table 1.4 shows their distribution as "best spoken language" among individuals of the various ethnic groups, aged six years and older, in 1964.

Research by the *Sociografisch Instituut* of the University of Amsterdam in 1969, among a sample of 500 family heads in Surinam, produced a roughly similar breakdown. Regarding the principal language spoken in the home, 33 percent answered Dutch, 18 percent *Sranantongo*, 28 percent *Sarnami Hindostans*, 17 percent Javanese, and 3 percent both Dutch and *Sranatongo.*[29] Going a step further, the interviewers asked for all the languages the family heads spoke. To this question, 68 percent answered Dutch, 78 percent *Sranantongo*, 36 percent *Sarnami Hindostans*, 21 percent Javanese, and 3 percent other Surinamese languages.[30] Assuming that the sample was reasonably representative, one can conclude that *Sranantongo* and Dutch both serve as *linguae francae* in the Surinam society, with large portions of the Asian groups able to use them. *Sranantongo* is the dominant language of the marketplace and on the streets, while Dutch is the language of government, education, and the communications media (press, television, and, with some exceptions, radio).

C. Residence. In terms of population settlement, there are no figures available on the urban-rural breakdown, per se. It is estimated, however, that as much as 85 percent of the population is settled within a 25-mile radius of the capital, Paramaribo,[31] making urban services and amenities available to many who might otherwise be classified as "rural." Smaller urban centers include Nieuw Nickerie (near the mouth of the Corantijn River on the border with Guyana), Moengo (in the center of the bauxite mining region of East Surinam), Albina (on the Marowijne River on the border with French Guiana), and Paranam (in the center of the bauxite mining region on the Suriname River, south of Paramaribo).

As the map on the frontispiece reveals, Surinam is divided into nine jurisdictional districts: seven located along the coastal plain, the remaining two further in the interior. From West to East, the coastal plain districts are Nickerie, Coronie, Saramacca, Suriname, Paramaribo, Commewijne, and Marowijne. (Nickerie, Saramacca, Commewijne, and Marowijne also include large interior regions.) The two wholly interior districts are Para and Brokopondo, to the South of Paramaribo.

[29] Kruijer, *op. cit.*, p. 120.

[30] *Ibid.*, pp. 120-21. For a similar analysis, see E. Sluisdom, "De Best Gesproken Taal in Suriname," *Geografisch Tijdschrift van het Koninklijk Nederlandsch Aardrijkskundig Genootschap*, 4, no. 4 (1970), pp. 349-53.

[31] "Surinam," *Focus* (The American Geographical Society), 21 (September 1970), p. 5.

Table 1.5. Surinam Population, by District and Ethnic Group, 1964.

District	*Creole*	*Hindustani*	*Javanese*	*Amerindian*[a]	*Chinese*	*European*	*Bush Negro*	*Amerindian in Tribes*	*Other*	*Unknown*	*Total*
Paramaribo	67,544	25,437	7,963	1,342	3,869	2,197	668	106	1,631	110	110,867
Suriname	31,641	55,208	18,292	920	776	1,587	1,013	854	991	412	111,694
Nickerie	5,900	17,973	4,887	185	303	294	130	719	81	–	30,472
Coronie	3,344	47	336	3	42	4	–	–	6	–	3,782
Commewijne	1,613	6,717	11,233	190	97	90	591	87	82	–	20,700
Saramacca	780	6,589	3,294	62	68	22	486	634	17	–	11,952
Marowijne	3,328	567	2,336	270	173	102	14,408	1,887	142	–	23,213
Brokopondo	811	95	122	7	11	26	10,402	21	36	–	11,531
Total	114,961	112,633	48,463	2,979	5,339	4,322	27,698	4,308	2,986	522	324,211

[a]Not living in tribal groups.

Source: Algemeen Bureau voor de Statistiek, *Derde Algemene Volkstelling*, *op. cit.*, Table 1A, n.p.

Table 1.6. Surinam Population, by District and Three Largest Ethnic Groups (in Percentages), 1964.

District	*Creole*	*Hindustani*	*Javanese*
Paramaribo	60.9	22.9	7.2
Suriname	28.3	49.4	16.4
Nickerie	19.4	59.0	16.0
Coronie	88.4	1.2	8.9
Commewijne	7.8	32.4	54.3
Saramacca	6.5	55.1	27.6
Marowijne	14.3	2.4	10.1
Brokopondo	7.0	0.8	1.1

Source: Table 1.5.

The 1964 figures on population by ethnic group for the districts include the population of Para under the district of Suriname, as the former did not become a separate district until 1966. According to these figures (Tables 1.5 and 1.6), we can see that in most of the districts some group other than the Creoles held the majority: in Nickerie, Saramacca and Suriname it was the Hindustanis; in Commewijne, the Javanese; and in Marowijne and Brokopondo, the Bush Negroes. Only in Coronie and Paramaribo were Creoles ascendant, though the new district of Para has a Creole majority. Nevertheless, although each district has one ethnic group in a majority or near-majority, only Coronie and Brokopondo come close to being homogeneous. At least one large minority (and usually two) can be found in most districts.

Of greatest importance, politically, is the fact that the most populous districts – Suriname and Paramaribo – feature little of what we might call ethnic ghettoization. Apart from the farming areas, where Hindustanis and Javanese greatly outnumber the remaining Creoles, residential settlement involves a remarkable degree of intermingling among the groups. The same may be said of the other urban areas in the country. Contacts, cultural borrowing, and opportunities for increased tolerance are facilitated by such conditions; but interethnic frictions have, at times, also been the result.

D. Occupation. The 1964 Census provides an ethnic breakdown of the economically active population according to economic sector (Tables 1.7 and 1.8). As the tables indicate, the largest percentages of Hindustanis and Javanese were active in agriculture, while the Creoles were spread more evenly across the economic spectrum, controlling the largest number of positions in government, mining, industry, construction, public utilities, commerce, and

Table 1.7. Surinam's Economically Active Population (Excluding Unemployed) by Economic Sector and Ethnic Group, 1964.

Economic Sector	*Creole*		*Hindustani*		*Javanese*		*Other*		*Total*	
	N	%	*N*	%	*N*	%	*N*	%	*N*	%
Government	11,508	40.1	3,667	15.1	1,911	13.6	1,302	25.1	18,388	25.5
Agriculture and Fishing	2,195	7.6	10,714	44.2	6,638	47.4	375	7.2	19,922	27.6
Mining	3,141	10.9	783	3.2	1,258	9.0	388	7.5	5,570	7.7
Industry	2,635	9.2	2,457	10.1	1,594	11.4	457	8.8	7,143	9.9
Construction	1,023	3.6	796	3.3	353	2.5	78	1.5	2,250	3.1
Electricity, Gas and Water	415	1.4	175	0.7	134	1.0	80	1.5	804	1.1
Commerce	3,107	10.8	2,995	12.4	969	6.9	1,787	34.4	8,858	12.3
Transportation and Shipping	700	2.4	967	4.0	161	1.1	78	1.5	1,906	2.6
Services	3,365	11.7	840	3.5	695	5.0	555	10.7	5,455	7.6
Unclassified	637	2.2	832	3.4	297	2.1	90	1.7	1,856	2.6
Total	28,726	99.9	24,226	99.9	14,010	100.0	5,190	99.9	72,152	100.0

Source: Algemeen Bureau voor de Statistiek, *Derde Algemene Volkstelling*, *op cit.*, Table 24, n.p.

Table 1.8. Surinam's Economic Sectors by Ethnic Group (in Percentages), 1964.

Economic Sector	*Creole*	*Hindustani*	*Javanese*	*Other*	*Total*
Government	62.6	19.9	10.4	7.1	100.0
Agriculture and Fishing	11.0	53.8	33.3	1.9	100.0
Mining	56.4	14.1	22.6	7.0	100.1
Industry	36.9	34.4	22.3	6.4	100.0
Construction	45.5	35.4	15.7	3.5	100.1
Electricity, Gas and Water	51.6	21.8	16.7	10.0	100.1
Commerce	35.1	33.8	10.9	20.2	100.0
Transportation and Shipping	36.7	50.7	8.4	4.1	99.9
Services	61.7	15.4	12.7	10.2	100.0
Unclassified	34.3	44.8	16.0	4.8	99.9

Source: Table 1.7.

services. Only in the field of transportation did they take a secondary position to the Hindustanis.

Nevertheless, it is improper to speak of a clear, ethnically-determined, division of labor in Surinam, as the percentages of positions for the Asian groups in each sector are well above the 10 percent point in almost all cases. (The Javanese, who, after all, constituted only 15 percent of the population, fall close to or below this figure only in government, commerce, transportation, and services.)

The drive of the Asian groups to become economically, if not socially, integrated has been very strong. In particular, the characteristic propensity of Hindustanis to work hard and save money to assist their children's advancement has led to striking advances for many members of this group, providing grounds for resentment and envy by the Creoles. Most significantly, the position of the government as the major non-agricultural source of economic livelihood for Surinamers has been a source of continuous political struggle.

It is important to note that, as each ethnic group becomes occupationally diversified and no longer dependent upon one main source of activity, opportunities begin to emerge for ethnically neutral economic, and other, interests to develop, uniting individuals across ethnic lines. A number of authors have pointed to this phenomenon, hoping alternatively for the reduction of ethnic rivalry and creation of greater social pluralism, or for the consolidation of class consciousness as prelude to social revolution.[32]

[32] Lamur, *The Demographic Evolution...*, pp. 160-62; Rudi F. Kross, "Onafhankelijkheid in Suriname, Rassen- of Klassenstrijd," in *Suriname van Slavernij naar Onafhankelijkheid: De Geschiedenis van Suriname 1674-1974* (Amsterdam: Stichting ter Bevordering van de Studie der Geschiedenis in Nederland, 1975), pp. 113-23; and Kruijer, *op. cit.*, pp. 199-202.

E. Acculturation. Surinam's educational system has served as the most important force for socialization and, at least partial, acculturation. Attendance is very high at the lower grades, compared to most Third World countries.[33] However, opportunities for advanced study, at the high school, university, and technical school levels, are far more limited. Although resentment of the Dutch orientation of education and cultural life has been strong among young Creole nationalists, the socializing effects of education are such that many young people from each ethnic group go, or are sent, to the Netherlands for further study.

Beneath the official orientation and pull of western values, a number of other cultural poles exert their own force upon the society. The result is a mixing of values and behavior, through cultural borrowing, that promises to give Surinam its own distinct national identity. Although all groups are involved in this process, the group most impacted by the conflict between official westernization and their own traditional behavior are the Creoles. The reason for this is that no "great tradition" serves to legitimize Creole folk culture, as it does the behavior of the Asian and other groups. Consequently, traditional Creole culture was subjected to almost continual deprecation or ridicule in the past century, with articulate defenders outnumbering detractors only in the past decade or so.

M.G. Smith and others have described the differences between social strata in Jamaica and other Caribbean territories in terms of distinct sets of institutions possessed by the westernized elite and Creole folk mass.[34] In Surinam, some of the institutions of the Dutch-oriented upper strata deviate from the overall pattern found in the West Indies. However, the Dutch-derived religious, linguistic, and educational patterns presumably guide the behavior of the Surinam elite to the same end as in the British islands: i.e., the achievement of respectability. Yet, rather than being defined in terms of inherent value, one suspects that their value lies more in their contrast to the "traditional Creole" institutions of family, religious belief, language, economic activity, recreation, etc. Despite elite pressures for greater conformity to "western" practices, the latter have persisted and gained strength over the years.

The "traditional Creole" family structure involves the prevalence of concubinage or "visiting relationships" as the basis of early child-bearing, with a strong tendency for a resultant matrifocality in child-rearing. In a sample of

[33] Kruijer, *op cit.*, p. 198; and Economic Information Service, *op cit.*, p. 5.

[34] M.G. Smith, "Social and Cultural Pluralism," in Smith, *The Plural Society in the British West Indies* (Berkeley: University of California Press, 1965), pp. 81ff; and David Lowenthal, *West Indian Societies* (London: Oxford University Press, 1972), pp. 100-23.

lower class households in 1965, Willem Buschkens found that 43.5 percent of co-residing Creole couples lived in concubinage, while among heads of households in his sample, 43.2 percent were women.[35] In contrast, the "European" pattern of family structure involves the practice of legal marriage before child-bearing and a larger role by the father in child-rearing and family life. Both systems may involve utilization of extended family connections for various purposes, but the "traditional Creole" family institution heavily utilizes the extended family in child-rearing.

A "traditional Creole" way of life also involves the exclusive or, at least, extensive use of *Sranantongo* along with various Afro-American practices (identified with, but not entirely the same as, those practiced by the Bush Negroes) – e.g., spiritualism, healing, etc. Economic activity and recreation follow the pattern of behavioral adjustments to poverty that Oscar Lewis has more generally called "the culture of poverty."[36] Its local form in Surinam involves a hustler-style (*hosselen*) of job-seeking and -abandonment, resignation regarding efforts at self-improvement, and a low propensity to save. The latter, affected by a strong need to achieve peer recognition, results from status-oriented consumption, entertaining, and promiscuity.[37]

In contrast, the "European" way of life normatively involves social moderation, a dedication to self-improvement (and especially that of one's children), and a high propensity to work hard and save money. Generally, it frowns upon *Sranantongo* and the Afro-American folk beliefs and usages, embracing the Dutch language as more advanced, and the "established" Dutch denominations of Christianity, as being more respectable.

The Creole group is not the only one divided according to "traditional" and "European" cultural norms. Upwardly mobile members of the Hindustani, Javanese, Chinese, and other ethnic groups are faced with making adjustments between the cultures of their origin and those of the Surinam elite. Moreover, because of the strength of "traditional Creole" institutions, lower class Asians and others have "borrowed" elements from this source.

Although the existence of concubinage among Hindustanis is not uncommon (Speckmann's 1959-61 sample showed an incidence of 18 percent in the districts and 14 percent in Paramaribo, while in 1969, 22 percent of a sample

[35] Buschkens, *op. cit.*, pp. 127, 136.

[36] "The Culture of Poverty," in Lewis, *Anthropological Essays* (New York: Random House, 1970), pp. 67-80.

[37] Buschkens, *op. cit.*, pp. 162-63, 268; H.C. van Renselaar, "De Houding van de Creoolse Bevolkingsgroep in Suriname ten Opzichte van de Andere Bevolkingsgroepen," in *Bijdragen tot de Taal-, Land- en Volkenkunde*, 119, no. 1 (1963), 104; and J.D. Speckmann, "De Houding van de Hindostaanse Bevolkingsgroep in Suriname ten Opzichte van de Creolen," in *ibid.*, pp. 89-90.

of Hindustani households in Nickerie involved concubinage[38]), this is not necessarily an adaptation to the "traditional Creole" pattern, as most of these cases involved the second union for the woman, which by traditional Hindu and Moslem practice is seldom accompanied by formal wedding rites.[39] Nevertheless, Speckmann indicates a number of not-so-traditional "secondary wife" (*buitenvrouw*) relationships with, and supporting their offspring from, women other than their marriage partners.[40] Kruijer adds the information that "no fewer than 13 percent of the Hindustani... households in Paramaribo are headed by a self-supporting woman."[41] Other changes reported by Speckmann and Anke Dew, most likely deriving from "European" influences, are the greater freedom of young Hindustanis in choosing their mates, increased age at marriage, the declining influence of caste, increased tendency to live as nuclear (instead of joint) families, etc.[42] Areas of cultural borrowing involve language (both Dutch and *Sranantongo* being widespread), religion (involving many conversions to Catholicism, as well as a few to Protestantism), and the "traditional Creole" practices of healing and folk medicine.

Both G.D. van Wengen and Parsudi Suparlan have pointed out that acculturational forces have similarly led many Javanese either towards the "traditional Creole" or "European" patterns of family structure and way of life.[43] Probably moreso than among Hindustanis, intermarriage and other forms of direct social adaptation have occurred between the Javanese and other groups. Suparlan says that some Javanese rationalize this behavior as "a matter of strategy." According to one of his informants,

> the Creoles are rough. If we treat them with politeness, as we treat other Javanese, and with *ngalah* (yielding) behavior to whatever they are doing to us, they tread on us. We have to respond to them in their ways of treating us.[44]

But, as Suparlan and Van Wengen point out, many go still further than the "strategy" rationalization requires, e.g., accepting *Sranantongo* or Dutch as the more appropriate languages for their home lives, repudiating the waste of traditional Javanese religious and life-cycle rituals, and adopting the

[38] Speckmann, *Marriage and Kinship...*, pp. 127-28; Kruijer, *op. cit.*, p. 181.

[39] Speckmann, *Marriage and Kinship...*, p. 127.

[40] *Ibid.*, p. 125.

[41] Kruijer, *op. cit.*, p. 181.

[42] Speckmann, *Marriage and Kinship...*, pp. 261-62; and Anke Dew, *op. cit.*, pp. 71-80, 83-85, 91-92, 93-95.

[43] Suparlan, *op. cit.*, pp. 92-94; and Van Wengen, *op. cit.*, pp. 215-35.

[44] Quoted in Suparlan, *op. cit.*, p. 157.

European practices of thrift, hard work, and educational advancement for their children in defiance of communal pressures against such individualistic striving.[45]

* * *

The political significance of these internally differentiating social characteristics for Surinam's ethnic groups is that calls for solidarity along ethnic lines have often been blunted by the number of rival leaders making them. Thus, while ethnicity remains paramount in the structuring of politics in Surinam, intra-ethnic cultural and other divisions provide both the issues and resources for factionalism.

[45] *Ibid.*, pp. 93-94, 155-57, 172, 183-89, 210-11; Van Wengen, *op. cit.*, pp. 222ff; and G.D. van Wengen, *The Cultural Inheritance of the Javanese in Surinam* (Leiden: E.J. Brill, 1975), pp. 49-51.

CHAPTER TWO

THE ROOTS OF ABRASA

> Like a cancer, the worm of slavery gnawed at every budding shoot, which, with proper care, could have brought the colony to well-being and prosperity.
> An ill-advised Immigration, a continued stream of Heathen coolies. . . .in order artificially to lower wages, . . . can only lead to disappointment, and the Negro, encountering no more fairness among the whites as a free laborer than trembling before them as a slave, will be compelled as a consequence to retreat to the woods. J. Wolbers (1861)*
> The loneliness of these Hindus is all the greater, in that they are scorned by the rest of the population. Their songs, therefore, always ring of broken despair. Albert Helman (1926)**

I. THE FIRST TRANSPLANTS

From the beginning of its contact with the West, Surinam's history may be told in terms of ethnic relations. Initial contacts between Europeans and Indians were apparently accommodating where exploration and superficial trade were the objectives; but where settlement was attempted, the Indians were much less hospitable. The first successful settlement of Surinam was made in 1651 by an English expedition from Barbados. Failing to enslave or secure adequate labor from the indigenous Caribs, the English proceeded to import African slaves to open and cultivate the land for tobacco and, later, sugar production.

The first years of the colony were marked by heavy interaction between the whites, Indians and Blacks. Although the whites' hegemony after 1651 was never broken, it was severely challenged by warfare with the Indians in the

* *Geschiedenis van Suriname* (Amsterdam: S. Emmering, 1970; original edition, 1861), pp. 296 and 778.

** (Lou Lichtveld), *Zuid-Zuid-West* (Amsterdam: Em. Querido's Uitgeverij, 1961), p. 27.

1670s,[1] and by slave revolts and sporadic warfare with well-organized bands of escaped slaves thereafter, reaching a climax in the 1770s.[2] A divide-and-rule pattern of political control in Surinam's plural society was quickly established, even before the Dutch seized the colony in 1667; and while the European settlers became nearly as heterogeneous as the Indians and African slaves they exploited, their superior resources and ideological cohesion surpassed that of their more numerous potential rivals. Following the Dutch evacuation of Brazil in the 1660s, Jews skilled in the technology of sugar production arrived to open new plantations along the Suriname River above the administrative center of Paramaribo.

When the Indian threat was finally overcome by the Dutch in the 1680s, the colony quickly developed as a major supplier of tropical produce – especially sugar – for the European market. Until the rise of the Dutch East Indies (now Indonesia) in the late 1700s, Surinam was the most important overseas holding of the Netherlands, providing considerable wealth to the booming mercantile houses of Holland and Zeeland.

As in all Caribbean plantation colonies, differentiation occurred over time among both the European and slave groups along social and occupational lines. Miscegenation between the two groups produced a colored population which gradually achieved an intermediate position in the society, legally reenforced in many cases by manumission.[3] The Maroons, or runaway slaves, remained a separate element in the picture, threatening the colony severely at times, and constantly encouraging, by their example as well as active intervention, the further flight of slaves. But this flight was also encouraged by the planters themselves, whose harshness was almost legendary throughout the Caribbean.[4]

J. Wolbers and others, who have chronicled Surinam's early history, portray a vicious circle of political struggle through most of this period: (1) ruthless planters calling for, but not themselves very willing to support, better

[1] See Raymond T.J. Buve, "Governor Johannes Heinsius – The Role of Van Aerssen's Predecessor in the Surinam Indian War of 1678-1680," in Peter Kloos and Henri J.M. Claessen, eds., *Current Anthropology in the Netherlands* (Rotterdam: Nederlandse Sociologische en Antropologische Vereniging, 1975), pp. 39-47; and J. Wolbers, *Geschiedenis van Suriname* (Amsterdam: S. Emmering, 1970, original edition, 1861), pp. 49-51, 62-64.

[2] See Wolbers, *op. cit.*, pp. 137-57, 319-52; J.G. Stedman, *Narrative of a Five Years' Expedition Against the Revolted Negroes of Surinam* ... (Amherst: University of Massachusetts Press, 1972); and Silvia W. de Groot, "The Boni Maroon War 1765-1793, Surinam and French Guyana," *Boletín de Estudios Latinoamericanos y del Caribe* 18 (June 1975), pp. 30-48.

[3] On the characteristics and evolution of the Creole group, see Rudolf van Lier, *Samenleving in een Grensgebied: Een Sociaal-Historische Studie van Suriname* (Deventer: Van Loghum Slaterus, 1971). Ch. 5.

[4] *Ibid.*, pp. 92-105; Wolbers, *op cit.*, pp. 128ff, 567; and Stedman, *op. cit.*, pp. 57-58, 63, 73 and *passim.*

military protection against the Maroons; (2) well-meaning colonial officials (in Holland and Surinam), calling for, but unable to effect, better treatment of the slaves; and (3) slaves steadily fleeing the estates to join the Maroons. The logical (and ethical) resolution of such a triangle should be obvious. But as J.S. Furnivall points out, "the fundamental character of the organization of a plural society [under colonial rule] is indeed the structure of a factory, organized for production, rather than a State, organized for the good life of its members."[5] The conflict that was inherent in this effort to maximize production would "be settled by will rather than by reason,"[6] and the "closed compartment" of those representing the cultural and moral standards of the West would become "narrower ... and degenerate in regions where 'there ain't no ten commandments'...."[7] According to calculations made by Captain John Stedman, a member of the expeditionary force sent out by the Netherlands in the 1770s to put down the most recent revolts, the annual number of deaths among the slaves exceeded births by 2500, about the number that were imported each year, proving "that the whole race of healthy slaves, consisting of 50,000, are totally extinct once every twenty years."[8]

The vicious circle of slavery in Surinam was transformed, though not substantially ameliorated, by the successful negotiation of peace treaties between the Dutch and two of the Maroon tribes in 1760,[9] their combined (Dutch and Maroon) pacification of another Maroon band in 1777 and again in the 1790s,[10] and England's termination of the slave trade in 1807, which may have instilled greater pragmatism among slave-owners and plantation overseers towards their declining work force. But, as Eric Williams points out for the British West Indies,[11] the relative decline of planter influence in metropolitan politics compared to other capitalist interests would ultimately lead to the abolition of slavery, itself.

Following the collapse of the Amsterdam stock exchange in 1773, many planters (especially the Jews) lost their estates to absentee ownership, and credit for further agricultural expansion was sharply reduced thereafter.[12]

[5] J.S. Furnivall, *Netherlands India: A Study of Plural Economy* (Cambridge: University Press, 1944), p. 450.

[6] *Ibid.*, p. 464.

[7] *Ibid.*, p. 458.

[8] Stedman, *op. cit.*, p. 373.

[9] Wolbers, *op. cit.*, pp. 156-58; Stedman, *op. cit.*, pp. 38-40. The model for such peace treaties had already been established by Cornelius van Aerssen van Sommelsdijk, Surinam's Governor at the end of the Indian Wars in the 1680s. See Wolbers, *op. cit.*, p. 64; and Buve, *op. cit.*, pp. 44-45.

[10] De Groot, *op. cit.*, pp. 45-47; and Wolbers, *op. cit.*, pp. 361-62, 373.

[11] Eric Williams, *Capitalism and Slavery* (New York: Capricorn Books, 1966), Chapters 8-10.

[12] Wolbers, *op. cit.*, pp. 302-15.

The Napoleonic Wars, interrupting trade and spurring the development of sugar beet cultivation on the European continent, confronted plantation owners with new uncertainties.[13] The number of plantations in Surinam fell from 452 in 1791 to less than 250 in 1860, and, despite some consolidation, cultivated acreage declined from over 50,000 in 1848 to under 40,000 in 1862.[14] The Dutch did nothing to help the situation. R.M.N. Panday points out that only 0.1% of the Dutch budget in 1842 was allocated to all the Dutch colonies combined (including the then more important East Indies).[15] "The fear," he writes, "that plantation farming would be annihilated if no alternative corrective measures were taken to replace [the declining slave force], was all the more being justified by the rapidly deteriorating conditions in the British and French colonies [where slavery was abolished in 1833 and 1848, respectively]."[16]

Local governmental efforts to encourage small farming among the free population of Paramaribo,[17] and experimental colonization efforts involving Dutch and German peasant groups in 1845[18] and 1853[19] had only limited success and were no direct answer to the plantation owners' problems. Of greater relevance was the importation of Chinese contract laborers, beginning in 1853. But although some 5000 arrived in the following two decades,[20] they never adequately solved the labor shortage. Their contracts were too short, and their desire to renew them was not great. Many drifted into other occupations or left the country.

Moral pressures for abolition in the Netherlands now rivalled the planters' more complicated appeals for slavery's maintenance and new labor supplies. The debate simmered for over a decade, as various arrangements were considered that would benefit both the slaves and their owners.[21] The Abolition bill which finally passed in 1862 established government compensation for the owners and required the ex-slaves to remain under state supervision for ten years (presumably signing labor contracts with their former owners).[22]

[13] R.M.N. Panday, *Agriculture in Surinam – 1650-1950: An Enquiry into the Causes of Its Decline* (Amsterdam: H.J. Paris, 1959), pp. 72-74.

[14] *Ibid.*, p. 82, and Van Lier, *op. cit.*, p. 23.

[15] Panday, *op. cit.*, p. 48.

[16] *Ibid.*, p. 46.

[17] Wolbers, *op cit.*, pp. 710-14.

[18] C. de Jong, "The Dutch Peasants in Surinam," *Plural Societies* 5, no. 3 (Autumn 1974), pp. 19-42.

[19] Wolbers, *op. cit.*, pp. 737-38.

[20] J.H. Adhin, *Development Planning in Surinam in Historical Perspective* (Utrecht: H.J. Smits, 1961), p. 71.

[21] Johanna Maria van Winter, "De Openbare Mening in Nederland over de Afschaffing der Slavernij," *West-Indische Gids* 34 (1953), pp. 61-90.

[22] Van Lier, *op. cit.*, pp. 132-33.

Support was also approved for efforts to foster immigration, but this was far more limited than the planters had hoped for. Abolition alone would cost over 10 million florins (at f 300 per slave for an estimated 36,484 slaves).[23] Viewing this as a sufficient stimulus for Surinam's economy, the Dutch Parliament rejected a government proposal to subsidize further immigration, and, in its place, set up a small experimental fund to offer premiums for private efforts in this direction.[24]

In 1791, the population in the Dutch-controlled areas of the country had been 58,120. Of these, approximately 5,000 were free (including whites, coloreds and Blacks).[25] In addition, another 6000 Bush Negroes and between 4000 and 5000 Amerindians populated the remote or interior regions.[26] By the eve of Abolition (July 1, 1863), the colony's population was down to 52,963, of which 16,479, including the Chinese and some other contract laborers, were free.[27]

II. THE LATER TRANSPLANTS

Opposition to further immigration was voiced in both the Netherlands and Surinam. J. Wolbers concluded his *Geschiedenis van Suriname* (History of Surinam) in 1861 with the warning cited at the outset of this chapter. In Surinam, too, at least one member of the Colonial *Staten* (legislature) denounced the efforts to stimulate immigration as leading the Negro population "to a condition of barbarity worse than they had ever before experienced."[28] Yet, despite these warnings, the planters felt their position following the State Supervision period would be untenable without the infusion of a fresh, new, working force. They were convinced the Negroes would abandon the plantations, ruining their owners in the process.

The fears of a massive internal migration from plantation to city seemed quickly to be borne out. Despite the terms of the State Supervision period, an estimated 20 percent of the work force left the plantations in the first year.[29] As the ten-year period neared its end, and with the report that Chinese ports were now closed to recruiters,[30] the planters grew desperate. Between 1862

[23] *Ibid.*, pp. 23, 132.

[24] Adhin, *op. cit.*, pp. 8-9; and Fred Oudschans Dentz, *Geschiedkundige Aantekeningen over Suriname en Paramaribo*, 2nd edition (Paramaribo: De West, 1972), pp. 85-86.

[25] Wolbers, *op. cit.*, pp. 442-43.

[26] *Ibid.*, pp. 538-39.

[27] Van Lier, *op. cit.*, p. 23.

[28] S. van Praag, quoted in C.J.M. de Klerk, *De Immigratie der Hindostanen in Suriname* (Amsterdam: Urbi et Orbi, 1953), p. 118.

[29] Panday, *op cit.*, pp. 91-94; and Van Lier, *op. cit.*, *p. 134.*

[30] Oudschans Dentz, *op. cit.*, p. 90.

and 1872, 77 plantations closed down, and the total acreage under cultivation declined still further, from 40,000 to 25,000.[31]

A. The Hindustanis. In 1868, the planters petitioned the Colonial *Staten* and Dutch Parliament to set up an Immigration Fund to facilitate further efforts at immigration.[32] The Dutch government responded by negotiating a treaty with Great Britain in 1870 to allow the recruitment of laborers from British India. Despite the absence of a governmental subsidy, the planters quickly took advantage of the new arrangement with the passage from India in 1873 of 399 men, women, and children on board the sailing vessel *Lalla Rookh*. Thousands more arrived that year and the next.[33]

According to the terms of the treaty with Great Britain, Surinam appointed an Agent-General to oversee the allotment and care of the new workers and their families. The first such official, J.F.A. Cateau van Rosevelt, took his duties seriously and, with the help of the British Consul in Paramaribo, campaigned energetically to provide better medical care and living conditions on the plantations.[34] Perhaps to compensate the planters for the new investments required of them, an Immigration Fund was finally set up in 1878.[35]

Between 1873 and 1916, roughly 34,000 Hindustanis migrated to Surinam.[36] About one-third of this number (11,690) returned to India after their contracts ended.[37] But, as many of the return migrants found their reintegration to Indian society difficult, a sizeable number re-migrated to Surinam.[38] Thus, the net immigration figure, roughly 22,500, is a more realistic measure of the demographic base from which the Hindustani population group developed.

Most Hindustanis came from the United Provinces and Western Bihar in North-Eastern India, an overpopulated and poverty-stricken area where the recruiters from Calcutta found the least resistance to their efforts.[39] De

[31] Van Lier, *op. cit.*, 1949 edition, p. 190. There is a misprint in the 1971 edition, where the 1862 figure is given as 10,562 hectares (p. 137) instead of 16,562.

[32] Oudschans Dentz, *op. cit.*, p. 90.

[33] De Klerk, *op. cit.*, p. 117.

[34] De Klerk, "De Komst en Vestiging van de Brits-Indiërs in Suriname," in E.G. Azimullah, ed., *Van Brits-Indisch Emigrant tot Burger van Suriname* (The Hague: Surinaamse Jongeren Vereniging "Manan", 1963), p. 23.

[35] De Klerk, *De Immigratie...*, pp. 126-27.

[36] There is some confusion in the exact total who made the passage. De Klerk gives the total figure 34, 304, but his own figures for the 64 ship transports add up to only 34,284 (*Ibid.*, pp. 71-73). Van Lier, Panday, and Adhin give the figure 34,024, without an accompanying breakdown (Van Lier, *op. cit.*, p. 160; Panday, *op. cit.*, p. 138; Adhin, *op cit.*, p. 158).

[37] Panday, *op. cit.*, p. 158).

[38] De Klerk, *De Immigratie...*, pp. 156-58.

[39] *Ibid.*, p. 50.

Klerk's examination of selected registration figures showed that approximately 82 percent of the migrants were Hindu and 18 percent Mohammedan. Of the former, all castes were represented (18 percent from high, 33 percent middle, and 9 percent low castes, with another 22 percent classified as pariahs, or, as they are usually called in Surinam, *chamars*).[40] As the caste system in India originated in an occupational division of labor (with racial differentiation also playing a part), it is surprising that so many Hindustanis from the higher castes would have been recruited. Yet, as De Klerk points out, caste was no longer a reliable indication of profession in India. The registration materials he examined indicated that the vast majority of incoming Hindustanis claimed to be agriculturists.[41]

Despite the apparent occupational homogeneity among the newcomers, the social adjustment of different castes to the relentless equality imposed by the migration and plantation experiences must have been formidable. After a visit to Surinam in 1891, D.W.D. Comins, Surgeon-Major in the Indian Medical Service, observed that

> The influence and restrictions of caste are much modified, and in some cases disappear altogether, though certain traditions and superstitions always remain.... Their belief is that no man can call himself a Hindu who has crossed the sea; so they lose their respect for the caste and religion of their fathers, which they neglect, and acquire no other in their place. They still wear amulets and charms, and believe in the evil eye, ghosts and devils innumerable, but in no God....[42]

Nevertheless, as Speckmann points out, efforts were made to restore the rudiments of Hindu culture among the immigrants:

> The highest group, the *Brahmans*, in particular, endeavoured to restore the old situation, while on the other hand the prestige of the various depressed castes, such as *Dhobis* and *Chamars*, remained low in the new community. But it was no longer possible to speak of the existence of castes in the native Indian sense. The corporative nature of the original castes and the caste *panchayat* were lacking; the connection between profession and caste had quite disappeared; the regulations regarding preparation of food, and the ban on eating meals with members of other castes, were only partly observed. Nor could caste endogamy be maintained, in view of the small percentage of Hindu women in Surinam. The fact that the caste system in India functioned as a point of reference did not make its restoration in the new country any less incomplete and defective.[43]

[40] *Ibid.*, pp. 98-108. De Klerk speculates that some "upward mobility" may have occurred in the registration process, as Hindustanis tried to disguise their lowly origins. It should be noted, too, that the *chamars* are only one of several categories of pariahs or Untouchables.

[41] *Ibid.*, p. 110.

[42] D.W.D. Comins, *Note on Emigration from the East Indies to Surinam or Dutch Guiana* (Calcutta: Bengal Secretariat Press, 1892), p. 17.

[43] J.D. Speckmann, *Marriage and Kinship Among the Indians in Surinam* (Assen: Van Gorcum and Co., 1965), pp. 32-33.

Indeed, as De Klerk points out, the new situation in which they found themselves led "all British Indians (to unite) collectively in a new sort of *national Indian caste* closed off from the other population groups."[44] It is interesting to note that the first organizations of Hindustanis were secular. The *Surinaamsche Immigranten Vereeniging* was set up in 1910 to defend the interests of contract laborers and "free" settlers alike, significantly changing its name to *Bharat Oeday* (Upcoming Hindustani) in 1922. A group of more educated young Hindustanis set up the *Nawa Yuga Oeday* (Beginning of a New Age) in 1924.[45] In contrast, the first religious organization, the *Sanatan Dharm* (Eternal Religion) was founded in 1929 "to stimulate the social welfare of the inhabitants of this country and to spread and maintain the Hindu religion...."[46] In the same year, the *Surinaamsche Islamietische Vereeniging* was founded; and a year later, the reformist *Arya Samaj* movement among the Hindus set up *Arya Dewaker* (Aryan Sun) to combat the orthodoxy of the *Sanatan Dharm.*[47]

The consequences of these organizational efforts, combined with the phenomenal growth rate of the Hindustani population and its economic development, would later transform Surinam's politics.

B. The Javanese. While migration from India continued steadily, another stream of migration began from the Dutch East Indies (nowadays Indonesia) in 1890. For some years, a number of plantation owners had sought permission to bring Javanese peasants to Surinam, but the Dutch government had resisted this under the belief that their labor was necessary in Java. Finally, in 1889 a license was given to the *Nederlandse Handel Maatschappij* (Dutch Trading Company) to recruit 100 Javanese on an experimental basis for its Marienburg sugar plantation. They succeeded in bringing 94 Javanese men, women, and children to Surinam in 1890.[48] Despite their initial difficulties adjusting to field labor, they sufficiently impressed their overseers that requests for 600 more Javanese were made in 1893.[49] Between 1893 and 1912,

[44] De Klerk, *De Immigratie...*, p. 168.

[45] *Ibid.*, p. 192.

[46] *Ibid.*, p. 193.

[47] *Ibid.*, pp. 194-95. The Aryan movement, begun in Bombay in 1875, attacked the hereditary caste system of orthodox Hindus as well as their polytheism, and urged a "return to the Vedas." Its challenge to the authority of the Brahman Pandits, who were often poorly trained, was particularly successful in immigration lands such as Surinam. See Speckmann, *op. cit.*, pp. 47-49 and Dhanpati Panday, *The Arya Samaj and Indian Nationalism (1875-1920)*. (New Delhi: S. Chand and Co., 1972).

[48] Joseph Ismael, *De Immigratie van Indonesiërs in Suriname* (Leiden: "Luctor et Emergo," 1949), pp. 27-31.

[49] *Ibid.*, p. 31.

10,590 Javanese and 16,006 Hindustanis joined the Surinamese work force.[50]

Immigration from the Dutch East Indies doubled in the next period, as nationalists in British India began to demand an end to the indentured labor contracts. Between 1912, when the Indian Legislative Council unanimously voted to ban such migration, and 1917, when the British Government finally stopped it,[51] only 2,815 Hindustanis migrated to Surinam, while in the decade 1913 to 1922, 10,567 Javanese arrived.[52] Between 1923 and 1932, another 10,715 came from Java, while in 1939, on the eve of the Second World War, the last contingent of 990 arrived.[53] In all, the Javanese migration totalled just over 33,000. Subtracting the number who returned to their homeland (8,441 by 1947),[54] the demographic base to their development was even higher than the Hindustanis (approximately 24,500).

Nevertheless, as Ismael point out, the Javanese experienced a far lower growth rate than the Hindustanis. The ratio of male to female was larger than the Hindustanis, for one thing.[55] Moreover, the medical care provided the Javanese was inferior to the Hindustanis, resulting in a higher mortality rate among Javanese children.[56] But in addition, Ismael argues that Javanese women were reluctant to have children (utilizing various traditional methods of contraception and abortion), and that the already weak structure of the Javanese family was aggravated by the shortage of women with the result that

> Weddings were very seldom entered into, exchange of partners was not unusual, concubinage and prostitution occurred often. Sexual diseases were the consequence, which to a large degree produced sterility among the women.[51]

Although recent figures, reported in Chapter One, indicate a fairly normal growth rate at present among Javanese, it is obvious that the initially low fertility among Javanese must have expressed the general social and emotional difficulties undergone by this group in adjusting to Surinamese conditions. None of the first generation informants interviewed by De Waal Malefijt explained their decision to remain in Surinam in terms of liking it there. Most spoke of a fear of being ridiculed or shamed if they ever returned

[50] *Ibid.*, p. 95 and De Klerk, *De Immigratie...*, pp. 72-73.

[51] De Klerk, *De Immigratie...*, p. 20.

[52] Ismael, *op. cit.*, p. 95 and De Klerk, *De Immigratie...*, p. 73.

[53] Ismael, *op. cit.*, p. 95.

[54] Panday, *op cit.*, p. 158.

[55] Ismael, *op cit.*, p. 105.

[56] P.H.J. Lampe, "Suriname – Sociaal-hygienische Beschouwingen," *Mededelingen Kon. Ver. Koloniaal Instituut Amsterdam*, 23, Afd. Trop. Hyg., no. 14 (1927), cited in Ismael, *op. cit.*, pp. 106-107.

[57] Ismael, *op. cit.*, pp. 105-106.

to Java. And almost all described their initial recruitment in terms of "being tricked."[58]

Despite the feelings of disillusionment and demoralization with their new circumstances, the Javanese managed to reconstitute many of the traditional folk institutions they had known in Java. These, perhaps more than the formal practice of Mohammedanism, provided bonds that held the Javanese community together *vis à vis* the other ethnic groups.[59] While some have lamented the wastefulness of traditional life-cycle ceremonies and feasts,[60] others have noted that the Javanese "underdog" position in the society makes such shows of social solidarity essential.[61]

C. From Contract Laborer to Small Farmer. Although their economic and social conditions were bad, and their adjustment to their new social and cultural surroundings was undoubtedly slow and painful, the new Asian immigrants constituted little threat to the other groups. In viewing this period of Surinam's history, one can no longer speak of the planter-laborer relationship as a *central* political polarity in the society's political development. There were, of course, occasional incidents involving organized confrontation and even violence between Hindustani and Javanese contract laborers and their plantation overseers; in a few cases the police were needed to restore order.[62] But none of these acquired significance for the society at large. Thus, we can speak of a compartmentalization of politics along ethnic lines through this period, with the problems of the Asian groups gradually being resolved by the government's accommodative social and agricultural policies, and by the

[58] Annemarie de Waal Malefijt, *The Javanese of Surinam: Segment of a Plural Society* (Assen: Van Gorcum, 1963), pp. 29-31.

[59] *Ibid.*, pp. 151-75.

[60] Such was the orientation of one of the first Javanese civic organizations, the *Pergerakan Bangsa Indonesia Suriname*, set up in 1947. See Parsudi Suparlan, *The Javanese in Surinam: Ethnicity in an Ethnically Plural Society* (Doctoral Dissertation, University of Illinois, 1976), p. 328.

[61] As Kruijer argues (*op. cit.*, p. 76): "the upward-striving group cannot permit any internal divisions and will strongly repudiate any effort, in the language of bicycle-racing, 'to escape from the platoon'."

[62] De Klerk refers to incidents involving Hindustanis in 1874, 1879, 1884, 1891 and 1902 (*De Immigratie...*, pp. 139-43). See also Anton de Kom, *Wij Slaven van Suriname* (Amsterdam: Uitgevers Mij. Contact, 1934), pp. 158-59. D.W.D. Comins, a surgeon-major in the Indian Medical Service visiting Surinam in 1891, described the 1879 and 1884 incidents in detail (*op. cit.*, pp. 24-25). The most serious of these incidents, the Marienburg "uprising" in 1902, involved considerable bloodshed (24 killed and 32 wounded). De Klerk attributes the causes to various abuses by the overseers (including sexual advances towards Hindustani women), as well as wage and labor grievances (*De Immigratie ...*, p. 142). Ismael doesn't mention dates, but refers to incidents of Javanese unrest at several plantations, as well as individual acts of violence against plantation overseers (*op. cit.*, pp. 124-25).

social adjustment of the two groups themselves. In fact, the Hindustanis' acceptance of their new situation was sufficiently optimistic that when the British Government abolished Indian contract labor, many Hindustanis appealed the decision. A group of them even went to India in 1920 to plead with Gandhi and other influential Indians to restore the program.[63]

To facilitate the Hindustani and Javanese adjustment, the government set up special schools in selected locations, with instruction in their native language. The Hindustanis particularly made use of this facility to acquire literacy and training for their children.[64] One of the first accredited Hindustani teachers was J.P. Kaulesar Sukul, a Hindu Brahman. Although he later became an influential political figure himself, while a schoolteacher, he assisted a number of young Hindustanis in acquiring higher education – among them, Jagernath Lachmon, who later mobilized and led the dominant Hindustani political party. More than the Javanese, the Hindustanis were quick to learn Dutch and *Sranantongo* and to make the social adjustments needed to leave agriculture for other activities in the society.

Nevertheless, the initial Hindustani drive was to possess land. Here, too, the government tried to assist them by the parcellization of plantations in 1877 and 1878, and the land settlement policy of 1895. Like the earlier parcellizations, the 1895 policy transformed old plantations into "settlement centers" (*vestigingsplaatsen*) whose lands were leased – not sold – to interested families. Although the parcels were too small (between three and five acres) for an extended family to operate at more than subsistence level, the Hindustanis, and later the Javanese, took them fairly eagerly.[65]

While we may speak of a gradual transition in government policy from providing laborers to promoting colonization, the interests of the planters

[63] De Klerk, *De Immigratie...*, pp. 178-79.

[64] J.H.E. Ferrier, *De Surinaamse Samenleving als Sociaal-Paedagogische Opgave* (Groningen: J.B. Wolters, 1950), p. 80; and W.E. Juglall, "Het Onderwijs aan Nakomelingen van Brits-Indische Immigranten in Suriname," in Azimullah, *op. cit.*, pp. 83-89.

[65] Panday, *op. cit.*, pp. 164-69. This program was instituted as a consequence of British and Indian pressures. The planters' demand for ten-year (as opposed to five-year) residence for East Indian laborers led to the visit of D.W.D. Comins (see note 62). Using the Dutch/Surinam request as "a very favourable opportunity" to make new counter-demands, Comins concluded that;

"If the period of indentured labor is limited to the five years for which the cooly immigrated, and if after that time he is permitted to enjoy the freedom common to the negroes, emancipated slaves and other sections of the population, and to purchase on reasonable terms, as in Demerara, Trinidad or other colonies, the freehold of some of the immense tracts of land now lying waste, or to choose for himself any legitimate occupation which may be suitable to him, I am satisfied that it would be both to the advantage of future immigrants, as well as to those now in the colony and to the colony itself, that the period of residence should be extended to ten years – the latter five years not to be necessarily industrial residence in estates." (*op. cit.*, p. 3).

were still dominant in the government's calculations. As Panday points out, "the main aims of the State [in the land-settlement policy] appear to have been (1) to keep the people together for the sake of efficient control, and (2) to establish these *vestigingsplaatsen* in the neighbourhood of [still-functioning] plantations so as to serve the original purpose of reservoir centre for the supply of labour."[66] Even as the plantation economy continued its steady decline, the sale or liquidation of plantations was more easily and profitably accomplished through this program. But agriculture, as such, was not stimulated. The small size of the parcels and the absence of adequate extension, credit, or marketing services made the progress of small-scale agriculture very difficult.[67]

Nevertheless, the impact of the Second World War upon agricultural prices helped many farmers (particularly Hindustanis) to advance economically. Increased urbanization and schooling among the Asian groups had the effect of breaking down the ethnic division of labor and increasing the competition between Asians and Creoles, at just the moment when class competition within the Creole group was reaching its peak. The light-skinned Creole elite, as Governor J.C. Kielstra (1933-1944) would later put it, became trapped between an Asian anvil and a Black hammer.[68]

III. COLOR-LINE CONFLICT AMONG THE CREOLES

Whatever the shortcomings of government policy in the long run, the relatively smooth transition of Asian workers into a settled peasantry may be considered a success. Only as the second and third generations of Hindustanis and Javanese began to drift to the cities and compete with Creoles for more prestigious and lucrative occupations did the ethnic and geographical division of labor break down. But in this period, from Abolition to the Second World War, political affairs were almost exclusively the concern of the colony's Creoles, Jews, and Dutch. The central polarities were between these three groups, on the one hand, and internally, within the Creole group, according to lines of class, color, and culture, on the other.

Political participation was extremely limited. Although the Dutch had set up a colonial legislature (*Staten*) in the new Constitution of 1865, and al-

[66] *Op cit.*, p. 165.

[67] De Kom, *op. cit.*, pp. 166-70. In 1911 and 1919, officially-sanctioned study commissions advocated a variety of agricultural reforms, but none of these recommendations were heeded by the Dutch Government (Adhin, *op. cit.*, pp. 93-101).

[68] Quoted by J. van de Walle, interview, Hilversum, April 2, 1976.

though nine of the thirteen seats in this body were to be taken by elected representatives, the electorate numbered only between 200 and 500 during the course of the nineteenth century.[69] Because suffrage was restricted to adult males paying f 40 or more in taxes, Van Lier writes that for many years, "Surinamese politics was managed chiefly by the well-to-do, who above all else represented the interests of the planters."[70] With some relaxation of the suffrage requirements in 1901,[71] the electorate grew to 800 in 1905 and about 2,000 in 1940.[72] In this latter period, the middle class, consisting mostly of colored officials, teachers, journalists, and professionals, became more influential.

A. "Dutchification" of the Volkscreolen. The lower class of freedmen and liberated slaves (sometimes called *volkscreolen* or *nengre*) were denied an effective voice in the new political order, like their Asian counterparts. Indeed, we can speak of the lower class Creoles' adjustment problems as being as severe and politically debilitating as those undergone by the Asian immigrants. "In order to protect the Dutch character of the territory," writes Van Lier, the freed slaves "had to be 'Dutchified' (*vernederlandst*) as quickly as possible..."[73] In 1874, the practice of traditional African religious ceremonies among the *volkscreolen* was strictly forbidden.[74] In 1876, free compulsory education was introduced for all Creole children between 7 and 12. Until this time, most schools were under the control of Surinam's largest Protestant sect, the Moravian Brethren (or *Herrnhutters*), and the Catholics, with classes frequently conducted in *Sranantongo*. But henceforth, all lessons had to be in Dutch.[75] This rule was carried out with what can only be called a passion. R.D. Simons describes the attitude of the first Inspector of Education, Dr. Herman D. Benjamins (a Dutch-educated Creole):

[69] *Verslag van de Commissie tot Bestudering van Staatkundige Hervormingen in Suriname* (The Hague: Staatsdrukkerij, 1948), Vol. I, p. 114.

[70] Van Lier, *op. cit.*, p. 255.

[71] C.D. Ooft, *Ontwikkeling van het Constitutionele Recht van Suriname* (Assen: Van Gorcum, 1972), p. 79.

[72] *Verslag van de Commissie tot Bestudering...*, Vol. I, p. 114.

[73] Van Lier, *op. cit.*, p. 142.

[74] *Ibid.*

[75] Ferrier, *op. cit.*, pp. 14-16, 54. This caused great difficulties. Many of the teachers (e.g., German *Herrnhutters*) spoke no Dutch and had done their teaching in *Sranantongo*. Voorhoeve and Lichtveld point out that new Dutch materials had to be imported to replace those in *Sranantongo* that had already been developed (and printed) by the missionaries (Jan Voorhoeve and Ursy Lichtveld, eds., *Creole Drum: An Anthology of Creole Literature in Surinam* (New Haven: Yale University Press, 1975), p. 8).

One can differ with him in opinion and find his objections too severe, but Benjamins happened to think that [*Sranantongo*] was disastrous for the improvement of good Dutch and that therefore it must be outlawed and disappear as completely as possible....

The struggle of Benjamins has not been without success: the native [sic] population came to be ashamed of its own language and considered it inferior. Countless are the number of children who were sent home with the "hundred lines" [to write]: "I may never speak *Neger-Engels* at school (or: in the schoolyard)."[76]

With slavery's abolition, the prohibition of Christian marriage between slaves was also abolished. Now the *Herrnhutters* themselves contributed to the "Dutchification" of the *volkscreolen* by demanding that all couples be lawfully married or lose their church membership. Enjoying only limited success in this policy, they finally "excommunicated" over 5,000 men and women in 1880.[77] This action aroused a tremendous protest and produced serious conflict within the church leadership. The Catholic Church also made such a requirement, but was never as strict in its enforcement.[78]

Economic adjustment was also difficult. After the period of State Supervision ended, many ex-slaves left the plantations to settle as small farmers in Coronie and Para, and along the Saramacca, Commewijne and Cottica Rivers. But many also abandoned agriculture altogether and made the trek to town. By 1890, an estimated 51 percent of Surinam's population was settled in Paramaribo.[79] Although this figure was to decline with the continued immigration of contract laborers, the trek of Creoles to the city was renewed after 1895, when witchbroom disease devastated the production of cacao, forcing many of the remaining Creole small farmers to abandon agriculture.[80]

Living conditions in the city were especially deplorable and continued to be so until after the Second World War. Tiny one-room wooden shacks abounded, and sanitary facilities were improved only gradually.

In their search for employment alternatives, many families were separated for long periods, as men joined the mini gold rush from the 1880s through the turn of the century, entered the crews of balata-bleeders thereafter, or migrated to Curaçao to work in the oil refineries there in the 1920s and 1930s.[81] The wages for unskilled labor in Paramaribo were little better than what the

[76] R.D. Simons, "Dr. Herman Daniel Benjamins, 1850-1933," in Surinaamsche Historische Kring, eds, *Emancipatie 1863/1963: Biografieën* (Paramaribo: Lionarons, 1964), p. 84.

[77] Van Lier, *op. cit.*, p. 216.

[78] *Ibid.*

[79] *Ibid.*, p. 189.

[80] *Ibid.*, p. 171.

[81] *Ibid.*, pp. 180-81, 186.

plantations could offer, and most women were obliged to work to make ends meet.[82] Still others were forced into prostitution. Like the ubiquitous *hanga-lampoe* (hybiscus), wrote De Kom in 1934, "*hangt de roode lamp der ellende voor het huis der armen*" (the red lamp of misery hangs in front of the home of the poor).[83]

Color-line discrimination was an additional problem. Van Lier writes that "the lighter skinned [Creole] considered himself automatically superior to those darker than himself...," and marriages between the two groups were rare, although concubinage was not.[84] De Kom recalls "how the sister of one of my friends refused to go walking with her own brother because his skin was a shade darker than hers."[85] Blacks struggled to gain respectability through hard work and study, but their effort, though aided by some, was complicated by a general air of discrimination.

> The *bakra* (white) [writes Van Lier] was considered by the negro population, much more than by the coloreds, to be a superior and more powerful being. The Jews and outstanding coloreds were also surrounded by an aura of superiority in the eyes of the lower class. This submissive attitude, however, could suddenly give way to aggressiveness – in words or deeds – whenever a man or woman from the masses felt they had been treated without the civility that was owed them.... In spite of their submissiveness towards their betters, the Negro possessed a strong feeling of his own worth.[86]

Worked up by the colored-dominated press, or encouraged by events that seemed to weaken the system's authority, the *volkscreolen* could easily mobilize to express their "latent animosity" towards the upper classes or the regime.[87]

B. The Coloreds' Struggle. The colored middle sectors, themselves, were hard-hit in the period following Abolition. Many skilled tradesmen, clerks and others on the lower fringe of the middle class were left unemployed by the closure or decline of the plantations, and their number increased with the addition of ex-slaves with similar skills and expectations. As Van Lier points out:

> The job opportunities for the Creole middle class are smaller than for such classes elsewhere, in that significant medium-scale agriculture never developed in Surinam

[82] Willem F.L. Buschkens, *The Family System of the Paramaribo Creoles* (The Hague: Martinus Nijhoff, 1974), pp. 120-21; and De Kom, *op. cit.*, pp. 173-75.

[83] De Kom, *op. cit.*, p. 212.

[84] Van Lier, *op. cit.*, p. 207.

[85] De Kom, *op cit.*, pp. 58-59.

[86] Van Lier, *op. cit.*, p. 210.

[87] *Ibid.*

and the Creole has not taken up an independent position of importance in commerce. The Creole appeared unfit for trade because he lacked economic skills, and his extended family and circle of friends too often exhibited a parasitic tendency. As a rule, the Creole lacked the necessary businesslike temperament to counteract this. Since the middle of the 19th century, the retail trade in foodstuffs has been wholly in the hands of Chinese....[88]

The extension of free basic education, and the development of middle-level schooling, despite (or even because of) its Dutch bias, led to a scramble among the lower middle class for diplomas and hoped-for social mobility.[89] Yet the chances for employment being few, frustrations among this group were also considerable. Van Lier states that many of this class migrated to the Netherlands, Indonesia and the Netherlands Antilles, where opportunities were better.[90]

Again, discrimination was an aggravating factor. "The colored individual developed a feeling of great personal insecurity through the discrimination to which he was exposed... by [the whites] whom he considered his reference group."[91] For their part, many Dutch were equally insecure, worrying about their career chances back in the Netherlands, trying to be liberal, but irritated by the aggressiveness and alleged deficiencies of the Creoles.[92] In particular, the competition between whites and coloreds for appointive and elective posts was intense. In 1905, when a Dutch candidate for the Colonial *Staten* was endorsed in a campaign advertisement by several coloreds, Van Lier reports that another advertisement promptly followed, asking "How can a Surinamer in his right mind – especially a colored one – vote for a Dutchman these days, since almost all Dutchmen do nothing else ... than scoff at those 'niggers' and 'that land of monkeys'?"[93]

Social mixing between coloreds and whites was very limited, and "newcomers from Holland, who were taken into the group of their countrymen in Surinam, received the warning on their arrival in the colony, to maintain the greatest reserve in their association with Surinamers [i.e., Creoles] and to limit their social intercourse as much as possible."[94] Nevertheless, some mixing was possible, especially on the neutral ground of the Dutch Reformed and

[88] *Ibid.*, p. 187.

[89] H.C. van Renselaar, "Het Sociaal-Economisch Vermogen van de Creolen in Suriname," *Tijdschrift van het Koninklijk Nederlands Aardrijkskundig Genootschap*, 80, no. 4 (1963), p. 480; and Van Lier, *op. cit.*, pp. 186, 212.

[90] Van Lier, *op. cit.*, p. 188.

[91] *Ibid.*, p. 206.

[92] *Ibid.*, p. 207.

[93] *Ibid.*, p. 204.

[94] *Ibid.*, p. 199.

Lutheran Churches and the Masonic Lodge, "Concordia."[95] *Max Havelaar*, Multatuli's famed nineteenth-century novel about Dutch abuses in the East Indies, provided some intellectuals of both groups with a kind of ideological bridge,[96] and collaborative efforts in journalism and literary work occurred from time to time. But the dominant force between whites and Creoles was polarization.

Further complicating the picture were the relations of all three groups (*volkscreolen*, coloreds and whites) with the Jewish population. While the Dutch, influenced by changing attitudes in the Netherlands, were more liberal in their attitude towards the Jews than towards the coloreds, they were still reserved. The coloreds were somewhat more antagonistic, accusing the Jews of nepotism and a lust for power and resenting their more fortunate circumstances.[97] A latent anti-semitism also existed among lower class Creoles who identified them with the old Jewish slave masters, reputedly the cruelest of the planters.[98]

The basis of these feelings was the considerable economic and political influence exercised by the Jews in the last third of the nineteenth century. Before 1863, Van Lier finds that despite their large numbers, only one Jew had ever been appointed to the Political Council of the colony.[99] Yet, in the years following 1866, with only about one-third of the electorate, their solidarity regularly gave them a near-majority of the elected seats in the *Staten*.[100] Moreover, Jews were frequently appointed to such positions as District Commissioner, Medical and Education Inspector, President of the Court of Justice, Police Commissioner, etc. In the period before 1920, nearly all the lawyers in the colony were Jewish.[101]

On one occasion, in 1891, an unruly mob of *volkscreolen* raged through Paramaribo, breaking the windows of Jewish homes, protesting the behavior of Jewish *Staten* members towards a Governor (M.A. de Savornin Lohman) who had proposed liberalization of suffrage requirements.[102] As Van Lier points out,

> The behavior of the mob was caused by the agitation of the members of the lower middle class, who acted from strong rancor against the better-situated groups. ... But

[95] *Ibid.*, p. 209.
[96] *Ibid.*
[97] *Ibid.*, p. 197.
[98] *Ibid.* Elsewhere, Van Lier finds this popular image of the Jewish planters to be greatly exaggerated ("Notes" in Stedman, *op. cit.*, p. 415).
[99] Van Lier, *Samenleving...*, p. 192.
[100] *Ibid.*, pp. 263, 192.
[101] *Ibid.*, p. 192.
[102] *Ibid.*, p. 264. For the full story of this complicated incident, see *ibid.*, pp. 256-69.

> the violent character of the lower class, which had no special interest in the retention of this Governor nor which would have benefitted from the proposed broadening of suffrage, is only explainable ... as a result of a strong latent animosity..., ordinarily not noticeable, but which, stirred up by such an occasion as this, easily manifested itself in acts of violence.[103]

Following the introduction of compulsory education in 1876, and the subsequent rise in the level of literacy among Creoles, the political influence of the press rose dramatically, contributing much, as C.D. Ooft points out, "to the democratic character of the Surinamese government."[104] Yet the press, like the colored middle class in general, suffered from contradictory impulses towards the Dutch. On the one hand, there was a keen local interest in following the affairs of the Netherlands. J. van de Walle recalled that

> before the [Second World] War, the papers in Surinam were thoroughly dependent upon articles borrowed from the Dutch press. *De Telegraaf* and other papers took two or three weeks to reach the West [Surinam], but no matter how stale or outdated the Dutch news might be, it found its way into the Surinamese papers. Articles, essays and news items from Surinam itself took up the remaining space.[105]

And yet, the press frequently expressed bitter resentment against both the Dutch Government and their representatives in Surinam. In the words of one editor, they do

> everything possible to antagonize the local inhabitants. Probably deluded by visions of the Dutch East Indies, where they confront a conquered, slavish people, or a wholly different race and culture than they, their conceitedness is a slap in the face for the Surinamers.[106]

In 1911, after a comic-opera attempt at a *coup d'état* by a disgruntled Hungarian police officer (Frans Killinger) and a small band of Creole and other collaborators,[107] Creoles of the middle and lower classes treated the defendants as heroic martyrs, gathering to cheer their appearance at the trial. One of Surinam's leading newspapers at the time, *De West*, while stating that the plot could only be the result of a deranged mind, duly noted the sympathetic response of public opinion:

[103] *Ibid.*, p. 269.

[104] Ooft, *op. cit.*, pp. 101-102.

[105] J. van de Walle, *Een Oog Boven Paramaribo: Herinneringen* (Amsterdam: Em. Querido, 1975), p. 29.

[106] Harry Johan van Ommeren, "Eenige besprekingen," in *Suriname* (Sept. 16, 1904), reprinted in Surinaamse Historische Kring, *op. cit.*, p. 173.

[107] D.G.A. Findlay, ed., *Het Politiek Complot van Killinger c.s. in Suriname* (Paramaribo: De West, n.d.), pp. 3-10.

...There exists a great deal of well-grounded dissatisfaction. The sympathy for Killinger and the others – which is present at the moment among the masses – grows out of the fact that he is seen as a man, who by an action – albeit a crazy one – tried to give expression to this existing dissatisfaction.

In our opinion, ... we hope this sad affair will be a warning to the Government.[108]

C. The Depression and Anton de Kom. Apart from the cultivation of rice and the nascent bauxite industry, Surinam's economy was generally stagnant throughout the inter-war years. Thus, the Great Depression meant a shrinkage of an already limited job-market, and the reduction of everyone's livelihood – from the small farmer peddling his meager surplus to the last few sugar and coffee plantation owners (sharing their hardship with their workers in the form of wage cuts). From Curaçao, hundreds of workers let go by the oil refineries streamed back to Surinam.[109] Since unemployment and underemployment were persistent factors of life, the wages of those who *had* work often supported more than their immediate families.[110] These were now stricken with even greater hardship. Finally, with the liquidation of the *Balata Compagnie Suriname* in 1931, over a thousand more workers entered the ranks of the unemployed.[111]

The political manifestation of discontent was quick in coming. Among the Creoles returning from Curaçao, many had some labor union experience and were influenced by Socialist and Communist ideas. One of these, Louis Doedel, had been expelled from Curaçao for his allegedly revolutionary activities.[112] In May and June 1931, Doedel organized several mass meetings, at one of which the then Governor, A.A.L. Rutgers, was petitioned, among other things, to establish a labor-exchange, set up a public works program, open new farm lands, and free more jobs in the civil service to benefit Surinam's unemployed. Governor Rutgers met with a committee of the organizers, while a large mass of demonstrators waited on the *Gouvernementsplein.* The talks were evidently fruitful, and after a march through the city, the crowd broke up. A few weeks later, Rutgers announced that most of the called-for projects would be carried out.[113] But, in the meantime, hundreds of workers were laid off at Moengo, with only twelve days severance pay, as the bauxite company cut back production.[114]

108 *Ibid.*, p. 46-47.
109 Van Lier, *Samenleving...*, pp. 186, 273-74; and Buschkens, *op. cit.*, pp. 121-23.
110 Van Lier, *Samenleving...*, p. 273.
111 *Ibid.*, pp. 184-85.
112 *Ibid.*, p. 274.
113 *Ibid.*, pp. 274-75.
114 De Kom, *op. cit.*, pp. 201-202.

Before the Governor's new programs could be implemented, another mass meeting was held in October 1931. The Governor, and his *ad hoc* "Support Committee" of prominent Surinam leaders, were accused of insensitivity and hypocrisy. Despite efforts to calm the crowd, they left the meeting full of bitterness. A march towards the Governor's Palace was turned back by the police, and the crowd was told to disperse. But bands of demonstrators roamed the streets, breaking windows, stoning houses of the well-to-do, and plundering shops. The women, says Van Lier, were especially violent, showering the police with stones and bottles.[115] Early the next day, new riots occurred, and carts of food on their way to the market were plundered. The police, now armed with sabers and rifles, and supported by a decree forbidding public assembly, had greater success clearing the streets. But at 3 p.m., a crowd gathered in the central square (*Gouvernementsplein*), defying the prohibition. The police, for the first time, opened fire on the assembled demonstrators, killing one and wounding several others.[116] Though order was quickly restored, the bitterness of the crowds remained.

In February 1932, the leaders of the 1931 demonstrations and others set up the *Surinaamsche Arbeiders en Werkers Organisatie* (Surinamese Laborers and Workers Organization, SAWO). Distributing Socialist and Communist literature supplied by Anton de Kom, a Surinamese Black teaching in the Netherlands, the SAWO held a number of mass meetings, at which, according to Van Lier, "strong anti-religious propaganda was often expressed", seemingly directed at the Calvinism of the white and colored elites. Because this violated its own officially-sanctioned statutes, SAWO was outlawed in July 1932.[117]

Finally, De Kom set out for Surinam to take the leadership of the workers' movement. Arriving January 4, 1933, he was met by a large crowd at the dock, and a team of plainclothes policemen, who apparently followed him during his short stay,[118] convinced, as were the newspapers, that he was a Communist. In this famous book, *Wij Slaven van Suriname* (We Slaves of Surinam), written after the affair, he denied the charge.[119] But there was no denying his popularity. Hundreds of workers, of all ethnic groups, lined up daily outside his house to tell him their troubles.

After the Government had foiled his attempts to hold a public meeting to reorganize the labor movement,[120] he evidently changed his tactics, con-

[115] Van Lier, *Samenleving...*, p. 276.
[116] *Ibid.*, p. 277, and De Kom, *op. cit.*, pp. 202-203.
[117] Van Lier, *Samenleving...*, p. 278.
[118] De Kom, *op. cit.*, p. 207.
[119] *Ibid.*, pp. 81-82.
[120] *Ibid.*, pp. 209-210.

centrating his attention on the Asian groups. He later wrote that his goal was to cultivate their sense of common proletarian unity with the Creole masses.[121] Van Lier notes, however, that the strong following De Kom developed among the Javanese had another basis:

> The agents of De Kom took advantage of the desire for remigration . . . circulating rumors that his action would provide an opportunity to return free-of-charge to Java – even for those who had surrendered this right. . . . The rumors increased. . . ; it was said that all plantations would be closed and that ships, to take the Javanese home, were already waiting offshore, so that it was necessary to report to De Kom as quickly as possible. . . . On January 29, 1933, 700 reported, and on January 31, 1350. . . .[122]

On February 1, De Kom was arrested before his activities got further out of hand.[123] For the next few days, great crowds gathered outside the offices of the Attorney General to demand De Kom's release. A rumor, published in one of the papers, that De Kom would be freed February 7, led a large group of Javanese, Hindustanis and Creoles to gather in the *Gouvernementsplein*. Van Lier describes the ensuing scene:

> Within the Javanese crowd, there was little sign of aggressiveness. However, small groups of Creoles provoked the crowd and got them moving . . . in the direction of the Attorney General's office. . . . The crowd was summoned three times to turn back, after which two rounds were fired above their heads. On the third round, some fell wounded. But here, too, as in the disorders of 1931, the crowd didn't believe that the police were really serious, jeering that they had only had blanks. . . . But the fourth round sobered them up. The crowd scattered in all directions, pursued by the police from the center of town. Thirty were left wounded at the scene of the shooting, two of them fatally.[124]

De Kom later noted that even the papers that had been most opposed to his presence in Surinam condemned the police action as unwarranted.[125] After the government evidently failed to assemble an adequate case against De Kom, he was exiled with his family to the Netherlands.[126]

Despite the physical violence involved in these incidents, Van Lier emphasizes that the crowds' aggressiveness was never expressed in terms of violence against individuals. Even in their confrontations with the police, "a kind of sporting element" was always present.

[121] *Ibid.*, p. 209.
[122] Van Lier, *Samenleving*. . . , p. 280.
[123] *Ibid.*, pp. 280-81, and De Kom, *op. cit.*, p. 217.
[124] Van Lier, *Samenleving*. . . , p. 282.
[125] De Kom, *op. cit.*, pp. 219-220.
[126] *Ibid.*, p. 220. He was later arrested by the Nazis for his underground activities during the war and died in a concentration camp in April 1945 (*Suriname Bulletin*, 4 no. 1 (February 1973), p. 18).

The outbursts were serious, but the sporting element was such that the mass considered the discharge of its aggression ... as a goal in itself and were not inclined to make the necessary sacrifices to achieve the concrete objectives which they had originally set for themselves.[127]

Compared with other areas in the Caribbean,[128] Surinam's record of conflict in the post-Abolition period was relatively mild. And, in contrast to the sort of unrestrained violence that had marked the period of slavery, the nature of conflict in Surinam since Abolition suggests that "Dutchification" – in a behavioral sense – was at least moderately successful. Nevertheless, this policy would now be revised in light of the society's other cleavages.

IV. KIELSTRA AND THE CHANGE IN CULTURAL POLICY

From the 1870s through the 1920s, Dutch colonial policy towards the ethnic groups of Surinam encouraged assimilation to a western cultural standard. Although there was some initial caution and sensitivity exhibited with regard to the adjustment of rural Asian school children to the Dutch culture,[129] it was limited and did not extend beyond the first grades. By the 1920s, these children, if they received education at all, were instructed primarily by Creoles or European missionaries in the Dutch language.[130] Asian religious practices were generally tolerated (with the exception of Hindu cremation and Javanese coffin-less burials), but none of the Hindu or Moslem sects received governmental subsidies as did the Christian and Jewish religions, nor were marriages, conducted solely according to Hindu or Moslem ceremonies, given legal recognition. Officially sanctioned holidays (both religious and secular) were patterned after the Netherlands. And, although translators were provided to assist the Asian groups in their dealings with the government, all formal transactions were conducted in Dutch. Despite the failure to attract many Dutch immigrants to the colony, the belief remained that Surinam's earlier prosperity was the work of the Dutch, *ex nihilo*, and it was accordingly ruled thereafter as a *volksplanting* (land of colonization), in Van Lier's term.[131] The gradual acculturation of the *volkscreolen* only served to confirm the appropriateness of this cultural policy.

The Dutch had followed a very different cultural practice in Indonesia. For

[127] Van Lier, *Samenleving...*, pp. 282-83.

[128] See, for example, Paul Blanshard, *Democracy and Empire in the Caribbean: A Contemporary Review* (New York: The Macmillan Company, 1947), pp. 22-28.

[129] Juglall, *op. cit.*, pp. 85-86.

[130] *Ibid.*, pp. 88-89.

[131] Van Lier, *Samenleving...*, pp. 141-42.

three centuries, the colonial policy there had simply been to procure tropical produce, without tampering with the culture of the inhabitants. This was accomplished by "a system of Indirect Rule, with ... native chieftain[s] in charge of native affairs, and ... European agent[s] to look after the business of the [Dutch East India] Company."[132] Despite changes of the system over time, particularly after the British interregnum during the Napoleonic wars, its principal characteristics were the maximization of economic yield and an indirect administration that allowed for, and to some extent safeguarded, local customs and traditional patterns of authority.[133] Van Lier refers to this colonial model as that of an *exploitatiekolonie* (exploitation colony).[134]

With both the *volksplanting* and *exploitatiekolonie* models in practice under the Dutch, the wisdom of Surinam's assimilation policy began to be questioned in the Dutch Parliament. In answer to a question whether an *apartheid*-like protection of the Asian cultural groups might be advisable, the Minister of Colonies, A.W.F. Idenburg, requested the Surinam authorities in 1903 to report on the progress of Hindustani assimilation. Their report was pessimistic. Although the Hindustanis had accepted some local practices (e.g., acquiring some use of *Sranantongo* and Dutch, and adopting Western dress), there was little mingling and almost no intermarriage with the Creole population. Still, the authors concluded, it was too early to predict the final outcome, and no change in policy was recommended.[135]

Over the following years, the assimilation policy was maintained. In 1928, in response to criticism in the Dutch Second Chamber regarding this policy, Minister of Colonies J.C. Koningsberger defended the principle of a unified Western code of law, declaring that "departures from this principle on behalf of one or another population group, with the purpose of protecting the customs of that group for posterity, should fundamentally be rejected."[136] Surinam's Governor in this period (A.A.L. Rutgers) later defended this policy as aiming "to do everything possible to fuse the whole population, white and brown, black and yellow, regardless of whether they be Europeans or Americans, Africans or Asians, to one, undivided, linguistic and cultural society, with one administration of justice...."[137]

Nevertheless, beginning in 1934, the Dutch began to reverse their assimilation policy. The two men most responsible for the new policy were C.J.I.M.

[132] J.S. Furnivall, *Colonial Policy and Practice: A Comparative Study of Burma and Netherlands India* (New York: New York University Press, 1956), p. 218.

[133] *Ibid.*, pp. 221-51.

[134] Van Lier, *Samenleving...*, pp. 141-42.

[135] De Klerk, *De Immigratie...*, pp. 209-10.

[136] Quoted in Ooft, *op. cit.*, p. 122.

[137] Quoted in Van Lier, *Samenleving...*, p. 142.

Welter, Minister of Colonies, and Johannes C. Kielstra, the Governor of Surinam from 1933 to 1944. Both men had had field experience in the Dutch East Indies and were deeply concerned about the condition of the Javanese in Surinam. The De Kom affair (1933) had, if nothing else, revealed the degree of anomie and homesickness that prevailed among this group, as well as the unsettling consequences they could have, if exploited by others for ulterior motives.

As a professor of Indonesian studies at the Agricultural University of Wageningen, Kielstra had turned his attention to Surinam in the 1920s and been particularly influenced by proposals made during the Abolition debates of the 1850s regarding the need to transfer plantation lands directly to the liberated slaves to help their economic adjustment. Although these proposals had been deemed too costly and were voted down, Kielstra rejected the continuing emphasis of "Western-tinted intellectual development" and advocated a new effort in this direction that would help Surinam develop strong village community life based on small-scale agriculture.[138] After his appointment as Governor, Kielstra set to work, with the full support of the Dutch government, applying these policies. But now, given the Creoles' large- scale urban migration and the immigration of Asians since 1873, the would-be beneficiaries of such policies were quite different from those intended in the Abolition debates.

In April 1934, Kielstra sent instructions to all the district commissioners that in their policies of land distribution and creation of new settlements, they "should strive as much as possible to create homogeneous population clusters... according to ethnic and/or religious unity."[139] This immediately precipitated sharp criticism in the Creole-dominated *Staten*.[140] But Kielstra remained undeterred. In August 1936, after the Dutch Government established new criteria for the appointment of district-commissioners in Surinam, Kielstra made it clear that henceforward he would only appoint civil servants to these posts with experience in the Dutch East Indies.[141] But, as these were among the few important posts to which capable Surinamese civil servants could aspire, "it was therefore understandable that Kielstra's appointment

[138] J.C. Kielstra, "De Economische Mogelijkheden van Suriname," *Haagsch Maandblad* 4, no. 5 (November 1925), p. 562. See also Van de Walle, *op. cit.*, p. 60. In a report written for the Dutch Government in 1945, Van de Walle describes Creole unemployment of the 1930s and notes ironically that, at the same time, plantation owners were pressing for further contract laborers from Java to work in the new banana plantations, because Creoles refused to do this work. (J. van de Walle, *Suriname: Rapport uitgebracht door het Hoofd van den Gouvernements Pers Dienst in Suriname* (Paramaribo, 15 Juli 1945), p. 30.)

[139] Quoted in Ooft, *op. cit.*, p. 123. See also Van de Walle, *Suriname...*, p. 31.

[140] Van Lier, *Samenleving...*, pp. 345-46, note 1.

[141] *De West* (Paramaribo), December 31, 1936. See also Ooft, *op. cit.*, p. 128, note 2.

policy created great displeasure among the bureaucratic corps."[142] Members of the Staten strongly denounced this "*verindisching*" (East Indianization) of their government, but without effect.

Still more opposition was expressed to changes in Surinam's Constitution which had been debated in the Dutch Parliament for over a year and were finally enacted in 1936.[143] The new fundamental laws (called the *Staatsregelingen*) seemed to mean a backward step in Surinam's constitutional, and political, development. The two most important changes were (1) the restoration of appointed members to the *Staten* (which had been wholly elective since 1901), and (2) the extension of decree-making powers to the Governor under certain conditions.[144] The restoration of appointed members was defended specifically as a means to provide the Hindustanis and Javanese with "independent representation."[145]

The Governor's powers under the new *Staatsregelingen* were quickly put to the test. Late in 1936, the Governor introduced legislation to establish local governments (*dorpsgemeenten*) at the village level, with the hope that the Asian groups, especially the Javanese, could develop a greater sense of belonging and involvement if they enjoyed a modicum of self-government.[146] The *Staten* amended the bill to require legislative approval for each case. Kielstra rejected the amendment, issuing the law on his own authority in August 1937, pleading "*dringende omstandigheden*" (pressing circumstances) according to Article 101 of the *Staatsregelingen*. The *Staten*, challenging the Governor's questionable use of this provision, immediately appealed this decision to The Hague, and in April 1938, Kielstra was overruled.[147] Yet, because he enjoyed the full backing of Minister of Colonies Welter, he remained in his post, pressing the Asians' cause.

At the same time as Kielstra pushed through the *dorpsgemeenten* law, he introduced an even more controversial proposal to the *Staten* – the so-called "Asian Marriage Laws." Since 1913, the Hindustani Surinam Immigrants Association had periodically appealed for legal recognition of those marriages performed by their religious leaders, but not accompanied by a civil

[142] Van Lier, *Samenleving...*, p. 246.

[143] Ph.A. Samson, "Parlementair Geschiedkundige Beschouwing," in *Gedenkboek: 100 Jaar Staten van Suriname, 1866-1966* (Paramaribo: Staten van Suriname, December 1966), p. 135.

[144] See A.L. Gastmann, *The Place of Surinam and the Netherlands Antilles in the Political and Constitutional Structure of the Kingdom of the Netherlands* (New York: Columbia University, Doctoral Dissertation, 1964), pp. 77-81; and Ooft, *op. cit.*, pp. 78-79, 89-91.

[145] Ooft, *op. cit.*, p. 78.

[146] Ismael, *op. cit.*, p. 148.

[147] Ooft, *op. cit.*, pp. 128-30. The only elected Hindustani member of the *Staten*, C.R. Biswamitre, a Catholic teacher, was one of Kielstra's bitterest opponents on this issue. See his criticisms in *De West* (Paramaribo), August 20, 1937.

ceremony as the law required.[148] In 1920, a member of the Dutch Parliament had echoed this request, and the assimilation debate in 1928, referred to above, reflected the continued concern of many "old Indies hands" regarding the imposition of Dutch practices on an alien population.[149] The major consequences of Asian marriages under the existing marriage laws was the illegitimacy of offspring and the accompanying problems of inheritance.

C.R. Biswamitre, a Hindustani Catholic (the sole elected Hindustani in the *Staten*), criticized the bills (one for Hindu weddings, and another for Islamic ones) as both unnecessary and dangerous. Where a problem of inheritance was foreseen, he argued, a civil ceremony (perhaps long after the religious one) could be arranged, as well as legal recognition of one's children. He felt that the bills had little popular support among Hindustanis, and that the few who championed the bills were concerned primarily to win legal recognition and subsidies for their religious organizations. Surely a better way could be found to achieve these ends, he argued, than by breaking the *rechtseenheid* (legal unity) of the society. The result would be that "we would always be considered more or less as foreigners, non-Surinamers... [while others would] use this as a pretext to close [us] off from the political and social affairs [of the colony]."[150] Others warned that Kielstra's policies were making "our 'most Dutchified colony' into a small piece of Asia in tropical America."[151]

The legislation, introduced by the Governor on January 27, 1937, was unanimously rejected by the *Staten* on March 24, 1938.[152] Four months later, the Governor resubmitted the legislation to the *Staten*, with the warning that he would use his special decree powers to enact it if it was again rejected.[153] In the meantime, new elections had been held, and, implementing the terms of the *Staatsregelingen*, the Governor appointed five additional *Staten* members to represent the Asian groups. On March 30, 1939, after considerable debate, the *Staten* again rejected the bills by a vote of 8 to 6.[154] Kielstra then proceeded to enact the laws on his own authority. He did this first according to

[148] Speckmann, *op. cit.*, p. 54; and C.R. Biswamitre, "Miskenning," *West-Indische Gids* 19 (1937), pp. 176-77.

[149] Van Lier, *Samenleving...*, p. 145.

[150] Biswamitre, *op. cit.*, p. 186.

[151] "Kroniek," *West Indische Gids* 19 (1937), p. 190. For a detailed discussion of the laws and their implications for Surinam, see Ismael, *op. cit.*, pp. 140-47.

[152] C.D. Ooft, "Drie Eeuwen Vertegenwoordigend Stelsel in Suriname," in *Gedenkboek: 100 Jaar Staten...*, pp. 45-46. In response to the *Staten*'s charge regarding the breaking of *rechtseenheid.* Kielstra argued that the legislation would achieve greater legal unity by removing the unnatural discrimination to which properly married Asians were subjected (*De West*, August 27, 1937).

[153] Ooft, "Drie Eeuwen...," *op cit.*, p. 46.

[154] *Ibid.*

Article 100 of the *Staatsregelingen*, which permitted the Dutch Parliament to review the case. But with the German invasion of the Netherlands, this review was never completed. He then used another constitutional provision (Article 32), which provided decree powers "in times of emergency." This was done October 14, 1940, with the marriage laws going into effect January 1, 1941.[155]

Yet another policy of Governor Kielstra and Minister of Colonies Welter to "Indianize" (*verindischen*) Surinam was interrupted by the War. This would have involved the migration of another 10,000 or more Javanese – not as laborers on plantations, but as colonists. Whole *desas* (communities), complete with their religious and civil leadership, would be resettled in Surinam on new lands provided by the government.[156] In fact, 990 Javanese arrived in Surinam under this program in 1939, before the war in Europe and rising tensions in the Pacific caused suspension of the program.[157]

It is still difficult to assess the impact of Kielstra's decade-long departure from Surinam's established assimilation policy. Surinamers of Asian and African ancestry still disagree strongly about the wisdom of his actions.[158] Undoubtedly, the social and political mobilization of the Hindustanis and Javanese was stimulated by the sympathetic behavior of Kielstra and his administration. But it was given an even more direct boost by the outbreak of the Second World War and the economic prosperity that came along with it. The war also precipitated Creole demands for self-determination and a series of new conflicts with the Governor that finally led to his ouster. An indirect effect of Kielstra's policies (and the aloof, stubborn manner with which he applied them) was to dampen the color-line frictions among Creoles that had been growing since abolition. His reversal of Surinam's assimilation policies unwittingly forged a greater sense of Creole solidarity than had existed before.

* * *

Surinam's society has been compared to the *abrasa*, a native vine that coils around a tree, gradually choking it, but gaining needed support for its own survival.[159] The transplanting of many ethnic groups to Surinam under European domination has produced a society in which the indigenous popu-

[155] *Ibid.*, pp. 46-47.

[156] Ismael, *op. cit.*, pp. 76-79.

[157] *Ibid.*, p. 95.

[158] For more on Kielstra, See Van de Walle, *Een Oog Boven Paramaribo...*, pp. 11, 22, 26, 27, 59ff. In 1973, the dispute over the Asiatic Marriage Laws was resolved by the simple expedient of abolishing the requirement of civil ceremonies for *Christian* weddings (*De Ware Tijd* (Paramaribo), August 23, 1973).

[159] I am indebted to former Economics Minister Just Rens for suggesting this metaphor.

lation (the Amerindians) have all but disappeared amid the newer arrivals. The colonial plantation system provided them their initial hold, and, as they grew, fueled by their own cultural resources, they each found a measure of assistance (economic, religious, educational, etc.) from the Europeans that enabled their move upwards. Then, one by one, each runner that made its way to the top (the white planters, the Jews, and then the coloreds) was overtaken by new runners from below – the result being a coiled tangle of independent, living forces, bound together in an interdependent effort to flower and survive.

CHAPTER THREE

NATIONALISM, CULTURAL MOBILIZATION, AND THE EMERGENCE OF POLITICAL PARTIES (1942-1948)

> Sinsi mi de, noiti mi jere na worto "toekomst" na ini Sranan Tongo. Joe sabi san ede? Bikasi Sranan no habi toekomst, efoe ala sani sa tan na fasi disi.
>
> Emile de la Fuente (1946)*

The period from December 1942 to December 1948 marks the watershed of political development in Surinam – as the years of cat-and-mouse impotency for the *Staten* came to an end and the promise of full local autonomy drew near. On December 6, 1942, largely in response to the Japanese occupation of Indonesia and the need to fortify the local resistance there, Queen Wilhelmina went on the radio from her exile in London to pledge a new internal order in the Kingdom of the Netherlands, one "in which the Netherlands, Indonesia, Surinam and Curaçao will all take part, and in which each will look after its own internal affairs, reliant on its own power, yet with the will to assist each other."[1]

The Queen's pledge was greeted enthusiastically in Paramaribo, where new efforts were immediately made to oust Governor Kielstra. But once this was accomplished, the question of autonomy almost immediately became a divisive one. How much autonomy? and for whom? In particular, the issue of universal suffrage sharply divided the Creoles, turning Catholics against Protestants, while at the same time it led to political mobilization among the

* "Never have I heard the word 'future' used in *Saranantongo*. Do you know why? Because Surinam has no future if everything stays the way it is now." (Quoted in *De West*, January 28, 1946).

[1] Rede van Hare Majesteit Koningin Wilhelmina uitgesproken op zondag 6 december 1942 voor Radio Oranje, Londen, in *Koninklijke Woorden over Nederland-Indonesië van Hare Majesteit Koningin Wilhelmina en Koningin Juliana* (Amsterdam: Wereld Bibliotheek Vereniging, 1950), p. 7. Cited also in F.E.M. Mitrasing, *Tien Jaar Suriname, van Afhankelijkheid tot Gelijkgerechtigdheid: Bijdrage tot de Kennis van de Staatkundige Ontwikkeling van Suriname van 1945-1955* (Leiden: Drukkerij "Luctor et Emergo", 1959), p. 1; and Ooft, *Ontwikkeling... p. 139.*

Hindustanis and Javanese. Parties emerged – first along religious, then along more clearly ethnic lines. By 1948, when Surinam's period of local autonomy finally began, political alignments existed that would remain through independence 27 years later.

I. THE SOCIO-ECONOMIC EFFECTS OF THE WAR

With the German occupation of the Netherlands in May 1940, Surinam was thrust unexpectedly and directly into the Second World War. A German ship, the *Goslar*, which had earlier entered Surinamese waters, seeking sanctuary from British pursuit, was purposely scuttled in an attempt to block the Suriname River's bauxite traffic.[2] Thereafter, U-boats appeared frequently off Surinam's coast and elsewhere in the Caribbean and North Atlantic, creating havoc in the Allies' efforts to supply themselves with bauxite and other vital resources.[3]

Because of these circumstances, American troops were sent to Surinam in November 1941 to protect the colony. President Roosevelt defended this action (under a special agreement with the Dutch government in London) declaring that "the bauxite mines in Surinam furnish upwards of 60 per cent of the requirements of the United States aluminum industry, which is vital to the defense of the United States..."[4] American blimps, planes and ships were assigned to search out the U-boats, and the airport facilities at Zanderij were expanded to accommodate the "Flying Fortresses" on their route to Natal and North Africa.[5] In addition to the foreign troops, approximately 5000 Surinamers were mobilized for a territorial army as well as for service overseas.[6]

Economically, the war was a great boon to the local economy. Van Lier estimates that roughly Sf. 68 million worth of investments took place between 1940 and 1945.[7] In particular, the production of bauxite grew spectacularly. The *Surinaamse Bauxiet Maatschappij* (SBM) increased its activities, and the Dutch *Billiton Maatschappij* began operations near the SBM's new Paranam

[2] Van de Walle, *Een Oog...*, p. 78. The effort failed, and the hulk of the Goslar became a kind of island in the river off Paramaribo. Interestingly, the German crew was taken as prisoners of war and forced, during their internment, to clear the ruins of Joden Savanne in the interior (*ibid.*, p. 21).

[3] Blanshard, *op. cit.*, p. 273.

[4] Quoted in *ibid.*, p. 274.

[5] Van de Walle, *Een Oog...*, pp. 78, 81.

[6] Van Lier, *Samenleving...*, p. 305.

[7] *Ibid.*

site on the Suriname River. Despite the recovery of agricultural prices in the war, the plantations went through a new crisis, as many Javanese and Hindustanis left to work in the bauxite mines, or in defense-related jobs.[8] As Van Lier relates

> There was now much money in circulation. Yet there was no exhorbitant rise in wages or prices because the import of consumer goods was restricted and maximum prices were fixed on basic commodities. If the standard of living in 1939 was indexed at 100, it rose in the war to an estimated 160-165.[9]

In contrast to the plantation owners, small farmers – in particular those settled within easy access of Paramaribo – profitted greatly from the additional demand for rice and other foodstuffs.[10]

> Throughout the war, [writes Speckmann] the Hindustani consolidated his economic position.... From the money they accumulated, parents were able to give their children a better education, even to the extent of sending them abroad to complete their studies.[11]

The Javanese, though equally affected by the war, were not always so fortunate. Van Wengen writes that many Javanese began to drift both geographically and occupationally.[12] The social controls of the community were weakened, and adjustment to non-agricultural work was difficult. Prostitution, generally involving Javanese girls, flourished near the American bases.[13]

If the Creoles' desire to assimilate other population groups to Dutch-Surinamese standards had been temporarily set back by Governor Kielstra, the wartime conditions in turn foiled the Governor. Young people of all races mingled in the army camps, road-building crews, and mines, as well as in Paramaribo. Urban migration rose sharply for all groups – the Hindustanis and Javanese in Paramaribo roughly doubling in number.[14] Kruijer points out that the occupational division of labor according to cultural groups that existed before the war now began to break down, as Hindustanis began to practice medicine and law and to compete for the higher posts in teaching and

[8] *Ibid.*, Van de Walle, *Suriname ..., pp. 83, 86; and G.D. van Wengen, De Javanen in de Surinaamse Samenleving* (Leiden, mimeographed, 1972), p. 111.

[9] Van Lier, *Samenleving ...*, p. 305. Van de Walle indicates that prices *did* rise considerably between 1939 and 1942 (*Suriname...*, p. 76).

[10] See Van de Walle's comparison of 1936, 1942 and 1943 prices of selected agricultural commodities in the Paramaribo open market in his *Suriname...*, App. VIII and IX.

[11] Speckmann, *op. cit.*, p. 56.

[12] Van Wengen, *op. cit.*, p. 111.

[13] *Ibid.;* and Van de Walle, *Een Oog...*, p. 115.

[14] Speckmann, *op. cit.*, p. 57.

government.[15] The Creoles were now trapped by the logical consequences of their assimilation ideology. In business, the Hindustanis made sharp inroads against both the Creoles and Chinese between 1940 and 1949 (Table 3.1), and increasingly became urban property holders – often as the Creoles' landlords.[16]

Table 3.1. Stores Registered by Owner's Nationality, Paramaribo, 1940-1949.

Year	*Dutch & Creole*	*Chinese*	*Hindu-stani*	*Syrian*	*Java-nese*	*Others*	*Total*
1940	215	276	63	26	2	30	612
1943	291	289	141	21	2	42	786
1946	366	338	241	29	19	33	
1949	221	329	261	41	22	31	

Sources: *Jaarverslag 1940*, Kamer van Koophandel en Fabrieken (Paramaribo, n.d.), p. 29: *Jaarverslag 1942-43*, Kamer van Koophandel en Fabrieken (Paramaribo, n.d.), p. 41: *De West*, March 21, 1947; *De West*, May 17, 1950.

Moreover, in terms of cultural assimilation, the sudden rise in urban migration and competition reversed an earlier pattern. The first Hindustani and Javanese intellectuals were frequently Catholic or Protestant (or had at least studied in private Christian schools), and often were married outside of their race. They had, in other words, become "marginal men" and potential brokers between their group and the dominant Creole and Dutch elites. But with the sudden (and for most, shortlived,) prosperity, educational opportunities were broadened, and the Asian communities within the larger urban community grew sufficiently so that their members' contacts with, and dependency upon, others for social and intellectual stimulation were relatively reduced. Cultural exogamy declined, and interest-group organization along cultural lines (as we shall see) was stimulated. Thus, *both* Kielstra *and* the Creoles were thwarted. The agricultural boom of the war years lured Asians *out of*, not *into*, agriculture, while the urbanization, and even westernization, of Asians led to their *competition*, not *amalgamation*, with the Creoles. Perhaps these developments would have been inevitable in the long-run. But the war served to telescope their arrival, intensifying the political struggles that accompanied the advent of Surinam's political autonomy.

[15] Kruijer, *Suriname...*, p. 143.

[16] Van de Walle reports that in 1944 alone, Hindustanis acquired Sf. 750,000 worth of urban property, most of it purchased from Creoles (*Suriname...*, p. 69).

II. UNIE SURINAME AND THE BOS VERSCHUUR INCIDENT

When word reached Surinam of the German invasion of the Netherlands, Governor Kielstra promptly declared a state of siege under Article 31 of the *Staatsregelingen*, thereby increasing his powers to rule by decree.[17] The *Staten* did not protest at first, as attention was rivetted upon the plight of the Motherland and the uncertain threat to Surinam itself. Yet the manner in which the Governor utilized his powers to override and ignore the *Staten* soon led to renewed struggles. Protests were made to visiting officials of the Dutch government-in-exile in 1941 and 1942, but to no avail. One of Kielstra's close aides, the District-Commissioner of Paramaribo (J. Hagen) denounced the protests as the work of "professional malcontents and pseudo-intellectuals" and said "the *Staten* produced a dreary lot of second-hand demagoguery and lame quibbling."[18] Aside from his appointment policy at the top level of the civil service, however, there is no proof of racial discrimination on the part of Kielstra. Yet most of the Creole informants for this study who had been involved in politics at this time felt that the Governor underestimated their intelligence and abilities. Kielstra's and his aides' relations with the *Staten* seemed to bear this out.

Nevertheless, until the time of the Queen's December 1942 speech, the *Staten*'s elected members seldom enjoyed any coherent public backing. Because of limited suffrage, elections were generally contests between strong personalities within the Creole elite. On occasion, candidates received the backing of small, *ad hoc kiesverenigingen* (election clubs), but these were usually dissolved after elections, having minimal impact on the shaping of public policy.[19] The only steady influence on politics from outside the government, as pointed out in the preceding chapter, was that of the press. Surinam's three Creole newspapers (none of them dailies as yet) were the liberal *De West* and *Suriname* and the Catholic *De Surinamer*. All were opposed to the

[17] *Ibid.*, pp. 92-93.

[18] *Ibid.*, p. 98. The words were found to be defamatory and Hagen was fined Sf. 75 (*De West*, Dec. 31, 1943).

[19] Two exceptions to this were the group "*Eendracht maakt Macht*" (Unity is Strength), which was active from 1908 to 1926, and the "*Surinaamsche Kiesvereniging*", which gave the former some competition in the years 1918 to 1924. The last of the *kiesverenigingen* before the war was the "*Sociaal Democratische Vrouwen Bond*" (Social Democratic Women's League), set up by a group of Creole market women before the elections of 1938 to support the candidacy of Mrs. G.R. Schneiders-Howard, an elderly health inspector who had long been a champion of better conditions for the rural poor. Although women did not yet have the vote, the group's efforts were successful, and Mrs. Schneiders-Howard became the first woman to be elected to the *Staten*. (Mitrasing, *op. cit.*, pp. 78-79; and Fred Ormskirk, *Twintig Jaren N.P.S.*: "*Groei temidden van beroering*", (Paramaribo: n.p. 1966), p. 11.)

Governor's policies of *verindisching*, and each gave backing in one form or another to the *Staten*'s protests.[20] But aside from the press, Surinam's political life was largely unorganized, clearly strengthening the conviction of the Governor that the *Staten* hardly represented the people he had been appointed to serve.[21]

Following the Queen's speech, however, a new organization emerged, called *Unie Suriname* (the Surinam Union). It embodied the Creoles' effort to counter the Governor's autocratic methods and *apartheid* policies. The organizers, led by a colored government engineer and journalist for *De West*, A.L. Smit, included a number of Creoles, along with two Hindustanis, a Chinese and Javanese, giving credence to its expressed goal of promoting "the feeling of oneness and the love for a just and purposeful social order among all classes and groups of the Surinamese population."[22] But while formally committed to the social goals of integration and national unity, it quickly became apparent that the members had political objectives as well. By organizing public meetings and sponsoring radio talks, the *Unie* focussed attention on a range of social and economic problems confronting Surinam. Drawing an ever-growing following, especially among urban Creoles, the *Unie* picked up the slogan "*baas in eigen huis*" (boss in our own house)[23] and began to champion Surinam's autonomy within the Kingdom as the only means for achieving the reforms they advocated. In the process, the *Unie* quickly became the *Staten*'s major organized supporter in the effort to have Governor Kielstra removed.

The climax to this struggle came in the summer and fall of 1943. In May 1943, an article entitled "*Dank Zij Adolf*" (Thanks to Adolf) was published in *Onze Gids*, a teachers magazine. Attacking "democracy for the big", it warned that many members of the working class in countries untouched by actual warfare were likely to credit their recent prosperity to Hitler and the War rather than to the operating principles of democracy and free enterprise. The article concluded by calling for more meaningful social, economic and political reforms.[24] In response to the article, Governor Kielstra had the magazine confiscated and the Creole editors and author suspended from their teaching posts.[25] He charged them with being "anti-national" and "anti-

[20] Van de Walle indicates that *De Surinamer* felt the charges of "dictatorship" made in the most recent protests were exaggerated, however (*Suriname*..., p. 98).

[21] *Ibid.*, p. 97.

[22] Cited in Ormskirk, *op. cit.*, p. 13; also interview A.L. Smit, March 16, 1976, Epse, Netherlands.

[23] The phrase was reportedly coined by Johan Wijngaarde, editor of *Suriname* (Van de Walle, *Een Oog*..., p. 127).

[24] *De West* (hereinafter *DW*), June 15, 1943.

[25] *Ibid.*

social", and went so far as to threaten the *Hernhutters* with withdrawal of any subsidy for their primary schools if such an incident were repeated.

Although the teachers were soon restored to their posts, opposition to the Governor's autocratic behavior gained new momentum as Kielstra, himself, was charged with harboring pro-Nazi sentiments. Wim Bos Verschuur, a Creole teacher and union leader, and, since April 1942, an elected member of the *Staten*, declared that he had proof that the Governor was sympathetic to the Dutch pro-Nazi *Nationaal Socialistische Beweging* (NSB).[26] Although he never revealed his "proof", he renewed the ironic arguments of the "Thanks to Adolf" article, demanding that the Governor support higher salaries for all workers as proof of "Democracy for All".[27] Warned that his language in the *Staten* was ill-becoming a teacher and that his qualification to teach would be withdrawn by the authorities if he persisted, Bos Verschuur only intensified his attacks.

In July 1943, he drafted a public petition to the Queen calling for Kielstra's removal:

> The people have lost all respect for the Administration.... And this, alas, is now beginning to affect the bond with the House of Orange. Majesty, Highest Ruler, You we approach with respect and confidence, that it may please You to replace Governor Kielstra with an administrator who will be more sympathetic with the problems and needs of our people.[28]

Going around the government offices and center of town, he collected 780 signatures in one day. The following day, July 30, he was arrested and told that he had violated a wartime rule requiring that petitions to the Queen first be approved by the colonial authorities. The petition was especially upsetting to them, because it was written in English as well as Dutch. According to Bos Verschuur, the authorities suspected him of "collaborating with the

[26] Van de Walle, *Suriname...*, p. 96. Bos Verschuur and other informants have repeated the charges to the author, citing an occasion before the War in which the Governor wrote excerpts from a Nazi marching song in the guest book of a Coronie hotel. and interference with efforts to sell or hang anti-Nazi posters in Paramaribo. One informant emphasized the naiveté of Kielstra – as a specialist (and civil servant) in the East Indies, and later during his period in Surinam, he was quite out of touch with European realities. Others have argued that he, and some of his aides, were under the influence of the East Indies version of the N.S.B. Still, it must be concluded, that once the Germans had overrun the Netherlands, his patriotism was above suspicion. His announcement of the German occupation was accompanied by strong words of condemnation, and the *Staten* applauded his show of determination to support the Kingdom in every way possible (*Handelingen*, Staten van Suriname, Zittingsjaar 1940-41, pp. 11-12). His treatment of the German prisoners-of-war (note 2, above) seemed keenly appropriate.

[27] *DW*, June 15, 1943.

[28] Cited in Blanshard, *op. cit.*, p. 300.

Americans for the take-over of the colony."[29] Stripped of his seat in the *Staten*, he was placed in an internment camp in the interior.[30]

Because no charges had been formally made, his arrest precipitated a strong protest in the press and a heated debate in the *Staten*, following which all of the elected members resigned.[31] Although he may have realized what lay in store for him, Kielstra had no alternative but to call new elections. Relying upon *Unie Suriname*'s organizational efforts, the demissionaire legislators stood *en bloc* for re-election against limited opposition, winning easily. Together with *Unie Suriname* they interpreted this as a "vote of no-confidence" against Kielstra and signalled this to the Dutch government-in-exile. On October 8, 1943, the new *Staten* met and renewed their criticism, pointing out that the Attorney General had brought no charges against the defendant, no trial had been scheduled, and no formal explanation had been given. Speaking for the re-elected members, William Kraan (the old, respected editor of *De West*) announced that they would "take no part in the legislative work" of the *Staten* "until there would be a solution to the conflict" with Kielstra, and he appealed to the Queen for mediation.[32]

In November, in evident response to this unsettled situation, Princess Juliana, the Queen's only daughter and heir to the throne, made an official visit to Surinam. As this was the first formal visit to Surinam in over a century by so high a member of the royal family, it was treated by the general public with great enthusiasm. But its political consequences were unmistakable: in December, the Queen announced that Kielstra would be replaced January 3, 1944.[33]

III. DEFINING THE TERMS OF AUTONOMY

After Kielstra's removal, *Unie Suriname* continued to press for Bos Verschuur's release and the removal of the curfew and other laws promul-

[29] Interview, Bos Verschuur, Pad van Wanika, Surinam. Van de Walle writes that the Americans were clearly looked upon with anxiety and distrust by Kielstra (*Een Oog...*, pp. 76-77), and the possible consequences of the petition reaching their hands deeply alarmed him (*Suriname...*, p. 97).

[30] For more details, see Ooft, "Drie Eeuwen...," *op cit.*, pp. 70-74.

[31] *DW*, August 13, 1943.

[32] Ooft, *Ontwikkeling...*, p. 137, and "Drie Eeuwen...,", *op. cit.*, pp. 72-73.

[33] Van de Walle describes the Governor's wariness in handling the Princess' visit (*Een Oog...*, pp. 26-27). Although he was present at virtually all of the Princess' activities, making any direct appeals difficult, she was still able to get a fairly clear picture of the local situation. As she had studied at Leiden University, a group of former Leiden students sent her flowers, whereupon she invited them to a private tea. Among their number was one of the protesting *Staten* members who, together with the others, used the occasion to make their grievances known. (Interview, Dr. J. Einaar, July 19, 1974, Delft).

gated by Kielstra under the state of siege. With most of these objectives achieved by the end of 1944, *Unie Suriname* turned its attention to the post-War reorganization of the Kingdom. In a public meeting on January 1, 1945, Bos Verschuur was a featured speaker. Now a member of the *Unie*, and a candidate for re-election to the *Staten*, he stated the group's position regarding political reforms: broader suffrage, extended to all taxpayers; a representative assembly without nominated members; and a lower voting age.[34]

While this was not a radical departure from the pre-1936 (i.e., pre-*Staatsregelingen*) conditions, its proponents expected it to produce a substantial widening of the electorate as a first step towards the goal of universal suffrage. Eligibility to vote at this time was limited to males over 25, with a ULO (ninth grade) diploma, and/or a taxable yearly income of Sf. 800 (approximately $ 425).[35] This limited the electorate in 1945 to 2945 (or about 3 percent of the adult population), of which only a little over 100 were Hindustanis.[36]

In response to the *Unie*'s "progressive" proposals, the more radical advocacy of universal suffrage was quickly picked up by the Catholic newspaper, *De Surinamer*, with the encouragement of the Redemptist Father, Leonardus Josephus Weidmann, an energetic and socially-conscious Dutch priest. Weidmann had helped to organize the first unions of Catholic workingmen and was clearly concerned about the dominance of Protestant Creoles and Jews in the *Staten* and civil service. Weidmann and *De Surinamer* may also have been given some encouragement in their demands by the fact that Kielstra's successor, Johannes C. Brons (1945-48), was a Catholic. This broke a long tradition of Protestant governors in Surinam and produced an initial uneasiness among the *Staten* members.[37] However, Governor Brons proved to be highly sympathetic and cooperative in his relations with the *Staten*.

To clear the air on the question of universal suffrage, *Unie Suriname* conducted a straw-ballot opinion poll in June 1945. A great deal of publicity was given in the press to the questionnaire and everyone was encourage to fill it out. While the limited number (174) of responses "satisfied" *Unie Suriname*'s expectations, they cannot in any way be called representative of the total

[34] *DW*, January 2, 1945.

[35] Mitrasing, *op. cit.*, p. 143.

[36] Blanshard, *op. cit.*, p. 299. according to figures published in 1946, 1937 voters were located in Paramaribo, 169 in Moengo, 152 in Nieuw Amsterdam (Commewijne), 128 in Nieuw Nickerie, and 138 elsewhere in the districts, for a total of 2,524 (*DW*, March 11, 1946). A.L. Smit (*Unie Suriname*'s founder) later recalled that "we opposed universal suffrage, because we feared a loss of influence to the (Hindu) pandits, since we knew the Creoles were then, and would continue to be, divided." (Interview, March 16, 1976, Epse, Netherlands).

[37] Mitrasing, *op. cit.*, p. 27.

population. They did, however, reveal certain divisions within the elite itself: 44% of the respondents favored the direct introduction of universal suffrage, while 54% favored a more gradual approach.[38] Despite the mixed findings, *Unie Suriname* concluded that its support of gradualism was affirmed.[39]

This must have been Governor Brons' conclusion as well, for in January 1946, he proposed legislation to the *Staten* that would lower the taxable income required for suffrage to Sf. 400. At the same time, he proposed dividing Surinam into several electoral districts, as a means of assuring minority group representation by some means other than appointed seats. His estimate was that these reforms would increase the electorate to about 14,000.[40] Mitrasing writes that the *Staten* was divided on the issue and, after heavy debate and 22 amendments, took no action. The principal position among the majority was that broadening the electorate "was senseless" until the powers of the *Staten*, themselves, were enlarged.[41] Nevertheless, the Catholic press sharply criticized the conservatism of the majority regarding even these modest reforms.

Over the next few years, universal suffrage would be at the heart of the debates on constitutional reform and would stimulate the growth of political parties in Surinam. In particular, as Hindustanis and lower-class Creoles mobilized, the role of *Unie Suriname* declined because of its relatively unpopular position on the issue. Because many of its members were also members of the exclusive Masonic Lodge "Concordia" and represented the higher echelons of the civil service and teachers' corps, they were frequently suspected of elitism. Despite the *Unie*'s support for his re-election, William Kraan warned them against their emphasis on intellectual assimilation at the elite level and called for a higher priority in the development of the Creole lower classes. We are, he wrote in *De West*, opposed to "any old or new tyranny."[42] But, ironically, as its membership became increasingly dominated by Creoles, even the *Unie*'s goal of assimilation began to lose its credibility.

Still the group had some influence left, which it revealed in the elections of February 1946 – the last "party-less" general elections in Surinam. In all, there were 22 candidates in the race for the *Staten*'s ten elective seats. Of these, eight were endorsed by *Unie Suriname* and the rest ran as independents. Most were Creole, Jewish, Dutch or Chinese. Only one Hindustani ran, as an independent, and was defeated. Seven of the *Unie* candidates were elected,[43] thus

[38] *Ibid.*, p. 37.
[39] *Ibid.*
[40] *Ibid.*, p. 143.
[41] *Ibid.*, p. 144.
[42] *DW*, February 14, 1944.
[43] *DW*, February 8, 1946; and Mitrasing, *op. cit.*, pp. 102-04.

maintaining the group's influence over the *Staten* through the autonomy struggle to come.

IV. CULTURAL MOBILIZATION AND THE RISE OF PARTIES

In August 1945, a "Commission of Inquiry into Dutch Views regarding the Place of the Overseas Territories in the Kingdom" had been called into being in the Netherlands under the chairmanship of the lawyer W.H. van Helsdingen; and in Surinam, a "Study Commission on Constitutional Reform", chaired by the lawyer R.H. Pos, was set up the following month and conducted hearings.[44] A proposal by *Unie Suriname* served as the Pos Commission's focus of deliberations.[45] As they proceeded with their work, the new *Staten* of Surinam convened and sharply protested the delay of the Dutch in proposing constitutional reforms.[46] In a mass meeting organized by *Unie Suriname*, it was proposed that a delegation be sent to the Netherlands to seek autonomy. The *Staten* accepted this proposal and, in a closed session, appointed three of its members to make the journey.

Angered by their exclusion from the delegation, a group of Hindustanis and Javanese, led by C.R. Biswamitre, Asgar Karamat Ali, S. Rambaran Mishre, and Ming Doelman, set up the "*Hindostans-Javaanse Centrale Raad*" (Hindustani-Javanese Central Council) and demanded that one Hindustani and one Javanese be added.[47] The *Staten* responded by adding a Chinese and a Hindustani.[48] This met with immediate protest from Moslem groups, who pointed out that the five delegates included four Christians and one Hindu (who, incidentally, were all identified with the *Unie Suriname*). One of the members of this *Centrale Raad*, Asgar Karamat Ali (a notary clerk and appointed member of the *Staten*), now went one step further, setting up the *Moeslim Partij* (MP) in May 1946 – Surinam's first political party. With Islam as "the foundation of its politics," the MP claimed to speak for both Javanese and Hindustani Moslems in calling for universal suffrage, and a form of autonomy that would begin at the village level first, before progressing to the district and national levels.[49] At the same time, the Hindustani and

[44] Ormskirk, *op. cit.*, pp. 39-40.
[45] Interview, Governor J. Ferrier, February 19, 1974, Paramaribo.
[46] Ooft, *Ontwikkeling...*, p. 141.
[47] *DW*, May 6, 1946.
[48] *DW*, May 13, 1946.
[49] Mitrasing, *op. cit.*, p. 80. Van de Walle takes some credit for the MP, having provided Karamat Ali with books about Dutch politics and political parties. (Interview, Hilversum, March 18, 1976).

Javanese Islamic associations sent off a telegram to the Queen, demanding representation on the *Staten* delegation for the "sixty thousand Muslims in Surinam."[50] On request of the Dutch Minister of Overseas Affairs, the *Staten* hastily added a Javanese Moslem to the delegation.[51]

By this time, the process of ethnic and religious mobilization was in full swing. As the *Staten*'s instructions to its delegates only demanded immediate self-government, the conditions of that self-government were the foci of organizational efforts by Catholics and Hindustanis. In a big meeting in the Luxor Theatre on June 9, 1946, the *Hindostans-Javaanse Centrale Raad* passed a number of resolutions regarding the political and socio-economic reforms considered urgent for their followers. They included:

- more civil service jobs for their groups, especially in the district government,
- outlawing of the words "*koeli*," "*koeri*," etc.,
- more new lands, roads, credit, and agricultural extension programs,
- more sympathetic attitudes towards the Hindu and Moslem religions in the schools,
- more investment in rural educational and medical services,

and, regarding political reforms,

- universal suffrage,
- proportional representation on a district basis,
- local self-rule in the districts, and
- more civics education in the schools.[52]

It is interesting to note that the secretary for these proceedings was the young lawyer, Jagernath Lachmon, the first Hindustani to practice law in Surinam, and later the leader of the United Hindustani Party. A more specifically religious political organization, the *Oranje Hindoe Groep*, was set up in July 1946 by a retired Hindustani policeman, J.D. Ponit, which echoed the demand for universal suffrage, while emphasizing the need to retain Surinam's ties to the House of Orange.[53]

The Catholics, led by Father Weidmann, quickly followed the Asians' lead by setting up the *Progressieve Surinaamse Volkspartij* (Progressive Surinamese People's Party, PSV). Advertisements for the first meeting of the PSV (held on August 25, 1946) declared: "all males above 18 can become members

[50] Mitrasing, *op. cit.*, p. 45.

[51] Yet another protest, by the Hindu *Arya Pratinidhi Sabha*, that they were being passed over in preference to the *Sanatan Dharm*, was ignored (*DW*, May 1, 1946).

[52] *DW*, June 11, 1946.

[53] Mitrasing, *op. cit.*, p. 82. In March 1947, Ponit's group changed its name to the *Hindostans Oranje Politieke Partij*. Although it didn't participate in the elections of 1949, it held frequent meetings and expressed its positions in the pages of *De West* and the Hindustani monthly, *Al Haq* (*ibid.*).

irrespective of race, color, belief, origins, class, occupation or whatever. Admission [is] for Catholics as well as non-Catholics."[54] Despite these disclaimers, the meeting had a distinctly religious overtone. Father Weidmann, chairing the proceedings, opened by calling on all present to rise and say, "*God zij geloofd en geprezen*" (God be glorified and praised). Coenraad Ooft, the party's young secretary, then read the program of the party:

- universal suffrage for men and women,
- government scholarships for study in the Netherlands,
- better salaries for teachers,
- stronger government measures against usury,
- legislation to restrict divorce,
- strengthening of the legal position of civil servants, and
- limitation of imports in favor of local production.[55]

Denouncing the inferiority complex felt by many Surinamers, another speaker said, to loud applause, "we don't hold each other in high enough regard. We must see in our own people what we see in the *bakra* [white man]."[56]

Whatever euphoria this organized show of political determination may have generated was undoubtedly dampened by the fact that across town another meeting was taking place. As *De West* noted, regarding the PSV inauguration, "there were few Roman Catholic intellectuals present."[57] The reason was that *Unie Suriname* had scheduled a homecoming reception for Surinam's most famous son, the novelist Lou Lichtveld.[58] Before a packed audience in the Bellevue Theatre, Lichtveld sketched his own political view for the future, advocating as much autonomy as possible "but within the Dutch Kingdom". "There must be a unity", he emphasized, "and the earlier mistakes such as the whites made against the Surinamers [sic] must not be repeated against the Hindustanis." Nevertheless, regarding suffrage, he favored a gradual extension to those who could intelligently use it, comparing its dangers to "a razor handed a child." By all means, he added, with clear reference to the cross-town meeting, Surinam must guard against "a Communist or Vatican-type exploitation of ignorance."[59]

A few weeks later, the positions of Lichtveld and the *Unie Suriname* were

[54] *DW*, August 23, 1946.

[55] *DW*, August 26, 1946.

[56] *Ibid.*

[57] *Ibid.*

[58] Under the pseudonym of Albert Helman, Lichtveld was the author of a series of well-received novels and other books, such as *De Stille Plantage* and *Zuid-Zuid-West*, as well as numerous essays and columns in *De West*. For many years he lived abroad in the Netherlands and the United States.

[59] *DW*, August 26, 1946.

given a more expressly political form with the establishment of the *Nationale Partij Suriname* (NPS). In later years, after the NPS had gone through a series of internal purges and policy changes, there was some debate over its origins and (in particular) its ties to the *Unie*. In the first meeting of the NPS, September 29, 1946, the founding chairman, G.J.C. van der Schroeff, explained that its "Initiative Committee" included none of the present *Staten* members. "We wanted to begin with people who weren't in the midst of politics." Regarding its ties to *Unie Suriname*, he was a little ambiguous. Some of the founders were members of the *Unie*, and hopefully, the NPS would attract other *Unie* members. But the two were separate entities, the *Unie* concentrating on economic and social problems and the NPS on politics. There was a clear coordination, however, in that the Initiative Committee had cleared its plans with the *Unie* and didn't want to impede the latter's work or cause any division in their overall strength.[60] As to the party's membership, he said,

> there is room for Christians, Jews, Mohammedans, Hindus, Confucians, etc. This is one of the important differences between it and the recently established Roman [sic] party.... This party is not a confessional party under the influence of a church.[61]

Mitrasing writes that the NPS must be considered the intellectual offspring of Dr. J.A.E. Buiskool, more than of the *Unie Suriname*.[62] Buiskool was a Dutch lawyer who, having spent much of his childhood in Surinam, returned there after his legal studies, rising quickly to become President of the *Hof van Justitie*. Writing at length on political and socio-economic matters – in books and the local press, he became a central force in the deliberations over constitutional reform.[63] As a Protestant, Buiskool was deeply alarmed at the creation of a Catholic party among the Creoles and began to press his Creole Protestant friends to establish a party that would serve as a counterforce to the PSV. As a Dutchman, he preferred not to take the initiative himself. Thus, the party was born in the law office of Van der Schroeff and included, as members of the preparatory committee, the Chairman of the *Staten*, H.L. de Vries, the journalist P. Wijngaarde, Dr. H. van Ommeren, and a number of Protestant school principals and civil servants, among others. Because Buiskool shared the assimilationist sentiments of the *Unie Suriname*, and believing the PSV could be out-flanked by a truly national party, he urged the

[60] *DW*, September 30, 1946.

[61] *Ibid.*

[62] Mitrasing, *op. cit.*, p. 82.

[63] His book *Suriname Nu en Straks: Een Sociaal-Economische en Staatkundige Beschouwing* (Amsterdam: W.L. Salm & Co., 1946) reads like a party program, and was undoubtedly intended to guide the NPS in its activities.

inclusion of non-Creoles in the initiative committee. W.E. Juglall, a Christian Hindustani school principal and *Unie Suriname* member, and A. Salimin, a Javanese civil servant, were included on the first governing board of the NPS, and in the early years of the party they brought a number of Hindustanis and Javanese into its ranks.[64]

The NPS reiterated the stand of the *Unie Suriname* regarding universal suffrage. Point six of their first party program proposed "Extension of active and passive[65] male and female suffrage on the broadest basis possible, as an introduction to final universal suffrage."[66] As Ormskirk later explained, the party felt the circumstances at that time were not sufficient: "the people as a whole had to be made ripe for it and that could best be achieved by making all Surinamers politically minded via party activities."[67] Buiskool shared this opinion, writing (in 1946), "There are far too many illiterates, or at least people who are insufficiently able to read and write and who don't know what's going on."[68] However, so as not to exclude the interests of less well-educated minority groups, he called for an electoral system that combined both proportional representation and district elections (a position that was similar to the *Hindostans-Javaanse Centrale Raad*).[69]

Despite the efforts of the NPS to become a cross-cultural mass party, the Asian groups were preoccupied by their own rivalries, and still more parties came into existence. The proselytizing rivalry between members of the orthodox Hindu *Sanatan Dharm* and the more reformist *Arya Samaj* had become intense by the 1930's and continued so through the 1940's. As the issue of universal suffrage arose, the high caste leaders of the *Sanatan Dharm* gradually distanced themselves from the position of the *Centrale Raad* (where they were outnumbered by Moslems, Aryans and Christians) and set up their own political party, the *Surinaamse Hindoe Partij* (SHP), on February 13, 1947. Among other things, they indicated a willingness to work with the NPS on a gradual extension of suffrage.[70]

Shortly thereafter, on February 25th, under the leadership of Jagernath Lachmon, members of the *Centrale Raad* set up the *Hindostans-Javaanse Politieke Partij* (H-JPP), and declared themselves ready to enter the political

[64] Reported by an anonymous informant.

[65] Active suffrage refers to voting, while passive suffrage refers to the qualifications of candidates.

[66] Cited in *Verslag van de Commissie tot Bestudering van Staatkundige Hervormingen in Suriname*, Vol. I ('s-Gravenhage: Staatsdrukkerij en Uitgeverijbedrijf, 1948), Appendix XI, p. 126.

[67] Ormskirk, *op. cit.*, p. 25.

[68] Buiskool, *op. cit.*, p. 210.

[69] *DW*, March 4, 1946.

[70] *DW*, February 14, 1947; and Mitrasing, *op. cit.*, p. 84.

arena in pursuit of the principles taken earlier by the *Centrale Raad.*[71] Regarding the new *Hindoe Partij*, the H-JPP argued that "in the present stage of development, the *religious* foundation is too narrow, and the *national* [i.e., as envisioned by the NPS] too vague for [our] groups."[72] More pointedly, the leader of the *Arya Pratinidhi Sabha*, J.S. Mungra, warned

> every Hindu, in particular every Aryan, against [joining] the ...Hindu Party.
> It is very striking that in its leadership there isn't a single Aryan.... It is virtually led by one family. And even worse, all but one of its leaders is a member of the *Sanatan Dharm.* [There is a great difference between these] and the Aryans... who have abandoned most of the outdated ideas such as caste differences.[73]

Amid the rivalry between the SHP and H-JPP, the Javanese were clearly shunted to one side. With only three members on the 16-man directorate of the H-JPP, Javanese interests were crowded out. Yet, because of the growing struggle for independence in Indonesia, the Javanese had suddenly become politicized – eager to show support for their countrymen abroad as well as to remigrate, if possible. A group called the *Persatuan Indonesia* (Indonesian Party) had been set up in 1946 by Iding Soemita and others to organize such a migration.[74] Feeling that these efforts would not benefit the majority of Surinam's Javanese, Salikin M. Hardjo (a member of the *Unie Suriname*) set up the *Pergerakan Bangsa Indonesia Suriname* (Union of Indonesians in Surinam, PBIS), in April 1947, explicitly dedicated to improving the position of the Javanese in Surinam by political means. Like the SHP, they expressed willingness to work with the NPS for the gradual expansion of suffrage.[75]

V. DELAYS AND STATEN IMPATIENCE

A major reason for confusion and delay in reaching an agreement with the Netherlands over constitutional reform was the struggle in Indonesia. An area of far greater size, population, and economic importance than Surinam, the "East Indies" had been the focus of Dutch colonialism since the decline of Surinam's sugar plantations early in the nineteenth century. Following Japan's surrender, Indonesian independence had been proclaimed by Achmed Sukarno in August 1945. British and Australian troops, supervising the Japanese evacuation, were in no position to effectively impede this na-

[71] *DW*, February 26, and March 5, 1947.
[72] *DW*, March 5, 1947.
[73] *DW*, March 7, 1947.
[74] Mitrasing, *op. cit.*, p. 87.
[75] *DW*, April 23, 1947.

tionalist movement, and Lord Mountbatten compelled the Dutch representative in the Allied mission to enter into negotiations with Sukarno's "Republicans".[76] After several military setbacks at the hands of the rebels in Java, the Dutch proposed establishment of a Commonwealth as a compromise to complete independence. Sukarno refused, and for over a year the situation was in flux as the Dutch attempted to re-establish control over the smaller islands, while making new proposals and seeking support for them from the British (still eagerly waiting to leave), as well as from representatives of the smaller islands.[77]

By November 1946, an agreement was reached with the Republicans which recognized the *de facto* authority of the Republic, but which committed both parties to form a Netherlands-Indonesian Union, consisting of "The Kingdom of the Netherlands – including the Netherlands, Surinam and Curaçao – and the U.S.I. [United States of Indonesia]", with the Queen at its head. The Union was to "set up its own agencies for the regulation of... foreign affairs, defense and certain financial and economic policies."[78] The position of Surinam and the Antilles in this Union was not clear, other than being mentioned as parts of the Kingdom of the Netherlands.

The Linggadjati Agreement, as it was called, created great resentment in Surinam. As early as November 1945, signs had appeared in Paramaribo saying that "if they push things to an extreme, there can also be Sukarnos here."[79] A year later, following announcement of the Linggadjati Agreement, the Surinam press and members of the *Staten* protested against the lack of prior consultation. Moreover, they were upset at the sweeping concessions that had been made. Purcy Wijngaarde, an NPS-member in the *Staten*, expressed the view of many when he asked, "must I assume that only through force can the Dutch Government be moved to make quick concessions?"[80] Posters were now reported around Paramaribo that read, among other things, "Self-Government Now", "Atlantic Charter's Four Freedoms for Surinam Too", and

BOSS IN OUR OWN HOUSE
NOT: NETHERLANDS
INDONESIA
SURINAM
CURAÇAO
BUT: NETHERLANDS-INDONESIA-SURINAM-CURAÇAO[81]

[76] Leslie H. Palmier, *Indonesia and the Dutch* (London: Oxford University Press, 1962), p. 48.
[77] *Ibid.*, pp. 50, 53.
[78] Cited in George McT. Kahin, *Nationalism and Revolution in Indonesia* (Ithaca: Cornell University Press, 1962), p. 196.
[79] *DW*, December 31, 1945.
[80] Quoted in Gastmann, *op. cit.*, p. 155.
[81] *DW*, January 13, 1947.

After June 1946, when the first delegation of Surinamese *Staten* members went to the Netherlands to petition the Queen for autonomy, a broad variety of proposals and counterproposals were made.[82] The Study Commission on Constitutional Reform narrowed the range down somewhat in March 1947 by rejecting both provincial status within the Netherlands and Dominion status – the one was too limiting, while the other granted too much independence, in their opinion. Their conclusion was to propose immediate autonomy as an equal member of the Dutch Kingdom, followed by the formulation of a new constitution.[83]

In April, Governor Brons announced that the political reforms for Surinam would be undertaken in two phases, but in the reverse order of that suggested by the Study Commission. In the first phase, to begin directly, there would be a reform of the *Staatsregelingen* to change the election laws, reduce the powers of the Governor and establish cabinet government. In the second phase, the fundamental law of the Kingdom, itself, would be revised, establishing the legal identity of the Surinam and Antillean territories and fixing their respective powers vis-à-vis the Kingdom.[84]

On May 1, an election was held for a *Staten* seat vacated by F.H.R. Lim A Po. It was contested by the NPS, the H-JPP and an independent. The NPS, chafing under a growing anti-Dutch sentiment, campaigned for the nationalization of the Dutch-owned water company and repeated its opposition to universal suffrage. (In an unfortunate variation on Lichtveld's earlier image, *Staten* member Bos Verschuur told a mass meeting of the NPS that for Surinam to accept universal suffrage now would be like "giving a knife to a monkey".)[85] In contrast, the H-JPP's ads read:

> Give the Voters Their Proper Due!
> 70,000 City Dwellers – 14 Representatives.
> 120,000 District Dwellers – 1 Appointed Representative – Truly!
> Replace the City-Legislature (*Stads-College*) – Paramaribo
> With a States (i.e., country-wide) Legislature (*Staten-College*) – Surinam![86]

But of 1643 votes cast, over a thousand went to the NPS and only 187 to the H-JPP.[87]

Irritated by the delays in reaching any accord with the Dutch, and en-

[82] Buiskool, *op. cit.*, pp. 173-79; and Mitrasing, *op. cit.*, pp. 55, 62-65.
[83] *DW*, March 19, 1947.
[84] *DW*, April 23, 1947.
[85] *DW*, April 28, 1947.
[86] *DW*, April 29, 1947.
[87] *DW*, May 2, 1947.

couraged by Governor Brons' legislative acquiescence, the *Staten* acted vigorously to nationalize the Dutch-owned water company, increase the taxes of Alcoa's *Surinaamsche Bauxiet Maatschappij*, and free the Surinam guilder from its Dutch counterpart. A former *Staten* member from this period recalls that "almost every night after work we would meet, often into the early morning, dealing with these and other reforms."[88]

One of the issues that added to the rising cultural strains of the period was a proposal for new large-scale immigration. Approached by the Freeland League for Jewish Territorial Colonization (a group financed largely from the United States), the *Staten* was asked to assist the resettlement of up to 100,000 Jewish peasants driven from their homes in Eastern Europe. All expenses – transport, land-clearing, and housing – would be handled by the Freeland League. After heated debate, the *Staten* voted 7-6 to allow a smaller group (30,000) to come. A study by health and agricultural experts was conducted in the winter of 1947-48, which recommended an area in the District of Saramacca for the settlement. The costs over a five-year period were estimated at $ 35 million. Despite the *Staten*'s approval, bitter protests from the NPS and *De West*, about the social and political consequences of such a new infusion into Surinam's already complex society kept the Governor from carrying it out. Despite repeated visits from Freeland League representatives (extending into the 1950's), the immigration never took place.[89]

Another event revealing the growing cultural tensions occurred in November 1947, when a number of Creole army veterans were arrested in Paramaribo and charged with planning a *coup* against the colonial authorities. The leader of the group, Simon Sanches, had organized his Killinger-like plan because of a general Creole resentment at the alleged pro-Asian prejudices of the authorities. He is reported as arguing that

> We Surinamers [sic] aren't advancing: the number of Chinese and British Indians is greater than the number of Creoles. The foreigners [i.e., Asians] are being supported and we children of the land are not. For years now we have been suppressed. No longer must we tolerate this. Though it cost us our lives, it has to happen. As long as no blood has been shed in Surinam, no change shall come. . . .[90]

In his trial in February 1948, Sanches was found guilty and sentenced to seven months in prison. Nevertheless, the issues he had raised were not untypical of

[88] Interview, A.L. Smit, March 16, 1976, Epse, Netherlands, and others.

[89] *DW*, October 21, 1946; January 31, February 14, March 31, April 9, 14, 21, June 20, 22, July 1, 2, November 24, 1947; February 4, October 4, 1948; February 2, 1949; March 11, 1952. See also *Rapport over de Mogelijkheid van Kolonisatie van Joden in Suriname* (Paramaribo?: Afdeling Suriname van de Freeland League, 1948).

[90] Quoted in Mitrasing, *op. cit.*, p. 72.

Creole sentiments at this time, and sympathetic voices in the press and *Staten* echoed his concerns and urged leniency in his case.[91]

VI. UNIVERSAL SUFFRAGE AND THE FIRST ROUNDTABLE CONFERENCE

It was under these circumstances that the first Roundtable Conference (RTC) took place between the Netherlands, Surinam and the Netherlands Antilles (January 27-March 18, 1948). In October 1947, on the eve of the Sanches affair, the *Staten* chose its eight-man delegation to the RTC. Inviting each established party to nominate two candidates, while nominating five more itself, the *Staten* proceeded to pick one nominee each of the NPS, MP, PBIS and PSV. Passing over the nominees of the H-JPP and SHP, it chose four of its own candidates (including Judge Buiskool and the Hindu scholar, J.P. Kaulesar Sukul).[92]

In December, the Second Chamber of the Dutch Parliament suggested the following amendments to the *Staatsregelingen* of Surinam and the Antilles for consideration by the RTC: (1) extension to each territory of full legislative and budgetary power over internal affairs; (2) increased size of the *Staten* (from 15 to 21 members), with all positions elective; (3) universal suffrage;[93] and (4) reduction of the Governor's powers by creation of an Executive Council (or cabinet) to be appointed by the Governor in consultation with the *Staten*. Regarding apportionment of *Staten* seats, this would be a matter for Surinam and the Antilles to decide themselves.[94]

In the subsequent meetings, both the Surinamers and Antilleans quickly agreed to the first two proposals, but joined in criticizing the ambiguous position of the cabinet, which was not made fully responsible to the *Staten*.[95] In addition, at least five of the eight members of the Surinam delegation opposed the proposal for universal suffrage, while only one unambiguously supported it.[96]

Although somewhat isolated within the Creole community, the PSV dog-

[91] *Ibid.*, pp. 71-73. See also *DW*, November 10, December 22, 1947 and April 5, 1948.

[92] *DW*, October 31, 1947.

[93] The Second Chamber (Lower House) originally suggested universal male suffrage, but this was amended with Catholic support by a Labor representative, Miss C. Tendeloo (*DW*, June 13, 1949).

[94] Gastmann, *op. cit.*, pp. 145-49.

[95] *Ibid.*, pp. 145-46, 149.

[96] The five opponents included G. van der Schroeff, F.H.R. Lim A Po, J.P. Kaulesar Sukul, S.M. Hardjo, and J.A.E. Buiskool. The member favoring universal suffrage was A. Karamat Ali. The two uncommitted members in the delegation were R.H. Pos and J.A. de Miranda. The latter, a Creole of Jewish descent, had been one of the PSV's two nominees.

gedly lobbied the Dutch Catholic People's Party by means of letters and telegrams, and pressed their own uncertain representative in the RTC to vote for it. Pressure was also exerted on Kaulesar Sukul (a member of the SHP) and the PBIS representative to give up their conservative positions and join in the lobbying effort.[97] Further challenge to the delegation's position came from the new *Neger Politieke Partij* (NPP), set up in January 1948 as a clear challenger to the NPS. Stimulated by the reform efforts of the Creole teacher, J.G.A. Koenders, to build pride in the Creoles' own language (*Sranantongo*), the NPP's members represented the first non-Catholic effort at mobilizing lower-class Creoles. Attacking the "elitism" of the NPS, it also came out for universal suffrage and bitterly protested the absence of a "true Negro" from the RTC delegation.[98]

As the RTC deliberations dragged on, a massive rally was organized on March 7, on the Catholic soccer field, by the PSV, H-JPP and MP to demonstrate support for universal suffrage. According to *De West* (which, under the new editorial direction of David Findlay, opposed their position), "order and organization were excellent, and this is certainly a compliment, given the fact that the crowd consisted for 95% of the lower class of over five different ethnic groups."[99] One by one the speakers explained their position in the various languages of the crowd (estimated by the organizers at between 20,000 and 25,000, and by the police at around 7,500[100]). In particular, Jagernath Lachmon, the lower caste leader of the H-JPP, made a striking impression.[101] At the end, the crowd enthusiastically approved a telegram calling on the PSV and MP representatives to leave the RTC if universal suffrage was rejected, and to notify the Dutch Government "of the steadily growing bitterness of a considerable portion of the population."[102] On March

[97] *DW*, January 14, February 23, 1948.

[98] *DW*, March 15, 1948. Although Koenders was not, to my knowledge, involved in the formation of the NPP, his monthly paper, *Foetoeboi* (Servant), published from 1946 to 1956, was very influential in stimulating the further flowering of *Sranantongo* and pride in traditional Creole culture. See Voorhoeve and Lichtveld, *op. cit.*, for more on Koenders' contributions (pp. 10, 135-63).

[99] *DW*, March 8, 1948.

[100] *Ibid.*

[101] As Lachmon spoke, it began to rain, and many began to leave the field. Evert Azimullah describes what followed:

"Almost helpless, the young man yelled through the microphone: 'Countrymen, where are you going? You've come here to listen to the plan of struggle that we've organized on your behalf... and for a few raindrops you're leaving us in the lurch.... Why, they could fire bullets at us, and we'd still keep on fighting for your interests!' To his amazement,... the crowd began applauding and reassembled on the field, and on this critical moment the political leader Jagernath Lachmon was born."

("Lachmon: Kwart Eeuw in de Politiek," *Vrije Stem*, March 16, 1972).

[102] *DW*, March 10, 1948.

17, the Dutch Lower House reaffirmed its support for universal suffrage in Surinam by a vote of 57-19,[103] and the next day the RTC adjourned.

As the delegates returned, preparing for the *Staten* debate on the RTC decisions, Governor Brons announced his resignation. This led to a widespread request, echoed in the *Staten*, that Judge Buiskool be appointed to replace him. Buiskool, who was viewed by many as highly sympathetic to the needs of the Creoles, was seen by the Dutch as having committed himself too politically in his writings and behavior in the RTC. He was, as they put it, too "Surinam-oriented" in his outlook, and was thus passed over for the Dutch Representative to the Allied Mission in Berlin, Dr. Willem Huender.[104] Shortly after Huender officially replaced Brons, Queen Wilhelmina gave the throne over to her daughter, Juliana. In her inaugural address from the throne, Queen Juliana pledged that "freedom, equality and autonomy shall be the inalienable right of Surinam and the Antilles in the new Kingdom."[105] For the *Staten* of Surinam, these were encouraging words, since the new constitutional relation between that body and the Governor was ambiguous, at best, and since, even before it would be instituted, the *Staten* and Governor would undoubtedly have to fight it out over electoral reform.

In the period before the *Staten* debates began, the NPS changed its position on the central question of universal suffrage, and chose instead to promote an electoral system that would safeguard Creole (and hopefully NPS) hegemony in the new order. They were strengthened in this reappraisal by separate by-elections in May, June and August, in which three new NPSers were elected to the *Staten*. The NPS now had five men (one of them, an appointed representative) in the fifteen-member body, while five others were closely identified with the *Unie Suriname*. What may have been particularly important in promoting the NPS shift in tactics was the success its organizers were having among lower-class Protestant Creoles, especially the Moravian *Herrnhutters*. The unavoidably Catholic character of the PSV (like it or not, its leader *was* a priest) tended to rally Protestants to the NPS, even though the latter's program was avowedly secular. A *Christelijke Sociale Partij* (set up in 1948) tried to undermine the NPS by more explicit appeals to the *Hernhutters*, but, like the NPP, it lacked the leadership, organization, and resources to offer serious competition. Thus, the NPS, reasonably confident of its strength in Paramaribo and several other districts, proposed a system of election districts (some to be multi-member districts) with elections by plurality, as opposed to proportional representation (PR). If universal suffrage was to be

[103] Mitrasing, *op. cit.*, p. 132.
[104] *Ibid.*, p. 157.
[105] *Ibid.*, p. 159.

extended to the Asian groups, their numerical advantage over the Creoles could be offset by giving them proportionally fewer seats.

But Governor Huender and his first appointed cabinet preferred the Dutch system of PR. In legislation submitted to the *Staten* in September 1948, they suggested, among other things, creation of five electoral districts, each with PR. The use of a list system would strengthen the growth of responsible parties and would also obviate the necessity of future by-elections.[106]

The *Staten*'s Commission of Reporters replied in their Provisional Report that, while in principle they rejected the adaption of universal suffrage as "a willful imposition of the Dutch State which carries all the markings of colonialism,"[107] they would abide by it. But they would not accept PR, demanding instead a simple majority system, with eleven districts instead of five. In addition, the NPS proposed an "*aanmeldingssysteem*" (a process which required voters to pick up voting cards in advance of an election), a 100 guilder deposit to run for office, and the inking of fingers to prevent repeated voting.[108]

As positions in the conflict between *Staten* and cabinet were publicized, the SHP finally swung over to the PSV/H-JPP/CSP/MP/NPP opposition, and a new party, the *Agrarische Partij* (which proposed a merger of the rural Asian groups), joined them.[109] To counterbalance this lineup, the NPS rallied nine largely Creole unions (representing miners, teachers, government workers, etc.) behind their own position, pointing out that the demographic preponderance of Asians (already over 50% of the population in 1946)[110] could lead to an Asian-dominated government if such an election system were established.

In the parliamentary debate that followed, the defenders of PR argued that the plurality election system would mean wasted votes and the denial of representation to minorities. In addition, the *aanmeldingssysteem* was seen as an impediment to the free exercise of the voting right. The Javanese member also complained that the 100 guilder deposit would bar Javanese from running. A more basic issue – the denial of fair representation to the Asian majority – was not mentioned, though it clearly pervaded everyone's thinking. The PSV was especially vulnerable to the charge that they were betraying the Creoles' interests by this demand. Though not mentioning this issue, the *Staten* majority was harsh in their response. One NPSer labelled the oppo-

[106] Memorie van Toelichting, cited in Mitrasing, *op. cit.*, p. 145.

[107] *DW*, November 1, 1948, special supplement.

[108] *Ibid.*

[109] *DW*, November 12, 1948.

[110] In 1946, it was estimated that there were 79,000 Creoles and 92,000 Asians (Hindustanis, Javanese and Chinese) (*DW*, October 17, 1947).

sition "reactionary" and, with a clear reference to Father Weidmann, sitting in the public tribune, added "their souls are as black as the clothing they wear."[111] In the final voting, the *Staten*'s amendments to the government's bill were approved 8-4.[112] The only concession by the majority was the establishment of nine, instead of eleven, electoral districts. But even here, the districts were constructed so as to overrepresent Paramaribo (with 34,234 voters and 10 seats) relative to the immediately surrounding districts (with 29,877 voters and only three seats). Table 3.2 gives the breakdown of eligible voters, seats, and cultural group distributions in the nine electoral districts established by this law.

Table 3.2. Voters, Seats, and Cultural Group Percentages, by Election District, in 1948/1950.

District	*Voters*	*Seats*	*Cultural Group Percentages*[a]
I (Paramaribo)	34,234	10	C-70, H-18, J- 7
II-IV (Suriname)	29,877	3	C-18, H-55, J-23
V (Commewijne)	15,900	2	C- 9, H-31, J-58
VI (Saramacca)	4,317	2	C- 8, H-52, J-37
VII (Nickerie)	8,396	2	C-21, H-57, J-20
VIII (Coronie)	1,681	1	C-89, H- 1, J- 9
IX (Marowijne)	2,061	1	C-56, H- 5, J-30

[a] Percentage of total population, 1950 Census; C-Creole, H-Hindustani, J-Javanese.
Sources; Mitrasing, *op. cit.*, p. 153, and D.B.W.M. van Dusseldorp, "Mobiliteit en Ontwikkeling van Suriname". *Bijdragen tot de Taal-, Land- en Volkenkunde* Vol. 119, no. 1 (1963), pp. 52-53.

It is interesting to note that, while the NPS *Staten* members intentionally surrendered the districts of Nickerie and Saramacca to the Hindustanis, and Commewijne to the Javanese, they were unwilling to do the same with the district of Suriname – the area around Paramaribo, which, though largely Hindustani, included the important mining area to the south, which was Creole. Thus, the District of Suriname was divided in three single-member electoral districts to assure one Creole representative in the *Staten*.

The opposition parties appealed to Governor Huender to overrule the *Staten*.[113] Sensitive to the desire of the Dutch Government to increase the *Staten*'s autonomy, the Governor was in a difficult position. Rejecting the amendments regarding the *aanmeldingssysteem*, electoral deposit, and color-

[111] Mitrasing, *op. cit.*, p. 150.

[112] For: H.L. de Vries (appointed member, NPS), G. van der Schroeff (NPS), W. Lauriers (NPS), O. Wong (NPS), W. Bos Verschuur (*Unie Suriname*), E. de la Fuente (*Unie Suriname*), D. Findlay (Independent), and P. Wijngaarde (NPS). Against: A. Karamat Ali (appointed member, MP), S. Rambaran Mishre (appointed, SHP), C.H.H. Jongbaw (PSV), and J.A. de Miranda (Independent).

[113] *DW*, November 26, 1948.

ing of fingers, he decided to accept the plurality election system, but requested a more equitable distribution of seats.[114] The *Staten* responded by letting the former amendments drop, but held firm on the districts as designed. The Governor then seemed to have no alternative but to put the law into effect.

As Douglas Rae points out, "Most single-party parliamentary majorities are 'manufactured' by electoral systems."[115] Such was clearly the strategy of the NPS-*Unie Suriname*-dominated *Staten*. But the key to their design was unique – a ten-member district, based on a plurality election, with no restrictions to the number of candidates a party might run. Thus, it was hoped that the NPS, even with a mere plurality of votes over the PSV and any other contending parties, could capture all ten seats. Together with just one other seat from the three remaining Creole-dominated districts, the NPS might then command a majority in the new *Staten*.

* * *

In this period, politically talented individuals discovered the sense of ethnic "territoriality" among Surinam's population groups, and explored its terrain for natural boundaries in order to stake their claims to group leadership. The compromise reached on the universal suffrage/electoral system issues, by creating a district system catering to ethnic strengths, validated ethnicity as a principle of political organization. But while it had become evident that common societal interests were unable to dissolve ethnic differences, they *could* be bridged. Moreover, the ethnic group, itself, could be fragmented. These facts emerged from the manner in which the constellations of group conflict shifted from (1) Creoles united against a Dutch-Asian alliance over cultural policy issues to (2) broad multicultural opposition to the local Dutch authorities during the war to (3) a multiethnic, multireligious opposition to the local Protestant elite (and its few Brahman and reform Javanese Moslem allies) over the issue of suffrage.

At the end of this period, with the NPS appearing to "snatch victory from the jaws of defeat," it probably should be emphasized that no group was very dissatisfied with the new order. An expanded legislature, elected on district lines, offered hope for many aspiring politicians. The prospect of self-government, together with the vigorous action of the *Staten* in these years, satisfied the anti-colonial, reformist instincts of still others, while the fears of ethnic political abuse that *full* independence would later arouse remained fairly subdued.

[114] Mitrasing, *op cit.*, p. 151.

[115] Douglas Rae, *The Political Consequences of Electoral Laws*, revised edition (New Haven: Yale University Press, 1971), p. 74.

CHAPTER FOUR

THE STRUGGLE FOR POWER IN THE NEW REGIME (1949-1954)

> The NPS is the focus of everyone's attention. She is being tugged and jerked in all directions. That she has remained firmly upright is certainly not to be credited to the good intentions of her opponents, nor, sadly, to the efforts of a few of her so-called supporters.
>
> Purcy Wijngaarde, 1949*

Although the color-line/class struggle among Creoles had been submerged to some extent in the Kielstra years, the NPS victories over its opposition in the electoral reform, and in the general elections of 1949, brought with them a new flare-up of Van Lier's "latent animosity." Ironically, but also logically, its locus was the NPS itself. A struggle for power between rival cliques within the party was quickly transformed into a color-line/class struggle, as the newest members of the party attacked the old guard for alleged elitism.

Kielstra had once predicted that the colored middle class would find itself "between the anvil (Asians) and hammer (Black lower class)."[1] Their ultimate collapse under these pressures would not come until the mid- and late-1950s, because the Hindustanis themselves were torn by internal conflict in this period, Yet the plight of the Creole elite had become clear within a year of the 1949 elections.

I. THE 1949 ELECTIONS

With the 1948 electoral law now in effect, the electorate jumped from 3,000 to 96,000 voters, and the most intensive political activity Surinam had ever known began. No less than forty-nine candidates entered the race for

* Commentary in *Suriname* (May 16, 1949), cited in Ormskirk, *op. cit.*, p. 49.

[1] J. van de Walle, interview, Hilversum, April 2, 1976.

Paramaribo's ten seats in the general elections of May 30, 1949. Eight ran as independents, and the remainder contested under eight separate party endorsements. Elsewhere in Surinam, thirty-six candidates (under nine different party labels or as independents) ran for the remaining eleven seats.[2]

With proportional representation rejected under the new law, the three largely Hindustani parties (MP, H-JPP, and SHP) recognized the necessity of joining together for those district races where the NPS or another party might take advantage of their division. Rejecting merger with the Dutch-led *Agrarische Partij*, they formed instead the *Verenigde Hindostaanse Partij* (United Hindustani Party, VHP) on January 16, 1949. In an attempt to resolve the internal religious divisions among their number, they allotted seats on the party's council proportionally – ten Hindus (including both Aryans and Sanatans), five Moslems, two Protestants, two Catholics, and two "who followed none of the major religions."[3] The chairman was Jagernath Lachmon (H-JPP), the vice-chairman was Asgar Karamat Ali (MP) and the first secretary was H. Shriemisier (SHP). Pointing out the risk of Creole domination if they didn't stick together, they adopted the slogan:

> Hindoe, Moeslim, Sikh, Isai;
> Sab hai bhai bhai;
> Bharat mata sab kie mai!
>
> (Hindu, Moslem, Sikh, Christian;
> They are all brothers;
> India is the mother of them all!)[4]

And in response to appeals by the NPS that racial or religious ideologies be avoided in the campaign, a young Hindustani schoolteacher (J.H. Adhin) answered:

> Why not be sentimental about India?... Why not form our own party? Has the Creole group ever thought of voting for a Hindustani? Have the Hindustanis ever found cooperation among the Creoles? Therefore, isn't it understandable why the Hindustanis want to avoid giving their votes to anybody else?[5]

While the Hindustanis united, the Javanese divided. Before the campaign was under way, the reformist PBIS declared that it would support NPS can-

[2] Ormskirk, *op. cit.*, pp. 66-68.

[3] Mitrasing, *op. cit.*, p. 161; *De West*, January 17, 1949.

[4] Mitrasing, *op. cit.*, p. 161.

[5] *DW*, February 21, 1949. *De West*, in response, noted that Creoles had indeed voted a Hindustani into the *Staten* (in 1930) – the ex-headteacher, lawyer, and civil servant, C.R. Biswamitre. Biswamitre, a Catholic, had been an early member of *Unie Suriname*. But after the war he had worked for *Radio Nederland* and had kept aloof from party politics (interview, Amsterdam, July 30, 1974).

didates in Creole districts, in the hope of getting NPS support in Commewijne and perhaps one of the districts on the edge of Paramaribo.[6] While this was still being negotiated, a rival social group, the *Persatuan Indonesia*, was reorganized as a political party, the *Kaum Tani Persatuan Indonesia* (Indonesian Peasants Party, KTPI), with the intention of contesting the election in the same, relatively strong, Javanese areas.

The *Persatuan Indonesia*, as mentioned before, had become prominent among Javanese by championing their right to return to Indonesia. As during the De Kom-affair in 1933, many were encouraged to sell their possessions and come to Paramaribo. Over 800 signed up for passage on the ship *Kota Gede* in 1947, and were disappointed when only 320 were taken aboard. After a shakeup in the *Persatuan Indonesia*, the KTPI was formed under the leadership of Iding Soemita, a former doctor's aide on the Marienburg sugar plantation, who began to refocus the group's activities towards seeking better conditions for Javanese in Surinam. Although actually a Sundanese, Soemita made use of traditional Javanese cultural and other interests to achieve his populist appeal. He attacked the PBIS' modernist orientation as elitist, pointing to their opposition to universal suffrage and their NPS ties. At one point, he accused the PBIS of working with Dutch interests who wanted to exploit the Javanese' cheap labor.[7]

To help the KTPI, M. Ashruf Karamat Ali (a younger brother of the VHP's Asgar Karamat Ali) organized the *Surinaamse Landbouwers Organisatie* (Surinam Farmers Organization, SLO) as an electoral ally, with the hope of drawing non-Javanese votes in these districts. Following the election, the SLO disappeared as an organization, and Karamat Ali joined the KTPI. In party rallies in Paramaribo, the PBIS instructed its followers to vote for the NPS there, while the KTPI and SLO told their supporters to vote for the VHP.[8] The VHP did not reciprocate this latter gesture, running its own candidates in Commewijne and other districts where the KTPI and PBIS contested for seats.

Within the NPS the first color-line conflict emerged over the selection of candidates. Ormskirk writes, "It was very much as if some people tried to close their ears to the *vox populi*. . . . and wished to pick the candidates from the narrow circle of the leadership and their followers."[9] In particular, the promotion by some NPSers of the candidacy of Johan Adolf Pengel caused a sharp polarization. A dark-skinned young man, Pengel had failed to qualify

[6] Letter from the PBIS executive committee to *De West*, July 14, 1947.

[7] *DW*, December 1, 1948.

[8] Mitrasing, *op. cit.*, p. 167.

[9] Ormskirk, *op. cit.*, p. 65.

for the bar despite his studies, for reasons that remain unclear but were often later interpreted as a matter of discrimination.[10] Bright and politically astute, he had become close friends with David Findlay, the young editor of *De West*, and had recently joined the NPS as Findlay's protege. (It should also be pointed out that Findlay, himself, was something of an outsider and latecomer in the NPS "establishment." Though born in Surinam of racially mixed parentage, he had emigrated to the Netherlands Antilles in the 1930s, where he became a teacher and journalist. Returning to Surinam to assist William Kraan in editing *De West*, Findlay had risen fast, being elected to Kraan's seat in the *Staten* when the latter retired in 1946. Though sometimes resented by the established Creole elite for his independence, the importance of his paper made him a necessary ally.)

At the NPS Party Congress of April 18-20, it became clear that the seven NPS members in the *Staten*[11] would all be renominated. Thus, the competition narrowed down to the three remaining Paramaribo seats. After three long nights of intense political activity by, and on behalf of, thirty-five nominees, the party accepted two Blacks (Pengel and his father-in-law, R.B.W. Comvalius, a respected school teacher,) along with one of the party's founders – H.C. van Ommeren, a colored gynaecologist and nephew of a prominent anti-Dutch journalist of the early 1900s. (Among the other seven, only one was dark-skinned and, with the possible exception of Findlay, all were members of the "narrow circle" referred to by Ormskirk.)

The PSV's candidates in Paramaribo included, among others, Father Weidmann and a former Chinese *Staten* member, C.H.H. Jongbaw, along with two women (there were none on the NPS list). Other Creole parties running candidates in Paramaribo were the *Neger Politieke Partij* (NPP), the *Christelijke Sociale Partij* (CSP), and groups called the *Internationale Werklozen Unie* (International Union of Unemployed) and the *Dames Comité* (Ladies Committee). After unsuccessfully trying to negotiate an agreement with the PSV, whereby the PSV would give up four seats on its Paramaribo list to the VHP in return for Hindustani support,[12] the VHP decided to run four candidates on their own list in Paramaribo. Others running in this critical district were the Dutch-led *Agrarische Partij* (with two candidates) and eight independents (including the former *Staten* members A.L.R. Smit, F.H.R. Lim A Po, and Mrs. G.R. Schneiders-Howard).

"Spectacular parades, massive demonstrations, banners and posters"

[10] Interview, Jacques Lemmer ("Pa Lem"), Paramaribo, February 5, 1974.

[11] G. van der Schroeff (the party's chairman), P. Wijngaarde, O. Wong, and L.A. Lauriers. E. de la Fuente, W. Bos Verschuur and Findlay had also joined the party by this time.

[12] Mitrasing, *op. cit.*, p. 162.

[13] *Ibid.*, p. 163.

marked this first campaign.[13] Renting a small plane, the NPS showered Paramaribo, Nickerie, Coronie and the mining district of Para with small parachutes, balloons and pamphlets,[14] while both the PSV and NPS toured the city and districts with sound trucks, announcing meetings and making propaganda. In Nickerie, the VHP went along the river and canals in a motorized launch with its own sound equipment. Everywhere little plays were staged in *Sranantongo* and *Sarnami Hindostans* instructing Surinamers of their duty to vote and showing them how.

The central contest, between the PSV and NPS, took place most directly in the pages of *De Surinamer* and *Het Nieuws* (pro-PSV) and *Suriname* and *De West* (pro-NPS). The latter repeatedly charged the PSV with being a branch of the Dutch Catholic People's Party, and warned voters of its religious fanaticism and dictatorial intentions. The Catholic papers rebutted with charges of the NPS' undemocratic elitism and obvious anti-Catholicism. Defending the NPS' democratic principles, *De West* pointed to the open selection of its candidates and declared that the PSV candidates were picked "in the German way" by Father Weidmann and his friends.[15] On more substantive matters, the PSV accused the NPS of opposing a policy of *kinderbijslag* (family allowances). The NPS, in response, announced their support of such a program, in turn accusing the Catholic Mission of not giving their own lay teachers family allowances, while paying their teaching clergy salaries equal to their lay staff.[16] The charge that the NPS was the party of the Moravian *Herrnhutters* was easily rebutted by pointing to the CSP, whose candidates were mostly *Hernhutters* and included at least one official of the church. The CSP's ironic failure to draw greater support from that source was already apparent before the election in the meager turnout to its meetings and undoubtedly caused relief in NPS circles. The NPP was having similar difficulties and had only been able to field four candidates.[17] The absence of newspaper support and experienced leadership undoubtedly hurt both parties.

Though the rhetoric and feelings aroused by the campaign were sharp and heated, no serious incidents were reported, and on May 30, 1949, long lines of voters waited outside the polling places to cast their ballots. The result (see Tables 4.1 and 4.2) was an overwhelming victory for the NPS, which swept all ten seats in Paramaribo by a large margin over its closest contenders, the PSV and VHP.

Had the latter two allied, as the VHP wished, they might have been able to

[14] *DW*, May 6, 1949.
[15] *DW*, May 13, 1949.
[16] *DW*, May 20, 1949. *DW*, May 25, 1949.
[17] Mitrasing, *op. cit.*, p. 165.

Table 4.1. Votes Cast in the 1949 Elections.

Election District		*NPS*	*PSV*	*VHP*	*NPP*	*CSP*	*KTPI*	*PBIS*	*Other (inc. independents)*
		Maximum and Minimum Votes by Party							
I. Paramaribo	maximum	11,341	5,988	4,377	469	1,589	—	—	2,849[a]
(10 seats)	minimum	9,117	3,935	3,701	286	437	—	—	376
II. Suriname (1 seat)		—	—	4,197	—	—	693	341	250
III. Suriname (1 seat)		—	—	4,953	—	—	927	—	—
IV. Para (Suriname) (1 seat)		889	353	—	—	—	522	—	563
V. Commewijne	maximum	791	—	1,698	—	—	2,325	884	347
(2 seats)	minimum	284	—	1,535	—	—	2,179	—[b]	—
VI. Saramacca	maximum	—	138	1,426	—	—	929	152	—
(2 seats)	minimum	—	—	1,412	—	—	912	146	—
VII. Nickerie	maximum	1,731	292	2,871	—	—	394	1,676	—
(2 seats)	minimum	—[c]	—	2,856	—	—	—	—[c]	—
VIII. Coronie (1 seat)		881	578	—	—	—	—	—	—
IX. Marowijne (1 seat)		1,007	244	—	—	—	—	—	—

[a] Tallied by the independent candidate, F.H.R. Lim A Po.
[b] Instead of running a second candidate, the PBIS instructed their followers to cast their second ballot for the NPS.
[c] The PBIS and NPS ran a joint slate in this district.
Source: Mitrasing, *op. cit.*, pp. 169-70.

Table 4.2. Seat Division in 1949 Elections.

	Election Districts	*NPS*	*VHP*	*KTPI*
I.	Paramaribo	10		
II.	Suriname		1	
III.	Suriname		1	
IV.	Para (Suriname)	1		
V.	Commewijne			2
VI.	Saramacca		2	
VII.	Nickerie		2	
VIII.	Coronie	1		
IX.	Marowijne	1		
	Total	13	6	2

win a few seats, for the sum of votes of their two leading candidates was more than that received by five of the NPS candidates.

It is also interesting to note that Pengel and Comvalius were among the lowest three vote-getters (the other was the NPS' sole Chinese candidate), polling up to a thousand or more fewer votes than the others. Pengel would later claim that this was a function of the elite's resentment of his candidacy and not his unpopularity within the party. On the contrary, he claimed credit for the victory, by bringing the Black lower class into the NPS.[18]

Outside of the city, NPS candidates won in the districts of Coronie, Marowijne (where the bauxite mining center of Moengo is located), and the Para region of the district of Suriname (site of the newer bauxite mines of Paranam and Onverdacht). The KTPI, pitting its leadership against that of the PBIS, won the two seats in the district of Commewijne. The closest competition here was from the VHP, which had hoped to take advantage of the division among the Javanese. The PBIS-NPS alliance made its best showing in Nickerie. But here, as in Saramacca and the two remaining races in the district of Suriname, the VHP easily triumphed.

Clearly, the distorted electoral system had served the NPS well, for with less than 17,000 votes in the country as a whole (about 32% of the vote), they had been able to win 13 seats (or 62% of the total), while the two leading Asian parties, with approximately 25,000 votes between them, could win only eight seats. This, indeed, was a handsomely "manufactured" parliamentary majority. Moreover, the PSV, with another 7,000 votes, was completely shut out. Popular independents, such as Lim A Po, Schneiders-Howard, and Smit, trailed far behind the front runners, as did the other party lists.

[18] *DW*, June 1, 1949.

The ethnic factor played a great role in determining voting in this election, as it would in subsequent ones. Hindustanis and Javanese rallied solidly behind their candidates. This is evident in Table 4.1 in the minimal deviation between maximum and minimum votes for the various Asian party lists in Paramaribo, Commewijne, Saramacca and Nickerie. A greater incidence of split-ticket voting can be seen among Creoles in Paramaribo, but this was

Table 4.3. Comparison of 1949 Election Results and 1950 Census, by Cultural Parties and Groups in Districts of Cross-Cultural Electoral Competition[a]

	Parties/Demographic Groups				
District	*Creole*	*Hindustani*	*Javanese*	*Other*	*Total*
Paramaribo					
1949 votes no.[b]	22,236	4,377			26,613
%	83.6	16.4			
1950 Census no.	49,872	12,857	3,645	5,124	71,498
%	69.8	18.0	5.1	7.1	
Suriname[c]					
1949 votes no.	2,055	9,150	2,483		13,688
%	15.0	66.8	18.1		
1950 Census no.	9,965	29,477	12,605	1,963	54,010
%	18.4	54.6	23.3	3.6	
Commewijne					
1949 votes no.[b,d]	631	1,698	2,578		4,907
%	12.9	34.6	52.5		
1950 Census no.	1,793	5,765	10,953	384	18,895
%	9.5	30.5	58.0	2.0	
Saramacca					
1949 votes no.[b]	138	1,426	1,081		2,645
%	5.2	53.9	40.9		
1950 Census no.	726	4,581	3,263	255	8,795
%	8.2	52.0	37.1	2.6	
Nickerie					
1949 votes no.[b,e]	1,200	2,871	1,200		5,271
%	22.7	54.6	22.8		
1950 Census no.	3,348	9,268	3,212	339	16,167
%	20.7	57.3	19.9	2.0	

[a] Coronie and Marowijne, where only Creole parties contested the 1949 election, are excluded.
[b] In multi-seat districts, the number voting for parties of any given cultural group was calculated by totalling the votes of the leading vote-getters (see Table 5.1) of each party in that group. As Independents generally appealed to Creole, as well as "Other" votes, they were included in the Creole column.
[c] To accommodate the census data, the three electoral areas in the District Suriname are here combined.
[d] Because the PBIS ran only one candidate and encouraged its followers to cast their second ballot for the NPS, the skewed figures of Table 5.1 are adjusted here.
[e] The PBIS-NPS alliance in this district also required adjustment. Both here and in Commewijne, the only reliable correlation is between Hindustani and Creole-Javanese figures.

Source: Table 4.1; and Van Dusseldorp, *op. cit.*, pp. 52-53.

restricted to the lists of Creole parties and Creole independents. If we total the votes received by parties identified with Creoles, Hindustanis, and Javanese and compare them district-by-district with the population figures of 1950, we find a close correlation between cultural groups and party votes (see Table 4.3).

Despite the obvious inequities in the system, the results were received with little protest. The PSV conceded defeat, but presciently advised its members to stand ready in case the NPS should split up.[19] The VHP accepted the results without protest, clearly pleased with the sharp increase in Hindustani representation. The KTPI, having denounced the PBIS throughout the campaign for their dealings with the NPS, reversed themselves after the election and approached the NPS for an alliance.[20] In the bright new world of self-government, the skills of maneuver were easy to learn.

II. THE INTERIM ORDERS AND THE CRISIS OF 1950-51

The new government began with an impressive show of unity – both within and between the NPS and VHP – on the matter of Dutch-imposed changes to the Surinam *Staatsregelingen*. Yet before the regime was a year old, a clash of personalities in the public health service had escalated into a national crisis, which burst both the NPS and VHP asunder and, by precipitating an ugly constitutional stalemate, placed Surinamese self-government in extreme jeopardy.

A. The Interim Orders. In order to confirm the principles of local self-government established by the RTC, and to facilitate further reforms, the Dutch Parliament was obliged to make revisions to its own constitution, as well as "provisional rules regulating the constitutional relations between each territorial government and the Kingdom Government."[21] The latter (called the Interim Orders) were submitted to the *Statens* of Surinam and the Antilles in 1949. Most of the provisions were fully in accord with the RTC agreements.

> The major new change was that the Governor's powers were constitutionally curtailed. In territorial matters the relation of the Governor to the Council of Ministers [i.e., cabinet] was supposed to be the same as those of the monarch and the cabinet in a parliamentary system, which meant that he would have no real power to rule, and

[19] Interviews, Jacques Lemmer, Paramaribo, February 5, 1974; A.L. Smit, Epse, Netherlands, March 16, 1976.

[20] *Ibid.*

[21] Gastmann, *op. cit.*, p. 179.

which signified that full autonomy had been granted through the introduction of parliamentary government and ministerial responsibility.[22]

Representatives of each government at the Hague would be able to participate in all ministerial consultations regarding Kingdom affairs, and all bills in the Dutch Parliament affecting one or both of the territories had to be reviewed by the governments concerned before they could become law. The tradition of judicial appointments by the Crown, on the advice of the local authorities, was to continue.[23]

In July 1949, several months after the main body of the Interim Orders had been approved, the Second Chamber (Lower House) of the Dutch Parliament proceeded to add two more amendments to the proposed new Surinam Constitution (now to be called the *Staatsregeling*) to bring it into conformity with the Kingdom's overall new order. Both touched highly sensitive issues. The first, establishing equal standing and government support for private and public schools – including teacher-training, was a provision already in effect in the Netherlands. The second, fixing the "marriage right" of all citizens, was an attempt to reconcile by legal terminology the separate practices established by the Kielstra government, without effectively altering them.[24] These actions produced a storm of protest in Surinam, and within a few hours after learning of them the *Staten* was called into session to hear criticism by all three parties (NPS, VHP, and KTPI) against this intrusion in Surinam's internal affairs. Protests were sent to the United Nations, the Pan-American Union and to a Dutch-Indonesian conference in Djokjakarta.[25] Surinam's cabinet met shortly thereafter and backed the *Staten's* stand.[26] In particular, as these matters had already been under negotiation by Surinam with the Minister of Overseas Affairs, the unilateral action of the Second Chamber was seen as a breach of faith,[27] as well as a violation of Surinam's supposed autonomy.[28]

Although, strictly speaking, there was no constitutional violation at stake, the angry response of the *Staten* provoked the Dutch First Chamber (Upper House) to advise withdrawal of the proposed amendments and fur-

[22] *Ibid.*, p. 180.

[23] *Ibid.*, p. 180-81.

[24] Ooft, *Ontwikkeling...*, p. 156.

[25] *DW*, July 25, 1949. See also Ooft, *Ontwikkeling...*, pp. 156-57.

[26] *DW*, July 29, 1949.

[27] *DW*, July 27, 1949; Ooft, *Ontwikkeling...*, p. 157.

[28] Technically, the Dutch Second Chamber had not violated any constitutional law. The Interim Orders, which would only go into effect in January 1950, safeguarded Surinam's control over legislation concerning internal affairs, but did not give it the power to amend its own constitution. This was one of the changes yet to be made (by the 1954 Statute). For an analysis of the constitutional issues involved in this matter, see Ooft, *Ontwikkeling...*, pp. 149, 153-61.

ther negotiation with Surinam on these matters. The Second Chamber acquiesced, and on September 10, 1949, the amendments were withdrawn.[29] Subsequent talks produced an agreement to leave any new formulation of marriage rights out of the Interim Orders, leaving the law as it was, subject to reformulation by the *Staten* at a later time. In return for this, the *Staten* conceded the constitutional establishment of educational equality between private and public school systems, provided that Surinam could change this provision as she saw fit. Thus, the final bill became law and the Interim Orders went into effect on January 20, 1950.[30] Leaders of the *Staten* spoke of Surinam now being "on the way toward Independence."[31]

During these negotiations, a number of other political developments had occurred. The NPS Chairman, Van der Schroeff, had been asked by the Governor to form a government "...on as broad a base as possible". After consultations with the VHP and KTPI, he chose a "non-political" Cabinet of "experts", including three members of the outgoing Cabinet.[32] Julius Cesar de Miranda, a distinguished Creole lawyer, was chosen as chairman, and the famed author, Lou Lichtveld, became Minister of Education and Public Health. Of the six ministers, only two were members of the NPS. (Lichtveld was to join, briefly, later in 1949.)[33] The reaction in the press to the new Cabinet was generally positive. *De West* complained only at the lack of more NPSers in it. The Asian parties registered no complaint, presumably viewing its non-partisan emphasis on expertise as the next best thing to an ethnically "broad basis." Van der Schroeff, in the meantime, was elected Speaker of the *Staten*, and, together with Lachmon, Wijngaarde, Pos and Buiskool, was chosen to carry on the talks over the Interim Orders with the Dutch during the fall of 1949.

Both the KTPI and VHP were shaken by events in 1949 affecting the Karamat Ali family. Ashruf Karamat Ali (KTPI) was denied his seat in the *Staten* on the basis that his brother-in-law, S. Jamaludin (VHP) had been elected in another district and had won more votes (which by law gave him priority to a seat). Thus Karamat Ali was obliged to run once more in Commewijne. This time the Creole community in Nieuw Amsterdam lured the PBIS leaders into supporting an NPS candidate rather than fielding one of their own. This new "sell-out" helped the KTPI consolidate its position among Javanese in Commewijne and hastened the PBIS' decline. Karamat

[29] *DW*, September 14, 1949; Ooft, *Ontwikkeling...*, p. 159.
[30] Ooft, *Ontwikkeling...*, p. 160.
[31] *DW*, January 23, 1950.
[32] *DW*, June 13, 1949.
[33] Ormskirk, *op. cit.*, p. 74.

Ali easily defeated his VHP and NPS competition, with 2527 votes to the others' 1110 and 719, respectively.[34]

In March 1949, the former *Staten* member Asgar Karamat Ali, Ashruf's older brother, who had founded the MP and had later become vice-chairman of the VHP, was charged with embezzling Sf 10,000 from the notary firm of the former *Staten* member, J.A. de Miranda (brother of the Cabinet chairman). In September, as the trial got underway (with Van der Schroeff as lawyer for the defendant), De Miranda himself was implicated in the irregularities, and both men were sentenced to 2½ and 3-year prison terms.[35] Lachmon admitted that the VHP had been hurt by the case, though the public seemed to sympathize with Karamat Ali as having been obliged to take the blame when the facts began to emerge.[36] The case was also embarrassing to the PSV, as De Miranda had been their choice as delegate to the RTC.

A new challenge to the VHP was the establishment by dissident Hindu and Christian Hindustanis of a "*Congres Partij*" in December 1949.[37] *De West* criticized the importation of such a name and questioned whether the members were real Surinamers.[38] But as time passed, and as Findlay found himself more frequently at odds with the VHP, he seemed to become more sympathetic with the new group, providing them space for their frequent criticisms of VHP actions.

B. The Van Ommeren-Lichtveld Affair. After his embarrassing loss as an independent in the 1949 elections, the lawyer F.H.R. Lim A Po joined the NPS and in December 1949 was chosen as chairman of its Paramaribo branch.[39] Perhaps unwittingly, he soon found himself in a hotbed of personal jealousies and budding conspiracies. As Ormskirk analyzed the NPS' problems,

> It is a lamentable fact that people who have set up a movement and have brought it through many personal sacrifices to growth and flowering often are not open to the ideas of newcomers.... [while] on the other side are people who can never accept the leadership of others and, in any organization where their word isn't law, they cause trouble.[40]

The lines of conflict were between the founders of the NPS (including its first members in the *Staten*) and the new members who had been drawn to it by the

[34] *DW*, December 7, 1949.
[35] *DW*, September 14, 1949; October 3, 1949; and March 29, 1950.
[36] *DW*, September 19, 1949.
[37] *DW*, December 5, 1949.
[38] *DW*, January 18, 1950.
[39] *DW*, December 12, 1949.
[40] Ormskirk, *op. cit.*, p. 83.

elections of 1949. The first signs of this conflict appeared in David Findlay's muted criticism in *De West* of the new De Miranda cabinet. Van der Schroeff's work was more enthusiastically defended by another NPS-supporting paper, *Suriname*, edited by Johan and Purcy Wijngaarde. Subsequently the divisions in the NPS found their reflection in the rivalry of these two newspapers.

Although there had been a show of unity by the parties and press regarding the Interim Orders problem (only the Catholic *De Surinamer* enthusiastically defending the private education guarantee), *De West* now began to attack elitist tendencies in the NPS leadership.

In response to criticism from Findlay that the leaders of the NPS Party Council should not include members of the NPS-fraction in the *Staten*, Van der Schroeff and Wijngaarde resigned their seats on that body. Subsequently Lim A Po was chosen as the new Chairman of the party.[41]

Findlay now turned his fire on Surinam's famed intellectual, Lou Lichtveld. Repeatedly, *De West* criticized Lichtveld's failure to assume his duties as Minister of Education and Public Health. (After going to the Netherlands to take care of personal matters, Lichtveld had lingered there to help negotiate the Interim Orders matter, then returned to Surinam after a speaking tour of the Antilles.) In particular, the announcement that Lichtveld would continue his travels by representing Surinam at the Pan American Union meeting in Lima (October 1949) provoked *De West*'s ire.[42] But, according to Bos Verschuur, the real motivation for Findlay's pointed attacks on Lichtveld was his fear that the latter might found his own newspaper (or help the Wijngaarde's *Suriname* to become more competitive with *De West*).[43]

Lichtveld was not one to dodge a fight. His letter of application for membership in the NPS in September 1949 clearly threw down the gauntlet. With an eye apparently on Findlay, Pengel, and others, he wrote "that since dangerous enemies of Surinam's well-being are not only outside the NPS, but are even to be found within the Party membership as wolves in sheeps clothing, the undersigned is therefore also compelled to repel them forcefully, since the nature of his job as member of the Cabinet for Education and Public Health is not only to set clear examples and perform constructive work wherever possible, but also to join the struggle against destructive elements..."[44]

41 *DW*, January 9, 1950.

42 *DW*, September 16, 1949.

43 Interview, Bos Verschuur, January 28, 1974.

44 "Indieningsbrief van Lou Lichtveld" (Paramaribo, September 28, 1949), cited in Ormskirk, *op. cit.*, p. 61.

The lines of combat were obvious now. Findlay charged that decisions on policy were being made by Van der Schroeff and Wijngaarde in "*onderonsjes*" (private understandings) with the Cabinet, disregarding the rest of the NPS-fraction in the *Staten.*[45] And these policies were not to their liking. In particular, Lichtveld's warning that teachers' salaries would have to be frozen and the education budget pruned of unnecessary expenditures upset many NPS members and caused protest among teachers and school officials.[46]

Then, on March 21, 1950, Lichtveld, responding to growing pressures by the administration and other staff members of the National Hospital, demanded that Dr. H. van Ommeren resign from the hospital's staff. No explanation was given.[47] After meeting with Lim A Po, Lichtveld postponed the deadline of his ultimatum, in order for a neutral commission to hear the charges. Nevertheless, the "opposition group" in the NPS was infuriated. Van Ommeren was not only a prominent member of the NPS, but also a member of the *Staten.* Although later testimony would reveal that his irascible personality had repeatedly provoked conflicts in the hospital, the hospital had never been free of political conspiracies and turmoil among its ambitious and individualistic personnel. The "opposition" in the NPS thus siezed upon this incident in an attempt to overturn its own government. In doing so, they deeply divided not only their own party, but that of the VHP as well.

Not satisfied with the neutral commission's investigation, Pengel, Findlay, Bos Verschuur, and H.W. Mohamed Radja (of the VHP) introduced a motion of interpellation calling upon Lichtveld to testify regarding the "abuse reigning in the Public Health Service."[48] Two days later, another interpellation was moved for Lichtveld to answer questions on education policy. Both motions were passed.[49]

On April 3, the neutral commission published its findings in the Van Ommeren case. Upholding Lichtveld's decision, they found Van Ommeren guilty of a number of acts of irresponsibility with regards to hospital equipment, and repeated incidents of insubordination towards the hospital administration. Van Ommeren's dismissal from government service was thereupon reaffirmed, with a "dishonorable discharge", costing him any chance for a pension.[50]

[45] *DW*, July 7, 1950.
[46] *DW*, March 20, 1950.
[47] *DW*, March 22, 1950.
[48] *DW*, March 27, 1950.
[49] *DW*, March 29, 1950.
[50] *DW*, April 3, 1950.

In preparation for the interpellation, the Paramaribo branch of the NPS now began to debate a motion of "no confidence" in Lichtveld. Accusing him of appointing relatives to posts in the Health Department, while threatening others with layoffs and other austerity measures, Pengel and Findlay mobilized a majority of votes for their motion in what *De West* called the "most heavily attended NPS meeting ever."[51]

J.C. de Miranda, Chairman of the Cabinet proposed an investigation of the case in terms of the broader charges made regarding the administration of the hospital.[52] But efforts in the *Staten* to get Pengel and Findlay to withdraw their interpellation motions failed, and in a heated exchange Pengel struck the Creole representative of the mining district of Para, L. Eliazer.[53]

On April 20, the interpellation began before a packed *Staten*. In a long extemporaneous address, Lichtveld criticized the general administration of the hospital, described the rivalries and rapid turnover of administrators that had occurred there, and condemned the steady pilferage of supplies by doctors and others. Van Ommeren, he said, recounting a series of incidents, "was the worst of the lot." Instructing the new hospital administrator to institute strict new standards, Lichtveld had been informed of Van Ommeren's persistent insubordination and had had no alternative but to make an example of him.[54] Others were called to testify, and the interpellation lasted for five sessions of angry debate and cross-examinations, during which time the Cabinet made one slight concession – they requalified Van Ommeren for his pension by granting him an "honorable discharge."[55]

By now, the lines were clearly drawn both within the *Staten* and the NPS and VHP. Eight NPSers, four VHPers and the two KTPI members supported the government, while five NPSers and two VHPers lined up with the opposition. Ominously, the four pro-government VHPers were all Hindus and the two aligned with the Pengel-Findlay group were Moslems. Lachmon, who collapsed and was hospitalized in the midst of the interpellation, later spoke of his agony in deciding the VHP position:

> De Miranda [Chairman of the Cabinet] was my guru – he taught me everything I know about law. Even though Van Ommeren may not have been given fair treatment, I couldn't bring myself to oppose my teacher.[56]

[51] *DW*, April 11, 1950.

[52] *DW*, April 14, 1950.

[53] *Ibid*, confirmed by F.E.M. Mitrasing in communication (February 1976).

[54] *DW*, April 21, 1950.

[55] *DW*, April 26, 1950.

[56] Interview, Jagernath Lachmon, January 16, 1974. Ironically, Dr. Van Ommeren was the first to treat Lachmon after his collapse in the *Staten* (interview, A.L. Smit, March 16, 1976, Epse, Netherlands).

Mitrasing also describes the affair as having a strong racial element, in that "the top figures in the party [i.e., NPS] were for the most part light-skinned,"[57] and in the January reorganization of the party, the three *Staten* members on the NPS Council were replaced by "pure Creoles."[58]

There were great pressures put on the VHP and KTPI by both sides in this issue. Just before the interpellation began, the *Staten* voted to subsidize all Hindu and Moslem temples according to the same standards as Protestant and Catholic churches.[59] A short while later, the *Staten* approved a law permitting cremations – a reform long demanded by the Hindus, but deemed "barbaric" by even that champion of special Asian laws, Governor Kielstra.[60] Earlier, Pengel had won credit with the VHP and KTPI by supporting their demands for a new land-distribution scheme,[61] while Van der Schroeff tried to win favor with the Moslems by defending Asgar Karamat Ali in the De Miranda embezzlement trial. When allegations were made that Iding Soemita had misused moneys given him by Javanese for passage to Indonesia, the KTPI organized a mass demonstration to show support for his leadership. NPSers from both sides of the growing cleavage participated in the testimonials.[62]

Nevertheless, when the chips were down, and the motion of "no confidence" against Lichtveld finally came to a vote in the *Staten*, only the two VHP Moslems joined the five anti-government NPSers in the opposition. The motion failed 13-7.[63]

But this was hardly the end of the affair. On the eve of the *Staten* showdown, the eight pro-government NPS members resigned from the party.[64] This produced two new, disruptive issues, equally as controversial as the Van Ommeren dismissal: (1) if a government enjoys a working-majority in parliament, does it lose its legitimacy if it is repudiated by the party that brought it to power? and (2) are not legislators obliged to resign their seats if they leave the party that elected them?[65] Immediately following the *Staten*'s defeat of the

[57] Mitrasing, *op. cit.*, p. 198.

[58] *Ibid.*, p. 199.

[59] *DW*, April 12, 1950.

[60] *DW*, June 12, 1950.

[61] *DW*, March 1, 1950.

[26] *DW*, March 20, 1950.

[63] *DW*, July 7, 1950. Lachmon was still hospitalized and was unable to vote.

[64] Emile de la Fuente, a shrewd, but well-liked, theatre showman, announced that, though he disagreed with the party and had to resign, he would continue to make his Bellevue Theatre available to the NPS for its meetings (*DW*, July 6, 1950). Mitrasing says that the NPS was ready to expel all those voting for the Government, and that, in addition, they would boycott De la Fuente's theatre (*op. cit.*, p. 204).

[65] For a discussion of these problems, see Ooft, *Ontwikkeling...*, pp. 244-47.

"no-confidence" motion, Pengel, Findlay and Van Ommeren made these arguments, demanding new elections as the only way to clear the air.[66] Though not agreeing to new elections, the Cabinet at least accepted part of this reasoning and tendered their resignations to the Governor.[67] Urging them to stay on temporarily, the new Governor, Jan Klaasesz (1949-56), called on Judge Buiskool and J.A. Drielsma, the Minister of Finance, to attempt to organize a new government. Representatives of the NPS, the ex-NPSers, the VHP (both Moslem and Hindu factions), the KTPI, and even the PSV were consulted.[68] After hearing demands for cabinet posts from all concerned, and finding the Asians impossible to satisfy without assigning each bloc its own ministry, Buiskool and Drielsma concluded that the standing government enjoyed a working majority as it was and recommended its retention.[69] Once again, the NPS rose up in protests, and a steady barrage of criticism filled the pro-NPS press (*De West* and two new papers, *Makka* and *De Volksstem*).[70]

Finally, in July 1950, as a gesture of conciliation, Emile de la Fuente, siding with the pro-government coalition, resigned his seat so that a by-election might show the balance of popular sentiments – at least in the district of Paramaribo.[71] The NPS applauded his action, wishing all the others would follow suit. They even invited De la Fuente to rejoin the party if he wished.[72]

The campaign, as De la Fuente had hoped, was concentrated on the issue of confidence in the government. The ex-NPSers now joined with the PSV (which had supported them throughout the conflict) behind an independent candidate, the widely respected medical practitioner, Mrs. Sophie Monkou-Redmond.[73] The NPS, confident of its mobilized strength and apparently eager to further split the VHP, ran W.E. Juglall, a Christian Hindustani school principal who had been one of the founders of *Unie Suriname* and of the NPS. Both the *Congres Partij* and the PBIS announced their support for the NPS.[74] Already torn by the conflict, and trying to mend themselves

[66] *DW*, July 7, 1950.

[67] *DW*, July 10, 1950.

[68] *DW*, July 11, 12, 13, 1950.

[69] *DW*, July 14, 1950.

[70] Besides criticism, appeals for reconciliation were also heard. In a letter to *De West*, A.J. MacMay, an NPS-member, wrote that "People say that the struggle now underway is between intellectuals and the people, meaning Creole intellectuals against Creole masses. They forget that there is only one interest that must bind all Creoles: SELF-PRESERVATION through UNITY." (*DW*, July 21, 1950)

[71] *DW*, July 29, 1950.

[72] *Ibid.*

[73] *DW*, September 11, 1950.

[74] *DW*, October 7, 1950; and Ormskirk, *op. cit.*, p. 88.

regardless of their potential spoiler effect, the VHP nominated a Moslem businessman, I. Husain Ali.

In October 1950, after a short, but heated, campaign that included overtones of racism and anti-Catholicism directed at the backers of Mrs. Redmond (who, ironically, was a *Herrnhutter*), the NPS got their "vote of confidence". Juglall received 10,225 votes to Mrs. Redmond's 5,289. The apparent confusion in the VHP cost Husain Ali dearly, as he trailed the others with only 654 votes.[75] Immediately, new demands were raised for the dissolution of the *Staten* and fresh elections.[76] In response to the outcome, the KTPI now announced its support for the Opposition, bringing the "working majority" of the government coalition to its barest possible margin, 11-10.[77] Reports that the Dutch military was on a stand-by alert underlined the seriousness of the situation.[78]

Continually disrupting *Staten* meetings by their behavior (including strategic walk-outs to break the quorum), the Opposition paralyzed debate on the budget (the 1950 budget had not yet been approved!) and other matters. All disciplinary measures against Van Ommeren were rescinded,[79] and still the obstruction went on, abetted by unruly crowds in the public tribune. The "latent animosity" between *volkscreolen* and the colored elites that Van Lier described as underlying politics in the post-Abolition period had emerged again, more potent than ever, with Pengel as its undisputed champion.

Finally, Governor Klaasesz threatened to seek Dutch approval for a temporary return to decree-legislation, so that the most important pending matters could be resolved.[80] These included, among others, authorization of the 1950 budget, and an election law to introduce PR and reduce the number of election districts to two (one for Paramaribo and one for the rest of the country).[81] Only after this legislation was in effect would he consider new elections. The Opposition immediately appealed to the Netherlands not to support any move towards decree-law.[82] Hostility was now directed at the Governor, and when he spoke at the Thalia Theatre on the observance of United Nations Day, military protection had to be summoned against the

[75] *DW*, October 10, 1950.
[76] *Ibid.*
[77] *DW*, October 20, 1950.
[78] *DW*, October 19, 1950.
[79] *DW*, November 10, 1950.
[80] This involved application of Article 174 of the 1950 Surinamese *Staatsregeling*, which declared that whenever an organ of the government was unable to fulfill its constitutional functions, a Dutch law can establish which law-making authority shall replace it (cited in Mitrasing, *op. cit.*, p. 210).
[81] *DW*, November 16, 1950.
[82] *DW*, November 18, 1950.

crowd of demonstrators that assembled outside.[83] In response to the Opposition's appeal, the Dutch government invited representatives from both sides of the conflict to come to the Netherlands to state their views.[84] The Opposition refused, at first, offering to work on the budget and other fiscal measures instead.[85] But the Governor held his ground, and as the Coalition's delegation prepared to depart for the Netherlands, the Opposition reversed itself and sent its own delegation.[86] Representing the government were Lichtveld, Wong, Shriemisier and Rambaran Mishre, while the Opposition was represented by Pengel, Findlay, Lim A Po, Mohamed Radja and Soemita.[87] The split among Hindustanis widened as the VHP wired the Dutch government that Mohamed Radja no longer represented that party,[88] and Lachmon declared in a meeting of the *Sanatan Dharm* that "if I, Lachmon, take no revenge on Radja and Jamaludin, then I am no son of a Hindu."[89]

After long talks, the Dutch finally imposed a settlement substantially in accord with the Opposition's position. They refused to approve the electoral reform, but, as a gesture to the pro-government Coalition, insisted that the *Staten* adopt new rules reducing the quorum for meetings to a simple majority and strengthening the Speaker's powers to maintain order and decorum in the meetings. All of the other measures should be handled by the present *Staten*, but immediately thereafter new elections should be called.[90] Following this decision, the delegates returned home, the *Staten* quietly passed the pressing legislation, De Miranda resigned as chairman of the Cabinet, and on January 15, 1951, the *Staten* was dissolved with new elections announced for March 14.[91]

How had the Dutch managed to produce an end to the conflict? As David Findlay later admitted, they dangled before the delegates the possibility of a multi-million dollar (Nf 250 million) hydroelectric dam on the Suriname River.[92]

[83] *DW*, November 25, 1950.
[84] *DW*, November 24, 1950.
[85] *DW*, December 5, 1950.
[86] *DW*, December 8, 1950.
[87] *DW*, December 9, 1950.
[88] *Ibid.*
[89] *DW*, December 18, 1950.
[90] *DW*, December 22, 1950.
[91] *DW*, January 12, 1951.
[92] *DW*, January 6, 1951.

III. THE 1951 ELECTIONS

On January 11, 1951, as the *Staten* completed its work, the Coalition government, in a last effort to buttress their electoral position, introduced a bill to strike all "aliens" from their voting lists.[93] What was at stake were the votes of the Javanese. In the period following full Indonesian independence in 1949, the Dutch had passed a law as part of the transfer of sovereignty to Indonesia whereby residents of the Netherlands, Surinam, or the Antilles of Indonesian birth or ethnicity must choose between Dutch and Indonesian citizenship.[94] Iding Soemita, while applying for Dutch citizenship himself, had not advised his followers to follow suit if they were interested in ever returning to their homeland.[95] And, though many had specifically taken Indonesian citizenship, many others didn't declare for either, thus legally becoming "aliens." A large majority of the Javanese in Surinam could thus have been disenfranchised by the Coalition's law.[96] With the *Staten* formally "dissolved" but still able to meet, the Coalition brought the issue to a vote, where by the abstention of one Coalition member, it was rejected by a 10-10 tied vote.[97] The KTPI protested to the Dutch and Indonesian governments against further action, and in a subsequent *Staten* meeting, with a large crowd of Javanese demonstrating outside, the Coalition declared it would defer to the Dutch for legal advice on the matter.[98] A cartoon in *De West* at this time depicted Van der Schroeff and Lachmon barring the door of a wooden hut, while a Javanese climbed through the roof. "Press harder, Jaggernath," ordered Van der Schroeff. "Yes, boss," Lachmon answered.[99] Both clearly might have gained from Javanese disenfranchisement. Commewijne, whose population was 58% Javanese and 31% Hindustani (with a pocket of Creoles in Nieuw Amsterdam) would have likely been won by the VHP, and Javanese support for the NPS in other, largely Creole, districts would have been weakened, giving the Coalition a better chance to hold power. Yet it was a desperate and unpopular gamble. When the Dutch advised against the bill, the Coalition withdrew it.[100]

[93] *DW*, January 15, 1951.
[94] Gastmann, *op. cit.*, p. 185; Mitrasing, *op. cit.*, p. 214.
[95] *DW*, August 18, 1950.
[96] Gastmann, *op. cit.*, p. 186.
[97] *DW*, January 20, 1951.
[98] *DW*, January 23, 1951.
[99] *DW*, January 29, 1951.
[100] The issue remained a thorny one, however. Those who had opted for Indonesian nationality *did* lose their right to vote – only those who had not opted one way or another could still vote. The Dutch passed another law in 1954 to enable Indonesian citizens to regain their Dutch nationality, and this was put into effect in Surinam later that year (Gastmann, *op. cit.*, pp. 186).

Having won these tactical confrontations, the NPS and KTPI now seemed assured of a fairly easy time in the elections. Indeed, the heat of division was now most intense among the Hindustanis. In the late summer of 1950, while Lachmon was still hospitalized, the two Moslem *Staten* members wrote a long letter to *De West* reporting that "dark forces" in the VHP were driving out the Christians and Moslems "who didn't want to submit to their caprice." Denouncing the absence of democratic organization in the party, they warned that these "forces" were violating the established principle of 2-1 proportionality between Hindus and Moslems. With apparent reference to the former SHP members, they charged that "those who were against universal suffrage, [are] now trying exclusively to dominate the VHP."[101] Although this protest may have stimulated the VHP to select a Moslem candidate for the October election, his poor showing (relative to VHP votes gathered in Paramaribo in 1949) seemed only further to inflame the Moslems' anti-Hindu passions. The bloodshed attending the partition of India and Pakistan, of course, may also have been a contributing factor in this, but Creoles on both sides of the NPS split aggravated the Hindustanis' division with actions of their own. For example, the Coalition government decided to raise the price of paddy rice and gave credit for its decision to the lobbying of Hindu *Staten* members. *De West* angrily replied that the credit should really have gone to Mohamed Radja, who had first made an issue of it.[102] "We sympathized with you in your sickness," Jamaludin wrote in December 1950 in an open letter to Lachmon,

> and now you present yourself as a martyr, blaming us.... You and Mungra are busy day and night pumping the Hindus full of hate and revenge against the Moslems. The consequence is that the Moslems are being boycotted in the districts and are being unnecessarily harassed and bothered by the Hindus. Mr. Mungra says openly "Radja and Jamaludin are traitors." "They've sold out the Hindustanis to the Negroes," etc. Any action against us will be against all Moslems.[103]

In January, the split was formalized as the VHP changed its name to the "*Verenigde Hindoe Partij*", and ran Hindu candidates in all districts but Commewijne, where it shared a ticket with a Coalition Creole, and the predominantly Creole districts of Paramaribo, Para, Coronie and Marowijne, where it ran no candidates.

Mohamed Radja and Jamaludin now joined the NPS. But ironically they found their reception was less than enthusiastic. In the NPS meeting that selected candidates for the March election, both men were denied the nominations they thought they had earned and were shunted off to the KTPI to

[101] *DW*, August 30, 1950.
[102] *DW*, September 23, 1950.
[103] *DW*, December 22, 1950.

stand in races in Saramacca and one of the largely Hindustani districts near Paramaribo. Not even W.E. Juglall was renominated in the rush of Creoles for the seats vacated by the Van der Schroeff group.[104] Those renominated by the NPS included Pengel, Findlay, Van Ommeren, Comvalius and P.A.R. Kolader (who had been elected from Coronie, but was renominated from Paramaribo). New candidates included Just Rens, F.H.R. Lim A Po, H.M.C. Bergen, S. Axwijk and A.J. MacMay.

In protest against the way the *Staten* was dissolved, the PSV and Van der Schroeff's group boycotted the elections in Paramaribo. Thus, with only 13 candidates (10 NPS, two CSP and one Hindustani independent) in the Paramaribo race, compared with 49 two years before, the campaign was mostly lacking in drama. Mitrasing described a sense of "disgust" against politics among many in the thinking public.[105] Compared to a voter turnout of over 53% in the 1949 elections, the turnout in Paramaribo in 1951 was only 27.7%. In the country as a whole, the turnout was 38.4% compared to 47.5% two years before. In particular, in the mining area of Para, where a five-way race occurred between various labor leaders and others for that district's single seat, the turnout was only 31.2%.[106] The results, in terms of seat allocation, was precisely the same as in 1949: the NPS returned 13 members, the VHP six, and the KTPI, two (see Table 4.4).[107]

Table 4.4. Seat Division in 1951 Elections.

Election District	*NPS*	*VHP*	*KTPI*
I. Paramaribo	10		
II. Suriname		1	
III. Suriname		1	
IV. Para (Suriname)	1		
V. Commewijne			2
VI. Saramacca		2	
VII. Nickerie		2	
VIII. Coronie	1		
IX. Marowijne	1		
Total	13	6	2

Even with the support of Javanese, Creole and Hindustani Moslem votes, Jamaludin and Mohamed Radja were badly defeated by the VHP in their

[104] *DW*, February 13, 1951.
[105] Mitrasing, *op. cit.*, p. 215.
[106] *Ibid.*, p. 218.
[107] *DW*, March 22, 1951.

Table 4.5. Votes Cast in the 1951 Elections.

Election District		*Maximum and Minimum Votes, by Party* *NPS*	*VHP*	*KTPI*	*CSP*	*Congres Partij*	*Other (incl. Independents)*
I. Paramaribo	max.	7,558	—	—	2,225	—	1,404
(10 seats)	min.	6,630	—	—	1,778	—	—
II. Suriname (1 seat)		—[a]	2,943	—[a]	—	139	1,259[a,b]
III. Suriname (1 seat)		—[c]	3,467	—[c]	—	166	1,286[c]
IV. Para (Suriname) (1 seat)		775	—	723	85	—	403[d]
V. Commewijne	max.	—	1,780	2,408	—	—	—
(2 seats)	min.	—	1,654	2,272	—	—	—
VI. Saramacca	max.	—	1,433	1,021	—	—	—
(2 seats)	min.	—	1,400	1,016	—	—	—
VII. Nickerie	max.	1,472[e]	2,669	1,240[e]	—	—	855[e]
(2 seats)	min.	—	2,303	—	—	—	—
VIII. Coronie (1 seat)		No election, NPS seat uncontested.					
IX. Marowijne (1 seat)		664	—	466	—	—	—

[a] H.I. Husain Ali, the VHP's candidate in the 1950 Paramaribo election, bolted from the party over its failure to support him sufficiently, and ran against the party's leader, Lachmon, as an independent in 1951. He enjoyed NPS and KTPI support in this effort.
[b] Another candidate in this race, from the *Agrarische Partij*, collected 437 votes.
[c] S.M. Jamaludin, the Moslem ex-VHPer, ran as an independent with NPS and KTPI support.
[d] There were two independent candidates, each sponsored by a miners union: L.E. Eliazer (a *Staten* member who had left the NPS; though chairman of the Paranam Mineworkers Union, and running under their endorsement, he received only 403 votes), and A.P. Lieuw Kie Song (Billiton Mineworkers Union, with 169 votes).
[e] The NPS and KTPI ran a common slate in this district.

Source: Mitrasing, *op. cit.* p. 214.

races. In Nickerie, where the NPS ran a Creole and a Javanese, party members there repudiated this strategy and split their vote between the Creole of the NPS and an independent Creole, giving the VHP an easy victory (see Table 4.5).

To the surprise of many, who expected a more partisan cabinet, the NPS *formateurs* (Findlay and Lim A Po) chose only two NPSers to the new body (W.E. Juglall and A. Smit). For the remaining posts they picked a group of independent experts, inviting one minister (J.A. Drielsma) to stay on. Judge Buiskool was asked to be Minister of General Affairs, presiding over the new body. As Mitrasing points out, the NPS was forced into such a selection by the fact that "the few 'ministeriable' figures in the NPS had distanced themselves from the job, not wishing to risk any political adventures."[108] The fact that the Governor felt obliged to pick two *formateurs* indicated that uncertainty and divisions in the NPS had not yet been resolved.[109] Following the next RTC, the party would once again be convulsed in conflict – this time between the supporters of Findlay (inheriting the "elitist" mantle) and those of Pengel (representing the darker-skinned lower class).

IV. THE LAST ROUNDTABLE CONFERENCES AND THE KINGDOM STATUTE

In June 1951, the Dutch announced they were adding a contingent of marines to the army units stationed in Surinam.[110] This provoked an angry protest by the *Staten* that they had not been consulted. Their demands for an explanation, set amid new anti-Dutch sentiments (directed also at the operations of the Dutch-financed Surinam Cultural Center[111]), provoked the Dutch Government into announcing plans for a new Round Table Conference.[112]

[108] Mitrasing, *op. cit.*, p. 220.

[109] A.L. Smit reports that Findlay and Lim A Po had their own list of candidates for the Cabinet and that the result was a series of difficult compromises. (Interview, March 16, 1976, Epse, Netherlands).

[110] *DW*, June 14, 1951.

[111] *DW*, May 9, 10, 22 *et passim*, 1951.

[112] With this announcement, the *Staten* quickly appointed a delegation composed of Lim A Po, Pengel, Bergen and Findlay (NPS), Lachmon and Shriemisier (VHP), M.A. Karamat Ali and Soemita (KTPI) and Jongbaw (PSV) (*DW*, July 27, 1951). But the Dutch weren't in any hurry to move, calling instead for a Study Commission to prepare an agenda for the meeting which would be held in 1952 (*DW*, October 11, 1951). To this "proto-delegation", the government named Buiskool, Lim A Po, Pos, Jongbaw and H. de Vries (who had replaced Pos as Surinam Representative in the Hague).

The primary consideration in this "second phase" of constitutional reform was the creation of a Kingdom government, distinct from, and "above", the three component units of the Kingdom. In the preliminary negotiations, it was agreed that a separate Kingdom-wide legislative body would be too costly and unwarranted by "the limited number and scope of matters falling within the definition of Kingdom affairs."[113] Instead, in the draft Statute submitted to the RTC, it was proposed that the Netherlands' own Council of Ministers and Parliament be utilized "with the proviso, however, that both these bodies would, when dealing with Kingdom affairs, be expanded to include representatives of Surinam and the Antilles, and follow special rules of procedure."[114] Other provisions regarding citizenship, economic cooperation, and the protection of judicial integrity and democratic institutions were also accepted without difficulty.[115]

But during the plenary meeting of the RTC that began April 3, 1952, criticisms that had been raised in NPS meetings in March 1952 were brought forward. One was related to the resolution of conflicts between the Netherlands and the Caribbean states over Kingdom matters. If the Surinamese or Antillean representatives to the Hague objected to decisions of the Council of Ministers on matters affecting the overseas territories, "a special cabinet committee consisting of the Dutch Prime Minister and an equal number of Dutch and Caribbean Ministers would have to find the solution."[116] Buiskool, speaking for the Surinam delegation, objected to the Dutch Prime Minister having the final deciding vote. This seemed to compromise Surinam's status and prestige as an autonomous part of the Kingdom.[117] The other criticism was the absence of a preamble stating that each state enjoyed the right of self- determination – i.e., the right of secession.[118] Again, although no real anticipation of secession as yet existed, the factor of prestige was involved. The Dutch refused to change either provision. Thus, on these two points the RTC was deadlocked, adjourning on May 29 to allow a smaller committee to deliberate further on these points.

The Dutch *Algemeen Handelsblad* reported that "Nationalism is rearing its head in Surinam."[119] In fact, the RTC delegation seemed to be reacting

[113] Quoted in Gastmann, *op. cit.*, pp. 205-06.
[114] *Ibid.*, p. 206.
[115] *Ibid.*, pp. 206-07.
[116] *Ibid.*, p. 207.
[117] *Ibid.*, pp. 207-08.
[118] *Ibid.*, p. 208.
[119] Reprinted in *DW*, June 25, 1952.

particularly to a mobilized protest by Surinamese students in the Netherlands who had condemned the draft of the new Kingdom Statute as neo-colonial. This group, called the *Nationale Comité Suriname*, demanded nothing less than complete independence. David Findlay, in *De West*, speculated that the students had been influenced by the Marxist ideas of Cheddi Jagan in British Guiana.[120] In any case, their demands had an impact on Johan Pengel, who was eager to attract young intellectuals such as these into the NPS, especially since a number of them had come from lower class backgrounds and could be expected to develop a popular following upon their return to Surinam.

After the Conference adjourned, Pengel began to pursue a more nationalistic course. He began by introducing a motion to declare July 1 "a national holiday", and followed this by calling for a competition to establish a Surinam flag, as well as a new national coat of arms and anthem.[121] Not only did these moves produce an angry reaction from the Hindustanis, it also began to split the NPS once again. David Findlay, a close ally of Pengel's in the earlier NPS conflict, now turned against him and, with four other NPS *Staten* members, joined with the VHP to defeat the "national holiday" motion.[122] Findlay defended his vote by calling for a national holiday that spoke for all Surinamers; but Pengel, arguing that this could have been just one of several "national holidays", grew more furious in the course of the debate, finally calling "no longer for autonomy, but complete independence.... Perhaps", he added, "blood will have to flow."[123]

Pengel especially directed his fire at Buiskool, whom he accused of compromising Surinam at the RTC. In a tense meeting at which Buiskool defended his policies, Pengel remarked bitterly that "we've considered him a Hercules, a Messiah..., [but] the more I got to know him the more questions rose in my mind, especially in his treatment of his colleagues." In particular, he denounced the way Buiskool had abstained, for reasons of being Dutch, in almost all votes at the RTC. Lachmon and Mungra echoed these criticisms

[120] *DW*, June 25, 1952. The group was led by E.A. Gessel, C. Defaris, and the young law student, Eddy Bruma (*DW*, June 11, 1952). A Surinam-Antillean bi-weekly, *De Westindiër*, published in The Netherlands, defended the students against the "Communist" charges, and warned critics of the Surinamese delegation's performance at the RTC against using "cheap" political charges. (July 4, 1952, p. 1; July 18, 1952, p. 1.)

[121] *DW*, July 4, 1952; August 12, 1952.

[122] *DW*, July 4, 1952.

[123] *Ibid.* A.L. Smit recalls that Pengel and Lim A Po visited him at this time, proposing full independence, with Lim A Po as President and Pengel Prime Minister. "I told them they were fools." Shortly thereafter Lim A Po had a severe heart attack and was forced to resign his seat in the *Staten*. (Interview, March 16, 1976, Epse, The Netherlands).

and Buiskool angrily tendered his resignation.[124] Comparing the treatment both Lichtveld and Buiskool had received, Mitrasing writes that both were "'hauled in' with hosannas and crowned, only to be shortly afterwards...'crucified'."[125]

For several months no new negotiations on the Statute were attempted. The Dutch, trying to repair the damage in Surinam-Netherlands feelings, quietly withdrew their Marines in June 1953, as Surinam had demanded.[126] Later, when the Dutch government invited Surinam and the Netherlands Antilles to send representatives to join the Dutch delegation to the United Nations General Assembly meeting, where their status as dependent territories was to be discussed, the two states responded that they would do so only on condition that the Dutch clarify their right of self-determination.[127] In negotiations with both governments, the Minister of Overseas Affairs, Professor W.J.A. Kernkamp, stated that an explicit provision for secession was unacceptable, but a preamble expressing the right of self-determination, and a simple provision for change of the Statute might have the same implicit significance.[128] Kernkamp was sharply criticized by his own government for this agreement, and after subsequent deliberations, the Hague announced a compromise solution on June 26, 1953, "in which it was proposed to shift the accent [on] the right of self-determination from the preamble to the amendment procedure."[129]

After a preliminary conference had ironed out other matters, this second RTC was reconvened in May 1954, and the Statute of the Kingdom of the Netherlands was quickly approved.[130] By October, the three legislatures had given their approval, and on December 29, 1954, the new Statute was officially promulgated by Queen Juliana.[131] It is remarkable that the Statute enjoyed such "smooth sailing" through the Surinam *Staten*, given the sharp divisions in the NPS. Apparently, the explanation for Surinam's acceptance of the Statute was economic. At stake, as the RTC met, was a Ten Year Plan of sizeable developmental assistance, plus the continued study of a hydro-

[124] *DW*, August 27, 1952.

[125] Mitrasing, *op. cit.*, p. 240.

[126] *DW*, December 31, 1953.

[127] Gastmann, *op. cit.*, note 2, p. 210.

[128] *Ibid.*, p. 211.

[129] *Ibid.*, pp. 211-13. No change was made in the other provision, giving the Dutch Prime Minister a tie-breaking vote in deadlocked Kingdom legislation.

[130] *Ibid.*, p. 213.

[131] Though the status of the overseas territories was less than sovereign, the United Nations accepted their argument that this had been a voluntary association, and thus exempted the Netherlands from the duty of reporting annually to the Secretary-General. Gastmann describes the United Nations deliberations on this, *ibid.*, pp. 215-32.

electric project on the Suriname River.[132] All parties now clearly recognized the need for Dutch aid and aspired to win credit for, and control over, the Plan's implementation. But first, the struggle for control over the NPS – and the Government – had to be resolved.

* * *

Despite their ability to contrive an electoral system beneficial to the Creoles, and to defeat all comers in the first national elections under universal suffrage, the NPS actually seemed to "snatch defeat from the jaws of victory" in the fratricidal battles that immediately followed. Once again, ethnicity, though a powerful force when under effective, cohesive leadership, proved to be fragmentable. The Creoles reverted to color-line conflict of the sort that had characterized Surinamese politics for fifty years or more, while Hindustanis experienced a mild version of the troubles then tormenting the Indian subcontinent itself. Again, cross-cutting ties emerged to subdue any rawer version of ethnic hostility among groups. Hindus and the Creole old-guard found each other now (bridging the universal suffrage cleavage), while Moslems and *volkscreolen* tried to do the same. As the Creoles' built-in advantage disappeared in the *Staten*, Hindustanis and Javanese could both aspire to roles as holders of the balance of power. But, with yesterday's enemy now conceivably tomorrow's friend, political opportunism would have to be accompanied by somewhat more circumspect application of the ethnicity principle – at least at the level of inter-elite relations.

[132] Adhin, *op. cit.*, pp. 115.

CHAPTER FIVE

VERBROEDERING: REJECTION AND APPROVAL (1955-1967)

> A nation is not formed by taking over the language, or religion, of others; that's not necessary to form a nation. A nation is formed by the feeling that Surinam is the soil on which we all find our existence and that this ground is dear to us; that is solidarity. No one can impose this feeling on you, no one can force it, you acquire this feeling from your Creator. Therefore, Mr. Speaker, let us do everything we can to allow this feeling of solidarity to come to fuller expression.
>
> Jagernath Lachmon, 1959*

Whether there is any truth to the charge that young Surinamers in Amsterdam were impressed by the nationalism and Marxism emanating from the Peoples Progressive Party (PPP) in British Guiana, another aspect of the political developments in Surinam's western neighbor may well have caught the attention of the NPS and VHP leaders – i.e., the formal collaboration within the PPP of British Guiana's two most popular political figures: Cheddi Jagan (an East Indian) and Forbes Burnham (a Black). Uniting to form the PPP in 1951, Jagan and Burnham had seemingly ignored potential ethnic divisions to ground their party in a nationalist, class struggle ideology.[1] In Surinam, it seemed possible to forge a similar alliance. Hindustanis still smarted from the Creole elite's attempt to limit their political participation, while the *volkscreolen* had also been aroused by the elite's discriminatory behavior. Thus, at the same time that the PPP won its greatest victory (in the 1953 elections), Lachmon and Pengel forged their own populist alliance in the name of ethnic *verbroedering* (fraternization). While this may have been the only way the two leaders could hope to achieve power, it was not simply an

* Staten van Suriname, *Handelingen 1959-60* (December 7, 1959), p. 321.

1 See Leo A. Despres, *Cultural Pluralism and Nationalist Politics in British Guiana* (Chicago: Rand McNally, 1967), pp. 180-92.

alliance of convenience. In contrast to the PPP, which split apart into irreconcilable Black and East Indian sections in 1954-55, both Surinamese leaders made great sacrifices to each other, and their personal relationship was genuinely warm for many years.

Although many Creoles appeared to reject this cooperation at first, dealing the NPS a serious blow in the elections of 1955, Pengel's and Lachmon's collaboration continued between 1955 and 1958 in the *Staten*, where, as leaders of the opposition, they won increasing respect for their parliamentary skills. From 1958 to 1967, despite attacks from more purist cultural forces within both the Creole and Hindustani population groups, the NPS and VHP shared power in a government that oversaw a period of steady economic development.

1. TROUBLE IN THE NPS

At the end of the struggle to oust Lichtveld from the government and purge Van der Schroeff's group from the NPS, Johan Adolf Pengel had taken over *De Volksstem*, a small weekly newspaper, in preparation for the 1951 elections. At the time, David Findlay welcomed the move, as it added force to the Opposition.[2] But Pengel became increasingly independent of Findlay, and over the next few years, though Findlay remained in the NPS, there were frequent verbal battles between their two papers.

Besides acquiring a forum in the media, Pengel sought to build a stronger base of electoral support in the working class. His means for doing this was in the labor movement, and to the surprise of many, he turned to Jagernath Lachmon for assistance. In January 1952, with Lachmon acting as legal advisor, Pengel organized the *Surinaamse Werknemers "Moederbond"* (Surinam Laborers "Mother Union", or Federation). At the inaugural meeting, representatives of a number of small industrial and civil service unions, as well as one of the powerful bauxite workers unions (the *Billiton Mijnwerkers Bond)*, expressed their willingness to affiliate.[3] Now Pengel concentrated his attention on the two remaining union strongholds at Alcoa's Moengo and Paranam mining sites. For the next five years, these unions were the scene of constant political conflict between the supporters and opponents of Pengel, but ultimately they affiliated with the *Moederbond* and contributed considerable voting strength as well as financial support to the NPS. *De West*

[2] *De West*, January 18, 1951. Pengel had written columns for *De Volksstem* anonymously for several months, but became co-editor with Maurits Ramlakhan on January 18, and sole editor and publisher on March 3, 1951.

[3] *De Volksstem*, January 23, 1952, and *DW*, January 21, 1952.

continually criticized these activities, and in particular questioned the use of union moneys to pay Pengel for his services.

During the 1952 RTC, Pengel and Lachmon strengthened their collaboration. As Lachmon later put it, Findlay's group "considered Pengel and me as second-class *Staten*-members." Thus they agreed that Lachmon, leading the farmers (mostly Hindustanis), and Pengel, leading the workers (mostly Creoles), would ally in an effort to win control over the *Staten* from Findlay and "the elite."[4]

Angered by the rough tactics of Pengel's group, such as their attack on Buiskool, and worried by their growing cooperation with the VHP and talk of independence, Bos Verschuur and a number of other ex-NPSers and independents established the *Partij Suriname* (PS) in December 1952. While acknowledging that "the ship is lacking a propeller (i.e., nationalism and idealism) and is floundering on the waves," the party opposed immediate independence. "...Surinam must first be economically strong before we can put our fist down on the table," they stated.[5]

The PS and others in the old Van der Schroeff group viewed the growing split between Findlay and Pengel in the NPS as potentially working to their advantage. Pengel was clearly driving for complete power in the party, and, with support from the VHP and the potential support of the KTPI, his group was within reach of power in the country as well.

At first, the Executive Committee of the NPS was split on Pengel's independent behavior. A Commission of Good Services within the NPS tried to mediate the split between the two factions but without much success. Then, in April 1953, Dr. G. Kletter, the Minister of Health, was swept up in a new scandal in his Ministry and was ordered by the Cabinet to resign. This prompted Pengel, Lachmon and M.A. Karamat Ali to call for an interpellation of the Minister of Justice, regarding the formal charges that had been made against Kletter.[6] The NPS Executive Committee, now backing Pengel, went even further and called on its *Staten* members to demand the government's resignation so that a new NPS government could be put in its place. Findlay's group refused to obey these instructions. When one of Pengel's supporters, Lim A Po, resigned for reasons of health, the anti-Pengel forces were given a chance once again to test their support in the district of Paramaribo.[7]

A small group of dissidents in the NPS Executive Committee promptly left the party. But instead of joining Bos Verschuur's PS (which represented ear-

[4] Radio address, reported in *De Ware Tijd*, June 16, 1970.

[5] *DW*, December 29, 1952.

[6] *DW*, April 14 and 16, 1953.

[7] *DW*, April 17 and 20, 1953.

lier defections from the NPS), they set up the *Democratische Eenheids Partij* (Democratic Unity Party, DEP) to take their case, in support of the present Cabinet, to the people.[8] Findlay and the other NPS dissidents in the *Staten*, while denouncing Pengel for demagoguery, had misgivings about following this example, and simply tried to ride out the conflict. Pengel, too, seemed uncertain about widening the breach. A motion of "no confidence", brought by the VHP, was defeated 10-5, with Pengel and his last ally, Just Rens, abstaining.[9]

No formal charges were brought against Kletter, yet he had been relieved of his post. Thus, Pengel encouraged him to join the NPS and be their candidate for the seat vacated by Lim A Po.[10] This action infuriated Findlay and the others, but they found no support among the *volkscreolen* in the NPS for an alternative candidate. Taking no position in the election, they may have hoped to see Pengel repudiated at the polls. Nevertheless, the opposition to the NPS within Paramaribo was hopelessly divided. The DEP and PS, after unsuccessful negotiations on a common candidate, each ran candidates against Kletter, while the PSV further hurt the opposition to Pengel by deciding to abstain altogether, demanding new general elections instead.[11] *De West*, without supporting any of the candidates, continued its biting attack on Pengel's opportunism and obstructionism. Smarting from charges in *De Volksstem* that *De West* had turned against the NPS, Findlay editorialized, "if someone gets in a polemic with Mr. Pengel, then he is against the NPS. Mr. Pengel is namely the NPS. What a conceit!"[12] But Findlay and the others were increasingly isolated within their own party.

In particular, Findlay was disturbed by the cooperative relationship developing between Pengel and Rens, on the one hand, and the VHP, on the other. Noting this even before the Kletter case, he observed that "the destructive forces present in the *Staten* . . . are only going to hurt the country and the party that helped them into the saddle." More specifically, he warned that leaning on the VHP to bring down the government "might lead to a VHP-dominated government."[13] In an attempt to halt *verbroedering* between the NPS and VHP, the Findlay group introduced a bill on the eve of the by-election, calling for a thorough revision of the Asiatic Marriage Laws.[14] Calculating that the Hindustani outcry would bring Pengel and Rens back

[8] *DW*, May 19, 1953.
[9] *DW*, May 27, 1953.
[10] *DW*, June 1, 1953.
[11] *DW*, June 19, 1953.
[12] *DW*, June 25, 1953.
[13] *DW*, April 11, 1953.
[14] *DW*, July 21, 1953.

into the fold, or cause the NPS rank and file to repudiate *verbroedering*, Findlay succeeded only in making the election of July 30 close, as some Hindustanis, misled by Findlay's actions, reportedly turned out to vote for the PS and DEP candidates. The PS candidate (I. de Vries) drew 6, 124 votes to Kletter's 7,270, while the DEP candidate (A. May) received only 668 votes.[15] Despite Kletter's victory, the *Staten* passed a new motion of confidence in the Cabinet, 12-6 (with only the VHP voting against it, and Pengel, Rens and Kletter abstaining).[16]

After the Findlay forces narrowly defeated a Pengel-VHP motion to withdraw the bill on Asian Marriages,[17] the VHP formally announced on August 14, 1953, that henceforth it would work together with the NPS (i.e., Pengel's group) in an effort "to strive for one people."[18] In response to prompt criticism from a number of Hindustanis that this decision was both "arbitrary" (i.e., taken without consultation with the party's rank and file) and "dangerous," a party spokesman defended the VHP's internal democratic structure and explained that "in order to become one people, racial assimilation isn't always necessary..." Instead, the party supported "an intellectual assimilation, such as had occurred in the United States."[19]

Indecision among the KTPIers about their position in the growing struggle was apparently resolved by continuing rivalry between Hindus and Moslems. In an emotional debate over a slaughterhouse ordinance, Lachmon demanded that Moslem butchers slaughter no cows in Hindu residential areas. In response, Soemita advocated a similar proscription against the slaughter of pigs in Moslem neighborhoods. As the pattern of settlement, at least in the more urbanized areas, was highly mixed, the definition of such religious districts was seemingly beyond the legislative powers of the *Staten*. Holding the balance of power in the *Staten*, the KTPI's religious dispute with the VHP drove them, at least for the present, to side with the government.[20]

But the stability of the Findlay group was shaken in May 1954, after Arnold Smit, the Minister of Public Works, haughtily refused to answer a long series of questions put to him by Just Rens in the *Staten*. Because this violated the constitutional "rules of the game," another motion of "no confidence" was introduced, and on this occasion, despite the loss of the two

[15] *DW*, July 31, 1953.

[16] *DW*, August 8, 1953.

[17] The vote was 10-2, with the KTPI voting for withdrawal and the VHP, Pengel, Rens, and Kletter either abstaining or absent (*DW*, August 13, 1953).

[18] *DW*, September 2, 1953.

[19] Poeniet Persad, letter to *DW*, September 9, 1953.

[20] *DW*, March 6, 1954. To hold their loyalty, Findlay's group quietly dropped its efforts to change the Marriage Laws.

KTPI votes, Pengel and Rens gained two additional allies from the Findlay ranks and the motion passed 11-8, forcing Smit's resignation.[21] Immediately after the vote, Findlay lamented that the country was now being run by the VHP. Lachmon angrily accused Findlay of trying to turn the Creoles against the Hindustanis and of preaching racial discrimination. With reference to Findlay's light skin, Pengel dryly noted: "Mr. Findlay shouldn't speak about Creoles. When he is abroad, he tries to pass as a Scot."[22]

Although the damage of these exchanges was temporarily papered over to permit representatives from both sides to participate in the reconvened RTC (where they unanimously accepted the revised Statute), the war of words resumed on their return. In June 1954, Arnold Smit printed 8,000 pamphlets calling for an *Eenheidsfront* (Unity Front) against the NPS and VHP. Noting the divisions among Creole opponents to the NPS, he urged that they be overcome if the NPS was to be ousted in the 1955 general elections.[23] As if to demonstrate Smit's point, a by-election was held in the district of Marowijne in July 1954. Like the earlier Paramaribo by-elections, it was won by the NPS against a divided (three candidate) Creole opposition.[24]

Increasingly harassed by charges of elitism and discrimination against the *volkscreolen*, Findlay's group made use of its own racial appeals to this group. In August 1954, Findlay called for an investigation of economic conditions among the Creole population, claiming that their position in the society had become increasingly vulnerable. "What does Mr. Findlay want from the Hindustanis?" asked Lachmon. "Does he want them to be massacred? Then let him shoot the first bullet at me..."[25] Findlay answered that he had said nothing about Hindustanis, but only that Creoles were being displaced in agriculture, lumbering, transport and construction. "And who are now the property owners in Paramaribo?" he asked. Pengel denounced the inquiry as inflammatory,[26] and later accused Findlay of doing more to hurt the Creoles himself by his refusal to heed party instructions, as these came directly from the Creole poor.[27]

[21] Smit later recalled that the Cabinet, like the NPS, was hopelessly divided and paralyzed. "As I was the most outspoken Findlay-supporter, Pengel's group selected me to show off their new strength." (Interview, March 16, 1976, Epse, Netherlands).

[22] *DW*, May 6, 1954. Findlay later recalled the source of this remark. Returning from the 1952 RTC meetings, the delegation had passed through England, where a customs agent had asked Findlay his clan. Not knowing the answer, he began to read about Scotland in his spare time, only recently discovering that the Findlays are clan Farquharson. (Interview, January 19, 1976, Paramaribo).

[23] *Eenheidsfront* (June 1954), p. 4; and *DW*, June 21, 1954.

[24] *DW*, July 23, 1954.

[25] *DW*, August 10, 1954.

[26] *Ibid.*

[27] *DW*, August 17, 1954.

With two groups of Hindustanis openly attacking *verbroedering* (the *Congres Partij* and a group of Catholic Hindustanis, led by C.R. Biswamitre), Findlay tried to weaken the VHP further by charging that Lachmon was just a figurehead and that the real leader of the party was the lawyer, H. Shriemisier, "by the simple fact that he is of a higher caste."[28] Emphasizing the power of the Hindu religious elite and the existence of caste and color divisions among Hindus, Findlay aimed for two objectives: harnessing Creole fears of religious domination (which had worked well against the Catholics), and reawakening the *Aryan-Sanatan* cleavages within the Hindu group.

Nevertheless, the VHP-NPS tie held strong in the *Staten*, and on September 6, 1954, Just Rens announced that the two parties would work together in the 1955 election.[29] In October, to strengthen their position, they began to plan a change in the election law whereby (1) lists would be introduced permitting vacancies to be filled by "shadow-candidates" – thus avoiding further costly, and risky, by-elections, and (2) three of the Hindustani districts (the two adjacent to Paramaribo plus the district of Saramacca) would be joined into one four-man district.[30] When the bill was introduced, Findlay called it an attempted "coup," and accused "certain VHPers" of conspiring with British Guiana's Cheddi Jagan to help the VHP dominate Surinam.[31]

The introduction of these electoral law changes seemed to swell the ranks of the NPS' opposition. Meetings of the PS and PSV were held, gathering large crowds, and the PSV announced in its meeting that it was willing to join an *Eenheidsfront* with other parties against the NPS-VHP alliance.[32] Feeling on the defensive, the NPS now called for a reaffirmation of adhesion from all its members, including Findlay's dissidents in the *Staten*.[33] In the subsequent debate on the electoral law, the KTPI's Karamat Ali denounced the changes, on the eve of an election, as "politically dirty," and called on Moslems to repudiate the VHP. The leader of the Aryans, J.S. Mungra (VHP), angrily answered that although the

> VHP has done everything possible to get Hindus and Moslems to work together again..., a Hindu can never tolerate a Moslem to threaten him and sit on him. We're not afraid of death. We can be born again.[34]

[28] *DW*, August 19, 1954.

[29] *DW*, September 7, 1954.

[30] The position of the VHP in Saramacca, where together there were more Creoles and Moslems than Hindus, was not as secure as in the two other districts. Presumably, excess votes in the latter two districts would safeguard the VHP's Saramacca seats (*DW*, October 22, and December 6, 1954).

[31] *DW*, November 2, 1954.

[32] *DW*, November 22 and 29, 1954.

[33] *DW*, December 2, 1954.

[34] *DW*, December 6, 1954.

The amendments merging the Hindustani districts and introducing shadow-candidates passed 12-7 and 12-6, respectively, with the KTPI and Findlay's shrinking group in the opposition. Besides the solid VHP Hindu vote, the number of NPSers siding with Pengel had now grown to eight.[35]

Finally, on January 4, 1955, David Findlay resigned from the NPS in protest of the VHP alliance and three days later announced the formation of his own party, the *Surinaamse Democratische Partij* (SDP).[36] A week later, Findlay's remaining allies in the *Staten* were expelled from the NPS and joined him in the SDP.[37] With the term of the government ending, the *Staten* was now dissolved and new elections scheduled for March 29.

II. THE 1955 ELECTIONS

The elections of 1955 were the closest and most heated of any Surinam had yet seen. In every district, the VHP and NPS were confronted by candidates of a new electoral coalition comprising the PSV, PS, SDP and KTPI, called the *Eenheidsfront* (EF). Aside from the *Congres Partij*, which also challenged the VHP in the new amalgamated district, there was virtually no other competition. In this polarized situation, the campaign was very intense.

The parties to the EF had divided the Paramaribo list as follows: four seats were allotted to the new SDP, three to the PS, and three to the PSV.[38] In addition, an SDP member was picked to run in Marowijne, a PSVer in Coronie and a PSer in Para. A *Nickerie Eenheids Partij* (NEP) was set up to oppose the VHP in *that* district, and a Creole and Hindustani were their candidates. In Commewijne, the VHP and NPS balanced their ticket with a Hindustani VHPer and a Javanese NPSer running against the KTPI's Karamat Ali and Soemita. In the new amalgamated district and Nickerie, the NPS instructed its voters to support the VHP, while the VHP reciprocated with support for the NPS ticket in Paramaribo. All the VHP candidates were Hindus, and with exception of the candidate in Commewijne, all were sitting members of the *Staten*.[39]

The campaign was, as Mitrasing puts it, "the most violent, sharp and tense in Surinamese history."[40] In particular, race and culture were involved as

[35] *Ibid.*

[36] *DW*, January 8, 1955.

[37] *DW*, January 12, 1955.

[38] *DW*, February 7, 1955.

[39] Lachmon, Mungra, H. Radhakishun, H.F. Sewberath Misser, K. Kanhai, and R.D. Oedayrajsing Varma.

[40] Mitrasing, *op. cit.*, p. 278.

never before. The EF charged that the leaders of the NPS were unfit to rule, violating all norms of decency and restraint. The NPS retaliated with charges of elitism, questioning the *eenheid* (unity) of the EF, and warning that it was out of touch with the people. Fair-skinned NPS candidates like De la Fuente felt obliged to use *Sranantongo* in the rallies to appeal to the *volkscreolen* ("I may be white," he declared, "but I have a black navel," – "*mi cumba blaka*").[41] The other NPS candidates, caught in the dilemma of appealing for lower class votes, while showing their "fitness" to rule, felt equally obliged to campaign in Dutch.

Sharp accusations of corruption, racism and political opportunism were aired in the partisan press and on the platforms. Both sides accused each other of eagerness to profit from the Dutch Ten Year Plan's development projects that were being planned, and both attempted to break each other's cross-cultural ties by a combination of racial slurs and character assassinations. The VHP accused the Hindustanis running on the EF list (the PSV's C.R. Biswamitre and the NEP's ex-VHPer L.B. Sitalsing) of racial betrayal,[42] while the EF responded with warnings that the VHP was telling its people to support only a few NPSers so that the VHP could dominate the new government.[43] Ads in *De West* asked "Do you want to be ruled by the VHP?" "Do you want mass immigration from a certain Eastern land?"[44] News of a conflict between Cheddi Jagan and Forbes Burnham leading to the collapse of the Black-East Indian People's Progressive Party coalition in British Guiana probably didn't help the political prospects of Surinamese *verbroedering*. *De West* reported extensively on the PPP's troubles throughout March 1955.

The election results (Tables 5.1 and 5.2) again showed the unrepresentativeness of Surinam's electoral system. With a total of nearly 30,000 votes, or 50% of the national total, the NPS-VHP was able to win only 8 seats (38%). In contrast, the EF (including the KTPI) had polled roughly 28,000 votes (47%) to gain a majority (13 seats or 62%) in the *Staten*. This time, the shoe was on the other foot.

When the results were tabulated, and it became apparent that the EF had won in Paramaribo, the supporters of the NPS went on a rampage, breaking windows, stoning cars and bicycles with EF flags, etc.[45] Crowds stormed the *Burgerlijke Stand* (Hall of Records) to protest the tally, and its director had a nervous collapse.[46] Homes of the newly elected *Staten* members were at-

[41] Interview, Emile de la Fuente, February 1, 1974, Paramaribo.
[42] *DW*, March 25, 1955.
[43] *DW*, February 25, 1955.
[44] Mitrasing, *op. cit.*, p. 271.
[45] *DW*, May 31, 1955.
[46] *Ibid.*

Table 5.1. Votes Cast in 1955 Elections.

Election District		Minimum and Maximum Votes, by Party NPS	VHP	EF	KTPI	Other
I. Paramaribo	max.	13,867	—	15,601	—	175[a]
(10 seats)	min.	13,587	—	15,342	—	106
II. New district	max.	—	9,099	—	5,400	375[b]
(4 seats)	min.	—	9,040	—	5,286	322
III. Para (Suriname) (1 seat)		1,383	—	771	—	937[c]
IV. Commewijne	max.	—	1,754	—	2,984	257[d]
(2 seats)	min.	—	1,726	—	2,966	—
V. Nickerie	max.	—	2,467	1,840[e]	—	—
(2 seats)	min.	—	2,440	1,817	—	—
VI. Coronie (1 seat)		767	—	629	—	—
VII. Marowijne (1 seat)		750	—	921	—	—

[a] The *Christelijke Sociale Partij* ran two candidates in this race.
[b] The *Congres Partij* ran four candidates in this race.
[c] H.W. Mohamed Radja ran as an independent in this race.
[d] H. Seljee ran as an independent in this race.
[e] L.B. Sitalsing and A.R. Wix ran on the ticket of the *Nickerie Eenheids Partij*, but it was allied with the *EF*.
Source: Fred Ormiskirk. *Twintig jaren N.P.S.: "Groei temidden van Beroering"* (Paramaribo: n.p., 1966), pp. 108-110.

Table 5.2. Seat Division in 1955 Elections.

Election District	NPS	VHP	EF	KTPI
I. Paramaribo			10	
II. New district		4		
III. Para	1			
IV. Commewijne				2
V. Nickerie		2		
VI. Coronie	1			
VII. Marowijne			1	
Total	2	6	11	2

tacked, and the police had difficulty restoring order. In an emotional gathering in front of his house, Pengel told a crowd of 3,000 that the NPS would have won but for the betrayal of some of its members ("Lord forgive them..."). Calling on his followers to contain their disappointment, he promised that the battle was not over and introduced Lachmon who had a startling announcement to make. To show that "they never leave their friends in the lurch," Lachmon announced that the VHP had decided to put two of their seats at Pengel's disposal, so that he and Rens, if they wished, might reenter the *Staten*.[47] Rens declined the gesture, but Pengel accepted.

[47] *DW*, April 2, 1955.

Lachmon had taken this initiative on his own, and it evidently caught the rest of his party off-guard. In a VHP meeting at the *Sanatan Dharm* temple, the executive committee of the VHP overruled Lachmon. Azimullah writes that

> after several influential pandits had had their say, strongly rejecting [his] decision, Lachmon reacted as follows:
>
> > Gentlemen, I have been elected a representative of the VHP in the Surinam *Staten*. No one can prevent me now from giving up my seat as a representative. I didn't mean to touch the seat of another VHP *Staten* member when I, as proof of my brotherhood feelings, offered a VHP seat to Mr. Pengel. I consider the presence of Pengel in the parliament so important that I have decided to step down myself, and I beseech the party to select Mr. Pengel as a candidate in my place.
>
> With this, Jagernath Lachmon had "thrown the cat among the pigeons." All the "contras" became "pros" as Lachmon was urged to keep his seat in the *Staten*.[48]

It was decided instead that another VHPer, H.F. Sewberath Misser, and all his shadow-candidates, would resign their seat, so that a by-election could be held.[49] The irony, and danger, of this move were obvious. Not only had the VHP and NPS made it more difficult to hold by-elections, but this attempt to get Pengel back into the *Staten* was attacked by many in both parties and ridiculed unmercifully by the EF.[50] *De West* ran a cartoon of Pengel, dressed as a beggar at the door of "Jack Lach" asking for alms.[51] *De Surinamer* called this a case of "masterful corruption" and "one of the most disgusting exhibitions and abuses of our electoral laws."[52] "If Mr. Lachmon doesn't feel capable enough to lead the opposition in the *Staten* without Pengel," argued a letter from "a group of VHPers" in *De West*, "then let him make place for another [Hindustani] leader..."[53]

Then, to everyone's surprise, Sewberath Misser's last shadow-candidate, K. Karagjitsing, refused to give up the seat.[54] Although Lachmon later spoke of this as "giving the VHP and NPS time to arrange things for the by-election,"[55] it clearly caused them consternation at the time, and they called for an investigation of Karagjitsing's credentials. After a *Staten* committee found no objection in awarding the seat to him, Pengel reportedly began

[48] Azimullah, *op. cit.*
[49] *DW*, April 4, 1955.
[50] *DW*, April 5, 1955.
[51] *DW*, April 6, 1955.
[52] Quoted in Mitrasing, *op. cit.*, p. 279.
[53] *DW*, April 20, 1955.
[54] *DW*, May 11, 1955.
[55] Interview, Jagernath Lachmon, Paramaribo, January 16, 1974.

negotiations with another VHPer, K. Kanhai, for his seat in Nickerie.[56]

In the meantime, reacting to the VHP-NPS plan for a by-election, the EF quickly introduced legislation to divide the amalgamated district back into its component parts. If Pengel *was* to try for Sewberath Misser's seat, this would force the election to take place in Saramacca, where the EF would have a better chance to defeat him with dissident Moslem, Hindu and Creole votes. This legislation passed on June 27, 1955.[57]

Finally, on January 16, 1956, Karagjitsing gave up his seat, and an election was scheduled in Saramacca on March 22.[58] In accepting the VHP-NPS nomination for the seat, Pengel promised that he would see to it that "new general elections would be possible within a year."[59] In an important coup, the VHP and NPS selected as his first two shadow-candidates, Islam Ramdjan, a Hindustani Moslem Leader who had run on the EF-supported KTPI ticket the year before, and H. Wongso, a Javanese candidate of the KTPI in the 1951 election. The EF chose as their candidate, L.B. Sitalsingh, a former VHPer (who had run in 1955 on the *Nickerie Eenheids Partij* ticket). His first two shadow-candidates included a Javanese KTPIer and a Creole.[60] Ironically, although *verbroedering*, as a symbol for the tie between the VHP and NPS, was under attack by those parties' opponents, the general principle of cross-cultural ticket-balancing, which the shadow-candidate rule had made possible, was quickly embraced by everyone!

Meanwhile, the "holders of the balance" had run afoul of the law. During the campaign, the two KTPI leaders, Karamat Ali (now Minister of Justice in the EF government) and Soemita, were accused of swindling Sf 25,000 in a rice deal. As both men exchanged charges regarding the other's complicity, the KTPI split into two groups. Hindustani Moslems who had sought a home in the KTPI now left it, while the Javanese rallied around Soemita.[61] The result was to bring many Moslem voters back into the VHP, allowing Pengel to sweep to victory in Saramacca, with 1759 votes against Sitalsingh's 831.[62]

This unusual by-election was frequently cited, in later years, by both Lachmon and Pengel as proof that their policy of *verbroedering* was not an alliance of convenience, but one of personal solidarity, and that the popular support it had been given revealed a deep desire at the grass-roots to find a political means to overcome the cultural divisions in this splintered society.

[56] *DW*, June 23 and 25, 1955.
[57] *DW*, June 28, 1955.
[58] *DW*, January 17 and 30, 1956.
[59] *DW*, February 13, 1956.
[60] *DW*, February 20, 1956.
[61] *DW*, March 7 and 8, 1956.
[62] *DW*, March 23, 1956.

III. THE EENHEIDSFRONT GOVERNMENT

The new Cabinet, chosen by *formateurs* D. Findlay and A. Sang A Jang (chairman of the PSV), was dominated by SDP members. Dr. J.H.E. Ferrier, a former chairman of *Unie Suriname* and Director of Education, became Minister-President.[63]

Aside from the flurry of political activity over the Saramacca by-election, the first year of the EF government was relatively quiet. The Dutch gave approval to the Ten Year Plan, and a number of school and road-building projects were launched, including a paved highway to eventually connect Paramaribo with Nieuw Nickerie (on the British Guiana border) and Albina (on the French Guiana border). Shortly after the elections, to honor the Statute's recent inauguration, Queen Juliana made the first visit ever by a reigning monarch to Surinam. At year's end, the United Nations General Assembly formally acknowledged the new status of Surinam and the Netherlands Antilles, removing them from the list of dependent territories falling under the purview of the Trusteeship Council.

But despite these evidently festive and unifying events, the political kettle soon heated up again. On the eve of the election in Saramacca in 1956, the EF had tried to push through its first significant and controversial piece of legislation: a regulation granting a ten-year tax exemption and fifteen-year monopoly for the export of shrimp and processed fish to E.S. Schweig, an American planning a large investment in Surinam.[64] Defending the bill for the government, C.R. Biswamitre explained that this was the first effort since the War to attract a major non-Dutch investment to Surinam. Therefore, a great deal would depend on it. Nevertheless, the proposal was attacked by the Opposition as well as by several members of the EF, who criticized the monopolistic position Schweig's company would get under the bill. Lachmon argued that, of the three ways to attract foreign investors – monopoly control, tax exemption, and provision of natural resources to exploit, Surinam was offering Schweig all three. A PS *Staten* member asked if the catches of Surinamese fishermen would be purchased and, together with two other EF representatives, expressed opposition to the tax-free and monopoly concessions. In answer to these criticisms Findlay compared Surinam with

[63] Ferrier's cabinet included M.A. Karamat Ali (KTPI) as Minister of Justice and Police; Dr. A.I. Faverij (SDP), Health; P.A.R. Kolader (SDP), Social Affairs; J.G. Kuiperback (unaffiliated), Public Works and Transportation; M.I. Lobato (unaffiliated), Agriculture; Dr. L.L.E. Rens (PSV), Education; W.G.H.C.J. Smit (SDP), Finance; and E.J. van de Veer (SDP), Economic Affairs (Ormskirk, *op. cit.*, p. 111).

[64] Staten van Suriname. *Bijlagen 1955-56* (21.2, 21.4 and 21.7) and *Gouvernementsblad van Suriname 1956*, No. 48.

Puerto Rico, emphasizing the need to create a favorable climate for investment. Moreover, the volume of exports intended would assure local fishermen of sales to the company in addition to the catches Schweig's own fleet would produce. Both he and Biswamitre emphasized the jobs Schweig would create as well as the symbolic importance the investment would have.[65] After two long *Staten* meetings, the debate ended without a decision on the bill.[66] Finally, on May 11, with an angry crowd demonstrating outside, and Pengel back in the *Staten*, the bill was narrowly passed 11-10, with two members of the EF voting against it.[67] Soemita's lawyer, Van der Schroeff (who was now an SDP supporter), later recounted how he got Soemita out of jail on the day of the meeting and rushed him to the *Staten* to cast the deciding vote.[68]

Seeing that the bill would pass, Lachmon challenged the government to try to implement it, and Pengel warned, ominously, that the government would quickly regret it, adding, "I call upon my political friends... to receive this now with jubilation. It will benefit us."[69]

Popular support for the EF *had* clearly shifted by this time. A number of Moslem associations had denounced the government for its treatment of Karamat Ali (who resigned as Minister of Justice on April 10 and was arrested April 13, 1956, in the rice swindle mentioned above). Within the Catholic PSV, division over the Schweig contract was bitter. After years of feeling discriminated against by the Creole Protestant elite, many Catholics now felt uncomfortable with their own role in what appeared to be "elitist" legislation. In a turbulent meeting in June, Father Weidmann, now retired to the background, warned that the EF was too much in the hands of David Findlay and not sufficiently responsive to the voters.[70]

Soon thereafter, the government set up a committee to coordinate popular support (*Comité Steun aan het Eenheidsfront*). After a week of meetings that were repeatedly disrupted by chanting and rock-throwing NPS members, its activities ceased.[71] Finally, the PSV executive council voted to leave the EF and ordered their *Staten* members to withdraw their support. In response, the PSV's one Minister in the Cabinet[72] resigned. But the three *Staten* members

[65] Staten van Suriname, *Handelingen 1955-56*, pp. 330-35, 344-46, 349-52, 382. See also *DW*, February 17, 1956.

[66] *DW*, February 17 and 22, 1956.

[67] Staten van Suriname, *Handelingen 1956-57*, p. 33; and *DW*, May 12, 1956.

[68] Interview, G. van der Schroeff, Paramaribo, February 18, 1974.

[69] Staten van Suriname, *Handelingen 1956-57*, pp. 31-32.

[70] *DW*, June 25, 1956.

[71] *DW*, July 18 and 29, 1956.

[72] L.L.E. Rens, Minister of Education.

refused to switch their support to the Opposition.[73] For this, they were finally "purged" from the party.[74]

In new tests of voting strength in the *Staten*, the government revealed that it still controlled 12 of 21 votes, and proceeded to take up new matters. The most important of these dealt with the long-planned hydro electric dam on the Suriname River. After studying the project for several years and fruitlessly hunting for financing in the Netherlands and elsewhere in Europe, the Surinam Government finally began to talk with their own single largest foreign investor, the *Surinaamse Bauxiet Maatschappij* (Alcoa). Findlay at the time indicated reluctance, saying "this concern already enjoys an immensely powerful position in our economic life.... Whenever one sees what role, for example, the United Fruit Company plays in Guatemala and elsewhere, then one can imagine what might happen in the much weaker Surinam."[75]

Nevertheless, desire for the project was strong on both Surinam's and Alcoa's side, and, with no other sponsors available, an agreement was reached in February 1957 by which, among other things, Alcoa would build the dam and a hydroelectric station in return for additional bauxite concessions (for 75 years) and free use of a large portion of the power generated by the dam.[76] Despite many warnings of the type that Findlay, himself, had earlier aired, and a long series of amendments that were all defeated, the *Staten* unanimously approved the "letter of intent," 21-0. However, members of the VHP and NPS warned that they would vote against the final agreement if some of their suggested changes (for construction of alumina and aluminum smelters and regarding employment guarantees, etc.) were not incorporated.[77]

Despite their tentative support of this so-called "Brokopondo Joint-Venture", the NPS and VHP continued their efforts to disrupt the *Staten* and force its dissolution. Interpellations and votes of "no-confidence" were repeatedly moved, slowing the business of the *Staten*, while petitions were sent to the Governor and Queen asking for new elections. In January 1957, the PSV announced that it would run a joint ticket with the NPS in the next election,[78] finally burying the old Protestant-Catholic cleavage among Creoles.

[73] *DW*, July 23, 1956.

[74] *DW*, December 29, 1956.

[75] *DW*, May 31, 1956.

[76] "Letter of Intent" (Richtlijnen Overeenkomst), Aluminum Company of America and the Government of Surinam, February 4, 1957, reprinted in *Brokopondo Gemeenschappelijke Onderneming Suriname-Suralco* (Paramaribo: 1959), pp. 1-29.

[77] Staten van Suriname, *Handelingen 1956-57*, p. 655. See the speeches of Radhakishun (VHP) and Pengel, pp. 606-11.

[78] *DW*, January 10, 1957.

In May, a popular local businessman and former member of the colonial *Staten*, H.J. de Vries, was appointed by the Dutch as acting-Governor. His efforts to mediate the conflict and to restore order to the *Staten*'s work seemed to bear some fruit.[79] But after an official of the semi-publicly-owned *Volkscrediet Bank* was discharged for his "overly liberal" lending practices toward Creoles, the Opposition pressed a new vote of confidence against the Government. This was narrowly defeated, 11-10.[80]

IV. THE 1958 ELECTIONS

In January 1958, the Government introduced its bill authorizing Alcoa's construction of the Brokopondo Dam. The most important change in the "Brokopondo Agreement" since its initial approval by the *Staten* was Alcoa's commitment to build alumina and aluminum smelters at its Paranam center within sixteen years. The *Surinaamse Bauxiet Maatschappij* would now become the *Suriname Aluminum Company* (Suralco). Despite this concession to the NPS-VHP opposition, the bill was heatedly debated. Pengel criticized the recent layoff of workers by the company at Paranam, and Lachmon warned of the increased influence that Suralco would have in Surinam's society. After five days of debate, the bill was passed 12-8.[81] Although the lack of unanimity was seen as somewhat insulting to Alcoa, the EF celebrated this as their greatest achievement.

Meanwhile, the NPS was busy negotiating terms for an alliance with the PSV, confident that they could soon topple the government. Several concessions were made by each party. Among other things, the PSV gave up its demands for proportional representation in elections, in exchange for four seats on an NPS-PSV Paramaribo list. The NPS in turn gave up its opposition to private (i.e., Catholic) school aid. Lachmon's own acceptance of these terms was denounced by a fellow VHPer, J.S. Mungra, who pointed out that the VHP had received no concessions of its own. He condemned Lachmon's "dictatorial methods", and was, in turn, threatened with expulsion from the VHP.[82]

[79] *DW*, June 1, 1957.

[80] *DW*, June 24, 1957.

[81] For the terms of the new bill, see Staten van Suriname, *Bijlagen 1957-58* (36.4), especially pp. 6-7. The debates are found in Staten van Suriname, *Handelingen 1957-58*, pp. 718-52, 754-74, 776-820, and 822-52. For a summary of these debates and general news regarding this critical issue, see *De Ware Tijd* (hereinafter *DWT*), January 13, 18, 20, 22, 25, 28, 1958.

[82] *DW*, April 15, 1958. According to several informants, Mungra was trying to get one of his sons appointed as the first Hindustani District Commissioner.

In April, when Soemita announced that the KTPI would no longer support the EF because of its neglect of Javanese interests, Findlay introduced a motion of confidence in the government. Despite the KTPI now being in the Opposition, the motion carried 12-9, as Mungra and another VHPer (Oedayrajsing Varma) had decided to support the EF, at least until the differences within the VHP were ironed out.[83]

An end to this odd coupling came a week later, when, in the midst of a debate on the budget, a report came into the *Staten* that Lachmon's house was on fire. Though the report later turned out to be false, Mungra quickly announced that he considered this symbolic for his party, and not wishing fire in "the VHP-house," he and Oedayrajsing Varma had decided to return to the Opposition. Minister-President Ferrier, who was present to defend his budget, called for an adjournment and two days later announced his government's resignation. After discussing the situation with representatives of various groups, the new Governor, J. van Tilburg, proceeded to call new elections for June 25, 1958.[84]

Once again, the parties lined up in two camps. The only changes from the 1955 elections were the disappearance of the *Congres* and *Christelijke Sociale* parties, the re-organization of the VHP's Nickerie opposition into the *Nickerie Onafhankelijke Partij* (Nickerie Independent Party, NOP), and the switch of the PSV to the side of the NPS and VHP. The three ex-PSV members in the EF ran for reelection as the Surinam People's Party (an inversion of the letters PSV: *Surinaamse Volks Partij*, SVP).

To the surprise of many, the KTPI, after helping bring down the EF, returned to support them in the election. At an EF rally later in the campaign, Soemita explained why he had become "the prodigal son": Around 1:00 AM on the morning of April 21 (the day the government fell), he had received a surprise visit from Lachmon, Pengel, Walter Lim A Po, and Harry Radhakishun. If the KTPI would stay with them, and if they could bring the government down, they proposed to form a coalition government in which Paramaribo would be joined to the largely Hindustani areas adjacent to the city, thus assuring permanent ascendancy of the NPS-VHP over the EF. The KTPI would get additional seats in this arrangement and thus extend its strength beyond the limits of Commewijne. If, together with the PSV, the NPS, VHP, and KTPI could win all 21 seats in the *Staten*, then, as one of them put it, "we can drop those 'proportional maniacs' [i.e., the PSV]." Soemita

[83] For Soemita's declaration, see *DWT*, April 11, 1958. For the vote of confidence, see *DW*, April 15, and *DWT*, April 16, 1958.

[84] Ooft, "Drie Eeuwen...," *op. cit.*, pp. 86-87; Ooft, *Ontwikkeling...*, p. 252; *DW*, April 22, and *DWT*, April 23, 24, 25, and May 2, 1958.

said he agreed to go along with their plan to topple the government, but in subsequent discussions, the NPS and VHP reneged on their agreement to give the KTPI additional *Staten* seats.[85] The NPS and VHP had then entered candidates against the KTPI in Commewijne, as did the disgruntled Hindustani Moslem followers of Ashruf Karamat Ali. Whether Soemita's story of the "midnight conspiracy" is true or not, he was confronted by such a formidable opposition that he had only one place to turn for help: the *Eenheidsfront.*

As the lineup in Commewijne illustrated, the Moslems were still divided and undecided what to do with their votes. Lachmon had promised Pengel's seat in Saramacca to a Moslem, and in fact gave it to Pengel's shadow-candidate there, Islam Ramdjan. But throughout the campaign, the EF featured Hindustani Moslem speakers who disputed the allegation that Moslems were returning to the VHP.[86]

Among the issues used by the NPS was the EF's "distance" from the people. Crowds of NPSers repeatedly disrupted EF meetings by chanting "N-P-S – N-P-S –," and "You can't beat Joe Louis twice" (their peculiar English-language slogan in this campaign). This continued harassment led the EF to publish advertisements such as "Don't vote for disorder, vote for stability. Don't vote for barbarity, vote for Surinam."[87]

The EF pointed to its record, especially "the promise of Brokopondo," and emphasized that its goal for society was real assimilation, not the "disguised *apartheid*" of the NPS and VHP.[88] Moreover, the Opposition's behavior during the Schweig and Brokopondo debates had hurt Surinam's image abroad, Findlay declared, and a government with Pengel in it would damage efforts to attract other foreign investments.[89] Biswamitre and other Hindustani supporters of the EF deplored VHP efforts to depict Findlay and others as Hindustani-haters, and they reminded their audiences of what Lachmon and Pengel had done to Mohamed Radja and Jamaludin after the crisis of 1950-51.[90] The NPS, charged Biswamitre, is a prisoner of the VHP,[91] and all the brotherly things Lachmon says in Dutch disappear in the "fierce hatred ... which he preaches [in *Sarnami Hindostans*]."[92]

Although their activists took pleasure in the disruption of the EF's rallies,

[85] *DW*, June 24, 1958.
[86] *DW*, May 17 and June 19, 1958.
[87] *DW*, June 24, 1958.
[88] *DW*, May 24, 1958.
[89] *DW*, June 4, 1958.
[90] *DW*, June 10 and 19, 1958.
[91] *DW*, June 17, 1958.
[92] *DW*, June 23, 1958.

the NPS and PSV made a serious effort to improve their image by attracting young Creole academics, recently returned from study in the Netherlands, to be candidates. Among those they recruited were the engineers Frank Essed (NPS) and Leonard H. Guda (PSV), the lawyers Walter Lim A Po (NPS) and Henricus F. Heidweiller (PSV), and the economist Paul A.M. van Philips (PSV). The only NPS candidates returning from past elections were Pengel, Rens and De la Fuente. As for issues, the NPS and VHP claimed that the original ideas for the Schweig and Brokopondo contracts had been theirs, but that they were improperly negotiated, and that, with the young talent now flowing into their ranks, these injustices would be corrected and sound economic development would be assured. Regarding assimilation, one candidate, E.M.L. Ensberg (NPS) honored

> the pioneers of the Roman Catholic mission and the EBG [i.e., Moravian *Herrnhutters*] who have contributed so much to the peaceful integration of different ethnic groups and uplifting of Surinam. Why must we fear that the Hindustanis will surpass us? What you don't want others to do to you, do ye not to them. The very struggle of the Hindustanis will be the stimulus for their assimilation.[93]

And L.H. Guda (PSV) added, "Surinam is at present an Asian land... Therefore the generation of racial conflicts is irresponsible."[94]

The cooler and more academic image projected by the NPS and its allies seemed to reduce the anxieties of those who had been offended previously; and in Paramaribo, the NPS-PSV list won handily, with roughly 19,700 votes to the EF's 13,200 (see Table 5.3). The NPS also won in Coronie, Para, and Marowijne, while the VHP won its races in the districts near Paramaribo and in Saramacca. The only surprise came in Nickerie, where the NOP dislodged the VHP from its two seats there. A special irony in this upset was the fact that the leader of the NOP, Dewnarain Poetoe, was arrested a few months before the election for embezzlement. As a bank clerk in Nickerie, he had made loans to many Hindustani farmers without following proper procedures. Such Robin Hood-like activities made him quite popular, and his arrest only enhanced his image as a man of the people.[95] After a short jail term, he entered the *Staten*, was an effective spokesman for his district, and was reelected in 1963. Thus, the EF's only voice in the Opposition would come from two independent, and very populist, Hindustanis from a district far removed from Paramaribo, together, presumably, with the Javanese KTPIers, Soemita and

[93] *DW*, June 3, 1958.

[94] *Ibid.*

[95] Interview, Fred Ormskirk, Paramaribo, January 15, 1974; also *DW*, April 24, 1958; *DWT*, April 24 and 25, 1958.

Table 5.3. Votes Cast in 1958 Elections.

Election District		*Minimum and Maximum Votes, by Party* *NPS-PSV*	*VHP*	*EF*	*KTPI*	*Other*
I. Paramaribo	max.	19,879	—	13,392	—	—
(10 seats)	min.	19,540	—	13,154	—	—
II. Suriname (1 seat)		—	4,100	2,746	—	—
III. Suriname (1 seat)		—	5,954	1,415	—	—
IV. Para (Suriname) (1 seat)		1,902	—	1,203	—	—
V. Commewijne	max.	—	1,160	—	2,519	1,816[a]
(2 seats)	min.	—	266	—	2,416	947
VI. Saramacca	max.	—	1,880	1,286	—	—
(2 seats)	min.	—	1,861	1,263	—	—
VII. Nickerie	max.	—	2,060	2,298[b]	—	—
(2 seats)	min.	—	2,046	2,290	—	—
VIII. Coronie (1 seat)		730	—	367	—	272[c]
IX. Marowijne (1 seat)		997	—	800	—	—

[a] M.A. Karamat Ali, expelled from the KTPI, ran his own ticket in this race.
[b] The *Nickerie Onafhankelijke Partij* ran in alliance with the *Eenheidsfront*.
[c] A third candidate, C.S.H. Sandvliet, ran as an independent.
Source: *Gouvernements-Advertentieblad* No. 48 (June 13, 1958) and No. 54 (July 4, 1958).

S. Soedardjo, who had won their three-way contests in Commewijne (see Table 5.4).

Table 5.4. Seat Division in 1958 Elections.

Election District	*NPS*	*PSV*	*VHP*	*EF(NOP)*	*KTPI*
I. Paramaribo	6	4			
II. Suriname			1		
III. Suriname			1		
IV. Para	1				
V. Commewijne					2
VI. Saramacca			2		
VII. Nickerie				2	
VIII. Coronie	1				
IX. Marowijne	1				
Total	9	4	4	2	2

Nevertheless, despite the humiliation of being "washed from the boards," the leaders of the EF took their defeat, as *De Ware Tijd* put it, "with good sportsmanship."[96] C.R. Biswamitre declared that "it is not a matter of win-

[96] *DWT*, June 27, 1958.

ning or losing. What's important is the program, whose continuity, for the sake of the country, must not be abandoned." Saying that the NPS, VHP, and PSV had as yet published no working program for the coming years, Biswamitre expressed the hope that they would follow the guidelines already developed by the *Eenheidsfront*.[97]

Like Findlay and Sang A Jang before him, Johan Pengel, as *formateur*, assembled a political Cabinet. Remaining as the leader of the NPS *fractie* in the *Staten*, Pengel chose the lawyer S.D. Emanuels (NPS) to chair the Cabinet, appointing four other NPSers to the posts of Finance, Development, Public Works and Social Affairs/Public Health. PSVers were given the Ministries of Education and Economic Affairs; and for the first time, VHPers entered the Cabinet, taking the posts of Justice and Police, and Agriculture. Three of these appointees had been elected to the *Staten* and gave up their seats to their shadow-candidates.[98]

V. VERBROEDERING IN POWER

The years from 1958 to 1967 mark the longest period of political stability Surinam has had under self-rule. Because of Dutch economic aid, good planning and the new investments of Alcoa, there was a healthy growth of the economy. The standard of living rose markedly and government services improved.

Yet, despite the close cooperation between VHP and NPS leaders at the government level, tensions and distrust remained strong at the grass-roots. Survey research conducted between 1959 and 1961 by the Dutch sociologists J.D. Speckmann and H.C. van Renselaar has confirmed this. Utilizing similar questionnaires, they asked Creole and Hindustani respondents to evaluate each of the other ethnic groups in the country. The findings (see Table 5.5) showed a striking degree of negative opinion by Hindustanis toward Creoles and vice versa. Follow-up questions revealed the basis for the negative opinions: Hindustanis frequently referred to the Creoles' authoritarian and aggressive behavior, their presumed position of privilege, their laziness and parasitic dependence, and "their refusal to pay their rents."[99] Creoles, on the other hand, cited the Hindustanis' economic aggressiveness, their stinginess, and their refusal to assimilate.[100] In contrast, the Javanese enjoyed a fairly

[97] *Ibid.*

[98] Ormskirk, *op. cit.*, pp. 116-17, 119.

[99] J.D. Speckmann, "De Houding van de Hindostaanse Bevolkingsgroep in Suriname ten opzichte van de Creolen," in *Bijdragen tot de Taal-, Land-, en Volkenkunde*, CXIX (1963), p. 90.

[100] H.C. van Renselaar, "De Houding van de Creoolse Bevolkingsgroep in Suriname ten opzichte van de Andere Bevolkingsgroepen," in *ibid.*, p. 104.

Table 5.5. Hindustani and Creole Attitudes toward Other Cultural Groups, 1959-1961

Hindustani Attitudes	*Positive* %	*Negative* %	*Neutral* %	*No Answer* %	*No Opinion* %
Creoles	9.5	63.0	9.5	2.0	16.0
Javanese	16.0	3.0	1.0	2.0	18.0
Chinese	46.0	16.0	12.0	2.0	24.0
Dutch	60.0	2.0	4.0	9.0	25.0
Creole Attitudes	*Positive* %	*Negative* %	*Neutral* %	*No Answer* %	*No Opinion* %
Hindustanis	2.8	83.3	13.9	—	—
Javanese	16.3	3.5	18.8	—	11.4
Chinese	15.9	33.3	5.5	—	45.1
Dutch	39.6	35.4	21.5	—	3.5

Source: J.D. Speckmann, "De Houding van de Hindostaanse Bevolkingsgroep in Suriname ten opzichte van de Creolen," in *Bijdragen tot de Taal-, Land-, en Volkenkunde*, CXIX (1963), p. 88; and H.C. van Renselaar, "De Houding van de Creoolse Bevolkingsgroep in Suriname ten opzichte van de Andere Bevolkingsgroepen," in *ibid.*, p. 103.

positive image with both groups, while the Creoles showed a somewhat mixed opinion regarding the Chinese and Dutch. Van Renselaar's Creole questionnaire included one question that was not replicated by Speckmann among Hindustanis: he asked Creoles for their opinions of themselves. The answers were surprisingly self-critical, probably revealing continued class- and color-line biases from the '40s and early 50's. Thirty-eight percent of the Creoles had a positive opinion of their group, 24 percent a neutral one, and nearly 35 percent were negative![101] Among their remarks: "Creoles are spendthrifts; they do not save; they never help their own people; they 'sport' too much (i.e. they spend too much time with their girl friends)."[102] But despite the internal differences among Creoles regarding their own qualities, they seemed to be nearly unanimous in their dislike and distrust of the Hindustanis. And these feelings were largely reciprocated. The soil was thus fertile for the emergence of more purist cultural movements within both the Creole and Hindustani camps seeking to repudiate the *verbroedering* of the two largest political parties.

In the mid 1950s, a nationalistic *Sranang* cultural group called *Wie Eegie Sanie* (our own things), led by the lawyer-playwright Mr. Eddy Bruma, began to draw large crowds to its plays and discussions. Though not initially oriented to politics, its championing of the *Sranantongo* language and indigen-

[101] *Ibid.*, p. 103.
[102] *Ibid.*, p. 104.

ous cultural themes gradually bore political fruit, as analogies were drawn between Dutch cultural discrimination against *Sranantongo* and Western exploitation of Surinam's natural resources. Attacking the schoolbook portrayal of certain Bush Negro leaders of the past as savages and revolutionaries, members of *Wie Eegie Sanie* launched a fund-raising program to build a statue of Boni, in their eyes, the greatest of these heroes. Aware of the growing influence of this group, the NPS made efforts to infiltrate and take it over, but were repulsed.[103]

After the victory of the NPS, VHP and PSV in 1958, *Wie Eegie Sanie* tried to attract the government's young ministers Dr. Jules Sedney (Finance) and Dr. Frank Essed (Development) to its meetings. Both men admired Bruma and his ideas. (Sedney had originally helped Bruma organize *Wie Eegie Sanie* in the Netherlands in the early 1950s,[104] and Essed had become an enthusiastic supporter of independence.) But now, they were under great pressure from Pengel not to lend official encouragement to Bruma's group.

Pengel's first action in response to these nationalistic pressures was to attempt to take over the fishing company of Schweig. Though the court rejected this effort, and the Government subsequently reaffirmed Schweig's contract, the latter agreed to enter new negotiations over the terms of his operations.[105]

Repeatedly referring to the Kingdom Statute as "*geen eeuwig edict*" (no eternal document), Pengel gave every indication of moving quickly towards independence. As a first step, the new Minister-President, S.D. Emanuels, promised quick adoption of a Surinam flag, new national coat of arms and revision of the national anthem.[106] But C.R. Biswamitre warned that these would hardly constitute a breakthrough from ethnic divisions to real national unity.[107]

In June 1959, a group of *Wie Eegie Sanie* members, led by the poet Robin Ravales ("Dobru"), organized the *Nationalistische Beweging Suriname* (Surinam Nationalist Movement, NBS), calling for independence and renewing the demand that July 1 be declared a national holiday.[108] The abolition of slavery, they said in their first manifesto, "was not intended for a specific

[103] *DW*, December 3, 1957.

[104] Sedney tried to persuade Pengel to offer a government subsidy to *Wie Eegie Sanie* for its cultural program, but Pengel "angrily refused." (Interview, Dr. Jules Sedney, Utrecht, August 1, 1974). For more background on *Wie Eegie Sanie* and Eddy Bruma, see John Jansen van Galen, "De Triomf van Meester Eddy Bruma," *Haagse Post*, November 29, 1975, pp. 6-10; and Voorhoeve and Lichtveld, *op. cit.*, pp. 11-12, 164-93.

[105] Schweig's company was now incorporated as the Surinam-American Industries Limited (SAIL). *DW*, September 23, 1958, and December 31, 1959, and *DWT*, November 18, 1959.

[106] *Regeringsverklaring*, reprinted in *DW*, September 15, 1958.

[107] *DW*, September 17, 1958.

[108] *DW*, June 10, 1959.

group, but for the Surinam nation as a whole." Subsequent changes in the society shouldn't mean a change in the historical significance of such a fact.[109] Although no action was taken by the Government, *Wie Eegie Sanie* organized a gala celebration for July 1, 1959, with nationalistic poetry, classical Hindustani and Javanese music and *Sranang Kawina* music and dances – all proceeds going to help erect the statue commemorating the revolutionary Bush Negroes.[110]

In a kind of race to "capture the flag" of nationalism among the Creoles, the Government quickly produced its proposals for the new national symbols of flag, coat of arms, and anthem. Before they were adopted in December 1959, they generated considerable debate and challenge not only from the young Creole nationalists and the Hindustani opponents to *verbroedering* but also from Surinam's largely-forgotten first inhabitants, the Amerindians. Already in February 1959, a delegation of 15 Amerindian leaders met with Minister-President Emanuels to discuss such things as their salaries, official titles, better lodgings in Paramaribo for their official visits, and the need for better educational opportunities for their people. In response to a question regarding their symbolic representation as shield-bearers on the existing coat of arms of Surinam, Emanuels answered vaguely that no change was expected except in the case of independence. The Amerindians insisted that whenever a new flag or coat of arms was introduced, it should have their approval.[111]

In November 1959, legislation was introduced to establish the flag, coat of arms and anthem. The coat of arms was somewhat modernized, as the schooner of the type that carried slaves in the early colonial period was replaced by a more recent sailing ship. The most drastic change, however, was the removal of the Indians. In a letter to the Indian leaders, Emanuels explained that

> the fact that the new coat of arms lacks shieldbearers has nothing to do with the rights of the Indians. The Indians have the same rights in this land as the rest of the population – not more nor less. Shieldbearers appear on a few coats of arms – mostly European ones – and these are of animals. In no land are the inhabitants depicted as shieldbearers, and I cannot see why only in Surinam should this be the case.[112]

De West promptly took up the Indians' cause and pointed to the coat of arms of Greece and a number of states in the United States (including New York,

[109] *Ibid.*
[110] *DW*, June 3, 1959.
[111] *DW*, February 27, 1959.
[112] *DW*, November 30, 1959.

whose coat of arms was very similar to Surinam's) as examples of human shieldbearers representing the indigenous population.[113] On December 2, a delegation of Indian leaders again visited the Minister-President, declaring that they felt so threatened by the change, they might emigrate to French Guiana.[114]

At the same time, an even wider controversy developed over the flag and anthem. The flag, a white field with five stars (red, brown, yellow, black and white) connected by a black ellipse, was widely criticized as ugly and plain. Perhaps more than most flags, considerations of symbolism were more important than esthetics, and in the *Staten* debates these symbols were a major factor in its adoption. The colors of the stars represented the five major racial groups in Surinam: red – Amerindians, brown – Hindustanis and Javanese, yellow – Chinese, black – Creoles and Bush Negroes, and white – Europeans and Lebanese. The ellipse symbolized "the unbreakable band with which the five elements are linked into a whole," while the white field symbolized "the peace in which all these various peoples live together in unity."[115] As the Government explained it, "this flag could not have been born in any other century than the twentieth, in which the peaceful coexistence of all the races and peoples of the earth must be the highest ideal of the world, and seeing that Surinam has set the example of this ideal, our flag will be greeted with honor and hopefulness in the ranks of nations."[116]

Nevertheless, the press remained critical. *De West* deplored the absence of any sign of a Dutch tie in the flag, *Onze Tijd* spoke of it as a "pirate flag," and *De Ware Tijd* warned that people would see it more as a puzzle than a "symbol into which people can pour out their love for their fatherland."[117]

The anthem also attracted controversy, especially within the Hindustani population, where the idea of a stanza in *Sranantongo* was offensive. *De West* reported that many Hindustani parents were saying they would refuse to let their children learn it. One group of young Hindustanis, calling themselves the "*Actie Groep* (Action Group) of the VHP," protested that the stanza in *Sranantongo* had a distinctly Creole character. Better that the song remain in Dutch, as that was more neutral and thus more appropriate for all

[113] *Ibid.*, and December 1, 1959.

[114] *DW*, December 3, 1959.

[115] "Memorie van Toelichting – Vlag Ontwerp," quoted in *DW*, November 26, 1959.

[116] *Ibid.*

[117] *DW*, November 28, 1959; *DWT*, November 30, 1959. The *Onze Tijd* remark was quoted in *DW*, November 30, 1959.

Surinamers.[118] This group, made up of young, urbanized Hindustani intellectuals, soon broke all ties to the VHP, denouncing its lack of internal democracy and protesting its neglect of the Hindustanis in the city. As a political party of its own it was to become very influential in the 1960s.

Rumors that the PSV might break away from the NPS over the new national symbols led to a packed *Staten* meeting on December 7, 1959 (the 19th anniversary of Queen Wilhelmina's 1942 promise of autonomy). All the members of the Cabinet were present for the debate. Speaking for the PSV, Coen Ooft aired many of the criticisms regarding the coat of arms, flag, and anthem. He would have preferred a referendum on them to a legislative enactment, and he resented the fact that the Government had already ordered thousands of guilders worth of the flags for the celebration of Statute Day later that month. But after several heated exchanges with Johan Pengel, Ooft's only action was to move restoration of the Indians to the coat of arms. His amendment was passed unanimously and the coat of arms was then accepted.[119]

If there had been any fears that the VHP might reverse its stand on the anthem, Lachmon quickly buried them. When debate began on this issue, he pointed to the Indian national anthem as being in a language other than Hindi – a language (Maradji) spoken by only a small percentage of Indians. In contrast, he argued,

> ...The Surinamese language is understood by 99% of the group which I represent here, [therefore] I consider it a privilege to be able to say, in the name of *verbroedering*: You [Creoles] are a great group; take this prerogative to have the anthem in your language,

[118] *DW*, December 1, 8 and 11, 1959. The old first stanza read: God zij met ons Suriname/Hij verheff' ons heerlijk land!/Doch dat elk zich dan ook schame/Die zijn ere maakt te schand/Recht en waarheid te betrachten,/Zedelijk rein en vroom en vrij,/Al wat slecht is te verachten/Dat geeft aan ons land waardij. (God be with our Surinam/Let Him elevate our wonderful land!/And let him be ashamed/Who harms his (country's) honor/Living in justice and truth,/Morally clean and pious and free,/Despising all that is bad/That gives our country worth.)

With changes by Henny de Ziel (penname Trefosa) to reflect Surinam's cultural pluralism, and to give the song a more positive meaning, the first stanza now reads:

God zij met ons Suriname/Hij verheff' ons heerlijk land!/Hoe wij daar ook samen kwamen,/Aan zijn grond zijn wij verpand./Werkend houden w'in gedachten:/Recht en waarheid maken vrij,/Al wat goed is te betrachten,/Dat geeft aan ons land waardij. (God be with our Surinam/Let Him elevate our wonderful land!/However we came here together/We are bound to its soil./And as we work, we keep in mind:/Justice and truth make free,/To do all that is good/That gives our country worth.) The second stanza, also by Trefosa, was in *Sranantongo* and read: Opo! Kondreman un opo!/Sranan gron e kari un,/Wans ope tata komopo,/Wi mu seti kondri bun./Stree de f'stree wi no sa frede/Gado de wi fesi man./Eri libi te na dede,/Wi sa feti dji Sranan. (Onward! Countrymen, let's go!/Surinam is calling us,/Regardless of our origin/We must set the country right./If there's a fight we mustn't fear/God is our leader./Our whole life 'til we die,/We shall fight for Surinam.)

[119] Staten van Suriname, *Handelingen 1959-60*, pp. 311-19.

because we understand it and think of it like our own.

Mister Speaker! Let us not debate this point further. As far as I'm concerned the important thing is the meaning of this song and the meaning of this song is not insulting to the group I represent. . . .[120]

Probably easing the VHP's acceptance of the anthem was a directive to school directors a few days before the *Staten* meeting announcing that the second stanza would not be obligatory in school assemblies.[121] The PSV's only criticism of the *Sranang* stanza was its spelling. To this, the Minister-President declared that a commission for an official spelling of *Sranantongo* had not yet finished its study, but any corrections deemed necessary would be made at that time. The anthem was then accepted unanimously.[122]

Finally, regarding the flag, Pengel admitted that the "beauty" of the flag may be debated, but its symbolism was its greatest attraction. Lachmon criticized the absence of a flag for the Dutch Kingdom as a whole, arguing that the Dutch flag did not suffice, and implying that rather than incorporate Dutch elements in the Surinam flag, what was needed was a Kingdom flag that incorporated elements from each of the component units' flags. The PSV, which had come prepared to oppose the flag, called a recess, then announced that it would give up its opposition. After another unanimous vote of approval, Minister-President Emanuels unfurled the new flag to the cheers of the audience.[123]

Even the young nationalists were reasonably happy. Though they objected to the separation of the stars, which seemed to mean that the policy of assimilation was being abandoned, Ravales, the leader of the NBS, wrote that "it's better to have a second-rate flag than none at all," for now they had a flag they could fight under. But, he added, they opposed inaugurating it on Statute Day, since they considered this the most colonial day of the year, and he reiterated their demand for outright independence.[124]

Encouraged by the anti-imperialist successes of Fidel Castro of Cuba, the NBS had increased its activities in 1959 and 1960. As the *Staten* debated a measure to take farmlands from Creoles and others in the Para area for new Suralco mining concessions under the Brokopondo Agreement, the radical lawyer, Eddy Bruma, vigorously began to champion the Para farmers' interests against the industry and its government supporters. Demonstrations were organized, and when they apparently failed, a bomb exploded near the home of Johan Pengel, in April 1959. Eight young Creoles, allegedly members

[120] *DW*, December 3, 1959.
[122] Staten van Suriname, *Handelingen 1959-60*, pp. 320-21.
[123] *Ibid.*, pp. 321-23.
[124] *DW*, December 14, 1959.

of the NBS, were arrested for this incident. Still, the *Staten* voted unanimously in May 1959 to dispossess the farmers of their lands.[125]

If the provision of new mining concessions to Suralco had been an embarrassing concession to make, Pengel's government later announced with pleasure the result of hard negotiations on another front: the Schweig fishing concern had agreed to surrender its monopoly over fishing, while at the same time increasing its investments.[126]

Despite the bomb incident, the young nationalists were gaining a positive reputation as skilled champions of the Creole underdog, and their position on independence acquired increased respectability as a result. Pengel now moved to have July 1 declared a national holiday, though as a compromise to the VHP, it was given the more appealing name "Day of Freedoms and Human Rights."[127] Yet Creole pressures for more substantial changes grew – even within the NPS itself.

Thus, when Lachmon indicated that he might accept independence for Surinam under a dominion status, Pengel eagerly called for a new Round Table Conference. By this time, a number of newspapers and party leaders in the Netherlands were prepared to see such a step taken, and the Dutch Government scheduled the new RTC for May 1961.

On the eve of departure for the Netherlands, a number of meetings were held by the smaller Asian parties. The leader of the *Nickerie Onafhankelijke Partij*, D. Poetoe, announced that his supporters were strongly opposed to independence in any form. The KTPI, meeting in Paramaribo, opposed "complete independence," but left their leader, I. Soemita, some leeway for making changes to the Statute. The *Actie Groep*, now fully independent of the VHP, posed the greatest threat, however, as its organizers were spreading out through the districts, "conducting an opinion poll on independence" while at the same time warning that independence would mean the selection of a "Negro President" and "Creole domination." The VHP organized a "*Reactie Groep*" to counter the other's propaganda and each side repeatedly disrupted the other's meetings.[128]

Finally, on May 21, the VHP held a mass meeting in the Bellevue Theater, to declare its own increasingly uncertain position. The crowd demanded that the speeches be in *Sarnami Hindostans*, but the leaders refused, providing a translator instead. Lachmon and the two VHP cabinet ministers defended

[125] *DWT*, February 18, April 15 and May 14, 1959. For the arrests in the bombing case, see *DWT*, March 12 and 26, 1960. *25 Juni*, to the contrary, identified the culprits as either independents or members of the *Eenheidsfront* (March 30, 1960).

[126] *DWT*, November 18, 1959.

[127] *25 Juni*, July 8, 1960.

[128] *DWT*, May 6, 8, 15, 18, 19, 23, and 25, 1961.

their government's policies as culturally balanced, and promised that they would continue to be so. Together with Soemita, who was present to declare his solidarity with the VHP, they assured the crowd they would leave the RTC if it went contrary to their expectations.[129] And in retrospect, it seems that their expectations were for failure.

On his arrival in The Netherlands, Surinam's Minister-President, S.D. Emanuels, declared that Surinam was not seeking independence, *per se*, but simply some (unspecified) changes in the Statute. Nevertheless, D. Poetoe reiterated the NOP's opposition to any changes, adding in a press conference in The Hague that the only way his party would accept a change in the Statute would be after new elections according to proportional representation, so that the Hindustanis would be better represented.[130]

The talks now seemed crippled before they began. Switching their demands from "Dominion Status" to merely achieving a degree of control over foreign affairs, the Surinamers found the Dutch more reluctant than they expected. Such a reform seemed constitutionally unviable, and after several weeks of meetings, a plenary session was finally held June 13 to adjourn the discussions. A working group was set up to continue study of the proposal, but no other actions were taken.[131] Returning disheartened, the NPS leaders now faced the thankless challenge of building nation-wide support before daring to try again.

Angered by the collapse of the RTC, the *Nationalistische Beweging Suriname* announced formation in September 1961 of the *Partij van de Nationalistische Republiek* (Nationalistic Republic Party, PNR), under the leadership of the lawyer, Eddy Bruma. Its announced goal was "to bring together all progressive men and women as well as all Surinamese youth into a well-organized political party, in order to give the Surinamese people a guiding body for the achievement of the nationalist revolution."[132]

Creoles were now badly polarized, especially along generational lines, over the independence issue. In December 1961, a Creole "Women's Committee Against Independence Now" (*Vrouwen Comité Anti-Onafhankelijkheid Nu*) announced it was planning a march and invited others to take part. The march took place in mid-January 1962. Despite a VHP warning against supporting such demonstrations, a sizeable contingent of Hindustanis also participated, led by the *Actie Groep* and featuring several young Hindustani intellectuals recently returned from studies in the Netherlands. This event pre-

[129] *DWT*. May 23, 1961.
[130] *DWT*, May 18 and 25, 1961.
[131] *DWT*, June 15, 1961.
[132] *DWT*, September 2, 1961.

sumably alarmed the VHP sufficiently that it reaffirmed its opposition to any change in Surinam's status and, in subsequent contacts with the young intellectuals, was able to lure some of them away from the *Actie Groep* and into the VHP.[133]

Faced with the growing mobilization of anti-independence forces, and recalling the NOP's demand for election law changes, Frank Essed departed from the NPS position on proportional representation, suggesting the creation of a PR district superimposed over the existing district system and adding 20 new seats. Conceivably, this concession – to increase Asian representation in the *Staten*, might pave the way for independence. The PSV applauded this suggestion, adding proposals of their own. But Pengel and other NPSers were cool to the idea.[134]

The NPS now demanded that the Dutch Governor, Van Tilburg, be replaced by a Surinamer. The *Actie Groep* came out flatly against this as a divisive move – better to leave the Queen's local representative Dutch, and thereby neutral on ethnic issues. The VHP, finding an issue where they could reaffirm their policy of *verbroedering*, came out in support of the Surinamese Governor suggestion.[135]

Meanwhile, the PNR announced that its target date for independence was July 1, 1963 – the 100th anniversary of the abolition of slavery.[136] Clearly, this idea might already have been the sentimental dream of Pengel and the NPS, and it was galling to have the newer PNR lay down the specific challenge in the open. For, if anything, the realistic prospect for independence had become more and more remote. In February 1962 British Guiana had experienced severe racial conflict,[137] and its impact on Surinam's own race relations was unavoidable. The destruction of large sections of Georgetown, and loss of life, were widely reported in Surinam's papers. Ferry service was halted between Nieuw Nickerie and Springlands, while Dutch ships patrolled the Corantijn River, and evacuated Surinamese and Guyanese refugees from the fighting. In April 1962, Governor Van Tilburg warned:

> Let the recent events in British Guiana serve as a warning example to Surinam. Surinam's position stands or falls not with the size of its population or its available

[133] *DWT*, December 29, 1961, and January 11 and 22, 1962; *CLO-Bulletin*, September 6, 1973. Also, interview, Evert Azimullah, Paramaribo, February 18, 1974.

[134] *DWT*, February 5 and 14, 1962; and interview, Frank Essed, Paramaribo, July 12, 1971.

[135] *DWT*, March 8, 1962; and *DW*, December 31, 1962 (Year's Review of News), p. 6.

[136] *DWT*, March 19, 1962. In a speech to the PNR in the Bellevue Theater, Eddy Bruma significantly added that he rejected the ideology of Communism. "We are nationalists who are ideologically committed only to building up the nation and the land." (*Ibid.*)

[137] *DWT*, February 17, 1962, and continuing coverage in *DWT* and *DW*. See also Despres, *op. cit.*, pp. 264-65.

capital. Only with the organized power of the people and their sense of unity will something new and original be brought into being.[138]

The position of the NPS on independence was further weakened in May with the defection of Pengel's close comrade, Just Rens, who announced that he too was against "Independence Now."[139] In the same month, the PSV declared that it would no longer "play second fiddle" to the NPS and introduced a bill similar to the proposal Essed had earlier made, to establish proportional representation.[140]

Pengel now began a strategic retreat from the independence issue. After a BBC program estimated the number of Communists in Surinam at 600,[141] Pengel grabbed at this issue to solidify the ranks of his government alliance and to seek to isolate and discredit the PNR. In a *Staten* meeting held immediately after the BBC announcement, all parties agreed that efforts must be made to stamp out Communist ideas in Surinam, and veiled references to the PNR made it clear that Bruma's group was the object of their concern.[142]

After stubbornly resisting Frank Essed's suggestion for PR, Pengel finally announced in December that he would accept it. There was a condition, however. New single-member districts would be set up in the interior in an effort to draw Bush Negroes into the political system (presumably in support of the NPS). As finally approved, the bill created four new districts. The Bush Negro districts were located along the Marowijne River (Boven Marowijne) and the upper Suriname River, where the Brokopondo Dam was being constructed (Brokopondo). The area immediately south of Paramaribo was divided in two single-member districts: Pad van Wanika, just south of the city, where Hindustanis were in the majority; and Para, the location of Suralco's Paranam operation and the Dutch Billiton mining company, where Creoles were ascendant. The fourth new "district" was the national list, comprising the nation as a whole, which would provide 12 additional seats, apportioned on the basis of PR.[143] Altogether, the changes enlarged the *Staten* from 21 to

[138] *DWT*, April 25, 1962.

[139] *DWT*, May 5, 1962.

[140] *DWT*, May 30, 1962.

[141] *DWT*, June 30, 1962.

[142] *Ibid.*

[143] In the 1963 elections, the problem of extra seats beyond those won by achieving the quota of votes (total votes divided by twelve) was handled as follows: the parties already winning at least one seat were ranked in order of their remaining number of votes (i.e., left over after achieving seats according to the quota number). The party with the largest vote-remainder was then awarded one extra seat. If there were as many extra seats as parties fulfilling the initial quota, they all got extra seats. In 1967, this method was changed to permit the awarding of seats according to average-voters-per-seat. (See Rae, *op. cit.*, pp. 31-33 and 34-36.) This later reform (modelled on the Dutch system) was clearly beneficial to the larger parties (NPS and VHP) at the expense of the smaller ones.

36 members and opened the doors not only for new candidates from the established political parties already represented in the Staten, but for their extra-parliamentary opposition (*Eenheidsfront*, *Actie Groep*, PNR, etc.) as well.

VI. THE 1963 ELECTIONS

In January 1963, before debate began on the new election laws, the *Eenheidsfront* made common cause with the opponents of *verbroedering*, the *Actie Groep* (AG), to form what they called an *Actiefront* for the March elections. After the election law was approved, the Nickerie Independent Party (NOP) joined the *Actiefront*, agreeing to share the ticket in Nickerie with the AG. Besides the *Actiefront*, eleven other parties registered for the elections, including the NPS, PSV, KTPI, VHP and PNR. Of interest was the appearance of a *Verenigde Indiaanse Partij* which ran Amerindian candidates in Saramacca and Marowijne.

Campaigning under the *Sranang* slogan "*tai hori, libi de*" (hold on, there's life), the NPS encountered spirited opposition from the *Actiefront*, who on several occasions drowned out the "*libi de*" of the NPS chants with "*batjauw de*" (there is *bakkeljauw*). A local salted fish, identified with the Creole lower class, *bakkeljauw* was symbolic of the government's relief program to poor families, as well as the idea of political spoils in general.[144]

Election day gave the NPS much to celebrate. In a surprise announcement that day, a former Minister-President in the 1951 Government, Archibald Currie, was appointed Governor – the first Surinamer to be so named.[145] And to the NPS' relief, the leftist, and highly vocal, PNR was unable to get a seat in the *Staten*. Running far behind the *Actiefront* and NPS in Paramaribo, the PNR was even unable to get a seat on the national PR list. With 3,140 votes, the PNR was far below the PR list's quota of 6,986 (see Table 5.6). The race in Paramaribo between the *Actiefront* and the NPS was closer than in 1958, but with the help of PSV votes, the NPS was able to win by roughly 17,000 to 14,400. The price they paid for this was steep, however, as the NPS had once again given the PSV four seats on its ten-man list. When it appeared that the PSV had been only slightly ahead of the PNR on the national list – coming in far short of the quota – it was clear that the PSV would be over-represented in the new *Staten* (see Table 5.7).

Although the NPS won its races in the smaller districts against Creole *Actiefront* candidates, it was edged out on the national list, as the *Actiefront*

[144] Ormskirk, *op. cit.*, pp. 132-33.
[145] *DWT*, March 27, 1963.

Table 5.6 Votes cast in the 1963 Elections

Election District		*Maximum and Minimum Votes, by Party* *NPS/PSV*	*VHP*	*Actie-front*	*KTPI*	*PNR*	*Other*
I. Paramaribo	max.	17,246	—	14,566	—	2,614	—
(10 seats)	min.	16,761	—	13,815	—	2,304	—
II. Suriname (1 seat)		—	4,457	4,068	—	—	—
III. Suriname (1 seat)		367	4,596	2,612	—	—	—
IV. Suriname (1 seat)		—	3,221	2,389	—	—	—
V. Para (Suriname) (1 seat)		1,838	—	904	—	—	800[a]
VI. Commewijne	max.	—	—	512	3,192	—	471[b]
(two seats)	min.	—	—	511	3,048	—	443
VII. Saramacca	max.	—	2,284	1,335	—	—	389[c]
(two seats)	min.	—	2,280	1,308	—	—	77
VIII. Nickerie	max.	—	3,597	4,016	645[d]	—	652[d]
(two seats)	min.	—	3,554	3,948	—	—	—
IX. Coronie (1 seat)		587	—	569	—	—	48[e]
X. Beneden Marowijne (1 seat)		1,769	—	757	—	—	167[f]
XI. Boven Marowijne (1 seat)		726	—	40	—	—	—
XII. Brokopondo (1 seat)		2,276	—	316	—	—	31[g]

	NPS	*PSV*	*Actie-front*	*PNR*	*VHP*	*KTPI*	*VIP*	*P v d Landbouw*	*Other lists*
National list (PR) (12 seats)	20,354	3,916	23,612	3,140	15,456	7,323	1,525	5,412	3,102

[a] R. Ramdjan, party affiliation not known. [b] *Kerngroep*, a Javanese party. [c] There were two additional lists- the *Verenigde Indiaanse Partij* (VIP) with nearly 400 votes was the stronger of these. [d] The KTPI and a group of independent Creoles ran a joint slate here. [e] There were two additional candidates. [f] The VIP ran the stronger of two additional candidates here. [g] There were two additional candidates.

Source: *Gouvernements-Advertentieblad* No. 26 (April 2, 1963) and No. 31 (April 19, 1963).

(aided by Hindustani votes in the districts) polled 23,612 to the NPS' 20,354 and the VHP's 15,456. In the division of seats on this list, the *Actiefront* was awarded 4, the NPS and VHP 3 each, and the KTPI (with 7,323 votes) 2.[146] Overall, with the loss of Nickerie again to the *Actiefront*, the new *Staten* was composed as follows: NPS – 14 seats, VHP – 8, PSV – 4, *Actiefront* – 6 (two SDP, including David Findlay; three AG and one NOP), and KTPI – 4.

A new provision in the electoral law provided that if a *Staten* member became a Minister and was censured as such, or otherwise resigned, he could be restored to his seat in the *Staten*. If Pengel had resisted the temptation to

[146] The KTPI's votes were barely over the quota for PR seats. But, because of the new electoral law's division of extra seats (see note 143 above), it was able to get one of the four extra seats.

Table 5.7. Seat Division in 1963 Elections

Election District	*NPS*	*PSV*	*VHP*	*Actiefront*	*KTPI*
I. Paramaribo	6	4	–	–	–
II. Suriname			1		
III. Suriname			1		
IV. Suriname			1		
V. Para (Suriname)	1				
VI. Commewijne					2
VII. Saramacca			2		
VIII. Nickerie				2[a]	
IX. Coronie	1				
X. Ben. Marowijne	1				
XI. Bov. Marowijne	1				
XII. Brokopondo	1				
National list	3		3	4[b]	2
Total	14	4	8	6	4

[a] divided between the NOP and *Actiegroep*
[b] divided between the SDP (2) and *Actiegroep* (2)

seek higher office with the fear that his enemies might drive him out of the government altogether, this new provision may have encouraged him to try his luck as Minister-President. Called on by the Governor to form the new Cabinet, Pengel awarded himself with three ministries (General Affairs, i.e., the office of the Minister-President; Internal Affairs and Finance); and divided the other ministries as follows: Education, Social Affairs, Public Works and Development, went to the NPS; Justice and Police, Agriculture, and Health to the VHP; and Economic Affairs to the PSV. The KTPI, which had announced its support for the Government, asked only for a high civil service post, saying it had no suitable candidates for minister.[147] But there were many who felt that Pengel was similarly unqualified to be a minister – let alone to do the work of three.[148] The VHP and PSV chose not to protest, however, because they had lost considerable strength. In particular, Lachmon was worried that to give up cooperation with the NPS would feed the fires of racial tension.[149]

[147] Ormskirk, *op. cit.*, p. 146.
[148] Ooft, *Ontwikkeling...*, p. 258.
[149] Interview, J. Lachmon, February 5, 1976, Paramaribo.

VII. THE SECOND VERBROEDERING GOVERNMENT

Pengel began his work dramatically, insisting upon new negotiations with Suralco, to speed up their timetable to build an aluminum smelter (the first to be constructed anywhere in the developing world). Moreover, to convey an impression of greater sovereignty, he set up an office in the General Affairs Ministry to deal with foreign affairs and began negotiations with the American State Department to receive financial aid under the newly operative Alliance for Progress and with the Government of West Germany and the European Common Market for similar aid.[150]

Having criticized his own government in the previous administration for failure to conclude an agreement for the development of bauxite resources in the West Surinam area, Pengel promised to make good these negotiations. But here, Pengel had his first setback. In October 1963, he announced that the contract to develop West Surinam would go to the so-called ORMET group (representing the American firms of Olin-Mathieson and Reynolds). The PSV attacked the contract for its lack of a clause to assure the local refining of the bauxite. In response, Pengel claimed that the agreement with ORMET had already been negotiated during the preceding government, and a binding commitment had been made. But, *Suriname*, Purcy Wijngaarde's daily, reported on October 24, 1963, that ex-ministers Essed, Sedney and V.M. de Miranda all denied the existence of such an agreement, while Minister Rens (of Development) reported he had searched his ministry's files and also couldn't find any record of it.[151]

With the credibility of his new government under attack, Pengel suddenly announced his resignation. As leader of the second largest legislative bloc in the *Staten*, Jagernath Lachmon was asked by the Governor to try to form a new Government. To everyone's surprise, Lachmon invited Pengel to remain as Minister-President, and the whole cabinet returned as formerly, with the exception of the PSV, whose Ministry of Economic Affairs was given to the KTPI.[152] It would appear that the entire affair was designed to end the NPS' ties with the PSV. But such a conclusion is unjustified. The price both Surinam and the NPS paid was too high. Not only was the contract with the ORMET group forfeited, but the prospects for West Surinam's development – on which Pengel had staked so much – was also lost for at least another decade.

Pengel's popularity further declined with his rough handling of a local radio station (AVROS), whose board of directors was dominated by mem-

[150] *DWT*, May 7, 10, 14, 30; June 11, 1963.

[151] *DWT*, October 15, 18, 22, 24, 25 and 28, 1963; and *Suriname*, October 24, 1963.

[152] *DWT*, November 23, 1963.

bers of the PNR. Charging that they had repeatedly failed to pay their licensing fees in time, Pengel ordered the station's license withdrawn. Most observers felt that the real issue was Pengel's anger at Eddy Bruma's sharp criticism of his government on a weekly program, aired by AVROS. In any case, the action produced a wave of criticism in the local press and a protest demonstration and march.[153]

Another source of protest was the inadequate provision made for Bush Negroes forced to move from the site of the lake created by the new dam. The *Actiefront*/PSV opposition in the *Staten* criticized the government's neglect in this matter, and the PNR's Eddy Bruma quickly picked up the Bush Negroes' cause, organizing the migrants and offering legal assistance. As construction on the dam ended and the waters began to rise, thousands of Bush Negroes were moved from the affected areas to resettlement camps, while others, who had enjoyed temporary employment in construction work were now left unemployed. Conflicts were frequently reported between Bush Negroes and the authorities in the Brokopondo area from 1963 through 1966, and delegations periodically visited Paramaribo to make demands of the Government. One proposed solution to the unemployment problem among Bush Negroes was an idea, attributed to Pengel, to add a Bush Negro detachment to the Dutch-Surinam Armed Forces for operations in the country's interior and along its borders with British Guiana. Pengel denied proposing such a force, but the Dutch press insisted that he had. In a sharp debate in the *Staten* the idea was criticized by the *Actie Groep*, as being threatening to the Hindustanis.[154]

Despite the setback to Pengel's plan for West Surinam's development, these were good times economically for Surinam. Queen Juliana made a return visit to Surinam to inaugurate the Afobaka Dam (as it was now called), and Suralco used the power it generated to begin processing bauxite into alumina (with the plants for processing alumina into aluminum shortly to follow). The significance of Surinam to the aluminum industry of the United States was underlined at this time by the promotion of Suralco's President to the presidency of the mother corporation, Alcoa.[155]

The Pengel government now promoted a new hydroelectric and irrigation project further down the Suriname River. Called the Torarica Project, it was the source of debate in the *Staten* between the PSV and NPS in 1966. No foreign investors appeared to be interested in it, though Pengel made several trips to Germany and the Common Market headquarters in Brussels for

[153] *DWT*, January 15, 18; February 6, 13, 14, 20 and 21, 1964.

[154] *DWT*, January 14, 31; February 5, 11, 13; October 16, 26, 30, 1964; and *DW*, December 31, 1964 (Year's Review of News), pp. 5, 11.

[155] Robert Overbeek (*DW*, December 31, 1965 (Year's Review of News), p. 6).

support. Eventually, after the 1967 elections, it was abandoned. Efforts to generate economic aid from the United States, the Common Market and the Dutch Government enjoyed greater success, however. Foreign investors showed an interest in bananas (the United Fruit Company in 1964-65), oil (the Colmar Oil Company in 1964), and West Surinam's bauxite deposits (the ORMET group, in conjunction with Alcoa, Alcan and Billiton, renewed negotiations in July 1965[156]). The KTPI was nominally in charge of the Ministry of Economic Affairs, the post that handled foreign investments such as these. Due to pressures from Pengel, as well as countervailing pressures from the KTPI, this post changed hands four times between 1964 and 1967, causing considerable conflict between the NPS and KTPI, and accompanying frictions within the KTPI itself.[157] Nevertheless, the new investments and foreign aid, together with the revenues from the sale of bauxite, alumina and finally aluminum, increased the government's capacity to provide more housing, schools and other services to the population.

Also in this period, following the collapse of the West Indian Federation, Eric Williams of Trinidad approached Surinam with the prospect of common market-type collaboration.[158] Despite some initial movement in this direction, countervailing talks took place between Barbados and British Guiana for creation of a free trade area in the Caribbean. In December 1965, the Carifta (Caribbean Free Trade Area) was designed, coming into being in 1968. This temporarily lured Trinidad away from its Surinam adventure.[159]

VIII. PENGEL, LACHMON, AND THE POLITICS OF VERBROEDERING

Ruthless in politics, as in play,[160] Pengel was nevertheless gracious in victory. Friends and enemies alike have reported countless incidents in which he contrived to remove or outmaneuver a rival, then saw to his needs in defeat. Raised in the Para district as the son of a schoolmaster, Pengel had few contacts with Hindustanis before he began to study law while working in the Paramaribo district court. But here, because of his outgoing nature, and the

[156] *DWT*, July 6, 1965.

[157] Ooft, *Ontwikkeling...*, p. 300; and *DW*, December 31, 1956 (Year's Review of News), pp. 7, 9.

[158] *DW*, December 31, 1962 (Year's Review of News), p. 14.

[159] *The Caribbean Community: A Guide* (Georgetown, Guyana: Caribbean Community Secretariat, 1973), pp. 18-21.

[160] A devotee of checkers, Pengel would play with anyone, but was not adverse to upsetting the board if he saw he would lose. As a youth, if his soccer team was defeated, he would contrive to join the winning side for the next match. (Anonymous informant)

contacts provided by his work, he made close friends with a number of individuals from other ethnic groups. Among them, F.H.R. Lim A Po, K. Kanhai, and H. Shriemisier are frequently identified as particularly influential in his later career. His failure to pass the law exams, a matter still shrouded in mystery, seems to have created a latent hostility towards both the Creole and white elites, and against intellectuals. Despite his membership in the NPS (which came on the eve of nominating candidates in the 1949 elections), he was not saddled with responsibility for the party's unpopular stand regarding universal suffrage and could legitimately take credit for getting the *volkscreolen* to support the party.

Later, while still engaged in bitter struggle with the Creole elite, his strategic alliance with the VHP (facilitated, most likely, by his friends Kanhai and Shriemisier – both active in the VHP) laid the foundations for an effective populist challenge to that elite. Though narrowly losing the 1955 elections to the *Eenheidsfront*, the NPS and VHP, in the opposition, disarmed their critics' objections to *verbroedering* by skilfully coordinated action and oratory – both in the *Staten* and in public rallies.

Lachmon, for his part, was committed to *verbroedering*, both politically and emotionally. Married to a woman of mixed Creole and Hindustani origins, and indebted for his career to a Black lawyer (J.C. de Miranda), he was trusted by many Creoles as able to "rise above" ethnicity for the sake of his country's interests. Nevertheless, *verbroedering* clearly meant something different to Lachmon than it did to Pengel. To Pengel, it meant gradual assimilation and intermarriage. To Lachmon, despite his own marriage, it meant unity through nonassimilation ("*eenheid in verscheidenheid*"[161]). Moreover, the period of Pengel's and his collaboration was never free of charges that the one had "sold out" to the other.

Once in power, the first real challenge to *verbroedering*'s political viability came in the selection of a Cabinet. Had Pengel or Lachmon (or both) taken ministerial positions, the image of "working in harness" might have been somewhat more strained. Moreover, new leadership in the *Staten* could emerge, as in the past, to challenge them. Both men chose to remain in the legislature, while those taking Cabinet posts, including S.D. Emanuels, the Minister-President, were increasingly viewed as having little power. With the 1963 change in the electoral law, giving a censured minister initially elected to the *Staten* the right to regain his seat, the threat of censure seemed reduced.

[161] J.H. Adhin, "Eenheid in Verscheidenheid," in L. Lichtveld, ed., *Culturele Activiteit in Suriname: Beginselen, Feiten en Problemen* (Paramaribo: Stichting Cultureel Centrum Suriname, 1957).

Nevertheless, Lachmon retained his seat in the *Staten* this second time around as well.

In neither Cabinet was power between Creoles and Hindustanis proportional to their numbers in the society, but it *was* roughly proportional to the number of *Staten* seats held by the alliance partners (see Table 5.8).

Table 5.8. Party Shares in Government, 1958 and 1963

	1958		*1963*	
	Staten seats	*Cabinet seats*	*Staten seats*	*Cabinet seats*
NPS	9	5/6[a]	14	5/7[b]
VHP	4	2	8	3
PSV	4	2	4	1[c]
KTPI	2	–	4	1[c]

[a] S.D. Emanuels held the posts of General Affairs and Internal Affairs.
[b] J.A. Pengel held the posts of General and Internal Affairs and Finance.
[c] After the ORMET affair, the KTPI replaced the PSV in the Cabinet.

Moreover, both parties shared in the distribution of civil service jobs to their followers. In particular, Pengel is credited with ending civil service discrimination against Blacks and opening doors to them at all levels of government. The rapid expansion of Surinam's civil service became a matter of great concern to the Dutch government, whose grants-in-aid largely went to this relatively unproductive end. However, many informants attributed the political tranquility of the 1960s to Pengel's jobs policy, pointing out that without it the ranks of the more radical PNR would have swelled. There is no adequate ethnic breakdown of the civil service on a year-to-year (or administration-to-administration) basis, but the 1964 Census figures, cited in Table 1.8, indicate that 63% of those employed in government service in that year were Creoles, 20% Hindustanis, 10% Javanese, and 7% "other." In general, Pengel and Lachmon used the ministries their parties controlled for rewarding their followers. Both men were careful to appoint qualified (even politically independent) candidates to the top positions, but such criteria were usually ignored at the lower levels. As the number of qualified Hindustanis grew out of proportion to the jobs available, many joined the *Actie Groep*, protesting that the top positions and promotions were more biassed towards the Creoles than to their own kind.[162] Alarmed by the unnecessary growth, as they saw it, of Surinam's civil service, the Dutch suddenly reversed their position of economic support to the government in 1966, demanding a halt to patronage and

[162] *DW*, November 6, 1964.

instituting stricter controls over the expenditure of their financial aid.[163]

As things became increasingly unstuck in the NPS-VHP alliance, the roof caved in on the KTPI. In 1966, as the term of this government neared its end, the sole Javanese party (at this moment) was convulsed in a struggle between its own charismatic leader, Iding Soemita, and its most recent Minister of Economic Affairs, G. Rakim. Soemita, clearly eager to augment his influence through a "balancing" role in Surinam's politics, was no more able than the others to command the solid loyalty of his group. Torn by intra-group religious and cultural rivalries, and not altogether confident in their leader's probity, the Javanese nevertheless admired Soemita's great oratorical skills and cunning ability to "play the fool" to good purpose in the *Staten*. Nevertheless, when Soemita demanded Rakim's expulsion for not following party (i.e., Soemita) directives, KTPI branches splintered into pro- and anti-Soemita groups. Finally, Rakim, retaining his ministerial post, joined the NPS, claiming to bring a following of 4,000 with him.[164] At the same time, a new party, the *Sarekat Rakjat Indonesia* (Indonesian People's Party, SRI) was set up (March 1966).[165] Some informants identified the SRI as a creature of the VHP, while others credited its emergence to the Indonesian Consul in Paramaribo who was dissatisfied with Soemita's traditional leadership.

* * *

Although ethnicity seemed a major force in this period, judging by the survey research of Speckmann and Van Renselaar as well as the activities of the NBS/PNR and *Actie Groep*/NOP opposition, there were clear signs of its limitations. For one, the alliance of major Creole and Hindustani parties continued to do well at the polls. For another, the *Actie Groep*, which had seemed to key its existence to questions of ethnicity, now revealed that it was not above forming cross-ethnic alliances of its own. In so doing, it could no longer effectively charge its intra-ethnic rivals with "selling out." Presumably the level of public oratory would now have to transcend ethnicity.

[163] A.H. Post, *et al.*, *De Sittewasie: De Velmekstaking en haar Konskwenties*, (Paramaribo: n.p., 1969), p. 9.

[164] *DW*, March 21, 1966.

[165] *DW*, March 2, 1967.

CHAPTER SIX

FLYING WITH A CLIPPED WING (1967-1973)

> Mr. Lachmon used to go around talking about how he "made" Ministers and Staten members. Well, he didn't make me, and he can't break me....
>
> J.A. Pengel, 1967*

Between 1958 and 1967, Surinam had enjoyed its most balanced and progressive period of development. In this period, control of the *Staten* was shared by the NPS and VHP, enjoying support from a clear majority of Creoles and Hindustanis, respectively. Beginning in 1967, as the VHP began to demand more ministerial posts, the NPS made an alliance with the smaller *Actie Groep*, which, ironically, had made its appearance as a protest movement against the VHP's dealings with the Creoles. Between 1967 and 1973, Surinam's government began to fly with one wing clipped: first, the NPS tried its luck with the smaller AG; then, after the abrupt collapse of that government in a teachers' strike in 1969, the VHP set off in uncertain flight with the smaller Creole *Progressieve Nationale Partij* (PNP). In both cases, the governments lacked the degree of legitimacy and support they had hoped for, and the NPS and VHP gradually discovered that reliance on a small ally from their rival's cultural group puts that ally through a severe "crisis of brokerage" – whereby it loses access to, and credibility among, its followers.[1] In both cases during Surinam's period of clipped-wing flying, the small allies of the NPS and VHP were virtually destroyed by their participation in the government.

* Quoted in *De West*, July 31, 1967.

[1] Edward Dew, *Politics in the Altiplano: The Dynamics of Change in Rural Peru* (Austin: University of Texas Press, 1969), pp. 12-13.

I. THE ELECTION LAW DEBATE

Although in May 1966, Pengel had declared that there would be no major changes in the election law for the 1967 elections, he began to reconsider his position in the fall of 1966. In 1963, the over-representation of the PSV (four places on the ten-man Paramaribo list) had been too high a price to pay for victory – especially since the subsequent expulsion of the PSV had made the net gain for the NPS from Paramaribo only two seats. Nevertheless, an alliance of the PSV – small as it was – with the *Actiefront* might cost the NPS the next elections. Clearly, proportional representation would reduce the risks and let the chips fall where they may. Thus, Pengel asked the VHP to support his plan to make Paramaribo's ten seats also distributable according to PR. Lachmon countered with the VHP's long-standing demand for the extension of PR to all seats in the *Staten*.[2] But as this would destroy Paramaribo's overrepresentation (and with it, that of the Creoles), Pengel refused. Lachmon then proposed rejoining the districts surrounding Paramaribo into one district, increasing its representation from three (the Para seat would be left aside) to eight, and making it a PR district as well. Pengel accepted this, though he insisted on six rather than eight seats for the new district. (The 1964 census, showing District Suriname to have nearly as many inhabitants as Paramaribo, was not released until 1969.)[3] Both parties agreed at the same time that there would be no pre-election deals between them – i.e., both parties would be free to run candidates in both Paramaribo and *Kieskring II* (the new election district). The VHP later indicated that it would continue to give its support to the NPS in the smaller, largely Creole districts, and the NPS reciprocated with support for the VHP (running in alliance with the Javanese SRI) in Saramacca and Commewijne.[4] Both parties ran candidates in Nickerie, however. The failure of an agreement in this latter district – already lost in two successive elections by the VHP – was to become a source of bitter discord.

When it was announced in December 1966, the proposed electoral law reform met with a mixed reception in the press. *De West* pointed to the ironic conversion of Pengel into a PR champion and hinted that it resulted from the poor results of house-to-house canvassing earlier in the year.[5] *De Ware Tijd*, on the other hand, applauded the prospect of Hindustani representation from

[2] *De Ware Tijd* (Paramaribo, hereinafter *DWT*), November 26, 1966.

[3] *New York Times*. January 28, 1966; and interview, Humphrey J. Lamur, Amsterdam, July 25, 1974.

[4] *DWT*, November 29, 1966 and May 18, 1967.

[5] *DW*, December 7, 9, 1966.

Paramaribo, since the number of urbanized Hindustanis had grown appreciably in recent years.[6] The PSV, quite naturally, was upset at the proposal. One of its leaders, Coen Ooft, denounced its consideration at the last-minute as "undemocratic."[7] Agreeing with this appraisal, the NPS Minister of Development, Just Rens, refused to join his fellow ministers in authorizing the bill's submission to the *Staten.*[8] To get around this act of defiance, Pengel promptly placed Rens on "sick leave" and had another minister endorse the legislation in his place.[9] Now a real storm erupted. Creole opponents to Pengel, ranging from the SDP and PSV to the PNR organized a Committee for Democracy and Civil Rights to protest the new election law. In a mass rally, Eddy Bruma denounced the extension of PR as permitting a division of the country into ethnic blocs. The more substantive issues and principles that parties raised would be overshadowed, he argued, by primordial fears and loyalties. Furthermore, he condemned the increased representation of *Kieskring* II in extreme ethnic terms:

> If you are lacking in political maturity, you vote for your tribe, your race.... Do you think that 50,000 people in Paramaribo have the same limited political development as 50,000 Hindustani *mais* and *baboens* [*Sarnami Hindostans* for mothers and fathers] who plant rice?[10]

(These words were widely quoted in the 1966 and subsequent campaigns to show that, worse than being a "Communist-sympathizer," Bruma was a dangerous "racist.")[11] Ironically, repudiation of the electoral reforms among

[6] *DWT*, December 7, 1966.

[7] *DWT*, December 10, 1966.

[8] *DWT*, December 12, 1966. Ever since 1958, Rens later recalled, his relationship with Pengel had been tense. He was, he said, the only other NPSer with a strong, loyal following. Efforts to purge Rens from the NPS' candidate list in 1958 and 1963 had failed, and in 1963, he was given the Ministry of Development, because "Pengel believed the job would break me." In fact, the failure of the ORMET contract might have led to his ouster, but for the intervention of Lachmon, the *formateur* of the second 1963 government. Pengel had announced the awarding of the ORMET contract before Rens' Ministry had completed its work on it. Lachmon warned that to make Rens a scapegoat in the affair would endanger the legitimacy of Pengel's government, as a Rens in the opposition would be far more damaging to the NPS than to keep him in the Cabinet. (Note: according to the new electoral rules, a *Staten* member who was appointed to a Ministry was allowed to take his seat back upon leaving the Cabinet.) Nevertheless, anticipating trouble from Rens regarding the latest electoral law reforms, Pengel had kept Rens out of his negotiations with Lachmon, and had presented the bill for his signature only after clearing it with all the other members of his Cabinet. "The insult," Rens recalled, "was too great for me to accept." (Interview, Just Rens, Paramaribo, December 1, 1973).

[9] *DWT*, December 13, 1966.

[10] *DWT*, December 17, 1966.

[11] At one rally in January, for example, Dr. Alwin Mungra, son of the *Staten* member J. Mungra (1951-58), said: "We'll fight Bruma and the others who hate the Hindustanis.... On

Creole opponents of the NPS had given Bruma a larger audience than his ideological positions had ever enjoyed. Signs appeared in Paramaribo now that read "Away with the racists," "Hands off Paramaribo!" "Away with the elephant dictatorship" (referring to the VHP's party symbol), "Think of your future and that of your children," and "No horse.trading [*koehandel*] with the Constitution."[12]

On December 23, 1966, the *Staten* debate began. As a two-thirds vote was needed to pass the bill, the NPS and VHP were two votes short, with 22 seats of a total of 36 (distributed as follows: NPS-14, VHP-8, PSV-4, SDP-2, AG-3, NOP-1, and KTPI-4). With the KTPI at odds with the Government over its retention of the ex-KTPIer, G. Rakim, as Minister of Economic Affairs, and with nothing to gain from the electoral change, they could not be won over. The NPS' and VHP's only hope was that the opposition Hindustani parties (AG and NOP) might break from the *Actiefront* to support the bill. Representatives of the AG reiterated the old Hindustani demand that all seats in the *Staten* be distributed by nation-wide PR, pointing to the disproportionality of representation and the wasted votes in past elections. But the NPS declared that national, single-district PR "would be a crime against different parts of the country which have specific social interests and for which the only guarantee to defend those interests is to have one or more representatives who maintain close contact with these areas and can be kept responsible by the people of these areas." In particular, the districts of Coronie, Nickerie, and the interior districts were areas likely to be ignored by a list system centering on Paramaribo. After last minute dealings between the NPS and the *Actiegroep*, including a promise that, if they broke out of the *Actiefront*, they would be considered as a possible ally in the new government, the bill was passed 25-6 (with only Findlay's SDP and the PSV opposed).[13]

II. THE 1967 ELECTIONS

With PR a fact now in Paramaribo, the opposition parties were confronted with tactical dilemmas. The collaboration of the SDP and PSV, which had earlier been agreed upon, was the first casualty, as the PSV advocated a large

March 15, we'll show them the power of the *mais* and *baboens*." (*DWT*, January 23, 1967). In 1973, I heard the same VHPer, in front of a large Hindustani crowd in Nieuw Nickerie, repeating this quote of Bruma's in conjunction with warnings about his radical ideas.

[12] *DWT*, December 20, 1966.

[13] The KTPI walked out before the vote, and Harry Hirasing, one of the founders of the AG, but now aloof from it and fervently opposed to the breakup of the *Actiefront*, abstained (*DWT*, December 28, 1966).

coalition, including several new political parties.[14] The SDP refused, feeling that with PR it might actually lose more ground than it gained if it had to share positions on the Paramaribo list with more than one additional party. Subsequently, the SDP entered the elections alone.[15] The PSV now proposed a National Liberation Front to include the small new parties, plus Bruma's PNR.[16] In the meantime, yet another new party, the *Progressieve Nationale Partij* (PNP), was formed by ex-Minister Rens and his followers within the NPS, including the former Ministers of Finance, Jules Sedney, and Development, Frank Essed, from the 1958-63 government. After initially inviting Rens' PNP to join their National Liberation Front, the PSV quickly reconsidered its position. Fearing that, in such a conglomerate, the PSV could get no more than one electable position on the Paramaribo list, members of that party totally reversed themselves and voted to enter the elections alone.[17] The PNP leaders, having formerly attacked Bruma as a Communist-sympathizer while in the NPS, were not about to make an alliance with the PNR at this point. However they easily wooed several smaller parties to join them, and entered the election with considerable momentum. Thus, in Paramaribo, eight lists were submitted: NPS, VHP, SDP, AG, PNR, PNP, PSV, and the *Actiefront Dihaat* (a small group of Creoles and Hindustanis, led by Dr. Harry Hirasing, the sole AGer who refused to betray the *Actiefront* in the election law vote, only to be abandoned by the SDP as too controversial).[18] The same group, minus the SDP, also competed in the *Kieskring* II elections, while on the *landelijke lijst*, they were joined by the two Javanese parties (KTPI and SRI).

With every party now a potential winner (and winner-take-all banished from all but the one- and two-member districts), the chances, and supportive atmosphere, for pre-election horse-trading were very limited. Yet it went on. The KTPI, which had been spurned by the VHP for an alliance, turned to the AG, and agreed to support them in Paramaribo, *Kieskring* II and Nickerie in return for a joint ticket in Saramacca and AG support in Commewijne.[19] Despite their suspicions about a possible understanding between the NPS and AG, the VHP told its supporters to vote for the NPS in Coronie, Para, Lower

[14] Among them were the National People's Party (led by the young Creole-Chinese geologist, Hans Prade), the Social Democratic Unity party (led by R. Dundas), and the group clustering around Just Rens (now discharged from the government).

[15] *DWT*, January 18, 1967.

[16] *DWT*, January 23, 1967.

[17] *DWT*, January 26, 1967.

[18] Interview, Harry Hirasing, Paramaribo, July 6, 1971.

[19] *DWT*, February 10, 1967.

and Upper Marowijne and Brokopondo. In return, they hoped for NPS support in Saramacca and Commewijne.[20]

In a rally in January, Lachmon spoke of the VHP now being a national party. The "Hindustani" in the name VHP was removed, and the acronym now stood for *Vatan Hitkari Partij* (a mixture of *Sarnami Hindostans* and Dutch meaning "Party to Promote National Welfare.") If this change was to mean a step away from cultural exclusiveness, the use of *Sarnami Hindostans* for the party's name was an obviously poor tactic. But the tie between the VHP and NPS was still affirmed. Regarding the electoral law's change, Lachmon declared:

> I am glad that I gave the hand of brotherhood to Pengel. His words still ring in my ears: "Lach, my brother, you have accused me of racism, but when the communique [i.e., proposing the new law] goes out, you'll see where the real racists are." . . .People call the *verbroedering* policy hypocrisy. That's nonsense! Let them try and put something else in its place![21]

Ironically, it was Pengel himself who was trying "to put something else in its place." Having already recruited a number of dissident Javanese from the KTPI into the party, the NPS placed several prominent Moslems (A.G. Karamat Ali, son of the ex-KTPI leader, and Islam Ramdjan, a VHP *Staten*-member from 1958-63) high on its lists in Paramaribo and *Kieskring* II. More than the VHP, with its name change, the NPS indeed was trying to become a national party. Moslem and Hindu religious leaders were featured speakers at many of its rallies. If *verbroedering* with the VHP could be replaced, Pengel felt it could only be done by a multi-racial party large enough to make post-election coalitions unnecessary. Instead of cross-cultural collaboration occurring *between* parties, it would now be institutionalized within *one* party, under the watchful, and presumably neutral, eye of Pengel himself. The NPS was restructured at the base to make this possible. Presidia were set up for each cultural group: Hindustani, Javanese, Chinese, Amerindian, Bush Negro and Creole. Each presidium had its own elected leadership, and was represented on the central Party Council of the NPS.[22] But this experiment in the name of *verbroedering* seems to have hurt the forces of integration and assimilation more than it helped them. For, as the NPS entered the elections in Nickerie with its own Hindustani candidates, both the VHP and AG retaliated with increasingly shrill appeals for cultural solidarity against the Creoles. While reiterating its support for *verbroedering* in Dutch (for the press

[20] *DWT*, May 18, 1967.
[21] *DWT*, January 23, 1967.
[22] Interview, Frank Essed, Paramaribo, February 13, 1976.

and mixed crowds at its larger rallies), the VHP's campaign in *Sarnami Hindostans*, especially in the districts and at the canvassing and small-group level, was highly racist and anti-Creole. After the election, *De Ware Tijd* told of the VHP displaying Hindustani women in Nickerie, allegedly mutilated by Creoles in Guyana's racial fighting, to show what might happen in Surinam.[23] Numerous Creole and Hindustani informants there and in Paramaribo repeated these and other charges, such as the warning that religious temples would be converted to grain warehouses, and more blatantly sexual charges regarding Creoles taking away the Hindustanis' daughters. The VHP later denied they had used racist propaganda, but levelled charges of their own at the AG, who they said had used anti-Creole slogans in Nickerie to slander both the NPS and the VHP (for its alliance with the NPS).[24]

If any of these allegations were correct, the campaign in Nickerie was more racial than in Paramaribo, where the five-way battle among Creole parties focussed on charges of mismanagement, corruption and dictatorial methods in the Pengel government, rather than against *verbroedering*. Both the NPS and PNP spent considerable sums of money: the NPS on trinkets and propaganda and the PNP on lavish rallies (where in one, for example, Trinidad's "Mighty Sparrow" was a featured attraction). The SDP charged that the NPS-PNP split was a fraud, that the parties would join together after the election,[25] while the PNP retaliated that the SDP in reality wanted such a deal with the NPS.[26] Pengel, in the meantime, had brought in Princess Alexandra von Hohenlohe, representing a consortium of German investors, presumably interested in the Torarica hydroelectric project.[27] Though he denied any political purpose of the visit, he announced, on the eve of the election, that an investment of Sf 50 million was being discussed.[28] The appeal of this investment was especially aimed at the Bush Negroes whose unemployment and dislocation caused by the Afobaka Dam had remained a serious problem. Another dam, at the Torarica site, would provide fresh jobs for these people, postponing their ultimate readjustment. After the election, it was alleged that Granman Aboikoni of the Saramaccaners had ordered his village *kapiteins* to produce large NPS majorities or face removal.[29] In any event, a large portion of the NPS' campaign expenditures were directed towards the Bush Negroes.

If the campaign was fairly peaceful and orderly, the reaction to the results

[23] *DWT*, May 17, 1967.
[24] *DW*, May 17, 1967; and *DWT*, May 18, 1967.
[25] *DW*, March 8, 1967.
[26] *DWT*, March 9, 1967.
[27] *DW*, March 8, 1967.
[28] *DWT*, March 14, 1967.
[29] *DW*, March 25, 1967.

Table 6.1. Votes Cast in the 1967 Elections

Election District	*NPS*	*SDP*	*PNP*	*PSV*	*PNR*	*VHP*	*AG*	*AFDihaat*	*KTPI*	*SRI*	*Other*
I. Paramaribo (10 seats, PR)	12,352	4,833	5,340	2,688	1,461	4,294	2,526	804	—	—	—
II. Suriname (6 seats, PR) ("*Kieskring* II")	7,329	—	2,134	596	1,389	9,593	8,689	319	—	—	—
III. Para (1 seat)	2,115	—	1,410	—	—	—	—	—	—	—	143[a]
IV. Commewijne (2 seats)	—	—	—	—	—	2,378[b]	—	—	2,157	2,674[b]	128[a]
	—	—	—	—	—	—	—	—	2,045	—	122
V. Saramacca (2 seats)	—	—	—	—	—	2,384[c]	1,688[d]	—	1,678[d]	2,445[c]	80[a]
	—	—	—	—	—	—	—	—	—	—	72
VI. Nickerie (2 seats)	1,724	—	—	—	—	4,179	1,754	—	—	—	640[a]
	1,678	—	—	—	—	4,155	1,739	—	—	—	608
VII. Coronie (1 seat)	617	—	591	—	—	—	—	—	—	—	—
VIII. Beneden Marowijne (1 seat)	2,149	—	407	566	132	—	—	—	—	—	—
IX. Boven Marowijne (1 seat)	1,058	—	—	—	—	—	—	—	—	—	17[a]
X. Brokopondo (1 seat)	1,928	—	1,542	—	—	—	—	—	—	—	—
National List (12 seats, PR)	30,135	7,242	8,506	5,373	2,396	20,725	11,614	889	5,825	3,064	—

[a] Independent candidates. [b] The VHP and SRI ran a joint slate here. [c] The VHP and SRI ran a joint slate here. [d] The AG and KTPI ran a joint slate here.
The electoral quotas necessary to win a seat in the PR districts were as follows: Paramaribo – 3,430; Kieskring II – 5,008; National List – 7,981.
Source: *Gouvernements-Advertentieblad* no. 34 (April 28, 1967).

was not. Although the NPS won only five of the ten seats in Paramaribo, it was able to win two of the six *Kieskring* II seats, four of the ten seats in the winner-take-all districts, and five on the National List (see Tables 6.1 and 6.2). Thus, with less than a third (31%) of the votes cast in the country the NPS had won 44% of the seats – three short of a clear majority in the *Staten* – hardly a "proportional" result! Charges of voting irregularities were made to the Governor by leaders of the PNP, PSV, PNR, and AG.[30] Findlay (SDP), writing in *De West*, refused to join in the protests, though he too acknowledged the possibility of fraud.[31] A noisy demonstration by the PNP and PNR was broken up by the police, using tear gas to clear the streets. Incidents of rock-throwing and scattered arson attempts against the homes of NPSers and a *Herrnhutter* warehouse were also reported.[32]

Table 6.2. Seat Division in the 1967 Elections

Election District	*NPS*	*SDP*	*PNP*	*VHP*	*AG*	*SRI*
I. Paramaribo	5	2	2	1		
II. Suriname	2			2	2	
III. Para	1					
IV. Commewijne				1		1
V. Saramacca				1		1
VI. Nickerie				2		
VII. Coronie	1					
VIII. Beneden Marowijne	1					
IX. Boven Marowijne	1					
X. Brokopondo	1					
National List	5		1	4	2	
Total	17	2	3	11	4	2

Despite its own doubts regarding the outcome's legitimacy, *De Ware Tijd* argued convincingly that the fragmentation of Pengel's Creole opposition had been far more damaging than any election fraud.[33] Together Creole parties had polled 56% of the total vote recorded on the national list, a far greater proportion than their demographic strength in the adult population (1964 Census) would seem to warrant (see Table 6.3). As in previous elections, the Creole parties tended to draw votes from the smaller cultural groups (Chinese, Europeans, Lebanese, etc.), while the NPS appeals among Hindustani Moslems and the defection of G. Rakim from the KTPI must have also brought the NPS many votes from these two sources.

[30] *DWT*, March 20, 1967. Some of these are recounted in A.H.C. Post, *et al.*, *De Sittewasie: De Velmekstaking en haar Konsekwenties* (Paramaribo: 1969), p. 10.

[31] *DW*, March 18, 1967.

[32] *DW*, March 18, 20, 1967.

[33] *DW*, March 20, 1967.

Although the opposition protests quickly died down, another outcry of a different sort followed the defection to the NPS of a Javanese member of the SRI, elected in Saramacca with VHP support. Amid allegations that the NPS had "paid him off," the SRI and VHP demanded his resignation.[34] With 18 seats now, the NPS needed only two more for a working majority.

Table 6.3. Comparison of 1967 National List Election Results and 1964 Census, by Ethnic Parties and Groups Age 15+

		Ethnic Parties/Demographic Groups				
		Creole	*Hindustani*	*Javanese*	*Other*	*Total*
1967 votes	no.	53,562	33,228	8,889	—	95,769
	%	56.0	34.7	9.3		100%
1964 Census	no.	59,299	51,109	25,838	26,944	163,190
	%	36.3	31.3	15.8	16.5	99.9%

Source: Table 6.1 and Algemeen Bureau voor de Statistiek, *Voorlopig Resultaat Vierde Algemene Volkstelling, Suriname in Cijfers* No. 60, p. 8.

III. THE NPS-VHP BREAK-UP

As Pengel headed the largest block of seats in the new *Staten*, the Governor invited him to consult with the other parties preparatory to assembling a Cabinet. In a press conference Pengel announced that he had no preference among the parties and would negotiate with them all, including the SDP and AG, previously his bitterest critics.[35] This produced a cry of dismay from the VHP, alarmed that he might break their long-standing alliance.[36] The strain between NPS and VHP now became even more apparent. Having increased their representation in the *Staten* (thanks to the electoral law), the VHP insisted on more seats in the Cabinet. As the proportions in that body had heavily favored the NPS in 1958 and 1963 (see Table 5.8), the VHP thought they deserved at least one additional ministry. Yet, with pressure already mounting from the Dutch to cut back on civil service spoils, Pengel was unwilling to give up the ministries he now controlled. Thus, after fifteen years of close collaboration with the VHP, he turned to the smaller *Actie Groep* as an alliance partner. Two ministries may have been a high price to pay for four legislative votes, but it was two less than the VHP had demanded, and it provided a working majority. In addition, Pengel invited David Findlay's SDP to join the government, offering him one ministry. Again Pengel re-

[34] *DWT*, March 22, 23, 1967.
[35] *DWT*, March 30, 1967.
[36] *DWT*, April 7, 1967.

served for himself three posts: the ministries of General Affairs, Internal Affairs and Finance.[37] In total, the NPS emerged with eight ministries under its control!

Because of his persistent criticism of Pengel's undue concentration of power, David Findlay's acceptance of an SDP role in the new government offended many of his followers. His fellow SDPer in the *Staten*, C.R. Biswamitre, publicly rejected the alliance and refused to sit with Findlay in the government benches.[38] The situation within the SDP was sufficiently strained that Findlay was unwilling for a long time to hold a party meeting to explain his position.

Pengel's working majority was much smaller than he had had in the years of collaboration with the VHP. Moreover, in their own way, his allies seemed more demanding than the VHP had been. Besides their resistance to independence, they demanded that the costly Torarica project be abandoned.[39] Obviously frustrated by the difficulties of Cabinet-formation, Pengel repeatedly threatened his prospective partners with new elections if they didn't accept his remaining terms.[40]

Following the announcement of his Cabinet, Pengel explained in a press conference that he could no longer work with the VHP because of their racial campaigning and demands for additional ministerial appointments. In particular, he decried the VHP's use of such ministries to provide jobs for their followers without consideration of competence.[41] Spokesmen for the VHP promptly called for an impartial investigation of the NPS' own appointment policy, assuring the press that, "if there was any bias, it was taught us by Pengel himself." Regarding the allegation that the VHP had abandoned the principles of *verbroedering*, Lachmon recalled how many Hindustanis had stepped down in 1955 to make way for Pengel in Saramacca. "We didn't do that for a person," he said, but for the idea that "without the cooperation of the different ethnic groups, life in Surinam would be untenable." The reason the VHP was excluded from this government was "our surprising strength." Pengel only wanted a weak Hindustani ally, according to Lachmon. "We are ready for new elections," he continued, "but only under an independent election tribunal."[42]

However, Pengel refused to acknowledge sole responsibility for the alliance's termination. After details were revealed in *De West* of an effort by

[37] *DWT*, May 16, 1967.
[38] *DWT*, May 13, 1967.
[39] *DW*, April 26, 1967; and *DWT*, July 19, 1967.
[40] *Suriname*, March 13, 1967; *DW*, May 5, 16, 1967.
[41] *DWT*, May 17, 1967.
[42] *DW*, May 17, 1967.

Lachmon to form a "counter-cabinet" to block Pengel's work as *formateur*,[43] Pengel declared that this unbrotherly violation of the "rules of the game" was the reason he could no longer work with Lachmon. "He didn't make me," Pengel declared, "and he can't break me." More threateningly, he added,

> Mr. Biswamitre has spoken about snakes in Paradise. Over the course of the years, I have smashed the heads of many snakes around me....[44]

The impact of this emotional and ill-chosen remark would linger on, poisoning his personal relations with Lachmon.

Later, Pengel spoke more philosophically about the changes that had occurred. Comparing Surinam's multi-party politics to the Netherlands, where each election is usually followed by shifting alliances, he called this "very healthy."[45] Pengel's choice of new alliance partners seemed popular within his own party. On the one hand, it buried the persistent belief that Pengel was under Lachmon's control, while at the same time indicating that the AG had dropped its parochial cultural purism and was now a pragmatic party. On the other hand, it mended an old NPS breach (with the SDP), partially compensating for the newer (PNP) one. Moreover, the system of government and opposition, as in the previous government, appeared to be healthily balanced. There were Creoles, Hindustanis, and Javanese in both the opposition and the government.[46] Pengel called this his "politics of breakthrough" and added that "the breakthrough idea now seems to be a blessing for the land and people, and I hereby predict that any party seeking power through the preaching of racial conflict is doomed to go under."[47]

The only danger in Pengel's "breakthrough" was that the opposition was larger than before, including the largest party of one of the ethnic groups. How strongly the AG could hold (or be held) up against the expected steady attack of the VHP was the key to the NPS staying in power. Presumably, with the Ministry of Agriculture in the AG's hands, they should be in a good position to deal favors and build up their following. Nevertheless, the Agriculture Minister (R.L. Jankie) warned his followers that there were limits to the jobs and other favors he could hand out.[48] And the Governor (H.L. de Vries, a popular Surinam businessman) warned in his speech opening the new

[43] *DW*, July 31, 1967.

[44] *Ibid.*, and *DW*, August 1, 1967.

[45] *DW*, November 13, 1967.

[46] The Javanese member in the majority in the *Staten* was the SRI renegade, and the Javanese in the Cabinet was the former KTPI Minister (Rakim) who was returned by Pengel to his post as an NPSer.

[47] *DW*, November 13, 1967.

[48] *DW*, August 16, 1967.

[49] *DW*, September 1, 1967.

legislative session in September, that rapid population growth was sharply increasing the cost of education and other social services.[49] Although a new Five Year Plan of Dutch aid was announced for 1967-1971, amounting potentially to Nf 240 million,[50] *De West* reminded its readers that the Treasury at that moment was empty and that if various stalled public works projects were to resume, greater austerity was required in governmental hiring, travel, and other nonessential expenditures.[51]

IV. THE STRIKES OF FEBRUARY 1969 AND PENGEL'S FALL

In October 1967, at the outset of the budget debates for 1968, Lachmon proposed a package of reforms headed significantly by a bill to establish a series of new national holidays to commemorate important Hindu and Moslem feast days, and to honor the Bush Negroes.[52] The VHP also called for the opening of new agricultural lands, construction of bridges, and other material benefits for the rural population.[53] As with most opposition initiatives of this sort, they were all defeated. But they gave the VHP issues with which to harass the AG in the coming years. Together with the PNP, with whom they shared the opposition, the VHP warned of dictatorial tendencies in the government and repeatedly reminded the AG that they held the fate of this government.[54] Nevertheless, at the outset, it appeared unlikely that the opposition could crack the government's solidarity.

But suddenly, on December 31, 1967, the leader of the AG, Persoewan Chandieshaw, died. Because the party had sought to contrast its internal democracy with the VHP's alleged one-man rule, it was now hopelessly caught up in a prolonged internal struggle among its ministers, legislators and party officials for the top position in the party.[55] *Suriname* wondered editorially if the NPS' abandonment of the VHP wasn't about to boomerang on them.[56] The VHP, for its part, now called for new elections.[57]

As the *Actie Groep* struggled to sort itself out, a new set of issues heated up

[50] Half of the money was an outright grant, and the rest were various low-interest loans (*DW*, October 2, 1967).

[51] *DW*, October 5, 1967.

[52] The holidays were *Holi Phagwa* and *Divali*, for the Hindus, *Idul Fitr* and *Idul Azha* for the Moslems, and *Brokodei* for the Bush Negroes (*DW*, October 21, 1967).

[53] *DW*, October 21, 1967.

[54] *DW*, November 28, 1967.

[55] *Suriname*, June 10, 1968.

[56] *Suriname*, May 2, 1968.

[57] *Suriname*, June 13, 1968.

which would eventually, but quite unexpectedly, precipitate the downfall of Pengel's government. Already in 1967, a number of PNP and politically independent higher civil servants began to criticize Pengel's methods of awarding engineering and other contracts to his friends, and formed an independent "Union of Higher Functionaries" (FEHOMA). In particular, several high officials in the Geological Mining Service protested unauthorized budgetary items as politically motivated and were summarily transferred from their posts.[58] During the 1968 budget debates in the *Staten*, Pengel displayed contempt for the opposition, pointedly leaving the room during the speeches of Jules Sedney and other PNPers, complaining that he couldn't understand them and "needed to sleep."[59] But, despite the acknowledged need for austerity, Pengel decided to award himself a triple salary (for the three ministries he headed), and then proceeded to organize a 70-man trip around the world, presumably to promote trade. These actions particularly aroused the country's school teachers, whose long-promised salary raises had been deferred in 1966 under pressure from the Dutch.[60]

A chain of incidents in the schools now occurred. The first involved a union dispute with the Ministry of Education involving the establishment of a new high school. The sudden removal of several of the union leaders from their posts during the dispute produced angry protests by both the teachers and their students, and a three-week strike.[61]

Sympathizing with the teachers regarding this evident abuse of their rights, another union, for grade school teachers, now entered the fray, demanding their salary raises. As many of the teachers were Dutch, on short-term contracts to work in Surinam, the government accused them of encouraging the Surinam teachers in their demands. By early February, this much larger union was also on strike, and sympathy protests by a number of other unions took place. A silent march by 3500 teachers through Paramaribo on February 13 was followed by the sudden announcement that Pengel's government had resigned.[62]

It must be noted that, at least to this point, the problems involved largely Creole protestors and Creole Ministers. Teachers of all cultural groups seem to have taken part in the strikes and marches, but the leaders were Creoles. It is likely, also, that Pengel expected to be urged to reconsider his resignation and stay on as in 1964 after the ORMET affair. But this time, nothing of the

[58] Post *et al.*, *op. cit.*, p. 13.
[59] *Ibid.*, p. 14.
[60] *Ibid.*, p. 51.
[61] *Ibid.*, pp. 22-24, 31-34.
[62] *DWT*, February 13, 14, 1969.

sort happened. The new Governor, Dr. J. Ferrier (former Minister-President, 1955-58), merely held Pengel's portfolio and waited for the air to clear. Meanwhile, the AG, which had had nothing to do with the strike, suddenly began to go into contortions. Splitting into several factions, it lost all coherence. After one of its members asked to return to the VHP, Governor Ferrier figured that the government's instability was sufficient to merit new elections. Thus, on February 24 he asked an independent lawyer (H.M.C. Bergen) to consult with the parties about the possibility of an Interim Cabinet to replace Pengel's until new elections could be held. As this would be an unprecedented move, Pengel and other NPS Ministers denounced the Governor's action and said they would not give up their posts after all, as long as they still enjoyed majority support in the *Staten.*[63] But this disappeared the following day (February 25), as the remaining AG members gave their support to the Governor's plan and severed their ties with the NPS.[64] With only Findlay left supporting the government,[65] the NPS was outnumbered 20 to 19. Pengel formally resigned February 27, while Findlay warned of the dangerous consequences of racial bloc-forming: "I can be wrong, but if the AG goes together with the VHP, we are heading towards a politics of racial conflict."[66]

The new government, like the first Cabinets in the late 1940s and early 1950s, was made up of professional men, most of whom had been politically inactive. Arthur May, a retired civil servant who had earlier headed the first Cabinet in 1948-49, was named Minister-President. During his eight months in power, May had the voting lists thoroughly reexamined and the Treasury audited. These studies found many irregularities among registered voters, and the budget deficit was found to be larger than Pengel had led people to believe.[67] Moreover, a government audit of the public-financed *Volkscrediet Bank* revealed a large number of loans outstanding to various leaders of the NPS, on many of which payments were long overdue.[68] These discoveries provided useful material for Pengel's opposition in the election campaign of October 1969.

[63] *DWT*, February 21, 25, 1969.

[64] *DWT*, February 27, 1969.

[65] His fellow SDPer, C.R. Biswamitre, had followed a generally independent course in the preceding two years.

[66] *DWT*, February 27, 28, 1969.

[67] Post, *et al.*, *op. cit.*, p. 10, 66; *DWT*, October 18, 1969.

[68] *Vrije Stem*, October 13, 1969.

V. THE 1969 ELECTIONS

After extensive debate, the *Actie Groep* finally agreed to an alliance with the VHP and SRI, receiving three seats on the various VHP lists nationwide.[69] A smaller group of AG dissidents sought admission to the NPS instead, denouncing the consolidation of Hindustanis as harmful for Surinam's future.[70] The AG-VHP-SRI combination tentatively agreed to a post-election alliance with the so-called PNP-bloc (comprising the PNP, PSV, KTPI and new *Progressieve BosNeger Partij* (PBP)), if they could get a clear majority. This conglomeration of parties (like the *Eenheidsfront* of 1955) clearly put the NPS on the defensive. Much of the latter's campaign strategy was focussed on racial issues, with arguments that a vote for the PNP was a vote for the Hindustanis,[71] and comparisons were made between their opposition's ethnic compartmentalization (*hokjespolitiek*) and South African *apartheid.*[72] Continuing its recruitment efforts among Asians, Bush Negroes and others, and featuring candidates on its lists and speakers at its rallies from all the major ethnic groups, the NPS may have hoped it would not be necessary to ally with anyone after the elections. But Pengel must have realized his hope for a cross-ethnic mass party was impossible. Moreover, he was also subject to the same kind of attack that he made against the VHP-PNP opposition. Eddy Bruma pointed out that ethnic compartmentalization was just as evident in the NPS' internal structure. Better to forget about *hokjes*, Bruma argued. Parties should be organized on the basis of issues.[73]

Bruma's idealism was just as unrealistic as Pengel's. For, despite Bruma's "ethnicity-free" ideas, his following was still largely Creole. But, that following had grown. In February 1968, Bruma had upset the incumbent (Pengel-backed) chairman of Surinam's most powerful union, the *Paranam Werknemers Bond* at the Suralco plant.[74] Like Pengel before him, Bruma saw that the best way to gain political influence was through a union base. And he did his best to make this base multi-ethnic – first organizing Bush Negroes on the Afobaka Dam, later giving legal advice to and organizing Asian and mixed unions on the Marienburg and Waterloo sugar plantations, the Jarikaba banana plantation, and the mechanized rice "plantation" at Wage-

[69] *DWT*, September 18, 1969.
[70] *DWT*, September 23, 1969.
[71] *Vrije Stem*, October 29, 1969.
[72] *Volksbode*, October 13, 1969.
[73] *DWT*, October 15, 1969.
[74] *DWT*, February 19, 1968.

ningen.[75] His services were clearly valued by each of these groups and the PNR hoped to translate this loyalty into votes. A number of Asian candidates were nominated by the PNR to run in the rural districts. But the party's greatest strength apparently remained in the city. After the February 1969 strikes, the PNR worked with the 47 unions (mostly of teachers and civil servants) that had been most closely involved, and encouraged them to unite in a new federation. Under Bruma's leadership progress was made through the summer and fall of 1969, and the new federation (*Centrale 47*) came into existence in January 1970.[76]

But growing even more dramatically than Bruma's PNR was the PNP. Led by the respected former Minister of Development, Frank Essed, the party conducted a vigorous campaign, hammering at the alleged corruption, authoritarianism and incompetence of Pengel and his immediate circle – carefully separating their attack on the man from any critique of the party. In particular, they interpreted a recent jump in the rate of Creole emigration to the Netherlands as a symptom of the government's lack of sympathy and imagination.[77]

Although both the PNR and NPS frequently campaigned on the need for independence, the NPS was less specific about a timetable. The PNP- and VHP-blocs were even more vague on the issue, though Lachmon drew a parallel between Surinam and Puerto Rico, pointing that the tie with the Motherland should be exploited as fully as possible for Surinam's economic development before independence was worth contemplating.[78]

There were complications in the cumbersome alliance of the VHP- and PNP-blocs. The two Javanese parties, SRI and KTPI, tried to mend their differences following the 1967 elections (which had seen their representation in the *Staten* decline from 4 to 1). Failing to reach an understanding, they continued to compete for seats in a number of districts, despite their respective alliances to the VHP and PNP. Although the PNP- and VHP-blocs won a large majority of seats in this election, Javanese representation remained disproportionally low (2 seats).

The results were a great disappointment to the NPS (see Tables 6.4 and 6.5), as they saw their representation drop to 11 and found themselves sharing the opposition with their long-time foe, Eddy Bruma, now elected as the PNR's sole representative. In fact, the outcome was proportionally more just than in 1967, at least as far as the NPS was concerned. With 27.8% of the vote, they

[75] *Vrije Stem*, October 25, 1969.
[76] *DWT*, January 11, 1970.
[77] *Vrije Stem*, October 6, 1969.
[78] *Vrije Stem*, December 3, 1969.

Table 6.4. Votes Cast in the 1969 Elections

Election District	*NPS*	*PNP-Bloc*[a]	*VHP-Bloc*[b]	*PNR*	*HPS*[c]	*SDP*	*Other*
I. Paramaribo (10 seats, PR)	9,941	8,817	7,560	3,416	183	979	
II. Suriname (6 seats, PR) ("Kieskring II")	6,861	5,500	17,900	1,837	742	434	
III. Para (1 seat)	1,433	1,084		898	37	306	
IV. Commewijne (2 seats)	924[d]	1,469[e]	2,078[f]	532[g]			
	852	1,393	2,050	515			
V. Saramacca (2 seats)	906[h]	902[i]	2,097[j]		163		
	867	879	2,084				
VI. Nickerie (2 seats)	2.380[k]	598[l]	4,371[m]	699[n]			
	2,344	580	4,359	669			
VII. Coronie (1 seat)	505	658					
VIII. Beneden Marowijne (1 seat)	1,492	1,368					416[o]
IX. Boven Marowijne (1 seat)	236	570					52[p]
X. Brokopondo (1 seat)	2,325	1,628					
National List	24,416	22,244	33,464[q]	7,377	1,029	1,433	3,189[q]

The electoral quotas necessary to win a seat in the PR districts were as follows: Paramaribo – 3,090; Kieskring II – 5,546; and National List – 7,943.

[a] PNP, PSV, PBP, KTPI. [b] VHP, SRI, AG. [c] Hindoe Partij Suriname. [d] Candidates: a Javanese and Hindustani. [e] Both candidates KTPI. [f] One SRI, one VHP. [g] Candidates: a Creole and Javanese. [h] Candidates: a Javanese and Hindustani. [i] Both candidates KTPI. [j] One SRI, one VHP. [k] Both candidates Hindustani. [l] Candidates: a Hindustani and Dutchman. [m] Both candidates VHP. [n] Candidates: Chinese-Creole and Javanese. [o] Combined vote tallied for three additional, unidentified, candidates. [p] Vote tallied for one additional, unidentified candidate. [q] The SRI had its own separate slate of candidates.

Source: *Gouvernements-Advertentieblad* No. 95 (November 17, 1969).

Table 6.5. Seat Division in the 1969 Elections

Election District	*NPS*	*PNP-Bloc*[a]	*VHP-Bloc*	*PNR*
I. Paramaribo	3	2 PNP, 1 PSV	3 VHP	1
II. Suriname	1	—	4 VHP, 1 AG	—
III. Para	1	—	—	—
IV. Commewijne	—	—	1 VHP, 1 SRI	—
V. Saramacca	—	—	1 VHP, 1 SRI	—
VI. Nickerie	—	—	2 VHP	—
VII. Coronie	—	1 PNP	—	—
VIII. Beneden Marowijne	1	—	—	—
IX. Boven Marowijne	—	1 PBP	—	—
X. Brokopondo	1	—	—	—
National List	4	3 PNP	3 VHP, 2 AG	—
Total	11	8	19	1

[a] In the final seat distribution, after the elevation of sóme Staten members to ministerial positions, one KTPIer took the seat of a PNPer.

had gotten 28.2% of the seats. Both the PNP-bloc and PNR were somewhat underrepresented (with 23.4% and 7.8% of the votes and only 20.5% and 2.6%

of the seats, respectively), while the VHP-bloc was now clearly over-represented (with 38.5% of the votes and 48.8% of the seats). Lachmon later spoke of the results as embarrassing. His party had not wanted to come so close to a majority in the *Staten*.[79]

The VHP's strong showing (3 seats) in Paramaribo also yielded a surprise: one of the party's few, presumably token, non-Hindustani candidates (a Creole) was elected. Only one of the many Asian NPS candidates was as lucky. Thus, despite the latter's greater effort to acquire a truly national appearance, the VHP could easily claim a national character as convincingly.[80]

When called upon by Governor Ferrier to form a new Cabinet, Lachmon cautiously divided the majority of portfolios equally between the PNP and VHP, additionally awarding one ministry each to the PSV, AG and SRI. As several ministries were awarded to elected *Staten* members, their seats were taken by shadow-candidates. In this way, a KTPI member was able to assume a place in the legislature, increasing Javanese representation to three. Lachmon's careful design – the closest approximation yet to Surinam's demographic distribution – was capped by Lachmon's selection of Dr. Jules Sedney (PNP) as new Minister-President, while Lachmon retained for himself the Speakership of the *Staten*. This balanced design was immediately criticized by the NPS and Findlay's *De West* as a misleading facade. Power was in the VHP's hands and would stay there.[81] The tactic the NPS would follow henceforth would be to treat the PNP as powerless pawns, dominated by their Hindustani partners. If the charge was similar to the one Findlay and others had levied against the NPS in the years of *verbroedering*, it did seem more credible now.

VI. THE VHP-PNP GOVERNMENT AND DEATH OF PENGEL

The first important policy innovation announced by the Sedney-Lachmon government was the replacement of two traditional Dutch Christian holidays (Easter Monday and Whit Monday) with Hindu and Moslem ones: *Holi Phagwa* (a Hindu holiday in the Spring) and *Idul Fitr* (a Moslem holiday in the Fall). In addition, May 1st was declared "Labor Day," and added to the list of official holidays.[82] Although the Committee of Christian Churches accepted the changes, most government and other labor unions did not.[83] Backing the

[79] Anonymous VHP Staten member.
[80] *Vrije Stem*, October 27, 1969.
[81] *DW*, November 17; *Volksbode*, November 24, 1969.
[82] *DWT*, February 4, 1970.
[83] *DWT*, February 12, March 2, 7, 1970.

workers, the NPS called for a formal interpellation of the ministers responsible for the holiday decree.[84] As Easter Monday (March 30, 1970) neared, workers threatened to stay home on that day, and Eddy Bruma filed a suit on their behalf which the court rejected.[85] The incident hardly enhanced either Bruma's or the NPS' reputations as culturally neutral. But the subsequent holiday transitions were uneventful – noone was reported protesting the closure of offices or factories on the Asian holidays.

Despite their stands on the holiday issue, the NPS and PNR resisted a more blatantly racial movement making its appearance in Surinam at this time. Visits to the Caribbean of Stokely Carmichael and other Black Power leaders in the late 1960s, as well as the Black Power riots in Trinidad in April 1970, had raised the question whether Black Power ideologies had any viability in the underdeveloped plural societies of the region.[86] Frustrations at the Hindustani ascension to power, envy at their restored cohesion, and a desire to achieve a similar reunification of the Creoles lay behind two movements undertaken by independent Creoles. The first, calling itself the Black Power Organization, was led by a journalist, Cyriel Karg.[87] Disassociating itself from Surinam's political parties, Karg's group concentrated on building up Black consciousness for the vaguely specified objective of breaking "institutionalized discrimination in this land." Karg pointed to the economic power of native and foreign whites, shared and managed in some cases by "coopted" Creoles and Hindustanis, but he was unclear as to where the non-Creole lower classes fit into his plans.[88]

An equal amount of press attention was given to a more purposeful new movement, calling itself *Krikomaka* (a shortened form of *Kriori Kon Makandra*, "Creoles Come Together,") which advocated efforts to bundle the existing Creole parties together to confront and force concessions from the "Asian bloc." It shared Karg's desire to awaken greater ethnic consciousness and solidarity among Creoles, but it denied charges that the consequence would be sharpened ethnic hostility. Its goals were simply tactical – to show "our Hindustani friends" that they mustn't abuse their power.[89]

The Creole press devoted considerable space to a debate over these efforts at ethnic bloc-forming. But the general reaction of the editors, as well as of the

[84] *DWT*, March 5, 13, 1970.
[85] *DWT*, March 25, 30, 1970.
[86] See, for example, David G. Nicholls, "East Indians and Black Power in Trinidad," *Race* XII, no. 4 (April 1971), pp. 443-59.
[87] *DWT*, July 15, 1970.
[88] *Vrije Stem*, July 27, 1970.
[89] *Volksbode*, July 31, 1970; *DWT*, October 10, 1970.

leadership of the Creole parties, was negative.[90] Neither movement was able to get off the ground, and by 1972, little more was heard of them.

Besides the shock of the VHP's victory, one of the reasons these movements enjoyed special, if brief, attention was that on June 5, 1970, Johan Adolf Pengel had died.[91] As *De Ware Tijd* later pointed out, Pengel's death created a vacuum not only in his own party, but in the political system as a whole.

> He always held his thousands of followers under control and prevented any disturbances. Of course, he knew well how to use racial emotions to keep his people together. But he never let tensions reach the point of exploding. [Moreover] Pengel... was personally opposed to bundling the Creoles together. But now that [he] is gone, people are openly talking about... forming a Creole bloc to prevent their falling at the mercy of the Hindustani bloc. This means that racial conflict and tensions, which til now were weak and of little significance, will be sharpened.[92]

Having already been convulsed by debate and recriminations over the causes for their defeat,[93] the NPS was now confronted with selecting new leadership. The changes that Pengel had made to rejuvenate the party's executive committee in November 1969 were sufficient to enable a younger generation of leaders to cast aside the "old quard" identified with Pengel. A Catholic bank official, and relative newcomer to the party, Henck Arron, was elected provisional Chairman in late June and confirmed as permanent Chairman in December.[94] Arron quickly reaffirmed the party's commitment to cultural integration, as opposed to racial bloc-forming, but his demand for independence by 1974,[95] coming on the heels of Lachmon's own statement that independence was out of the question for at least another 25 years,[96] seemed to rule out any resumed cooperation between the parties.

Yet, with Pengel gone, Lachmon now saw the resumption of an NPS-VHP alliance as extremely attractive. After the resignation, for personal reasons, of a PNP minister in September 1970, Lachmon offered the NPS this and several other Cabinet posts (presumably to be vacated by the PNP).[97] Arron refused

[90] *Vrije Stem*, July 27, 1970. For the PNR reaction, see *DWT*, September 18, 1970. For the NPS reaction, see *Vrije Stem*, July 10, 1970. A new, Communist-oriented, movement being formed at this time by Humphrey Keerveld also denounced ethnic bloc-forming as impeding the chances for revolution (*Vrije Stem*, July 21, 1970).

[91] *DWT*, June 6, 1970.

[92] *DWT*, July 4, 1970.

[93] *Vrije Stem*, November 10, 11, 1960.

[94] *Vrije Stem*, July 10, 1970 and *DWT*, December 14, 1970. Technically, Arron was made Chairman of the Executive Committee, while Olton van Genderen (identified with the party's old guard) was named Chairman of the larger Party Council. For details of the struggle between the two factions, see *Vrije Stem*, July 13, 1970.

[95] *Vrije Stem*, July 10, 1970.

[96] *Volksbode*, May 16, 1970.

[97] *DWT*, September 24, 2970.

to consider the offer, but Lachmon kept dangling it before the NPS through the Spring of 1972.[98] One result was to keep the NPS divided, as members of the "old guard" also desired restoration of the alliance. Another result was to seemingly confirm the weak position of the PNP in the government. As a consequence of growing insecurity vis-à-vis their Creole following, PNP *Staten* members became increasingly independent in their critique of government policies – particularly demanding that the VHP reconsider its conservative position regarding independence.[99] The Chairman of the PNP's Party Council, Willy Cairo, went so far as to propose merger with the NPS, and when this was rejected, he quit the PNP to go to work for *Krikomaka*.[100] In January 1972, Hans Prade, Chairman of the PNP's Executive Committee, also resigned, denouncing the PNP ministers' lack of initiative and feeling of dependence on the VHP.[101]

VII. ESCALATION OF STRIKES

Although these various currents kept the Creoles divided and weak relative to the Hindustanis, almost constant strike activity by a number of government workers unions, combined with the government's failure to relieve growing unemployment by its ambitious joint-venture and other development programs, gradually produced an image as discredited as that of the government they had replaced.

In the summer and fall of 1970, the police and *douane* (customs officers) carried out damaging strike actions, demanding higher wages and improved side benefits.[102] In addition, Creole teachers went on strike in October 1970 to protest the appointment of Hindustani school directors by the VHP's Minister of Education.[103] Black Power considerations had reportedly encouraged the protest, and the strike met with sharp criticism from the press.[104] Nevertheless, the government agreed to clarify its procedures for naming school officials, and the strike ended.[105] However, a rash of disturbances broke out in November, when a court backed the government's decision to withhold pay for the hours lost through the teachers' strike action.[106]

[98] *DWT*, April 13, 1972.
[99] *DWT*, August 31, 1970.
[100] *DWT*, October 16, 1970.
[101] *DWT*, January 29, 1972.
[102] *Vrije Stem*, July 8, 1970; *DWT*, July 21, 22; November 9, December 2, 12, 1970.
[103] *Vrije Stem*, October 12, 1970.
[104] *Ibid.*; *DWT*, October 20, 1970.
[105] *DWT*, October 24, 1970.
[106] *DWT*, November 7, 11, 16, 17, 1970.

PNR member, Harold Rusland, angrily proposed a massive resignation, while "sympathetic" students roamed the city breaking store windows and destroying government property.[107]

In January 1971, government workers unions were organized into a new federation, the *Centrale van Landsdienaren Organisaties* (CLO), under PNR direction.[108] Then, in September 1971, a general strike was organized to protest the government's failure to control rising prices, or to take other social measures called for by the unions.[109] Coordination between the four labor federations (*Moederbond*, PWO, C-47, and CLO) was now very close, and an estimated 50% of Surinam's work force, including many Hindustanis and Javanese, honored the three-day strike.[110]

Faced by the unprecedented coordination among union federations, as well as the growing restlessness of the PNP *Staten* members, the government (particularly its Minister of Development, Frank Essed) worked feverishly to attract new investments, or otherwise increase Surinam's control in existing foreign enterprises. Joint ventures were signed with Reynolds Aluminum (for the development of bauxite reserves in West Surinam), the Dutch *Overzeese Gas en Electriciteits Maatschappij* (for the expansion of electrification in the districts) and the United Fruit Company (for operation of the banana plantation, Surland), while others were demanded of the Dutch firms Bruynzeel (lumber) and Billiton (bauxite).[111]

Unemployment, estimated at 15% in 1971,[112] climbed steadily higher, as did migration to the Netherlands. Although several studies of the migration phenomenon in this period indicate that socio-economic and other personal motives were the primary causes of migration,[113] it can be argued that the exclusion of the NPS from power, with its cut-off of spoils (particularly promotion chances for those already in government employment), may have had a major influence on these decisions to emigrate.[114] The Census of 1971

[107] *Vrije Stem*, November 18, 1970.

[108] *DWT*, January 5, 1972.

[109] *Ibid.*

[110] Eric Paërl, *Klassenstrijd in Suriname* (Nijmegen: SUN, 1972), pp. 33, 35-36.

[111] *Ibid.*, pp. 25, 32, 44-50; *DWT*, August 13, 1971. For details of the Reynolds joint venture, see F.E. Essed, *Een Volk Op Weg Naar Zelfstandigheid* (Paramaribo: Stichting Planbureau Suriname, 1973), pp. 229-33; and on the other joint ventures, see E. Azimullah, *De Realisering van het Mogelijke 1969-1973* (Paramaribo: 1973), pp. 19-25.

[112] Essed, *op. cit.*, p. 73.

[113] L. Zielhuis and D. Girdhari, *Migratie Uit Suriname* (Paramaribo: Ministerie van Sociale Zaken, June 1973), Vol. I, pp. 16-40; J.M.M. van Amersfoort, *Immigratie en Minderheidsvorming: Een Analyse van de Nederlandse Situatie 1945-1973* (Alphen aan den Rijn: Samson, 1974), pp. 145-49.

[114] F.E.R. Derveld, "Politics and Surinam Migration," unpublished paper, University of Groningen 1976.

revealed that an estimated 62,000 Surinamers had left their country since 1964, with 57,000 going to the Netherlands.[115] The largest share of these (some 32,000) were Creoles.[116] But increasingly, these migrants encountered difficulties ranging from housing and job discrimination to instances of alleged police brutality.[117] Despite the progressive Dutch government's declared readiness to support Surinamese independence, the suspicion grew that racial prejudice was among the factors in their "liberal" calculations. Rumors, in October 1972, that the Dutch were considering legislation to restrict Surinamese (and Antillean) immigration, were confirmed in December, when the Dutch Minister of Justice, A. van Agt, threatened that

> Unless the talks over a change in the Statute can lead to another rule covering nationality pretty quickly, I find it – in the interests both of the Netherlands and of the Surinamese immigrants – necessary that the [Dutch] Constitution be changed to permit us to limit immigration.[118]

Undoubtedly, these threatening actions by the Netherlands increased the frustrations of Creoles. The NPS and PNR now became more and more aggressive. Their next action began with a strike by the NPS-controlled *douane* in January 1973. Demanding to negotiate directly with the Minister of Finance, Harry Radhakishun (VHP), the *douane*'s leaders rejected all efforts at mediation. After they defied a court order to resume work, the government began to levy fines and demotions against the leaders.[119] Sympathy strikes by a broad range of unions in both the public and private sectors quickly followed, and once again street disturbances broke out. Initially involving only students, they quickly got out of hand, and serious plundering and destruction occurred, accompanied by incidents of arson directed at public installations.

Day after day, through the month of February, the press reported new stories of disturbances. Telegraph communications to the outside world were cut for over a week,[120] and the offices of several leading newspapers, because of their criticism of the strikers' demands and behavior (in contrast to 1969), were attacked by demonstrators and damaged.[121] Not allowing the estab-

[115] A.B.S., *Voorlopig Resultaat Vierde Algemene Volkstelling, Suriname in Cijfers No. 60* (Paramaribo: 1973), pp. 9-10.

[116] *Ibid.*

[117] *Elsevier* (Netherlands), October 21, 1972; *Haagse Post*, (Netherlands), November 15, 1972.

[118] Quoted by *Het Parool* (Amsterdam), December 20, 1972.

[119] "*Analyse van een Crisis*"*: Suriname februari 1973* (Paramaribo: INFORMA, 1973), pp. 6, 16.

[120] *DWT*, February 8, 1973.

[121] These were the offices of *Vrije Stem* and *De Ware Tijd* (*Vrije Stem*, February 8, 1973).

lished press access to their meetings, and having no press of their own, the unions relied at first on the printing facilities of the new Marxist-Leninist Center for their communications. But this soon became an embarrassment,[122] and one of the labor federations, the CLO, began printing its own strike paper, the *CLO-Bulletin*.[123] Appeals were made to the various Dutch labor federations for support, and in fact over Nf 100,000 in financial aid was sent. This infuriated the Surinam government.[124]

Finding the government unwilling to negotiate further with the *douane*, the strikers organized massive marches to the *Gouvernementsplein*, aiming their strongest denunciations, at first, at the VHP Minister, Radhakishun (whose offices faced onto the square).[125] But soon the whole movement became one to drive the government from office, as in 1969.[126] Chanting crowds demonstrated before Minister-President Sedney's office calling for his resignation,[127] while others broke into the office of the PNP Minister of Public Works and raided his liquor cabinet.[128]

The police, often confronted by angry crowds and taking the brunt of their hostility, remained remarkably poised and professional. Although the ratio of Creoles to Hindustanis in the police was about 2-1,[129] they did not seem to falter in their efforts to keep order among the largely Creole demonstrators through the month or more of constant turmoil. At one point early in the struggle, a directive from the (mostly Creole) leaders of the police union in Paramaribo to their members declared

> We want to make it more clear than ever, that we stand not only behind this government, but behind every legally elected regime. Whether the government consists of RED, BLUE, YELLOW, GREEN, BLACK, BROWN or ORANGE SURINAMERS ... we are ready. We stand as one man and we fall as one man![130]

Their professionalism was even more evident in the limited number of casualties reported,[131] although hundreds were arrested for the countless acts of violence and destruction.

[122] *DWT*. February 9, 1973.

[123] *Vrije Stem*, February 17, 1973.

[124] *DWT*, February 17, 1973; *Vrije Stem*, February 22, 1973.

[125] *Vrije Stem*, February 8, 1973.

[126] *DWT*, February 13, 1973.

[127] *Vrije Stem*, February 14, 1973.

[128] *DWT*, February 14, 1973.

[129] The figures in December 1973 were 553 Creoles, 290 Hindustanis, 36 Javanese, 4 Amerindians, and 1 Dutchman (Personal communication, December 17, 1973).

[130] Cited in *Vrije Stem*, February 10, 1973.

[131] The CLO reported 22 cases of injuries in the first three weeks (*Vrije Stem*, February 21, 1973).

Outside of Paramaribo, the effects of the general strike were less apparent. A number of schools were closed in Nickerie, partial walkouts at the Moengo and Paranam bauxite mines took place, and a complete work stoppage occurred at the Marienburg sugar plantation.[132] Nevertheless, as the Surinamese historian, E.A. Gessel, pointed out at the time,

> It is clearer and clearer that the strike is mostly a Creole affair, and that the Hindustanis [in the unions] are staying out of it. If [the Dutch Minister of Justice] Van Agt doesn't get his restrictive legislation passed, KLM isn't going to have enough planes to bring the Creole refugees to the Netherlands.[133]

The NPS, which had stayed behind the scenes through most of this, now openly called on Governor Ferrier to dissolve the *Staten* and hold new elections, "considering that there is a clearly massive public revolt against the Government."[134] But the Governor refused to intervene. The NPS now raised the issue of independence. Talks on changes in the Kingdom Statute (related to possible migration restriction and long-range plans for independence for both Surinam and the Netherlands Antilles) had been urged by the Dutch Government, and were scheduled to begin in March in Curaçao. The NPS denounced the talks, calling for outright independence.[135]

After three weeks of uncompromising confrontation, representatives of the government and the four labor federations finally began constructive talks on February 21, 1973.[136] But still the street disturbances and scattered incidents of arson continued,[137] along with organized marches by the striking workers. Suddenly the level of violence shot upwards. A Creole was killed looting a store on the night of the 26th,[138] and the next day, a Bush Negro leader of the Geological Mining Service workers was killed by police as he tried to break through their barricade on the Gravenstraat near the Catholic cathedral.[139] The death of the latter, Ronald Kitty ("Abaisa") produced a great wave of emotion against the government, but also, ironically, against any further demonstrations. The strike had finally peaked.[140] And while the unions would continue to hold out in their negotiations with the government,

[132] *DWT*, February 13, 23, 1973; *Vrije Stem*, February 10, 12, 15, 1973.
[133] Quoted in *DWT*, February 17, 1973.
[134] *Vrije Stem*, February 20, 1973.
[135] *DWT*, February 21, 1973.
[136] *DWT*, February 22, 26, 1973; *Vrije Stem*, February 23, 1973.
[137] *Vrije Stem*, February 23, 24, 27, 1973.
[138] *DWT*, February 27, 1973.
[139] *Vrije Stem*, *DWT*, February 28, 1973.
[140] *Vrije Stem*, March 1, 1973.

officially not giving up the strike until mid-April,[141] many workers already began to filter back to their jobs in March, and schools reopened shortly thereafter.[142] The government had won the battle. And though Creoles increasingly chanted and sang "Abaisa *gowini*" (Abaisa's going to win), it was not clear how the "martyr's redemption" was going to be achieved.

VIII. THE 1973 ELECTIONS

After the strike had run its course, and most workers had returned to their jobs, Eddy Bruma (PNR) joined with the one defector from the VHP's ranks during the disturbances, Dr. Harry Hirasing, who was now organizing an "*Actie Groep '73*", and together they formed a "*Bevrijdings Front*" (Liberation Front) with the leaders of the C-47 and CLO.[143] It appeared as though the *Bevrijdings Front* would run a mixed list of Creole and Hindustani candidates in the next elections. But when the call for new elections was finally officialized, and the time arrived to post slates of candidates, Bruma and the unions accepted a last-minute invitation from the NPS to join in a so-called *Nationale Partij Kombinatie* (NPK), which also included the PSV and KTPI (both of which had quit the PNP-bloc in 1972).[144] Dr. Hirasing fulminated about the "opportunism" of his former partners and warned about the polarization of the races that Bruma's act might signify. Invited to join a new anti-VHP *Hindostaanse Progressieve Partij* (HPP) that was being set up as a potential post-election alliance partner for the NPS, he declined, saying this would be as bad racially as what the Creoles were doing. Instead, he stuck with the *Actie Groep '73* and ran candidates on its slate from all ethnic groups.[145]

Dr. Hirasing was not the only party leader to experiment with ticket-balancing. The VHP, still smarting from charges of "racialism," changed its name to the "*Vooruitstrevende Hervormings Partij*" (Progressive Reform Party) and placed a prominent Creole cultural leader, Eugene Drenthe, in its 4th place on the Paramaribo district list – confident that with him they could win four of the city's ten seats. Drenthe campaigned vigorously and effec-

[141] *Vrije Stem*, April 16, 1973.

[142] *Vrije Stem*, April 4, 1973.

[143] *DWT*, July 28, 1973.

[144] *CLO-Bulletin*, August 25, 1973; *DWT*, September 3, 7, 10, 1973.

[145] *Aktueel*, September 1, 1973. Hirasing was particularly angry that the NPS had only entered talks with the PNR and the predominantly Creole labor unions. This may have been a personal slight (as Hirasing is a volatile and highly independent leader), but it seemed to him a clear case of ethnic bloc-forming (*ibid.*).

tively (even using a bit of *Sarnami Hindostans* in his speeches), but was denied at the end, to everyone's surprise.

The Creole-Javanese NPK ran A.G. Karamat Ali, a distinguished Moslem lawyer and long-time NPSer in the more secure second place on its Paramaribo slate. But, among Hindustanis, his significance was disputed, as he is a *Dogla* (of mixed Creole-Hindustani parentage), and thus "not really" a Hindustani. Nevertheless, other Hindustani NPSers ran on NPK lists in several of the rural districts and on the National (PR) List.

Most of the smaller parties, like the AG-'73, were clearly mixed: the PNP, denied a chance to merge its lists with the VHP, ran Creole, Hindustani, European and Javanese candidates in top positions (along with a significant number of female candidates); a new coalition of small urban Creole parties and PNP dissidents, allied with a Bush Negro party and called the *Bosnegers Eenheids Partij* (Bush Negro Unity Party, BEP), ran candidates of all races and religions; the new *Verenigde Volkspartij-Surinaamse Vrouwen Front* (United People's Party-Surinamese Women's Front), representing the unlikely alliance of Chinese shopkeepers and militant women-liberationists, featured men of Chinese and Chinese-Creole ancestry, and women of a variety of origins; and the (Communist) *Demokratische Volksfront* (DVF) ran a variety of young radicals, who, given the recent lowering of the voting age to 21, were clearly aiming for the youth vote.[146]

The remaining political parties – the SDP, now renamed the *Democratische* (sic) *Unie Suriname*, the *Vooruitstrevende Moslims Partij*, and the *Hindostaanse Progressieve Partij* – were more homogeneous cultural organizations, aimed at conservative Creoles, Hindustani Moslems, and the dissident Hindu and Hindustani-Christian groups. Of these last three, only the HPP was considered in the running with the NPK, VHP, PNP and BEP.

The NPK lists were filled with veterans of the February strikes (thoroughly rejuvenating, but also apparently radicalizing, the NPS' and PSV's images). NPS candidates dominated the lists in the smaller districts, but in Paramaribo, *Kieskring* II, and the National List, the other NPK parties shared a number of top, electable positions. In Commewijne the KTPI faced off against the SRI in what proved to be the closest race in the whole election. Their competition in *Kieskring* II, where Javanese candidates were given high positions on both the NPK and VHP lists, was also intense.

The issues were fairly simple. Lachmon played heavily upon the alarm Hindustanis had felt during the strikes, warning that the "*terreur, brutaliteit en onzekerheid*" (terror, crudity and insecurity) of the "February days" was

[146] By lowering the voting age to 21 (in 1973), an estimated 22,000 new voters were added to the lists (*DW*, September 1, 1973).

bound to intensify if the NPK won. The PNR would demand independence and would push the government towards Communist dictatorship.[147] (The presence of an avowed Communist party, the DVF, that criticized Bruma and the PNR as "too bourgeois" didn't seem to restrain Lachmon in the least.)

The NPK, which said little about independence, focussed its campaign on the need to redistribute wealth through welfare programs and work-generating investments. Charges were levelled at the top leadership in the VHP (particularly Lachmon and Radhakishun) and PNP (especially Economic Affairs Minister Just Rens) for having enriched themselves at the expense of the people. Yet much of the rhetoric was almost professorial, as the NPK's candidates – especially Bruma – lectured soberly in *Sranantongo* on the problems and challenges of economic and social development. The coalition's initial image as a band of fire-eating strike leaders quickly changed to a more coolly professional one, effectively countering the VHP's propaganda stereotype – at least for those who were exposed to the rallies of both sides.

The smaller parties seemed to get lost in the competition. The attendance at their rallies was considerably less than at the NPK and VHP's, where, beside the speeches, live music and entertainment were also featured. Nevertheless, fairly large Creole crowds gathered to hear the PNP's fiery, but conservative, leader Just Rens respond to and overcome the jeering challenge of young anti-PNPers. Similarly, they proceeded on to the BEP rallies to hear Rens' energetic young Creole-Chinese rival, Hans Prade, whose resignation, together with several others, from the PNP in September had further split and weakened the party.[148] Both the HPP and AG-'73 meetings – at least in the districts – were frequently disrupted by Hindustani hecklers chanting insults and throwing rotten eggs. The VHP seemed to take some pleasure (if not responsibility) in its rivals' difficulties, as their nightly rallies featured a song in *Sarnami Hindostans* recounting these disturbances in satirical terms.

In the interior, the BEP took on the VHP's ally, the *Progressieve Bos Neger Partij* (PBP),[149] and the NPS, over their records of service (or non-service) to

[147] These themes were already introduced at a VHP-SRI meeting in August. SRI-leader J. Sariman declared that there would be little sense in raising the flag of independence "if directly thereafter it would fly in flames." Dr. Alwin Mungra, the VHP's most outspoken (and in Creole eyes, most extremist,) leader warned that if Bruma came to power, he would "force people [i.e., Hindustanis] to leave the country, just as in Uganda." (*CLO-Bulletin*, August 27, 1973). Later, throughout the campaign, Lachmon and others accused Bruma of being a Communist. E.g., Lachmon: "This will be the last election in Surinam, since Communism doesn't permit elections." (*Vrije Stem*, November 3, 1973).

[148] *DWT*, September 24, 1973.

[149] The PBP had been allied with the PNP in the 1969 elections, entering the *Staten* as part of the PNP-bloc. Other PNP-bloc parties (the PSV and KTPI) had also distanced themselves from

the Bush Negroes. As election day drew near, the BEP protested that the government was failing to distribute voting cards, especially in the district of Boven Marowijne. But here, as in previous elections, the *Granmans* (chiefs) seemed reluctant to encourage their people to get involved, and a low turnout was expected.

By the eve of the election, it seemed clear that the NPK was closing in on the VHP, and that the outcome would hinge on (1) how the Bush Negroes and Javanese would vote, (2) how many dissident Hindustanis would vote for the HPP in Nickerie and the country as a whole, (3) how many voters, of each ethnic group, would stay at home, and (4) how the small mixed parties would fare, especially after the NPK's and VHP's warnings that votes for rival parties from their ethnic groups would be "wasted." If neither the VHP nor the NPK received a majority of seats in the *Staten*, the largest would still be invited to form the government. Thus, what particularly interested political observers was which of the small parties would get candidates into the *Staten* to become possible alliance partners. As only the PNP had declared itself willing to ally with the VHP, for example, what would happen if the VHP won a plurality over the NPK, but could find no allies (i.e., if the PNP could get none of its candidates elected, or too few to make a majority)? Of even more widespread concern was the threat of post-election disturbances in the event of a VHP victory. Many openly predicted this, including Bruma and others in the NPK. Minister of Justice and Police, J.H. Adhin (VHP), announced shortly before the election that the police would be fully prepared to handle any problems.[150] And while party propagandists hustled to get out the vote on election day, shop-keepers cleared their showcases or boarded up their windows.

All the complicated worrying and contingency-thinking was tossed into a cocked hat by the outcome, as the NPK swept to victory with 22 seats, with all the others going to the VHP (see Table 6.6 and 6.7). The strongest small party showings were made by the HPP in Nickerie, the BEP in Boven Marowijne and Brokopondo, and the PNP in Beneden Marowijne and Paramaribo. But in none of these cases was there really a close race, per se. It is possible that many voters, attracted to the smaller parties, were swayed by the fear of wasting their votes, and thus hurting their ethnic group's chances for representation. Thus, only in the largely Javanese district of Commewijne was an intra-ethnic contest close – the VHP-SRI winning those two seats, 3019 and 3005 against the NPK's 2812 and 2800.

the PNP as early as 1971 (KTPI) and 1972 (PSV). Thus, the PNP entered the 1973 elections badly isolated.

[150] *Vrije Stem*, November 14, 1973.

Table 6.6. Votes Cast in the 1973 Elections

Election District	*NPK*[a]	*VHP*[b]	*PNP*	*BEP*	*DVF*	*DUS*	*VVP/SVF*	*AG*	*HPP*	*VMP*	*Other*
I. Paramaribo (10 seats, PR)	21,047	8,995	1,154	887	513	254	648	326	284	323	—
II. Suriname (6 seats, PR) ("Kieskring II")	20,286	25,316	983	567	987	—	302	207	1,059	388	—
III. Para (1 seat)	3,873	—	942	—	332	—	—	—	—	—	—
IV. Commewijne (2 seats)	2,812[c]	3,019[d]	—	—	—	—	—	—	—	—	32[e]
	2,808	3,005	—	—	—	—	—	—	—	—	—
V. Saramacca (2 seats)	1,863[f]	2,543[g]	—	—	—	—	—	—	—	—	133[e]
	1,794	2,493	—	—	—	—	—	—	—	—	125
VI. Nickerie (2 seats)	991[h]	5,263[i]	209	—	—	—	—	—	3,376	—	—
	955	5,243	183	—	—	—	—	—	3,275	—	—
VII. Coronie (1 seat)	873	—	315	—	—	—	—	—	—	—	
VIII. Beneden Marowijne (1 seat)	2,595	—	1,026	435	63	—	—	—	—	—	
IX. Boven Marowijne (1 seat)	633	138[j]	—	134	—	—	—	—	—	—	—
X. Brokopondo (1 seat)	3,578	526[j]	—	1,291	—	—	—	—	—	—	43[e]
National List (12 seats, PR)	61,760	47,931	3,908	3,198	676	334	1,215	628	3,121	—	—

Electoral quotas: Paramaribo – 3,443; Kieskring II – 8,349; National List – 10,231.

[a] NPS, PNR, PSV, KTPI. [b] VHP, SRI, PBP. [c] Both KTPI candidates. [d] One VHP, one SRI candidate, both Javanese. [e] Unidentified. [f] One NPS (Hindustani) and one KTPI candidate. [g] Both VHP and Hindustani. [h] One NPS (Hindustani), one PNR (Creole). [i] Both VHP and Hindustani. [j] Bush Negro (PBP).

Source: *Gouvernements-Advertentieblad* No. 100 (December 3, 1973).

Table 6.7. Seat Division in the 1973 Elections

Election District	*NPK*				*VHP-BLOC*	
	NPS	*PSV*	*PNR*	*KTPI*	*VHP*	*SRI*
I. Paramaribo	4	2	1	–	3	–
II. Suriname	1	–	1	1	3	–
III. Para	1	–	–	–	–	–
IV. Commewijne	–	–	–	–	1	1
V. Saramacca	–	–	–	–	2	–
VI. Nickerie	–	–	–	–	2	–
VII. Coronie	1	–	–	–	–	–
VIII. Beneden Marowijne	1	–	–	–	–	–
IX. Boven Marowijne	1	–	–	–	–	–
X. Brokopondo	1	–	–	–	–	–
National List	3	1	2	1	5	–
Sub-total	13	3	4	2	16	1
Total	22				17	

On the National List, none of the smaller parties came within half of the 10,000-vote quota number that would qualify them for a seat. In this race, the NPK confirmed the validity of its victories elsewhere, winning 61,760 votes to the VHP's 47,931.

Given a turnout of 67% in the country as a whole, compared to the 69% turnout in 1969, it would appear that voter alienation was fairly minimal. In the wake of his own's party's thorough defeat, Minister-President Jules Sedney (PNP) declared that the NPK victory could only have been accomplished with at least some votes of every ethnic group going to the winners.[151] While there may be some truth to this, a more obvious explanation of the victory is that the appeals for Creole solidarity (made earlier by the Black Power Organization and *Krikomaka*) had struck a responsive note, bringing this group together in a show of unity that was virtually unprecedented in Surinam's modern history. (The "sweep" of seats by the NPS against its Creole party rivals in 1949, 1951, and 1958 were achieved under the old 'winner-take-all" system. Had there been proportional representation in those elections, at least some of the other Creole parties would have been represented in the *Staten*.)

Moreover, the smaller population groups, especially the Javanese in the KTPI, as well as those still tied to the NPS, had apparently given considerable support to this Creole coalition. The NPS' efforts to forge a cross-ethnic mass party seemed more legitimate in 1973 than they did in 1967 or 1969, as non-Creole candidates (heads of the various NPS presidia) were given higher

[151] *DWT*, November 21, 1973. In particular, he identified young, urbanized Hindustanis as voting for the NPK (*ibid.*).

positions on the election lists and now entered the *Staten*. In addition to the Bush Negro representative from Brokopondo (S.H.R. Vreede), who had earlier been elected in both 1967 and 1969, non-Creole members of the NPS elected in 1973 included Charles Lee Kon Fong (Chinese), Salim Somohardjo (Javanese), and Eugene Arichero (Amerindian). Islam Ramdjan, a Moslem Hindustani who had been elected in 1969, was re-elected posthumously, having been an apparent suicide victim during the campaign.[152]

Thus, it is difficult to speak of the restoration of Creole unity, represented by the electoral "sweep" of the NPK, as stemming simply from racial or cultural chauvinism. Rather, it seemed to combine resentment and fear of the solidarity of Hindustanis with the desire for an alternative form of political organization as embodied in their integrated (though Creole-dominated) electoral lists. Also, because the PNR and many strike leaders were represented in the NPK coalition (a fact which, before, might have "turned off" many Creole voters and precipitated party fragmentation), we have to conclude that the desire for progressive reforms, including independence from the Netherlands, had grown considerably among most non-Hindustanis.

Nevertheless, the polarization of the *Staten* – with no Creoles in the opposition, and no Hindustanis in the majority – seemed fraught with danger. Only once before had there been such a political configuration of the ethnic groups: in 1949-50. But, on that occasion, the Hindustanis had made absolute gains in representation and were reasonably self-content. Moreover, the Creole bloc in the governing NPS quickly broke down, offering opportunities for power-sharing between these groups. Now, the Hindustanis had *fallen from power*, and resentment against their position and influence in Surinam society seemed to bar any return to power-sharing. Would the NPK remain cohesive? How far would they go in their reforms? And how safe would the Hindustani group be under an NPK government?

[152] *Vrije Stem*, October 15, 1973.

CHAPTER SEVEN

THE STRUGGLE FOR INDEPENDENCE (1973-1975)

Moeten wij in hokjes blijven leven?
Moeten wij altijd aan rassen kleven?
Moeten wij vechten tegen elkaar?
Ay, Surinamers! Bloeden maar!
Wie is er bang voor de Sranangman?

Thea Doelwijt (1973)*

The 1973 elections had produced a degree of polarization unmatched since the first year of self-government 25 years before. There were no Hindustanis in the NPK's government benches, and no Creoles in the opposition. In contrast to the earlier situation, in which Hindustanis had at least enjoyed a sharp increase in representation, they were now in the position of having been driven from power. Thus, the potential for intense confrontation was much greater. An NPK-VHP coalition, to provide the facade of *verbroedering*, was clearly out of the question, given the tone of the preceding campaign. Moreover, the Cabinet assembled by Minister-President Henck Arron included a number of radical PNR members in key positions, intimating that reforms were planned that might jeopardize the economic interests of the Hindustani community.

Arron's reasons for this risky polarization included the desire to push Surinam through to independence. But although their numbers in the *Staten* were initially too small to effect the outcome of this move, the VHP brought so much pressure to bear on the regime that fragmentation began to occur in the NPK's ranks, and the issue, as well as the government itself, was put in great jeopardy.

* Must we remain living in our cultural boxes? Must we always cling to race? Must we fight against each other? Ay, Surinamers! Bloody yourselves! Who is afraid of the Surinam man? (*Land te Koop*, musical cabaret, 1973.)

1. THE NEW GOVERNMENT

The election's "*verrassende uitslag*" (surprising result), as it was generally called, created an awkward dilemma for Henck Arron and the leaders of the NPK. The absence of any other parties or blocs in the *Staten* made post-election alliances impossible, aside from the unthinkable alternatives of breaking up the NPK, or joining it to the VHP. It had been hoped that the HPP would win at least a few seats to allow the facade of Hindustani participation in the government.[1] But with this now out of the question, Arron was faced with the choice of leaving Hindustanis out of the government altogether, or looking for a qualified, but independent, figure. Reportedly, he contacted Mohamed Radja, the former VHP member who had broken from the party in the 1950 crisis, and had since become the chairman of the Surinam Chamber of Commerce.[2] These, and possibly other, talks were unsatisfactory, leaving Arron no choice but to assemble a Cabinet that excluded Hindustanis. (As perceived by most Surinamers, A. G. Karamat Ali, a mixed Hindustani-Creole NPS member, who became Minister of Public Works, was a Creole – this being the general classification given in Surinam to such individuals.) The Cabinet was made up of members of the NPK parties, with five posts going to the NPS, three to the PNR, and two each to the PSV and KTPI. Arron became Minister-President.

Several newspapers warned that the absence of Hindustanis in the Cabinet seemed to reenforce the political polarization produced by the elections, and they expressed regret at Arron's failure to remedy it.[3] A weekly newspaper, the *Volkskrant*, edited by VHP members, now made its appearance, bitterly denouncing the composition of the new Cabinet as "unrepresentative" and thus unfit to speak for the nation as a whole.[4] Lachmon compared the Hindustanis' situation to that of Rama and Sita in the classic Hindu epic, the *Ramayana*. At a rally in the Pad van Wanika that drew an estimated 20,000 Hindustanis in late December, he assured his audience that he would fight for them as steadfastly as his namesake, Lakshmana, had fought for his brother Rama to save the beautiful Sita from the (dark-skinned) forces of the demon king, Ravana.[5] There was no misunderstanding such an allusion.

[1] Handbills were distributed at NPK rallies proposing this, with the phrase "*NPK moesoe wini na stree, Makandra nanga HPP* (NPK must win the race, Together with the HPP)" (personal observation).

[2] This was the unconfirmed report of an informant.

[3] *Ibid.*, and *DW*, December 24, 1973.

[4] *Volkskrant*, December 29, 1973.

[5] Anonymous informant. For a summary of the *Ramayana*, see James A. Kirk, *Stories of the Hindus: An Introduction through Texts and Interpretation* (New York: Macmillan, 1972), pp. 186-215, especially, pp. 196-201.

In contrast to Lachmon's pessimistic interpretation, Evert Azimullah, a Surinamese (and Hindustani) political scientist, suggested that in light of the earlier NPS-AG debacle it was more important for the Creoles to win the confidence of Hindustanis by deeds than by token symbols, and that Arron may be gambling with just this in mind.[6] If so, Arron's strategy of ethnic "breakthrough" was both more profound *and* risky than that of his mentor, Pengel.

Clearly the test of these contrasting interpretations would be the issue of independence, against which the VHP had campaigned so virulently but towards which the NPK had maintained a discreet silence. With the experience of the NPS-AG alliance in mind, Arron may have anticipated the unbearable pressures to which an independent Hindustani (or two) in the Cabinet would have been subjected, once the objective of independence was proclaimed. Yet, *without* such individuals to serve as brokers between the government and Hindustani community, Arron was inviting almost certain political collision. The question was whether this collision could be limited to the parliamentary arena.

II. INDEPENDENCE BY 1975

Arron made his challenge clear on February 15, 1974, when he declared it the policy of his government to seek independence no later than "ultimo 1975".[7] The announcement was greeted by the VHP opposition in the *Staten* with anger and defiance: any change in the Kingdom Statute, they argued, must be carried out by a two-thirds majority, and the NPK, being four votes short of that, would have to reach an accommodation with them before it could be guaranteed the necessary votes.

Lachmon stated that he was quite willing to debate the subject in the *Staten* with Arron. But in the meantime, he held a new series of mass meetings and warned his followers against letting Surinam "be dragged into a dangerous adventure by overexcited Utopians and unrealistic dilettantes."[8] Arron responded to these attacks by accusing Lachmon of sedition (*opruiing*) and inciting polarization within the population.[9] Other NPK members warned that the VHP might attempt to break up the NPK alliance by various tactics.

The VHP turned now to the Dutch government, asking them to use their influence to safeguard constitutional procedures. But these efforts were to no

[6] Quoted in *Vrije Stem*, February 14, 1974.

[7] *Regeringsverklaring 1973/1977* (Paramaribo: February 15, 1974), p. 5.

[8] *DWT*, March 22, 1974.

[9] *DWT*, March 25, 1974.

avail. The parties in control of the Dutch government had been on record since before 1973 as supporting Surinam's independence by the mid-1970s.[10] In May 1974, talks began between the NPK and the government of Premier Joop den Uyl in the Netherlands. Lachmon, protesting his exclusion from these talks, pointed bitterly at the Netherlands' support for opposition movements in Rhodesia, Chile and Brazil, and declared that Den Uyl's behavior was irresponsible and regrettable.[11]

Tensions were eased temporarily in June, when Lachmon, on the anniversary of his 25th year in the *Staten*, conceded that he would be willing to accept independence by 1975 under certain conditions.[12] While Arron hailed him for his decision, there were still no indications of what these "conditions" were, or when talks between the two might be held. Yet Lachmon seemed to be willing to put his cooperative spirit in practice. A few days after his announcement, the VHP gave its support to a bill requiring identity cards for all Surinamers. These, it was made clear, would be necessary for the later issuance of Surinamese passports, voting, etc.[13]

Nevertheless, great anxiety and opposition to independence remained at the grassroots among Hindustanis. An organization to seek a separate Hindustani state in West Surinam was set up, and a large demonstration was held in front of the Minister-President's office.[14] While Lachmon repudiated such a solution, he confessed that he was beginning to lose control over his followers.[15] Others, however, suspected that he was behind these moves. E. A. Gessel, in a commentary on the political polarization published in *De Ware Tijd*, complained that "we hang from the windows preaching integration, brotherhood [etc.], while privately we try to cut each other's throat, because the political death of the one is the political bread of the other (*de politieke dood van de een [is] het politieke brood voor de ander*...)."[16]

[10] N. J. Prinson *et. al.*, *Nederland en de Zelfstandigheid van Suriname en de Nederlandse Antillen: Een Standpuntbepaling Voorbereid door een Werkgroep van D'66, de PPR en de PvdA* (Amsterdam: May 1973), p. 2. The position of these parties was clearly backed by the Dutch public. In a "Nipo-Enquete" in March 1973, 78% of the Dutchmen polled favored Surinam's independence, and of these 11% felt it should be achieved gradually, 32% within a few years, and 56% as soon as possible (*Elseviers Magazine*, March 24, 1973). For a more general discussion of Dutch attitudes regarding Surinam, see E. Dew, "The Draining of Surinam," *Caribbean Review*, Vol. 5, no. 4 (October-December 1973), pp. 8-15.

[11] *DWT*, May 21, 1974.

[12] *DWT*, June 11, 1974.

[13] *DWT*, June 14, 1974.

[14] *DWT*, June 18, 1974.

[15] *Ibid.*

[16] *DWT*, June 22, 1974.

III. MIGRATION AND THE DOUBLE NATIONALITY PROBLEM

Although migration had already become a serious problem in Surinam, with an estimated 57,000 Surinamers in the Netherlands at the time of the 1971 Census, the rate of departure climbed steadily after the elections of 1973. In addition to socio-economic motives which earlier research had found behind most of the migration,[17] a new political motive – fear – was added. After 1973, the number of Creoles emigrating continued to rise, but the rate of Hindustani emigration rose still more rapidly. In 1974, for the first time, Hindustanis constituted a majority of those leaving the country.[18] In the summer of 1974, estimates by Dutch officials regarding the size of the Surinamese migrant community in the Netherlands expected by the end of 1975 ranged from 130,000 to 150,000 – fully one-third of Surinam's total population.[19] Yet neither the VHP-PNP government, nor the present NPK regime, were willing to see measures taken to dam the stream.

In fact, Lachmon now demanded that the Dutch permit *continued* emigration after independence, by instituting a double nationality for Surinamers – i.e., safeguarding their Dutch nationality – for an indefinite period.[20] Spokesmen for the NPK took the position that Surinamers in the Netherlands should be given an option period to choose their nationality, but that extending this to Surinamers in Surinam would only breed chaos. This was a position acceptable to a committee of the tripartite Kingdom Commission meeting in the Netherlands Antilles in August 1974.[21] Yet *De*

[17] See, for example, L. Zielhuis and D. Girdhari, *Migratie Uit Suriname* (Paramaribo: Ministerie van Sociale Zaken, 1973), Vol. I, pp. 16-40; J. M. M. van Amersfoort, *Immigratie en Minderheidsvorming: Een Analyse van de Nederlandse Situatie 1945-1973* (Alphen aan den Rijn: Samson, 1974), Ch. 9, esp. pp. 145-149; and Frank Bovenkerk, *Emigratie Uit Suriname* (Amsterdam: Antropologische-Sociologische Centrum, Universiteit van Amsterdam, 1975), Ch. 4.

[18] According to figures collected by the Dutch *Centraal Bureau voor de Statistiek*, which used religious affiliation rather than ethnic group for its figures, the number of Hindus, Mohammedans and Buddhists arriving from Surinam rose from 3362 in 1973 to 7930 in 1974, while those of all other (or no) religions rose from 5391 in 1973 to 7421 in 1974. Judging by newspaper reports and various eyewitness accounts by informants for this study, we may assume that the great majority of the first categorie were Hindustanis, while the second category included other groups (Chinese and Europeans) along with the Creoles. Javanese migration only began to rise sharply late in 1975. (See "Buitenlandse Migratie van Nederland met Suriname en de Nederlandse Antillen, 1965-1974," reprinted from *Maandstatistiek van Bevolking en Volksgezondheid* (C.B.S., August 1975), Table 5a, p. 253.

[19] Interviews with officials of the *Ministerie van Cultuur, Recreatie en Maatschappelijk Werk*, and the *Kabinet voor Surinaamse en Nederlands-Antilliaanse Zaken*, Rijswijk and Den Haag, July 1974.

[20] *DWT*, July 4, 1974, August 8, 1974.

[21] *DWT*, August 10, 1974.

Ware Tijd warned that massive migration would be further stimulated by this policy, unless the NPK government gave Surinamers more to be confident about.[22]

Although they were excluded from the high-level conferences between the Dutch and Surinamese governments, VHPers were permitted to sit on the various committees of the Kingdom Commission. In these forums, they began to state more clearly the conditions deemed necessary for independence. Besides the nationality question, VHP demands were raised for Dutch guarantees regarding Surinam's contested borders with Guiana and French Guiana,[23] and the passage of a new constitution before independence.[24]

IV. TENSIONS IN THE NPK

A political crisis within the NPK now seemed to be brewing. Three NPS members (a Creole, a Chinese and a Javanese) refused to attend the opening of the new legislative session in September 1974, protesting that the NPK leaders were ignoring them. Given the balance of power in the *Staten*, their defection to the opposition would mean the government's downfall. After hasty talks, they returned to the government's benches.[25] But discontent among Chinese storeowners remained strong regarding new import controls to combat inflation and strengthen Surinam's balance of payments, and the Chinese NPSer (Charles Lee Kon Fong) complained that he and his family were increasingly isolated in the Chinese community.[26]

Pressures for new elections in the party leadership of the NPS arose, and along with them a demand by many NPSers for restoration of the NPS-VHP alliance. The leaders of the party, Arron and Olton van Genderen, rejected these demands and said that new elections in the NPS would be held only after independence.[27] Salim Somohardjo (a Javanese NPSer) now threatened to leave the party, and several Creole NPSers (E. Vriesde, W. Zalmijn and Albertina Clarke) echoed Somohardjo's criticism of the government's economic and social policies.

Much of this discontent reflected continuing fear of the PNR among older members of the NPS. Although Eddy Bruma, as the new Minister of Economic Affairs, had not begun any radical reforms of the economy beyond

[22] *DWT*, August 14, 1974.
[23] *DWT*, August 23, 1974.
[24] *DWT*, August 31, 1974.
[25] *DWT*, September 3, 1974.
[26] *Ibid.*
[27] *DWT*, October 23, 1974.

the institution of import controls, his presence in the government was a cause of continued apprehension, and Arron was seen as being either under his influence, or too weak to control him.

V. ECONOMIC SELF-SUFFICIENCY

In the 1960s, when the subject of independence first came up, the VHP's stand had been that Surinam must first be economically self-sufficient before it should seek full sovereignty. Although negotiations with the Dutch had been conducted under assurances of continued financial aid after independence, the amount of that aid was not yet agreed upon. But another source of income was jubilantly announced by Arron in November 1974.

Following Surinam's participation in the creation of the International Bauxite Producers Association in the Spring of 1974, the government had pressed its own largest bauxite-aluminium company, Suralco, to pay higher taxes. An agreement was announced on November 21, in which Surinam's taxes on bauxite were quadrupled. Moreover, the agreement included back payments for 1974 of Sf. 50 million.[28] A week later, another agreement was signed between Surinam and the *Billiton Bauxiet Maatschappij* along the same lines.[29]

Still another agreement was being negotiated between the governments of Surinam and Venezuela. As finally announced in January 1975, Venezuela assured Surinam oil deliveries at a fixed level 25 percent below the world market price in exchange for deliveries of Surinamese bauxite and alumina to Venezuela's new industrial complex in Ciudad Guyana.[30] Bilateral negotiations between Surinam and the Netherlands over the Dutch aid package occurred amid these encouraging reports and continued through June 1975.

VI. NEW VHP DEMANDS

Feeling that he had begun effectively to satisfy the VHP demands regarding economic self-sufficiency, Arron now pledged that a new constitution would be adopted before Independence.[31] In January 1975, he installed a nonpartisan commission of legal experts (including several Hindustanis) to draw up a

[28] *DW*, November 22, and *DWT*, November 22, 1974.
[29] *DWT*, November 30, 1974.
[30] *DWT*, February 1, 1975.
[31] *DWT*, January 27, 1975.

working document, and the commission began its work by conducting hearings to which all interested groups were invited to testify and make their recommendations.[32]

But at the same time as the commission began its work, a massive rally of 20,000 Hindustanis was held in Paramaribo, threatening a series of actions if a direct dialogue between Arron and Lachmon didn't begin at once.[33] Governor Johan Ferrier was petitioned to intervene on behalf of the opposition, and Lachmon announced that 80% of the Javanese, 99.9% of the Hindustanis, and 50% of the Creoles were opposed to independence.[34]

A short while later, Lachmon made several new demands. In response to Arron's declaration that Surinam would become a parliamentary republic, with a president chosen by the parliament as head of state,[35] Lachmon demanded that the president be directly elected by the people.[36] Arron's vision was presumably predicated upon a continuation of the present system, with the president's powers being as circumscribed as the governor's. But Lachmon was thinking in terms of a stronger role for the president and proposed the creation of a constitutional court to resolve differences between president and parliament. It was not clear, however, how Lachmon intended the direct election to be structured to guarantee sufficient legitimacy to the new head of state.

Another demand was that the new Surinam army be a reflection (*weerspiegeling*) of the population, i.e., that its composition be proportional to the balance of ethnic groups in the society, so as to prevent its political misuse. Because the Kingdom Statute's provisions for amendment did not necessarily require a 2/3 vote,[37] Lachmon gave up his earlier demand on this score, but insisted that a 2/3 majority *was* required for approval of the constitution.[38] Finally, he insisted that independence be followed promptly by new elections.[39]

The demands for top-level cooperation between the NPK and VHP now received support from two predominantly Creole institutions: the Churches

[32] *Ibid.*

[33] *Ibid.* Eyewitnesses reported that the crowd of Hindustanis and others attending the rally filled the *Gouvernementsplein* to overflowing (Interview, Stan and Judie Martin, Paramaribo, January 30, 1976).

[34] *DWT*, January 28, 1975.

[35] *DWT*, February 3, 1975.

[36] *DWT*, February 5, 1975.

[37] Article 55 of the *Statuut* provides for immediate passage of amendments if a 2/3 vote is achieved in the legislatures of the three constituent member states. However, amendments may also be passed by simple majority, if given a second reading within one month.

[38] *DWT*, February 5, 1975.

[39] *Ibid.*

and the press. In March 1975, the *Comité Christelijke Kerken* (CCK, uniting Catholic and Protestant church leaders) issued an appeal for a new spirit of toleration and unity, warning that there was "uncertainty and even anxiety regarding [the] future, which expresses itself... in the rising migration to the Netherlands, growing fear engendered by the ongoing power struggle, and concern regarding the preservation of meaningful democracy in an independent Surinam."[40] Its members were especially concerned that the Hindu celebration of *Holi Phagwa* coincided in 1975 with Good Friday (March 28), and that the joyous celebration of the one might clash with the somber celebration of the other, leading to conflict. Both the CCK and Hindu leaders warned their followers to be tolerant and discreet in their observation of the (legal) holiday.[41]

At the same time, representatives of Surinam's three major papers, *De Ware Tijd*, *De West* and *Vrije Stem*, met with Arron to insist on opening talks with the VHP.[42] Apart from a "casual, nonpolitical" meeting in the Netherlands in September 1974,[43] no effort to resolve the growing differences had been made in the 12 months following Arron's Independence announcement.[44] But still, no meeting was scheduled.

In the meantime, the Javanese NPSer, somohardjo, had decided to quit the NPS, threatening a massive emigration of Javanese to the Netherlands. Together with two Javanese members of the opposition, he visited the Netherlands, warning of "a bloodbath" if the Dutch didn't politically intervene.[45] Lachmon, also in the Netherlands at this time, threatened actions in June and July "to cripple the economy" if Arron didn't agree to the requirement of a 2/3 majority for approval of the new constitution.[46] Speaking in The Hague, he declared "the chance of civil war in Surinam cannot be ruled out, if the Netherlands does nothing to prevent the constitution from being adopted without Javanese and Hindustani approval."[47] Still, Den Uyl was cool to Lachmon's warnings and refused to intervene.

[40] *DWT*, March 5, 1975.

[41] *Ibid.* No incidents were reported on this double holiday.

[42] *DWT*, March 8, 1975.

[43] *DWT*, September 28, 1974.

[44] Although the press was increasingly critical in its treatment of the political polarization, it had not lost its sense of humor. On April 1, *De Ware Tijd* reported the death of a Surinam millionaire, Dr. R. E. Manirus, in New York, who reportedly had bequeathed his estate of $ 200 million to the Surinam people. Although the report was an April Fools' Day hoax, *DWT* reported that its switchboard had been busy answering calls for more information about the "millionaire" (whose name was "Surinamer" spelled backwards)! (*DWT*, April 1 and 2, 1975).

[45] *DWT*, March 12, 1975.

[46] *DWT*, March 15, 1975.

[47] *DWT*, March 22, 1975. He later denied using the term "civil war" (*DWT*, April 9, 1975).

VII. THE TALKS, AND FIRES, OF MAY

In May 1975, as Den Uyl and his key ministers visited Surinam for the final phase of their bilateral negotiations, crowds of Hindustanis lined the road to Paramaribo from the airport, and 7,000 massed at the bridge over the Saramacca *Doorsteek* (Canal) to hand Den Uyl a petition calling for his intervention. Refusing to stop, the car sped dangerously through the crowd.[48] Many chased after it across the bridge, only to encounter a crowd of Creole counter-demonstrators. Rock throwing between the two groups injured dozens, and fighting was reported there and at other points in the city.[49]

At the same time that Den Uyl arrived for his talks with the Arron government, Arron and other top NPK leaders finally met briefly with Lachmon and the opposition. Lachmon presented his above-mentioned demands regarding the constitution and other issues, and after a short discussion, the meeting was adjourned for a week to allow the NPK to formulate a response.[50] The failure of any immediate agreement to be forthcoming, combined with the tensions aroused by the presence of the Dutch leaders, led a number of young Hindustanis to launch a wave of arson. Almost every night through the week of the Dutch visit, fires were started in government buildings, climaxing with the destruction, on May 21, of part of a downtown block of buildings, including the well-known Hotel Lashley.[51] Arson had earlier destroyed the Hall of Records on May 9, destroying all sorts of valuable data, as well as many passports and passport applications.[51] Minister C. Ooft of Internal Affairs didn't ease the political climate by his charges (before any arrests had been made) that blame for this first fire could indirectly be laid to Lachmon, because of his intransigent opposition to the government.[53] Although a number of young VHP activists were arrested in connection with the fires, no indication was found that they had acted except on their own initiative.[54]

Following the Lashley fire, Lachmon stated that he might now be willing to make some concessions to restore harmony.[55] Nevertheless, the aura of suspicion and hostility evidently gave the NPK a pretext to postpone further talks with the VHP for the time being.

[48] It appears that the passenger was the Minister of Development Aid, J. Pronk, and not Den Uyl, who arrived from the airport by helicopter.

[49] *DWT*, May 15, 1975.

[50] *DWT*, May 16, 1975.

[51] *DWT*, May 22, 1975.

[52] *DWT*, May 12, 1975.

[53] *DWT*, May 14, 1975.

[54] *DWT*, May 23, 1975.

[55] *DWT*, May 24, June 3, 1975.

Despite (or even because?) of the tense and nearly chaotic conditions surrounding the final Arron-Den Uyl talks, a handsome agreement was reached with the Dutch government whereby financial assistance of various kinds (including cancellation of debts) totalling over Nf 4 billion ($ 1.6 billion) was to be extended to Surinam over a period of from ten to fifteen years.[56] Between 1947 and 1974, the Dutch had given Surinam approximately Nf 950 million.[57] Independence, it seemed, was going to be a great deal more profitable than simple autonomy. But first, independence had to be achieved.

VIII. NEW NPK DIVISIONS

Although another meeting was held on June 17 between the NPK and VHP leaders, no agreements were reached.[58] The situation remained polarized, and several VHP leaders threatened to resume "democratic actions" against the government.[59]

At the same time, the Staten members Charles Lee Kon Fong and Albertina Liesdek-Clarke[60] demanded that the NPS step out of the NPK.[61] When a party meeting voted their proposal down, they formed their own fraction in the *Staten*, threatening to block the government's work by cooperating in certain areas with the VHP.[62] Together with the earlier NPK defector, Somohardjo, they provided the VHP the necessary votes to defeat the government on a vote of confidence. Protests and harassment from some elements of the NPS rank and file were directed at the two new defectors, and Lee Kon Fong began to waver under the pressure, finally leaving the country on an "extended vacation."[63]

The *Staten* was now stalemated at 19-19 – a situation permitting the VHP to block all legislative action, but not sufficient to enable the vote of no-confidence. Efforts to appoint a delegation to the Dutch parliamentary debates over Surinam's independence (initially scheduled in September) were frustrated, as was the opposition's procedural effort to give priority to deliberating on the new constitution (submitted to the government by the Constitutional Commission on August 21). For several weeks, the *Staten* was

[56] *DWT*, May 19, June 28, 1975.
[57] *DWT*, September 18, 1974.
[58] *DWT*, June 24, 1975.
[59] *DWT*, July 26, 1975.
[60] Albertina Clarke had gotten married in the meantime.
[61] *DWT*, July 26, 1975.
[62] *DWT*, July 31, 1975.
[63] *DWT*, August 23, 1975.

paralyzed as the opposition refused to provide a quorum for its meetings. Efforts to locate Lee Kon Fong failed, and the Dutch Parliament was forced to postpone its debate.

If the NPK was intent upon achieving independence by November 25 – the target date they had announced in June, time was running out for them. Yet neither side seemed willing to make a concession or to resume talks, while each continued to make use of their remaining power to thwart the other. The VHP, attending the opening of the new legislative session, September 1, listened to Governor Ferrier's opening address and then walked out, denying Arron a quorum for the presentation of his financial program. A threatening crowd waited outside the *Staten* to show their displeasure at Mrs. Liesdek-Clarke, the one NPK dissident who had attended the meeting, but she departed through a back door.[64]

Despite the inability to display a working majority in the *Staten*, Arron declared that his government would not resign,[65] and speculation began to grow that he would unilaterally declare Surinam's independence without use of any constitutional formalities, under pressure from Bruma and the PNR. A few days after the VHP walk-out, a large crowd of Hindustanis, but including many older Javanese and Creoles, paraded through Paramaribo with banners calling for the government to resign. They laid a wreath at the statue of Mahatma Gandhi and presented a petition to the Governor. When they also tried to lay a wreath at the newly erected statue of Johan Pengel, a crowd of younger Creoles threatened them, and the police were forced to intervene.[66]

IX. STRAINS IN THE VHP

The heightened tensions produced by the defections from the NPK now seemed to produce a defection in the VHP. Eager to demonstrate to the Dutch government that Arron had lost his majority, and locating Lee Kon Fong on the island of Aruba, Lachmon proposed that the entire opposition go to the Netherlands. One member of the VHP, George Hindorie, thought by many to be Lachmon's most likely successor to the party leadership, refused to join the delegation. Denying that he was parting ways with the party's standpoint on the issues, he remained hopeful that reconciliation might be achieved, and felt that the Netherlands trip would only polarize things further, wasting valuable time.[67]

[64] *DWT*, September 2, 1975.
[65] *DWT*, September 8, 1975.
[66] *DWT*, September 12, 1975.
[67] *DWT*, September 13, 1975.

In this volatile situation Arron promptly invited Lachmon for new talks. But these, too, failed, as Lachmon's demands remained unchanged, and Arron refused to make any concessions.[68] In a press conference in The Hague, Premier Den Uyl spoke of the "checkmate between government and opposition" as "an unpleasant development," and declared that "it will be extremely regretted if Surinam declares independence unilaterally."[69] Taking these words as encouragement, Lachmon and the remainder of the opposition flew to the Netherlands. Hindorie wavered momentarily, then decided to go along.[70]

Despite Dutch concern over the stalemate in Surinam, the opposition's visit was not well received. Dr. A. Vondeling, Speaker of the Dutch Second Chamber (Lower House) argued that "if... Lachmon wants to prove that he has the majority in the Surinam *Staten*, he must do that in Surinam and not in the Netherlands."[71] Despite the VHP's lobbying efforts, Vondeling scheduled the Dutch debate on Surinam's independence to begin on October 21.

The VHP now faced "the moment of truth." Lachmon, before leaving the Netherlands, declared that the opposition would introduce a motion of no-confidence on their return. Their intention would be to force the NPK to make way for a new "transitional cabinet," including the VHP (and presumably excluding the PNR), which would then attempt to see the independence issue through to a sound conclusion.[72] Yet, as the VHP delegation returned home, a government delegation departed for their own talks with the Dutch government, and the NPK refused to call the *Staten* into session.[73]

The effort to appoint a formal delegation of NPK and VHP representatives to attend the Dutch parliamentary debates had been blocked by the *Staten*'s inactivity since mid-August. Now, *Staten* Chairman Emile Wijntuin (PSV) informally appointed a seven-man NPK delegation and requested Vondeling to set aside an equal number of seats for the VHP.[74] But the VHP refused to attend.

At this point, George Hindorie again broke ranks from his party, deciding to extend his "cooperation to the NPK in the realization of Surinam's independence on November 25." He would again travel to the Netherlands to take one of the seats reserved for the VHP and to make the VHP's case before the

[68] *DWT*, September 18, 1975.
[69] *DWT*, September 20, 1975.
[70] *DWT*, September 29 and 30, 1975.
[71] *DWT*, October 1, 1975.
[72] *DWT*, October 11, 1975.
[73] *DWT*, October 13, 1975.
[74] "Brief van de Staten van Suriname," Paramaribo, October 4, 1975, Tweede Kamer der Staten-Generaal, Zitting 1975-76, 13473 (R990), nr. 15.

Dutch Parliament. He would also take part in the debates in the Surinam *Staten* on the consitution and other matters, to assure a quorum.[75] Although there was no indication that he would betray Lachmon's standpoint on any of these issues, his decision was bitterly condemned by the VHP and enthusiastically applauded by the NPK.[76] Distrusting what Hindorie might do in The Hague, Lachmon reversed his earlier decision and assembled his own delegation to fill the reserved VHP seats – notably excluding Hindorie.[77]

X. THE DUTCH PARLIAMENTARY DEBATES

The debates in the Second and First Chambers, from October 21-28, 1975, were a colorful and dramatic political extravaganza. With Premier Den Uyl and a number of his Cabinet in attendance, the Surinam legislators paraded to the rostrum to plead their separate cases. "Hail, Den Uyl!" began one of the Hindustanis, "we, who are going to die, salute you!"[78] Another spoke bitterly of the warm reception given by Den Uyl to the widow of Salvador Allende of Chile, and to the loud outcry in the Dutch press and government against the recent execution of Basque terrorists in Spain, while "there is a fire within their own Kingdom that they do not see."[79]

Each of the opposition's demands was thoroughly debated, and rejected by the majority of the Dutch legislators. Regarding the nationality question, one speaker wryly observed that Surinam's internal conflicts would be solved if all Surinamers were allowed to keep leaving their country.[80] But Somohardjo, a member of the VHP's delegation, emphasized that Dutch nationality, "purchased at the travel bureaus," was not available to the poor, and that their deprival of Dutch citizenship would be a violation of Article 15 of the Universal Declaration of the Rights of Man.[81] Several Dutch legislators disputed this, saying the Declaration's intent was to protect individuals from arbitrary actions that rendered them *stateless*,[82] and the Dutch Minister of Internal [including Kingdom] Affairs later asked Lachmon pointedly how

[75] *DWT*, October 16, 1975.
[76] *DWT*, October 16 and 17, 1975.
[77] *DWT*, October 18, 1975.
[78] Speech of Dr. Alwin Mungra, *Handelingen*, Tweede Kamer der Staten-Generaal, Zitting 1975-76, 11de vergadering, October 22, 1975, p. 540.
[79] Speech of M. S. A. Nurmohamed, *ibid.*, p. 535.
[80] *Ibid.*, 12de vergadering, October 23, 1975, p. 617
[81] *Ibid.*, 11de vergadering, October 22, 1975, p. 546.
[82] *Ibid.*, 10de vergadering, October 21, 1975, p. 469.

independence could occur without the Surinamers acquiring their own citizenship.[83]

On the issue of the Armed Forces, NPK delegates admitted that the Kingdom Commission on Defense Matters had recommended that the Armed Forces be a reflection of the population. But they argued that the cross-section upon which this was to be based was a "vertical" or social class one and not as the opposition argued a "horizontal" or ethnic one.[84]. Only a few Dutch legislators signalled their sympathy to the warnings of the VHP regarding the developments in neighboring Guyana, where the military was almost exclusively Black and thus a force of great potential abuse against the majority Hindustani population.[85] Regarding the disputed borders with Guyana and French Guiana, Den Uyl's government refused to give a guarantee of anything stronger than diplomatic support.

The most disturbing package of issues for the Dutch legislators was the absence of a constitution, and the possibility that Arron's government might declare Surinam's independence unconstitutionally. Den Uyl repeated his earlier statement that a unilateral declaration would be "regrettable," but stated that he had seen no indication that Arron had any such move in mind.[86] Yet both Lachmon and Mrs. Liesdek-Clarke pointed to statements by Arron and Bruma that kept these suspicions alive.[87] By the end of the debate, it was clear that the Dutch government would reconsider its aid agreement with Surinam in such an event.[88]

On the subject of the constitution, Dutch opposition legislators insisted that the protection of human rights in Surinam was the responsibility of the Dutch under the Kingdom Statute, and that there must be assurances from the Surinam government that a new constitution would be in place before independence could be voted on.[89] But Rufus Nooitmeer (NPS), legislative leader of the NPK fraction, declared in the Second Chamber's closing debate that "it is definitely the goal of the Surinam Government to have a constitution at the time of the independence declaration." Moreover, he added that

[83] *Ibid.*, 11de vergadering, October 22, 1975, p. 553.

[84] Speech of O. Rodgers, *ibid.*, 11de vergadering, October 22, 1975, p. 550.

[85] *Ibid.*, 12de vergadering, p. 615. See also, Cynthia Enloe, "Civilian Control of the Military: Implications in the Plural Societies of Guyana and Malaysia," paper presented at the Inter-university Seminar on Armed Forces and Society, State University of New York, Buffalo, October 18-19, 1974, pp. 25-40.

[86] Tweede Kamer, *op. cit.*, 12de vergadering, p. 574.

[87] *Ibid.*, 11de vergadering, p. 530.

[88] *Ibid.*, 12de vergadering, p. 612.

[89] *Ibid.*, 10de vergadering, p. 473.

the NKP can in no way give our support to a... constitution... with which we can have our own fingers cut. For what is today the coalition can be the opposition tomorrow...

We're not carrying out "*kalong*-politics." Let me explain what that is. The *kalong* is a kind of bat... You know that the bat has the habit of sitting or standing upside down. Consequently he thinks he can foul the things above him only to find that the mess he makes hits him in the face... We will never do anything which can later hurt us, as the *kalong* does.[90]

Still not assured of the NPK's intentions, the VHP proposed an amendment to delete the date of independence from the bill ending the Statutory ties with Surinam, so as to assure prior passage of the constitution. But the motion was defeated in a standing vote, and the bill to accept Surinam's independence was passed by roll-call, 106-5.[91] After a much shorter debate in the First Chamber, the bill was again passed 53-11.[92]

XI. THE "SHOWDOWN"

Following the decision in the Second Chamber, Lee Kon Fong announced he was giving up his seat in the *Staten* to his shadow-candidate, assuring the NPK restoration of its majority.[93] A few days later, it was announced that a Javanese member of the VHP (R. Dasiman) was leaving Surinam for the Netherlands with his family, but that he was *not* giving up *his Staten* seat.[94] Both he and Somohardjo accompanied large groups of Javanese emigrating to the Netherlands, while Somohardjo initiated a suit against the Dutch government to force issuance of passports to an additional 6000 Javanese desiring to emigrate.[95]

Returning somberly to Surinam, the VHP stubbornly repeated, and even expanded, its demands in a new summit meeting with Arron and several other NPK ministers: (1) new elections must be held within five months of independence, according to a country-wide system of proportional representation (PR), (2) an independent election authority must be set up, and voting machines must not be introduced, (3) there must be no absentee ballots for

[90] *Ibid.*, 12de vergadering, p. 619.

[91] *Ibid.*, 12de vergadering, p. 630.

[92] *Handelingen*, Eerste Kamer der Staten-Generaal, Zitting 1975-1976, 4de vergadering, October 28, 1975, p. 95.

[93] *DWT*, October 25, 1975.

[94] *DWT*, October 28, 1975.

[95] *DWT*, November 14, 1975.

Surinamers outside the country,[96] (4) a two-thirds majority must be required in the constitution for nationalization of any foreign enterprises, (5) the constitution must explicitly require the military to be an ethnic reflection of the population, never to be used for political purposes, and (6) the Vice-President of Surinam must be elected by the Parliament in the same manner as the President. (This last demand constituted a retreat from their earlier demand for direct, popular election of both office-holders.) Additionally, the VHP decried the proposed new flag for Surinam, objecting to its colors as those of the parties constituting the NPK.[97] Once again, all that the NPK leaders reportedly said was that they would study the VHP's demands.

To the VHP's relief, the first order of business when the *Staten* resumed work was the new Constitution. In a closed meeting, Friday, November 14, the *Staten* was presented with the document (*Ontwerp Grondwet*) as modified by the government. Actually, there were few changes from the bill submitted by the independent constitutional committee, and those that *were* made represented efforts to appease the opposition. For example, the ministers had added the clause (Article 121, section 1) "All Surinamers can take part on an equal basis in the military and be appointed to each function on an equal basis."

Members of both government and opposition benches generally applauded the wide-ranging list of fundamental human rights guaranteed in the Preamble and first nineteen Articles. Still, the members of the mixed *Staten* committee studying the bill found many points of disagreement. Their report was submitted to the Cabinet and the latter delivered their answer to the *Staten* members early Sunday morning, November 16. A few hours later, the *Staten* convened in an open session for the beginning of a marathon debate that lasted nearly 48 hours and was broadcast throughout Surinam by radio.

When *Staten* Chairman Wijntuin pointed out in his opening remarks that this wasn't the first time in Surinam's history that the legislature had met on a Sunday, the opposition's first speaker, former Minister of Justice J. H. Adhin (VHP) quickly pointed out that the only previous occasion (May 17, 1891) was during the De Savornin Lohman crisis which had followed "two years of the greatest chaos and confusion" Surinam had ever known.[98] Despite the obvious comparison, and though the speeches of the opposition generally

[96] This issue, like that of the military's composition, was one that had arisen because of the manifold abuses occurring in Guyana. See Alvin Rabushka and Kenneth A. Shepsle, *Politics in Plural Societies: A Theory of Democratic Instability* (Columbus: Charles E. Merrill, 1972), pp. 103-104.

[97] *DWT*, November 14, 1975.

[98] Staten van Suriname, *Handelingen 1975-76*, 6de vergadering, November 16, 1975, p. 21. See above, pp. 37-38.

began with protests about the haste with which they had to work and accusations that the government had mishandled the affair, the debate was orderly and generally constructive. Adhin's comments were typical:

> we shall ... extend our cooperation. We have already done so because we realize that it is a *fait accompli* .... But I might also state that this is a very incorrect procedure which bodes ill for our future .... Many of the important things that we would have liked to bring forward ... we are forced to leave aside .... But I do this under protest ....[99]

Besides the host of technical and legalistic observations raised by legislators from both the NPK and VHP, a number of fundamental criticisms were raised: those, already cited, by the VHP, as well as several from the side of the PNR. The latter included demands for an 18-year-old voting age, sanctions against legislative violations of party discipline,[100] and, most significantly, the workers' right to strike, which had not been included among the fundamental laws (*Grondrechten*) in Articles 1-19.[101] This latter demand, in particular, may have provided Arron leverage with the PNR to make some concessions to the opposition in the later stages of the debate.

In addition to the suggested changes, the VHP members repeatedly insisted upon passage of the Constitution by a 2/3 vote. As Lachmon pointed out, "juridical chaos" would exist if less than that vote was mustered, because the existing constitution (*Staatsregeling*) could only be *removed* by such a vote. Without a 2/3 vote, Lachmon warned, "you would get two fundamental laws for Surinam," accompanied by a host of legal contradictions and likely court cases.[102] This clearly was the last "trump card" the opposition could play, and while Lachmon's interpretation was disputed by members of the Cabinet and government majority, it was evidently effective.

In the second round of debates, Tuesday, November 18, Arron and Justice Minister E. Hoost (PNR) presented a long series of amendments to the Constitution reflecting minor corrections demanded by both the VHP and NPK speakers. Perhaps the most important of these, meeting one of the VHP's principal demands, was the assurance of an independent election bureau (Article 54, section 6). More dramatically, Arron concluded his formal remarks by addressing Lachmon:

[99] *Ibid.*, p. 22.

[100] Interestingly, the same demand was made by the VHPer R. Sardjoe (*ibid.*, p. 202). Although the government steadfastly refused to circumscribe the independence of legislators, members of both the NPK and VHP were clearly aggrieved by the behavior of their respective "defectors."

[101] Article 8 (1.8 in the *Ontwerp*) included only the civil rights of assembly, demonstration and association – with the right to set up and join labor unions expressly recognized under these clauses. For the PNR's demands, see speech of F. Derby, *ibid.*, pp. 51, 54, 55.

[102] *Ibid.*, p. 150.

It may well be that we both have sharpened our battle axes in the past. We have fought, Mister Chairman, but we have never been each other's enemy. Political struggle is hard, and when we are no longer here .... politics will go on and perhaps be conducted somewhat more rationally.

I am a man, Mr. Chairman, and the Opposition leader is also a man, and no man is born without human deficiencies .... Let us ... be prepared to accept each other with our human faults ... to break away the barriers that exist between Lachmon and me, because even with our shortcomings, we will have to set up a monument, and this monument must not be a Surinam torn apart by struggle, but a Surinam that is built up in unity and unanimity, through our cooperation ....[103]

Inviting Lachmon to accompany him to the United Nations on December 4 "to present the Sovereign State of Surinam to the world," Arron then walked across the *Staten* floor to shake his hand and embrace him.[104] The *Staten*'s Records, confirmed by newspaper accounts, reported that all those present broke out in applause and many were in tears.[105]

Later in the debates that day, Lachmon gave a bittersweet acknowledgement of Arron's moving gesture, but pointed out that there had still not been any response to most of his fundamental points.[106] If the government had hoped to prevent the VHP's efforts formally to amend the draft Constitution, they were mistaken. Announcing that they had reduced their demands to a bare minimum, Lachmon now stated the terms of his amendments. They would:

(1) replace the present mixed electoral system by a national system of proportional representation;
(2) provide for new elections within 6 months of Independence (in the provisional articles at the end of the Constitution);
(3) replace the "equal basis" language of Article 121 regarding the military with its description as "a cross-section of the whole Surinam people";
(4) require a 2/3 vote by Parliament for the nationalization of domestic or foreign enterprises; and
(5) select the Vice-President by the same procedure (i.e., 2/3 vote of Parliament) as the President.[107]

Although *Staten* Chairman Wijntuin periodically broke into the stream of debate to read telegrams of congratulations from individuals and organi-

[103] *Ibid.*, 7de vergadering, November 18, 1975, p. 15.

[104] *Ibid.*, p. 16.

[105] *Ibid. De Ware Tijd* wrote that "future historians will commemorate November 18, 1975, precisely one week before the independence of our land, as the day in which the most historic moment in the history of Surinam took place ...." "It was clear," they added, "that opposition leader Lachmon was deeply moved ...." (*DWT*, November 19, 1975).

[106] Staten van Suriname, *Handelingen 1975-76*, 7de vergadering, November 18, 1975, pp. 32-33.

[107] *Ibid.*, pp. 96-98.

zations for the "breakthrough" that had occurred, there was still no breakthrough to celebrate. When the VHP "dissident" Hindorie finally took the floor to comment on the Constitution, his declaration of neutrality on the VHP's proposed amendments[108] aroused bitter criticism from his fellow VHPers.[109]

Six hours after the second round of debates had ended, the *Staten* reconvened (November 19) for the final round. Arron now, for the first time, detailed his government's opposition to some of the VHP's amendments. The institution of national PR, he argued, would hurt the rural and interior districts, though he would not be opposed to a form of PR being instituted in the 2-seat districts (i.e., Nickerie, Saramacca, and Commewijne).[110] Expropriations, he continued, should take place under the more general terms of Article 15, guaranteeing property rights and fair compensation for dispossession. To write a specific provision regarding the nationalization of foreign or domestic enterprises might actually alarm those whom it was seeking to assure.[111] Regarding Lachmon's other proposals (and the PNR's still-unanswered demand for recognition of the right to strike), Arron requested a chance for talks during the morning recess. Another issue clarified at this time, by Minister Hoost, was the status of the old Bush Negro treaties.[112] They would no longer be valid, he declared, as they restricted both the Bush Negroes' and other Surinamers' movements. As the government had long ago ceased to restrict the movement of Bush Negroes *out* of their protected areas, it would not be in the Bush Negroes' interest to have the treaties enforced. Moreover, most of their traditional rights would be protected under the more general terms of the new Constitution's fundamental rights.[113]

At mid-morning, the *Staten* recessed to permit talks between Arron and Lachmon (as well as between Arron and the union leaders). When the recess ended, it was clear that the breakthrough had indeed occurred. Arron and

108 *Ibid.*, pp. 118-119.

109 *Ibid.*, pp. 130-134. At one point, when R. Sardjoe (VHP) denounced the "strange behavior" of the "crown prince," Minister Bruma (PNR) of Economic Affairs asked him what and whom he meant. Sardjoe answered that "until a short while ago" Hindorie had been the "VHP's crown prince," but now it was clear that he was the "crown prince of the PNR." (p. 133).

110 *Ibid.*, 8ste vergadering, November 19, 1975, p. 5.

111 *Ibid.*, pp. 14-15.

112 This issue, raised in the Dutch parliamentary debates by J. Gadden (PBP member of the VHP-bloc) was brought up again in the Constitution debates (*ibid.*, 6de vergadering, pp. 186-187, and 7de vergadering, pp. 120-127). For a discussion of the treaties and political relations between the Bush Negro tribes and national government, see J. D. Lenoir "Surinam National Development and Maroon Cultural Autonomy," paper presented to the Caribbean Studies Association meeting, San Juan, Puerto Rico, January 8-11, 1975.

113 Staten van Suriname, *Handelingen 1975-76*, 8ste vergadering, pp. 36-37.

Lachmon had each given up ground. Regarding the institution of national PR, Lachmon admitted that a careful study was needed before the problems of local and national representation could be reconciled. He was satisfied with Arron's promise to establish a study commission to this effect.[114]

Although the promise of new elections would not be written into the provisional articles, Arron had also promised that they would be held "within a reasonably short period." Now Lachmon asked him specifically what this meant. Arron answered that, although the various party organs of both the government and opposition would have to be consulted, the elections would be held "between now and not later than the coming eight months."[115]

Regarding the military's composition and use, Lachmon announced that the government had agreed to add the following to its interpretation (*Memorie van Toelichting*) of the "equal basis" clause in Article 121:

> the armed forces shall have that structure and composition which represents a cross-section of the total Surinam people and ... [it] may never be used as a power device by any group to impede its democratic functioning.[116]

The remaining two issues raised by Lachmon were resolved in a trade-off between the two leaders. Arron accepted the demand for parliamentary election of the Vice-President, while Lachmon surrendered the issue of 2/3 approval for acts of expropriation.[117] Finally, Arron announced acceptance by the government of the "right to strike" (which became Article 8, Section 2), but accompanied it with a *Memorie van Toelichting* restricting it to a measure of "last resort" after all other channels of labor negotiation and mediation had been exhausted.[118]

With Lachmon's withdrawal of his five amendments, the way was clear for unanimous approval of the Constitution, burying the issue of the old *Staatsregeling*'s status. Before the voting, both Hindorie and Mrs. Liesdek-Clarke gave short, emotional speeches praising their respective leaders (Lachmon and Arron) for their reconciliation, and Mrs. Liesdek-Clarke added that

> when they are older, my children will read in the history books that their mother has fought for integration and nearly lost her life in the process. [But now] if my party leader needs me and calls, I will be there .... It's up to him. God be with our beloved Surinam.[119]

[114] *Ibid.*, p. 45.
[115] *Ibid.*, p. 44.
[116] *Ibid.*, p. 45.
[117] *Ibid.*, p. 46.
[118] *Ibid.*, p. 47.
[119] *Ibid.*, p. 50.

The Constitution was then passed unanimously, with Lachmon calling it "as good a constitution as that of many democratic states."[120]

In the remaining few days, the *Staten* quickly passed the remaining bills on its agenda – voiding the Kingdom Statute for Surinam, and establishing the armed forces, nationality law, and new flag.[121] All were approved unanimously, amid a spirit of growing camaraderie (and exhaustion).[122]

Finally, at midnight, November 25, the Dutch and old Surinam flags were lowered, and Independence became a reality with the hoisting of the new. The next morning, before a host of visiting dignitaries (including Crown Princess Beatrix and Minister-President Den Uyl), the members of the *Staten* – now Parliament – of Surinam met once again to install Governor J. H. E. Ferrier as President and to formally proclaim the Republic of Surinam an independent state.

[120] *Ibid.*, pp. 52, 53.

[121] Several VHPers abstained from voting on the nationality law, despite provisions offered that would automatically grant Surinamership to those remaining "stateless" Javanese and Hindustanis (*ibid.*, 11de vergadering, November 20, 1975, p. 12). Regarding the NPK's party colors represented in the new flag, the spirit of *verzoening* was such that none of the opposition expressed objections. J. H. Adhin (VHP) emphasized that the red in the central stripe of the flag was "4 parts bright orange" (the color of the VHP) and "six parts carmen red" (the PNR's color), symbolizing, respectively, "renewal" and "productive love." (*Ibid.*, 12de vergadering, November 21, 1975, p. 9). All were apparently agreed that the single yellow star, symbolizing unity (the star) and sacrifice (yellow), were an improvement over the separate stars of the previous flag, with colors that stood for the separate ethnic groups.

[122] *Ibid.*, 9de vergadering, November 19, p. 8; 10de vergadering, November 20, pp. 82, 84; 11de vergadering, November 20, p. 27; and 12de vergadering, November 21, 1975, p. 13.

CHAPTER EIGHT

CONCLUSION

> While conflict itself has a propensity to force a dissolution, the *resolution* of conflict is an essential mechanism of integration. The whole experience of jointly looking for a way out of a crisis, of seeing your own mutual hostility subside to a level of mutual tolerance, of being intensely conscious of each other's positions and yet sensing the need to bridge the gulf – these are experiences which, over a period of time, should help two groups of people move forward into a relationship of deeper integration.
>
> Ali Mazrui*

Despite the fact that most non-Latin Caribbean societies are ethnically plural, few have suffered the severe communal bloodshed and/or lapse into authoritarian rule that has accompanied economic and political development elsewhere in the Third World. Surinam, I would argue, is second to none in the Caribean for bearing the strains of development without severe turbulence. Yet, its historical experience under self-government has revealed many features shared by other polities of this type. In this concluding analysis, we shall examine some of the propositions regarding the politics of ethnic pluralism and explore the conditions that have kept and, hopefully, shall keep Surinam's society essentially stable and accommodative.

I. THE PLURAL SOCIETY AND ETHNIC MOBILIZATION

"Pluralism," writes Pierre van den Berghe, "refers to a property, or set of properties, of societies wherein several distinct social and/or cultural groups coexist within the boundaries of a single polity and share a common economic system that makes them interdependent, yet maintain a greater or lesser de-

* "Pluralism and National Integration," in Leo Kuper and M. G. Smith, eds., *Pluralism in Africa* (Berkeley: University of California, 1971), p. 335.

gree of autonomy and a set of discrete institutional structures in other spheres of social life, notably the familial, recreational, and religious."[1] If ethnic pluralism is only one of many properties a society may have, how is it that this, rather than economic or social stratification, should become the organizing focus of politics? In fact, it need not be. As Crawford Young points out, the Indo-American states of Mexico, Guatemala and the South American Andes reveal cases where class identification has greater political salience than ethnicity.[2] The differentiating feature between these and other plural societies in Young's opinion is the Spanish destruction of a major institutional structure (i.e., Indian religion) essential to nourish and fortify the separate Indian identity.[3] The cross-cutting ties of Latin American Indians and mestizos to Catholicism, has rendered culture less viable than class as a focus for affirmative mobilization in these areas.

In many other societies, however, the presence of a full range of institutional structures to differentiate and nourish ethnic identities has allowed them to take the appearance of corporate groups.[4] Nevertheless, it is improper to treat such entities as if they have a "primordial," ascriptive power over their members.[5] As Young points out, the discovery of ethnicity as an issue and a resource for group mobilization generally *follows*, rather than *precedes*, "such social change processes as urbanization, the revolution in communications, and spread of modern education."[6] Clearly, the possibility exists that individuals benefitting from these processes may react unpredictably to the mobilization efforts undertaken by others of the same ethnic group. Nevertheless, as competition develops over the benefits made available by technological change, the most successful political entrepreneurs will be those to cultivate an instinct of protective *territoriality* with regards to the

[1] Pierre L. van den Berghe, "Pluralism," in J. J. Honigmann, ed., *Handbook of Social and Cultural Anthropology* (Chicago: Rand McNally, 1973), p. 961.

[2] Crawford Young, *The Politics of Cultural Pluralism* (Madison: University of Wisconsin, 1976), Ch. 11; see also Edward Dew, *Politics in the Altiplano: The Dynamics of Change in Rural Peru* (Austin: University of Texas, 1969), Ch. 4.

[3] Young, *op. cit.*, pp. 435, 456-59.

[4] For a treatment of the "corporate" character of ethnic groups, see M. G. Smith, "Institutional and Political Conditions of Pluralism," in Leo Kuper and M. G. Smith, eds., *Pluralism in Africa* (Berkely: University of California, 1971), pp. 35-53. For diverging views on the subjective vs. objective qualities of ethnicity, see Frederik Barth, "Introduction," in Barth, ed., *Ethnic Groups and Boundaries: The Social Organization of Cultural Difference* (Boston: Little Brown, 1969), pp. 9-38; and Leo A. Despres, "Toward a Theory of Ethnic Phenomena," in Despres, ed., *Ethnicity and Resource Competition in Plural Societies* (The Hague: Mouton, 1975), pp. 187-207.

[5] Young, *op. cit.*, pp. 23, 34-43.

[6] *Ibid.*, p. 65.

cultural institutions of the group, articulating an identity that differentiates "we" from "they," and luring – if not forcing – others to accept and commit themselves to these dichotomous categories.

Although Surinam is a fairly complex example of a plural society, it provides a clear confirmation of these principles. In the restricted political system of the post-Abolition period, crosscutting ties binding all Creoles to the whites' religious institutions tended to make conflict oriented more to class than ethnicity – as in the Andes. But as colonial policy regarding assimilation was reversed in the 1930s, intra-Creole conflict was temporarily smothered by common, if unorganized, resistance to the Dutch authorities and their Asian clients. The "we" of *Unie Suriname* purported to be "all Surinamers" and "they" were the Dutch. But in actuality only a few Asians joined it.

Granted, the Creole professional elite of the 1930s permitted some Asians to enter its ranks. Many of these were Christians, by virtue of the restricted educational opportunities at this time, and many married across ethnic lines, because of the absence of appropriately educated mates from their own group. These cross-cutting ties of religion, marriage, and/or patron-client indebtedness gave a certain cosmopolitan character to Surinam's society in the 1940s, and made *Unie Suriname*'s program seem legitimate and hopeful. But, as Cynthia Enloe points out, "[n]arrowly based integration among elites crumbles when change penetrates more deeply into all groups."[7] The economic consequences of the Second World War vastly broadened the opportunities of Hindustanis for education and social mobility, and the prospect of self-government and universal suffrage awakened new possibilities – both positive and threatening. "Although," as Young points out, "intensity of identity of individuals with cultural segments varies widely, in moments of communal threat the group pressures escalate and strongly constrain individuals to align their overt behavior with the interests of the cultural collectivity."[8] The arrival of self-government and establishment of the terms of suffrage (determining who would govern) were clearly seen by all groups in Surinam as such "moments of communal threat."

As political parties came into being, their definitions of in- and out-groups varied experimentally, undergoing sharp reduction from their initial broad appeals. The *Moeslim Partij* and *Hindostans-Javaanse Politieke Partij* both attempted to speak for the Javanese as well as their own Hindustani cores –

[7] Cynthia Enloe, *Ethnic Conflict and Political Development* (Boston: Little Brown, 1973), p. 163.

[8] Young, *op. cit.*, p. 162.

but with minimal results in terms of Javanese recruitment. The organization of the more homogeneously Javanese KTPI (albeit with the help of a Hindustani Moslem) finally led Hindustanis to amalgamate into the multi-religious, but exclusively Hindustani, VHP.

Among Creoles, the PSV, founded by Catholics, broadly defined "we" as all God-fearing Surinamers, and "they" as the Creole Protestant elite (identified with *Unie Suriname* and the NPS) that sought to keep suffrage restricted. As the PSV's operational "we" narrowed to its Catholic (and largely Creole) base, a neutral category emerged in its field of vision, occupied by other parties sharing its common enemy. Together, the PSV, H-JPP, and MP campaigned for universal suffrage in Surinam's first successful multi-ethnic alliance.

The NPS, striving for its own broad base, at first defined its membership exclusively in terms of its enemies – the Dutch and the Catholics – both conceived as anti-nationalistic and/or ultramontane (or really, ultramar). The appeal of Surinamese nationalism implicit in the name "*Nationale Partij Suriname*" did much to counter the PSV's charges of elitism, at least among Creole Protestants. But note: intra-Creole conflict, largely a class/color-line affair between 1890 and 1933, had now shifted to mirror the religious *verzuiling* (pillarization) of the Netherlands.[9] The PSV may not have intended this, building its initial organization on the vigorous labor unionizing of Father Weidmann and new social ethic of Roman Catholicism. But both the ethnically neutral ideologies of nationalism and working-class mobilization that the NPS and PSV championed were obscured by the ethnic (and denominational) following each party acquired.

The same may be said of subsequent efforts to break through Surinam's ethnic *verzuiling*. Eddy Bruma's radical PNR in the 1960s, and the Communist *Demokratische Volksfront* in 1973, tried valiantly to identify themselves as ethnically neutral, only to alienate many in their target audiences by unintended cues of ethnicity. Despite the possible validity of their analyses of Surinam's problems, the Creole leaders of these parties could not establish a viable new identity by which other ethnics could join them in large numbers; and Creoles, accustomed to the patron-client services which their avowedly ethnic parties could offer, also shunned this new class identity as being too risky.

Thus, Surinam's political tradition has been firmly based upon ethnic parties. Ideology – for better or worse – has been relegated to a relatively minor role in differentiating the programs of the NPS, VHP, PNP, AG, KTPI, SRI,

[9] See Arend Lijphart, *The Politics of Accommodation: Pluralism and Democracy in the Netherlands*, second edition (Berkeley: University of California, 1975), Ch. 2.

etc. Those who see the need for basic structural changes in Surinam's political economy view this ethnic fixation and attendant neglect of ideological questions as a kind of "conspiracy" to defend the status quo.[10] Yet, other than identifying suggestive evidence (the relative poverty of the masses, affluence of leaders, and similarities in the latters' politics), they provide no harder proof to indicate the "staging" of Surinam's ethnic politics.

In fact, such a "conspiracy theory" would be very attractive as an explanation for the independence struggle and its dramatic resolution. One might argue that the struggle was staged (with Arron's approval and Lachmon's cooperation) as a means (1) to limit the PNR's influence in the government by focussing attention on Arron, (2) to extract more financial aid from the Netherlands than might otherwise have been possible, (3) to correct the demographic (and electoral) balance by frightening Hindustanis into emigration, and/or (4) to socialize all Surinamers to the dangers of civil war and the need for more cooperative behavior in the future. But, while these may have been results of the conflict, there is no indication that they were ever intended. From top to bottom, both sides seemed thoroughly suspicious of and hostile towards the other's intentions. Moreover, none of the struggle's defectors from either side (nor, for that matter, any of the more radical onlookers) included the charge of "sham" in their criticisms of Arron or Lachmon. One must conclude that the conflict itself was very real – each side's leaders firmly supported, at least initially, by their followers, then just as strongly supported in their sudden reconciliation.

II. MULTIPOLARITY AND CONSOCIATIONAL DEMOCRACY

At the conclusion of their survey of politics in many of the world's plural societies, Alvin Rabushka and Kenneth Shepsle conclude with the question, "is the resolution of intense but conflicting preferences in the plural society manageable in a democratic framework?" Their answer: "We think not."[11] This conclusion seems to fly in the face of their own data, which included the

[10] Such is the contention of G. J. Kruijer, *Suriname, Neokolonie in Rijksverband* (Meppel: Boom, 1973), p. 206. See also Rudi F. Kross, "Onafhankelijkheid in Suriname: Rassen- of Klassenstrijd?" in *Suriname, van Slavernij naar Onafhankelijkheid: De Geschiedenis van Suriname 1674-1974* (Amsterdam: Stichting ter Bevordering van de Studie der Geschiedenis in Nederland, 1975), pp. 113-158; and Henk Herrenberg, "De Surinaamse Socialistische Unie," in *De Gids* 113, no. 9 (1970), p. 324.

[11] Alvin Rabushka and Kenneth A. Shepsle, *Politics in Plural Societies: A Theory of Democratic Instability* (Columbus: Charles E. Merrill, 1972), p. 217.

cases of Belgium, Switzerland, Trinidad and Malaysia, as well as Surinam.[12] Despite their evidence of the breakdown of democracy in still other plural societies, as well as continued ethnic conflict in some of the above-named lands, their sweeping pessimism is uncalled for.

Belgium, Switzerland, and Malaysia all illustrate a commitment to "consociational democracy," a normative model for politics defined by Arend Lijphart as "government by elite cartel designed to turn a democracy with a fragmented political culture into a stable democracy."[13] This model provides a useful framework for the analysis of Surinam's modern political development, although the model of majority domination, illustrated by Trinidad, may also be relevant to the most recent events there.

In his most recent formulation of the model, Lijphart lists four basic elements:

(1) Government by a grand coalition of the political leaders of all significant segments of the plural society....
(2) The minority veto, or... "concurrent majority" rule.
(3) Proportionality as the basic standard of political representation, civil service appointments, and allocation of public funds....
(4) Segmental autonomy; a special form of [which]... is federalism.[14]

In some cases, the last of these elements may appear inapplicable (i.e., where settlement of ethnic groups is intermingled rather than regionally clustered), and probably in all cases, dispute is bound to occur over the appropriate extent of proportionality and institutionalization of the minority veto. Nevertheless, as a normative set of goals for plural societies desirous of establishing or maintaining democratic rule, these constitute the structural arrangements that should be considered.[15]

[12] Crawford Young also takes the authors to task for failing to consider the case of India (*op. cit.*, pp. 308, 517). Canada's exclusion is also unfortunate.

[13] Arend Lijphart, "Consociational Democracy," *World Politics* 21, no. 2 (January 1969), p. 216.

[14] Lijphart, "Transplanting the Consociational Model to the Third World: The impact of the Colonial Heritage," paper delivered at the ECPR/CPSA workshop on "The Politics of Multi-Cultural Societies," Louvain, April 8-14, 1976. See also his *Democracy in Plural Societies: A Comparative Exploration* (New Haven: Yale University Press, 1977), Ch. 2. Elsewhere, Eric Nordlinger has identified six "conflict-regulating practices" for plural societies which follow the same lines: stable governing coalitions, the principle of proportionality, the mutual veto, purposive depoliticization of certain issues, compromise, and concessions. A seventh technique – federalism – was excluded for being too ambiguous in its results (Eric A. Nordlinger, *Conflict Regulation in Divided Societies* (Cambridge: Harvard University, Center for International Affairs, Occasional Papers, No. 29, January 1972), pp. 21-32). See also Charles Anderson *et. al.*, *Issues of Political Development*, second edition (Englewood Cliffs: Prentice-Hall, 1974), Ch. 5.

[15] In his first elaboration of the model of consociational democracy, Lijphart listed a number of factors which he felt were conducive to its establishment and persistence. These were divided

The most important condition supporting the emergence of consociationalism in Surinam has been the multipolarity of ethnic groups, combined with their almost persistent internal fragmentation. This condition, in the 1960s, virtually dictated the formation of pre- or post-electoral alliances among parties, automatically necessitating some measure of proportionality in services provided to the parties' clienteles as well as their mutual veto over policies. But it is interesting to note that such consociational arrangements took place before the election reforms of the 1960s made them mandatory.

At the beginning of self-government in 1949, the breakup of the NPS over the Lichtveld-Van Ommeren dispute forced both factions to seek alliances with the Asian parties in the *Staten*. By accident of Jagernath Lachmon's loyalty to his law teacher, J. C. de Miranda (now heading the government), the VHP's Hindus allied with the NPS elite, while the Moslems, irritated by Hindu domination in the VHP, joined the "anti-elitists", David Findlay and Johan Pengel. Findlay's subsequent criticism of the Hindus, and the Moslems' failure to find a home in the reconstituted (and "blacker") NPS, made it possible for the Hindus to shift their allegiance to Pengel a few years later, gaining control of the *Staten* after the fall of the De Miranda Cabinet. The Javanese KTPI, which had supported the De Miranda and subsequent governments, did not have enough leverage to offset these shifts, gaining little for their loyalty.

This wan't fully consociational government, as such. Cabinet positions were not shared among alliance partners, and proportionality remained limited because of resources and the practice of appointing non-political Cabinet

into conditions of elite commitment to and performance of cross-ethnic decision-making, and conditions identified with the social system itself. For their part, elites must (1) understand "the perils of political fragmentation," (2) be committed to the maintenance of the system through collaborative decision-making practices, and (3) be able to transcend the system's cleavages in doing so. This can only be done when (4) the elites have "the ability to accommodate the divergent interests and demands of the subcultures." ("Consociational Democracy," *op. cit.*, p. 216). Although Lijphart does not spell out this "ability" in greater detail, it presumably includes a responsive sensitivity to the nature of sub-cultural interests, as well as control over the resources necessary to service these interests.

Among the characteristics of the system itself that contribute to consociationalism, Lijphart has listed the following: (1) the duration of the experiment, (2) the balance of power of contending groups in the system, (3) limits in the range of conflict-laden issues and total load on the decision-making apparatus, (4) segregated settlement of groups with a low volume of transactions that cross group lines, (5) internal political cohesion within the groups, (6) clear articulation of ethnic and other interests in the society, (7) public approval of the "elite cartel" (i.e., consociational) system, and (8) the existence of a common external enemy. (*Ibid.*, pp. 216-222, and Lijphart, "Cultural Diversity and Theories of Political Integration," *The Canadian Journal of Political Science* 4, no. 1 (March 1971), p. 12). For a discussion of these conditions and their application to Surinam, see E. Dew, "Surinam: The Test of Consociationalism," *Plural Societies* 3, no. 3 (Autumn 1972), pp. 35-56.

members. However, political in-fighting among the Creoles led to a steady rise in demand-generation, and this pattern was repeated among Hindustanis and Javanese. As neutral brokers between these groups (and between Surinam and the Netherlands), the Cabinet members' lack of any clear constituency made them vulnerable to attack and repudiation.[16]

By 1955, the idea of politically neutral Cabinets had been abandoned. Yet, despite the possibility of setting up an exclusively Creole government, based on the *Eenheidsfront*'s simple majority of *Staten* seats, one ministry was given to the Hindustani leader of the KTPI, in recognition of that party's additional support. With the VHP and NPS already committed to consociationalism, this appointment provided the new government a chance to demonstrate its own readiness to serve all groups. Cabinets were now political, but they were not to be ethnically biassed.

Subsequently, in the ten years during which the NPS-VHP coalition dominated Surinam's government (1958-1967), an even clearer effort was made to share decision-making power. Although the Creoles were still over-represented in the *Staten* and Cabinet, their sharing of ministries, jobs, and benefits with the Hindustanis (and Javanese, from 1963 to 1967), apparently met with widespread approval. More importantly, there was clearly a minority veto available to the participating parties. This was illustrated in the VHP rejection of the move towards independence in 1961, and the PSV's (and apparently VHP's) rejection of the ORMET contract in 1963. Though precise data on the ethnic pattern of civil service jobs and other benefits awarded to the alliance-partners' followers in this period are not available, leaders of both the NPS and VHP later described each other as liberally using such spoils. The ethnic composition of the civil service in 1964 (Tables 1.7 and 1.8) was presumably a product of this. Similarly, the distribution of lands, agricultural credits, etc., to Hindustani followers of the VHP (facilitated by their control over the Ministry of Agriculture), indicates at least some commitment to proportional resource-sharing.

In the later period (1967-1973), shared decision-making, minority vetoes and proportionality also continued. But in the two governments in this period, large sectors of the population were excluded from the benefits and operation of the system. The abandonment by the NPS of its VHP ally came as a result of the latter's demand for a greater share of Cabinet posts (implying also a demand for a wider range of resources under its control). Thus, the NPS' alliance with the *Actie Groep* must be seen as a *step back* from consociational principles. This alliance obviously came at a cheaper price to the

[16] The "crisis of brokerage" experienced in this and other situations in Surinam's politics is given a schematic outline in my *Politics in the Altiplano* ..., pp. 12-13.

NPS in resource terms. Nevertheless, the *Actie Groep* was accorded a minority veto (by necessity, according to its crucial bloc of votes in the *Staten*). Its terms for the alliance included shelving Pengel's plans for independence as well as the costly Torarica project. The AG's share of new civil service jobs and other benefits was presumably more limited than that obtained by the VHP – both as a result of the fewer ministries it controlled and because of growing budgetary pressures exerted on the government by the Dutch.

Under the VHP-PNP government, the facade of proportionality in decision-making was greater than ever before. Ministerial posts were shared equally by the two allies despite the fact that the VHP-bloc's seats in the *Staten* were more than double those of the PNP-bloc (see Table 6.5). Nevertheless, it is harder to distinguish the operation of a minority veto in this government. The PNP *was* given leeway to pursue policies of industrial and mining development – a traditional Creole concern; but the impression grew throughout this period that Hindustani power in other areas was unchecked, or at least that the PNP ministers were unduly acquiescent, kept in line by the growing threat that the VHP might resume its alliance with the NPS at their expense. As in the previous regime, budgetary restraints kept the opportunities for substantial spoils allocations limited.

More significantly, the exclusion of major ethnic parties from these two last regimes left them unbalanced, and the smaller alliance partners were subjected to heavy attack. The *Actie Groep* succumbed to Hindustani pressures, toppling the NPS government in 1969, then rejoining the VHP. Creole opposition to the VHP-PNP government caused the PNP to become increasingly divided. It was then thoroughly repudiated by the Creoles at the polls in 1973. Bearing these two cases in mind, it would thus seem necessary to amend Lijphart's criteria for consociationalism to require the decision- making participation of the *largest parties* from each major ethnic group, if this model is to be accepted as a legitimate solution to the problems of ethnic pluralism. The opportunistic use of token consociationalism may simply invite the unnecessary hardening of cleavage lines and growing political instability.

Finally, a word must be said about the NPK government of the post-1973 period. Although leaders of the non-Creole *presidia* in the NPS were elected to the *Staten*, giving the government benches a multi-ethnic appearance, the absence of Hindustanis there, together with their exclusion from the Cabinet, makes the NPK an experiment in "anti-consociationalism." Even conceding the point by Suparlan, that the position of the Javanese as coequal government partners is unprecedented,[17] the political costs of Hindustani (as op-

[17] Suparlan, *op. cit.*, pp. 323, 325.

posed to Javanese) exclusion are much higher in Surinam's political system. Conflict-resolution in this configuration, following the pattern of the independence struggle, may only be possible after repeated and wasteful manifestations of power by the opposing groups and *ad hoc* summit negotiations between group leaders.

Nevertheless, the absence of consociationalism (at least between Creole and Hindustani parties) does not preclude the existence of a number of cross-cutting common interests among all ethnic groups: i.e., the commitment to civil liberties, preservation of the economic system, and respect for each other's cultural autonomy. These provide a basis for maintaining Surinam's civic order despite continued ethnic conflict. Selwyn Ryan's study of Trinidad, where a major group (East Indians) is excluded from governing power, illustrates the role such shared values may have in keeping ethnic conflict relatively civil.[18] Ali Mazrui's argument (at the beginning of this chapter) should remind us that political conflict can have an integrative effect in any society. This is all the more true where a deep commitment to democratic principles is present.

III. THE OUTBIDDING PHENOMENON

Despite the special contribution that consociational government can make in a plural society, Rabushka and Shepsle correctly identify the chief source of instability in such a system as "political outbidding":

> First, ambitious politicians not included in the multi-ethnic coalition have incentives to generate demand for communal rather than national issues.... Second, ... communal politicians can defeat candidates of the multi-ethnic coalition, whose positions on the ethnic issue is [sic] ambiguous, only by taking extreme positions.... In short, communally based political entrepreneurs seek to increase the salience of communal issues and then to outbid the ambiguous multi-ethnic coalition.[19]

The bases for outbidding are not only found at the elite level, in the ambition of rival leaders, but at the grass-roots level as well, in what Young calls "the apostasy suspicion – that elites have sacrificed community goals to achieve their own ambitions for political status."[20] As Enloe points out, frequently

[18] Selwyn Ryan, *Race and Nationalism in Trinidad and Tobago* (Toronto: University of Toronto, 1972).

[19] Rabushka and Shepsle, *op. cit.*, p. 83. The term "outbidding" is drawn from Giovanni Sartori, "European Political Parties: The Case of Polarized Pluralism," in Joseph LaPalombara and Myron Weiner, eds., *Political Parties and Political Development* (Princeton: Princeton University, 1966), p. 158.

[20] Young, *op. cit.*, p. 115.

"people in the lowest strata of two mutually hostile communities lose faith in their established leaders and become newly convinced that they are being cheated in any elite-to-elite negotiations."[21] The challenge to consociational democracy, Young concludes, is that "cultural politicians must compromise and bargain with... other groups to obtain material advantage, yet in so doing must not appear to betray their following."[22]

This, indeed, has been the most frequent challenge to stability in Surinam's politics – at least until 1973. The growing distrust and animosity between Creoles and Hindustanis at the grass-roots, measured in the survey research summarized in Chapter Five, strongly encouraged outbidding, while the internal fragmentation of ethnic groups over religious and other cultural matters provided the resources and potential leadership for it. The pattern was already set in the early 1950s by the color-line rivalry and religious disputes in the NPS and VHP, respectively. And the principle that groups *purged* from a major party could recover enough strength subsequently to win power was demonstrated by the *Eenheidsfront* victory over the NPS in 1955. As pointed out in Chapter Five, the leaders of the EF successfully linked the elitist charge that Pengel's group was "unfit" to rule with the allegation that he was controlled by the Hindustanis. Pengel's subsequent return to the *Staten* by the grace of Hindustani votes in 1956 seemed to add strength to this charge. But at the same time, Hindustanis increasingly accused their own leadership in the VHP with "selling out."

Both the *Actie Groep* and Creole nationalists in the NBS and, later, PNR drew strength from the ambiguous behavior of the VHP and NPS leaders regarding "independence" issues in the late 1950s and early 1960s (i.e., the flag, coat of arms, and anthem questions, and the ill-fated change of the Kingdom Statute). At the same time, these new parties spearheaded cultural revival movements that appealed to the younger generation of Hindustanis and Creoles. In response, the VHP and NPS sought to strengthen the trust of their constituencies by actions that increasingly strained their own relationship.

Election rule changes in 1963 and 1966 that sought to increase Hindustani representation while broadening the NPS' base of support (with the addition of Bush Negro districts) only led to new recriminations against the NPS by Creoles, leading to the formation of the PNP. The KTPI, for its part, with little to show for its maneuvering between the dominant parties, fell apart, and a new (less tradition-oriented) party, the SRI, emerged to challenge it.

VHP demands for more Hindustani Cabinet posts and civil service jobs

[21] Enloe, *op. cit.*, pp. 212-213.
[22] Young, *op. cit.*, p. 138.

finally led to the breakdown of the NPS-VHP alliance in 1967. The proliferation of political parties in the *Staten* permitted the NPS (1967-69) and VHP (1969-73) to preserve the facade of consociationalism, but the role of "outbidder" now passed dangerously into the hands of the larger parties excluded from the new coalitions.

Although still more extremist Creole groups, the Black Power Organization and *Krikomaka*, enjoyed little popular following, their message was studied by the Creole parties excluded from the VHP-PNP government. Their coalition (together with the KTPI) was broadly endorsed by the Creole electorate in 1973, while Hindustani and Creole parties identified as potential post-election allies of the NPK and VHP were decisively rejected. Ethnic voting continued to be as strong as ever, but now it had apparently become anti-consociational, as well.

This was not true for everyone, however. The resumption of party fragmentation that occurred during the independence struggle – with defectors leaving *both* the NPK and VHP, shows that at least a few Surinamers were clearly uncomfortable with the results of the 1973 polarization. More important theoretically, these defections (and their critical political impacts) show that the functional consequences of "outbidding" may be positive as well as negative. Those who left their blocs did so denouncing their leaders' intransigence and urging conciliation and compromise. The leaders, "outbid" in terms of losing their effectiveness in the *Staten*, were obliged to obey these demands. While it is impossible to predict the defectors' survival as leaders of new parties following the 1977 elections, it is at least conceivable that the political multipolarity restored to the Staten on the eve of independence (and continuing into mid-1977) may continue into the future.

By narrowly construing the concept of "outbidding," we may lose sight of the many efforts to resolve or transcend ethnic conflict in a plural society. Those that succeed (as the NPS-VHP-PSV alliance did against the Creole-dominated EF in 1958) did so by bidding their ideas against their opponents. Such contests can go either way – the ethnic extremist need not necessarily "outbid" the consociationalist. By expanding the concept of "outbidding" to include its functional, as well as dysfunctional, possibilities, we can save ethnic groups (and plural societies) from an unnecessary determinism.

* * *

What of Surinam's future political stability? Given the serious challenges that lie ahead – generation of new resources, creation of jobs, provision of greater welfare, etc. – it is at least reassuring to have the *precedent* of close, cross-ethnic, political collaboration. Moreover, few issues in the future should have the emotional impact for so large a number that independence had; and, despite hard bargaining and great social tensions to the bitter end, *this* struggle was resolved through political diplomacy of a very high order, leaving as its legacy a document of impressive quality for the regulation of future conflicts.

Clearly, the work of preserving democracy, of cultivating it and making it flower is extremely difficult in a plural society, and Surinam has proven to be no exception to this. Yet, there are certainly grounds for hope. Mocking the furious activities that surrounded the 1973 general strike, the poet Dobru declared that "flowers must not grow today."[23] For nearly three years after Abaisa's death in that strike, the slogan "Abaisa *gowini*" (Abaisa will win) drove Creoles on in their pursuit of independence. But, after the November 1975 embrace of Arron and Lachmon in the *Staten*, and their emotional call for others to follow their example, I heard a new slogan on the streets of Paramaribo – one which expressed hope instead of defiance, with a metaphor that meant both embrace *and* Surinam's flowering vine-tree: "*Abrasa gowini!*"

[23] Robin Ravales (Dobru), *Flowers Must Not Grow Today* (Paramaribo: "Afi-Kofi," 1973), p. 14.

BIBLIOGRAPHY

ABBENHUIS, FR.M.F. "Bonni." In *Emancipatie 1863/1963*, ed., Surinaamse Historische Kring. Paramaribo: Lionarons, 1964.

ADHIN, JAN HANSDEW. *Development Planning in Surinam in Historical Perspective (With Special Reference to the Ten Year Plan)*. Utrecht: H.J. Smits, 1961.

—. "Eenheid in Verscheidenheid." In *Culturele Activiteit in Suriname: Beginselen, Feiten en Problemen*, ed., L. Lichtveld. Paramaribo: Stichting Cultureel Centrum Suriname, 1957.

—, ed. *100 Jaar Suriname: Gedenkboek I.V.M. Een Eeuw Immigratie (1873-5 Juni-1973)*. Paramaribo: Nationale Stichting Hindostaanse Immigratie, 1973.

ALMOND, GABRIEL A. and POWELL, G. BINGHAM. *Comparative Politics: A Developmental Approach*. Boston: Little Brown, 1966.

ALUMINIUM-COMITE. *De Uitbuiting van Suriname*. Nijmegen: SUN, 1970.

AMERSFOORT, J.M.M. VAN. *Immigratie en Minderheidsvorming: Een Analyse van de Nederlandse Situatie, 1945-1973*. Alphen aan den Rijn: Samson, 1974.

—. *Surinamese Immigrants in the Netherlands*. The Hague: Staatsdrukkerij, 1969.

AMIRKHAN, M.S. *Surinaamse Clienten van de Gemeentelijke Sociale Dienst te Amsterdam*. Amsterdam: "Aemstelhorn" Katholieke Sociale Academie, January 1971.

ANDERSON, CHARLES, *et al. Issues of Political Development*. Englewood Cliffs: Prentice Hall, second edition, 1974.

ANDIC, FUAT M. and ANDIC, SUPHAN. "The Economic Background of Surinam." in *The Netherlands, French and British Areas of the Caribbean*, ed., T. Mathews. Rio Piedras: University of Puerto Rico, 1966.

ASSENDERP, ANDRE L. VAN. "Some Aspects of Society in the Netherlands Antilles and Surinam." In *The Caribbean: British, Dutch, French, United States*, ed., A.C. Wilgus. Gainesville: University of Florida Press, 1958.

AZIMULLAH, EVERT. "Lachmon: Kwart Eeuw in de Politiek," *Vrije Stem* (Paramaribo), March 16, 1972.

—, ed. *De Realisering van het Mogelijke: Een Greep uit de Prestatie van de Regering-Sedney*. Paramaribo: Kabinet van de Minister-President, 1973.

—, ed. *Van Brits-Indisch Emigrant tot Burger van Suriname*. 's Gravenhage: Wieringa, 1963.

BAGLEY, CHRISTOPHER. *The Dutch Plural Society: A Comparative Study in Race Relations*. London: Oxford University Press, 1973.

—. "Racialism and Pluralism: A Dimensional Analysis of Forty-Eight Countries," *Race* 13, no. 3 (1972): 347-54.

BAHADOORSINGH, KRISHNA. *Trinidad Electoral Politics: The Persistence of the Race Factor.* London: Institute of Race Relations, 1968.

BARTH, FREDRIK, ed. *Ethnic Groups and Boundaries: The Social Organization of Cultural Difference.* Boston: Little Brown, 1969.

BAYER, A.E. *Surinaamse Arbeiders in Nederland.* Assen: Van Gorcum, 1965.

BENJAMINS, H.D. and SNELLEMAN, JOH. F. eds. *Encyclopaedie van Nederlandsch West-Indië.* 's Gravenhage: Martinus Nijhoff, and Leiden: E.J. Brill, 1914-1917.

BERGHE, PIERRE L. VAN DEN. "Pluralism." In *Handbook of Social and Cultural Anthropology*, ed., J.J. Honigmann. Chicago: Rand McNally, 1973.

—. "Pluralism and the Polity: A Theoretical Exploration." In *Pluralhih in :frica*, eds., Leo Kuper and M.G. Smith. Berkeley: University of California, 1971.

BIERVLIET, W.E., *et al.* "Surinaamse Immigratie: Overheidsbeleid en de Rol van het Sociale Onderzoek," *Beleid en Maatschappij* 2, no. 12 (1975): 337-341.

—. "Surinamers in Nederland: Absorptie of Isolement?" *Internationale Spectator* 28, no. 16 (Sept. 22, 1974): 552-559.

BISWAMITRE, C.R. "Miskenning," *West-Indische Gids* 19 (1937): 176-188.

BLANKENSTEIJN, M. VAN. *Suriname.* Rotterdam: Nijgh and Van Ditmar's, 1923.

BLANSHARD, PAUL. *Democracy and Empire in the Caribbean: A Contemporary Review.* New York: Macmillan, 1947.

BOVENKERK, FRANK. *Emigratie uit Suriname.* Amsterdam: Antropologisch-Sociologisch Centrum, 1975.

—. "Surinamers in Nederland: Uitzicht op Terugkeer?" *Internationale Spectator* 28 no. 16 (Sept. 22, 1974): 560-563.

—. *Terug Naar Suriname?* Amsterdam: Antropologisch-Sociologisch Centrum, 1973.

— and BOVENKERK-TEERINK, L.M. *Surinamers en Antillianen in de Nederlandse Pers.* Amsterdam: Antropologisch-Sociologisch Centrum, 1972.

BRAAMS, S. *Suriname en de Surinamers als Maatschappelijke Vreemdelingen in Nederland.* Den Haag: Kruseman's, 1973.

BRANDSMA, J.K. "Werkgelegenheid in een Plantagemaatschappij," *Beleid en Maatschappij* 2, no. 9 (1975): 232-240.

BREMAN, J.C. "Beleid en Maatschappij in Suriname: De Systematiek van 'Hosselen en Pinaren,'" *Beleid en Maatschappij* 2, no. 9 (1975): 214-225.

BRONS, J.C. *Het Rijksdeel Suriname.* Haarlem: F. Bohn, 1952.

BUISKOOL, J. *Suriname Nu en Straks: Een Sociaal-Economische en Staatkundige Beschouwing.* Amsterdam: W.L. Salm, 1946.

BUSCHKENS, WILLEM F.L. *The Family System of the Paramaribo Creoles.* 's Gravenhage: Martinus Nijhoff, 1974.

BUVE, RAYMOND, T.J. "Governor Johannes Heinsius – The Role of Van Aerssen's Predecessor in the Surinam Indian War of 1678-1680." In *Current Anthropology in the Netherlands*, eds., Peter Kloos and Henri J.M. Claessen. Rotterdam: Nederlandse Sociologische en Antropologische Vereniging, 1975.

CARIBBEAN SCHOLARS CONFERENCE. *Caribbean Studies Special Report 1962.* Rio Piedras: Institute of Caribbean Studies, 1962.

CHIN, H.E. "Welke Economische Ontwikkelingsstrategie voor Onafhankelijke Suriname?" *Beleid en Maatschappij* 2, no. 9 (1975): 241-247.

COMINS, D.W.D. *Note on Emigration from the East Indies to Surinam or Dutch Guiana*. Calcutta: Bengal Secretariat Press, 1892.

COMMONWEALTH CARIBBEAN REGIONAL SECRETARIAT. *From Carifta to Caribbean Community*. Georgetown: Guyana Lithographic Co., 1972.

CONNOR, WALKER. "Nation-Building or Nation-Destroying," *World Politics* 25, no. 3 (April 1972): 319-355.

COX, OLIVER C. "The Question of Pluralism," *Race* 12, no. 4 (April 1971): 385-400.

CRASSWELLER, ROBERT D. *The Caribbean Community: Changing Societies and United States Policy*. New York: Praeger, 1972.

CROSS, MALCOLM. "On Conflict, Race Relations, and the Theory of the Plural Society," *Race* 12, no. 4 (April 1971): 477-494.

DAALDER, HANS. "The Consociational Democracy Theme," *World Politics* 26 (July 1974): 604-621.

—. "On Building Consociational Nations: The Cases of the Netherlands and Switzerland," *International Social Science Journal* 23 (1971): 355-370.

DAHL, ROBERT A. *Polyarchy: Participation and Opposition*. New Haven: Yale University Press, 1971.

DERVELD, F.E.R. "Politics and Surinam Migration." Unpublished paper, University of Groningen, 1976.

DESPRES, LEO A. *Cultural Pluralism and Nationalist Politics in British Guiana*. Chicago: Rand McNally, 1967.

—. "Toward a Theory of Ethnic Phenomena." In *Ethnicity and Resource Competition in Plural Societies*, ed., Leo A. Despres. The Hague: Mouton, 1975.

—, ed. *Ethnicity and Resource Competition in Plural Societies*. The Hague: Mouton, 1975.

Developments Towards Self-Government in the Caribbean. The Hague: W. van Hoeve, 1955.

DEW, ANKE VAN DIJK. *Fertility and Culture Among Hindus in Surinam*. New Haven: Yale University Department of Epidemiology and Public Health, Master's Thesis, 1975.

DEW, EDWARD. "Anticonsociationalism and Independence in Surinam," *Boletín de Estudios Latinoamericanos y del Caribe* 21 (December 1976): 3-15.

—. "De Beheersing van Raciale en Culturele Polarisatie in een Onafhankelijk Suriname," *Beleid en Maatschappij* 2, no. 9 (1975): 226-231.

—. "The Draining of Surinam," *Caribbean Review* 5, no. 4 (October-December 1973): 8-15.

—. *Politics in the Altiplano: The Dynamics of Change in Rural Peru*. Austin: University of Texas Press, 1969.

—. "Surinam – The Struggle for Ethnic Balance and Identity," *Plural Societies* 5, no. 3 (Autumn 1974): 3-17. Published in abridged form as "Elections Surinam Style," *Caribbean Review* 6, no. 2 (April-June 1974): 20-26.

—. "Surinam: The Test of Consociationalism," *Plural Societies* 3, no. 4 (Autumn 1972): 35-56.

—. "Surinam's Independence: Zero-Sum or Negative Sum?" Paper presented to the Second Annual Conference of the Caribbean Studies Association, St. Lucia, January 9, 1976.

—. "Testing Elite Perceptions of Deprivation and Satisfaction in a Culturally Plural Society," *Comparative Politics* 6, no. 2 (January 1974): 271-285.

DISHMAN, ROBERT B. "Cultural Pluralism and Bureaucratic Neutrality in the British Caribbean." Paper given at the Annual Meeting of the American Political Science Association, Chicago, August 29-September 2, 1974.

DODGE, PETER. "Ethnic Fragmentation and Politics: The Case of Surinam," *Political Science Quarterly* 81 (December 1966): 593-601.

DOELWIJT, THEA, *et al. De Vlucht: Suriname-Holland, Holland-Suriname*. Paramaribo: H. v.d. Boomen, 1968.

DUNN, JAMES A. "'Consociational Democracy' and Language Conflict," *Comparative Political Studies* 5, no. 1 (April 1972): 3-39.

DUSSELDORP, D.B.W.M. VAN. "Een Classificatie van de Occupatievormen in Suriname," *Tijdschrift v.h. Koninklijk Nederlands Aardrijkskundig Genootschap* 79, no. 2 (April 1962): 128-147.

—. "Mobiliteit en Ontwikkeling van Suriname," *Bijdragen tot de Taal-, Land- en Volkenkunde* 118, no. 1 (1963): 1855.

EISENSTADT, S.N. *The Absorption of Immigrants*. Glencoe: Free Press, 1957.

ELST, DIRK VAN DER. *The Bush Negro Tribes of Surinam, South America: A Synthesis*. Evanston: Northwestern University, Doctoral Dissertation, 1971.

EMMER, PIETER CORNELIS. *Engeland, Nederland, Afrika en de Slavenhandel in de Negentiende Eeuw*. Leiden: E.J. Brill, 1974.

ENLOE, CYNTHIA H. "Civilian Control of the Military – Implications in the Plural Societies of Guyana and Malaysia." Paper presented at the Interuniversity Seminar on Armed Forces and Society. State University of New York, Buffalo, October 18-19, 1974.

—. *Ethnic Conflict and Political Development*. Boston: Little Brown, 1973.

ESSED, FRANK. *Analyse Bij Commentaar*. Paramaribo: D.A.G., 1961.

—. *Een Volk op Weg Naar Zelfstandigheid*. Paramaribo: Stichting Planbureau Suriname, 1973.

—. *Frank en Vrij: Voor en Tegen van de NPS*. Amsterdam: Rotaprint, 1966.

FERRIER, JOHAN H.E. *De Surinaamse Samenleving als Sociaal-Paedagogische Opgave*. Groningen: J.B. Wolters, 1950.

FINDLAY, D.G.A., ed. *Het Politiek Complot van Killinger c.s. in Suriname*. Paramaribo: De West, n.d.

FOUNDATION FOR THE PROMOTION OF INVESTMENT IN SURINAM. *Doing Business in Surinam*. Baarn: Bosch and Keuning, 1968.

FREELAND LEAGUE. *Rapport over de Mogelijkheid van Kolonisatie van Joden in Suriname*. Paramaribo: Afdeling Suriname van de Freeland League, 1948.

FURNIVALL, J. S. *Colonial Policy and Practice: A Comparative Study of Burma and Netherlands India*. New York: New York University Press, 1956.

—. *Netherlands India: A Study of Plural Economy*. Cambridge: University Press, 1944.

—. "Some Problems of Tropical Economy." In *Fabian Colonial Essays*, ed., Rita Hinden. London: George Allen and Unwin, 1945.

GASTMANN, ALBERT LODEWIJK. *The Place of Surinam and the Netherlands Antilles in the Political and Constitutional Structure of the Kingdom of the Netherlands*. New York: Columbia University, Doctoral Dissertation, 1964.

—. *The Politics of Surinam and the Netherlands Antilles*. Rio Piedras: University of Puerto Rico, 1968.

Gedenkboek: 100 Jaar Staten van Suriname, 1866-1966. Paramaribo: Staten van Suriname, December 1966.

GEERTZ, CLIFFORD. "The Integrative Revolution: Primordial Sentiments and Civil Politics in the New States." In *Old Societies and New States: The Quest for Modernity in Asia and Africa*, ed., Clifford Geertz. Glencoe: Free Press, 1963.

GRAAF, H.J. DE, ed. *Nederlanders over de Zeëen: 350 Jaar Geschiedenis van Nederland Buitengaats*. Utrecht: W. de Haan, 2nd ed., 1955.

GROOT, SILVIA W. DE. "The Boni-Maroon War 1765-1793, Surinam and French Guyana," *Boletín de Estudios Latinoamericanos y del Caribe* 18 (June 1975): 30-48.

—. *Djuka Society and Social Change: History of an Attempt to Develop a Bush Negro Community in Surinam, 1917-1926*. Assen: Van Gorcum, 1969.

—. *Surinaamse Granmans in Africa*. Utrecht: Spectrum, 1974.

HANDLER, BRUCE. "Surinam," *Atlantic Monthly* 224 (November 1969): 38ff.

HANSEN, HAN and WAGT, GABRI DE. *Wat Doen We in Suriname?* Hilversum: Paul Brand, 1967.

HAUG, MARIE R. "Social and Cultural Pluralism as a Concept in Social System Analysis," *American Journal of Sociology* 73 (1967): 294-304.

HELLINGA, W.G. *Language Problems in Surinam: Dutch as the Language of the Schools*. Amsterdam: North Holland Publishing Co., 1955.

HELMAN, ALBERT. See Lichtveld, Lou.

HERMANS, HANS G. "Constitutional Development of the Netherlands Antilles and Surinam." In *The Caribbean: British, Dutch, French, United States*, ed., A.C. Wilgus. Gainesville: University of Florida Press, 1958.

HERRENBERG, HENK F. *De Reële Onafhankelijkheid voor Suriname*. Paramaribo: Lionarons, 1972.

—. "De Surinaamse Socialistische Unie," *De Gids* 133, no. 9 (1970): 322-324.

HERSKOVITS, MELVILLE J. *Acculturation: The Study of Culture Contact*. New York: J.J. Augustin, 1938.

— and HERSKOVITS, F.S. *Rebel Destiny: Among the Bush Negroes of Dutch Guiana*. New York: McGraw-Hill, 1934.

— and HERSKOVITS, F.S. *Suriname Folklore*. New York: Columbia University Press, 1936.

HISS, PHILIP HANSON. *Netherlands America: The Dutch Territories in the West*. London: Robert Hale, 1943.

HOETINK, HARMANNUS. *Caribbean Race Relations: A Study of Two Variants*. London: Oxford University Press, 1967.

—. "Change in Prejudice: Some Notes on the Minority Problem, With References to the West Indies and Latin America," *Bijdragen tot de Taal-, Land- en Volkenkunde* 119, no. 1 (1963): 56-75.

—. "Diferencias en Relaciones Raciales entre Curaçao y Surinam," *Revista de Ciencias Sociales* 5 (1961): 490-514.

—. "National Identity, Culture, and Race in the Caribbean." In *Racial Tensions and National Identity*, ed., Ernest Q. Campbell. Nashville: Vanderbilt University Press, 1972.

—. *Slavery and Race Relations in the Americas: An Inquiry Into Their Nature and Nexus*. New York: Harper and Row, 1973.

HOLLANDER, A.N.J. DEN, *et al. De Plurale Samenleving: Begrip Zonder Toekomst?* Meppel: J.A. Boom, 1966.

HOPPE, R. "Het Politieke Systeem van Suriname: Elite-Kartel Demokratie," *Acta Politica* 11, no. 2 (April 1976): 145-77.

HOROWITZ, DONALD L. "Three Dimensions of Ethnic Politics," *World Politics* 23 (January 1971): 232-244.

HUNT, CHESTER L. and WALKER, LEWIS. *Ethnic Dynamics: Patterns of Intergroup Relations in Various Societies.* Homewood: Dorsey Press, 1975.

INFORMA. "*Analyse van een Crisis*": *Suriname Februari 1973.* Paramaribo: Informa, 1973.

ISMAEL, JOSEPH. *De Immigratie van Indonesiërs in Suriname.* Leiden: "Luctor et Emergo," 1949.

JANSEN, P. and JANSEN-VAN NES, D. *Arm Suriname: Land van Onmogelijkheid.* Voorburg: Actuele Informatie, 1974.

JANSEN VAN GALEN, JOHN. "De Triomf van Meester Eddy Bruma," *Haagse Post* (November 29, 1975): 6-10.

JAYAWARDENA, CHANDRA. *Conflict and Solidarity in a Guianese Plantation.* London: Athlone Press, 1963.

JONG, ANDRIES DE. *Suriname Onafhankelijk.* Amsterdam: Nieuw Schrift, 1974.

JONG, C. DE. "The Dutch Peasants in Surinam," *Plural Societies* 5, no. 3 (Autumn 1974): 19-42.

KAHIN, GEORGE MCT. *Nationalism and Revolution in Indonesia.* Ithaca: Cornell University Press, 1962.

KAMER VAN KOOPHANDEL EN FABRIEKEN. *Jaarverslag 1940, 1942, 1943, 1944, 1945.* Paramaribo: J.H. Oliviera, 1941, 1944, 1945, 1946.

KIELSTRA, J.C. "De Economische Mogelijkheden voor Suriname," *Haagsch Maandblad* 4, no. 5 (November 1925): 551-563.

KLERK, C.J.M. DE. *De Immigratie der Hindostanen in Suriname.* Amsterdam: Urbi et Orbi, 1953.

KLOOS, PETER. *The Maroni River Caribs of Surinam.* Assen: Van Gorcum, 1971.

Knipselkrant van het Kabinet voor Surinaamse en Nederlands-Antilliaanse Zaken, 1972-1975.

KOM, ANTON DE. *Wij Slaven van Suriname.* Amsterdam: Contact, 1934.

KROEF, JUSTUS M. VAN DER. "The Indonesian Minority in Surinam," *American Sociological Review* 16 (1951): 672-679.

KROSS, RUDI F. "Onafhankelijkheid in Suriname, Rassen- of Klassenstrijd." In *Suriname van Slavernij Naar Onafhankelijkheid: De Geschiedenis van Suriname 1674-1974.* Amsterdam: Stichting ter Bevordering van de Studie der Geschiedenis in Nederland, 1975.

—. *Rebel op de Valreep: Een Analyse na de Persconferentie v.d. Heer J. Lachmon.* Paramaribo: Biswakon and Biswakon, 1972.

KRUIJER, G.J. *Suriname en Zijn Buren: Landen in Ontwikkeling.* Meppel: J.A. Boom, 1968.

—. *Suriname, Neokolonie in Rijksverband.* Meppel: J.A. Boom, 1973.

KUPER, LEO. "Ethnic and Racial Pluralism: Some Aspects of Polarization and Depluralization." In *Pluralism in Africa*, eds., Leo Kuper and M.G. Smith. Berkeley: University of California Press, 1971.

—. "Plural Societies: Perspectives and Problems." In *Pluralism in Africa*, eds., Leo Kuper and M.G. Smith. Berkeley: University of California Press, 1971.

— and Smith, M.G., eds. *Pluralism in Africa*. Berkeley: University of California Press, 1971.

LAGERBERG, C. and VINGERHOETS, J. "Ontwikkelingssamenwerking met Onafhankelijk Suriname," *Internationale Spectator* 28, no. 16 (September 22, 1974): 529-545 and 559.

LAMUR, H.E. "De Bevolkingsgroei van Suriname 1964-1973," *Internationale Spectator* 28, no. 16 (September 22, 1974): 546-551.

—. *The Demographic Development of Suriname, 1920-1970*. The Hague: Martinus Nijhoff, 1973.

—. "Fertility Decline in Surinam, 1964-1970," *Boletín de Estudios Latinoamericanos y del Caribe* 16 (June 1974): 28-49.

LAND, SIPKE VAN DER. *Ratjetoe: Het Bonte Leven van Suriname*. Kampen: J.H. Kok, n.d.

LENOIR, J.D. "Surinam National Development and Maroon Cultural Autonomy." Paper presented to Annual Meeting of Caribbean Studies Association, San Juan, Puerto Rico, January 8-11, 1975.

LEWIS, OSCAR. "The Culture of Poverty." In *Anthropological Essays*, ed., Oscar Lewis. New York: Random House, 1970.

LICHTVELD, LOU (pseud. Albert Helman), ed. *Cultureel Mozaiek van Suriname: Bijdrage tot onderling begrip*. Zutphen: De Walburg Pers, 1977.

—.*Merchant, Mission and Meditation: The Romance of a Two Hundred Year Old Suriname Company*. Paramaribo: C. Kersten, 1968.

—. *Suriname: A New Nation in South America*. Paramaribo: Radhakishun, 1959.

—. *Zuid-Zuid-West*. Amsterdam: Em. Querido, 1964.

—, ed. *Culturele Activiteit in Suriname: Beginselen, Feiten en Problemen*. Paramaribo: Stichting Cultureel Centrum Suriname, 1957.

LICHTVELD, W.H. "Lou Lichtveld Neemt Afscheid," *El Dorado* 1 (1949): 386-389.

LIER, R.A.J. VAN. "Cultuurconflict in de Heterogene Samenleving," *Sociologisch Jaarboek* 8 (1954): 36-56.

—. *The Development and Nature of Society in the West Indies*. Amsterdam: Koninklijke Vereeniging Indisch Instituut, 1950.

—. "Introduction." In *Narrative of a Five Years' Expedition Against the Revolted Negroes of Surinam in Guiana on the Wild Coast of South America from the Years 1772 to 1777*. by J.G. Stedman Amherst: University of Massachusetts Press, 1972.

—. *Samenleving in een Grensgebied: Een Sociaal-Historische Studie van Suriname*. Revised edition, Deventer: Van Loghum Slaterus, 1971. (Also published as *Frontier Society: A Social Analysis of the History of Surinam*, The Hague: Martinus Nijhoff, 1971.)

—. "Social and Political Conditions in Suriname and the Netherlands Antilles: Introduction." In *Developments Towards Self-Government in the Caribbean*. The Hague: W. van Hoeve, 1955.

—. "Le Suriname et les Antilles Néerlandaises en tant que Sociétés Plurales." In *Pluralisme Ethnique et Culturel dans les Sociétés Intertropicales*. Bruxelles: INCIDI, 1957.

LIJPHART, AREND. "Consociational Democracy," *World Politics* 21 (January 1969): 207-225.

—. "Cultural Diversity and Theories of Political Integration," *Canadian Journal of Political Science* 4, no. 1 (March 1971): 1-14.

—. *Democracy in Plural Societies: A Comparative Exploration*.New Haven: Yale University Press, 1977.

—. "The Northern Ireland Problem: Cases, Theories, and Solutions," *British Journal of Political Science* 5 (1974): 83-106.

—. *The Politics of Accommodation: Pluralism and Democracy in the Netherlands*. Berkeley: University of California Press, 1968, second edition, 1975.

—. "Transplanting the Consociational Model to the Third World: The Impact of the Colonial Heritage." Paper presented at the ECPR/CPSA Workshop on "The Politics of Multi-Cultural Societies," Louvain, April 8-14, 1976.

—. "Typologies of Democratic Systems," *Comparative Political Studies*, 1 (April 1968): 3-44.

LOGEMANN, J.H.A. "The Constitutional Status of the Netherlands Caribbean Territories." In *Developments Towards Self-Government in the Caribbean*. The Hague: W. van Hoeven, 1955.

LOWENTHAL, DAVID. "Post-Emancipation Race Relations: Some Caribbean and American Perspectives," *Journal of Inter-American Studies and World Affairs* 13, nos. 3 and 4 (July-October, 1971): 367-377.

—. *West Indian Societies*. London: Oxford University Press, 1972.

LYMAN, STANFORD M. and DOUGLASS, WILLIAM A. "Ethnicity: Strategies of Collective and Individual Impression Management," *Social Research* 40 (1973): 344-365.

MATHEWS, THOMAS. "The Caribbean Kaleidoscope," *Current History* (January 1965): 32-39.

—. "The Political Conditions in Surinam." In *The Netherlands, French and British Areas of the Caribbean*, ed. Thomas Mathews. Rio Piedras: Institute of Caribbean Studies, University of Puerto Rico, 1966.

—. "The Three Guianas," *Current History* (December 1966): 333-336.

—. "What Ever Happened to Polarization in the Caribbean?" *Caribbean Review* 5, no. 1 (January-March 1973): 26-30.

MAZRUI, ALI A. "Pluralism and National Integration." In *Pluralism in Africa*, eds. Leo Kuper and M.G. Smith. Berkeley: University of California Press, 1971.

MENKMAN, W.R. "Nederland in Amerika en West Afrika." In *Nederlanders over de Zeëen: 350 Jaar Geschiedenis van Nederland Buitengaats*, ed., H.J. de Graaf. Utrecht: W. de Haan, 1955.

MEYER, H. "Suriname en het Wereldbevolkingsvraagstuk," *Nieuwe West-Indische Gids* 41 (1961): 38-45.

MITRASING, F.E.M. *The Border-Conflict Between Surinam and Guiana: A Legal Research*. Paramaribo: C. Kersten, 1975.

—. *Proeve van een Grondwet voor Suriname*. Paramaribo: D.A.G., 1974.

—. *Tien Jaar Suriname – Van Afhankelijkheid tot Gelijkgerechtigdheid: Bijdrage tot de Kennis van de Staatkundige Ontwikkeling van Suriname van 1945-1955*. Leiden: "Luctor et Emergo," 1959.

MITRASING-SITALSING, S.A.S. "Sophie Redmond 1907-1955." In *Emancipatie 1863/1963*, ed., Surinaamse Historische Kring. Paramaribo: Lionarons, 1964.

MORSE, RICHARD. "Report on the Netherlands Caribbean." In *Caribbean Reports and Papers*, ed., Richard Morse. Rio Piedras: University of Puerto Rico, 1959.

MULTATULI (pseudonym of E. Douwes Dekker). *Max Havelaar: Or, the Coffee Auctions of the Dutch Trading Company*. New York: British Book Center, 1967.

NATIONAAL BERAAD. *Memorandum van het Nationaal Beraad*. Paramaribo: n.p., 1975.

NELEMANS, B. *De Arme Landen Latijns America: Aardrijkskunde voor het Voortgezet Onderwijs in Suriname*. Paramaribo: El Dorado, 1973.

THE NETHERLANDS. Adviescommissie Inzake Migratie van Surinamers en Antillianen. *Rapport*. The Hague: October 17, 1972.

—. Centraal Bureau voor de Statistiek. *Buitenlandse Migratie van Nederland met Suriname en de Nederlandse Antillen, 1946-1972*. The Hague: Staatsuitgeverij, 1974.

—. —. "Buitenlandse Migratie van Nederland met Suriname en de Nederlandse Antillen, 1965-1974," *Maandstatistiek van Bevolking en Volksgezondheid*, August 1975.

—. Koninkrijkscommissie ter Voorbereiding van Alternatieven voor de Huidige Staatkundige Verhouding tussen Nederland, Suriname en de Nederlandse Antillen. *Rapport ter Voorbereiding van de Onafhankelijkheid van Suriname*. The Hague: October 1974.

—. *Het Statuut voor het Koninkrijk der Nederlanden*. The Hague: 1954.

—. Tweede Kamer der Staten-Generaal. *Handelingen, Zitting 1975-1976, Beeindiging van de Statutaire Band met Suriname*. 10de, 11de en 12de vergadering (October 21-23, 1975).

NICHOLLS, DAVID G. "East Indians and Black Power in Trinidad," *Race* 12, no. 4 (April 1971): 443-459.

NORDLINGER, ERIC A. *Conflict Regulation in Divided Societies*. Cambridge: Harvard University Press, 1972.

NURMOHAMED, M.S.A. *De Aziatische Huwelijkswetgeving*. Paramaribo: Reprocentrum, 1971.

OCHSE, J.J. "Economic Factors in the Netherlands Antilles and Surinam." In *The Caribbean: British, Dutch, French, United States*, ed., A.C. Wilgus. Gainesville: University of Florida Press, 1958.

OEDAYRAJSINGH VARMA, C.C.S. "Een Sociometrisch Onderzoek Naar de Etnische Factor bij de Keuze van Klasgenoten op Enkele Scholen in Suriname," *Sociologische Gids* 15, no. 6 (November/December 1968): 367-378.

OMMEREN, H. VAN and JONG, C. DE. "Julius E. Muller, 1846-1902, Om het Goud van Suriname." In *Emancipatie 1863/1963*, ed., Surinaamse Historische Kring. Paramaribo: Lionarons, 1964.

OOFT, C.D. *Aanloop voor een Rechtsvergelijkende Studie van het Nederlands en het Surinaams Staatsrecht*. Alphen aan de Rijn: N. Samson, 1966.

—. "Drie Eeuwen Vertegenwoordigend Stelsel in Suriname." In *Gedenkboek: 100 Jaar Staten van Suriname, 1866-1966*. Paramaribo: Staten van Suriname, December 1966.

—. *Kort Begrip v.d. Staatsinrichting v. Suriname*. Paramaribo: Leo Victor, 4th ed., 1973.

—. *Ontwikkeling van het Constitutionele Recht van Suriname*. Assen: Van Gorcum, 1972.

—. *De Staten: Geschiedenis, Rechtskarakter en Samenstelling*. Paramaribo: De Ware Tijd, 1963.

ORMSKIRK, FRED W. *Over Zelfstandigheid en Integratie*. Paramaribo: Regeringsvoorlichtingsdients Suriname, 1974.

—. *Twintig Jaren N.P.S.: "Groei Temidden van Beroering."* Paramaribo: n.p., 1966.

OUDSCHANS DENTZ, FRED. *Geschiedkundige Aanteekeningen over Suriname en Paramaribo*. Paramaribo: De West, second edition, 1972.

PAËRL, ERIC. *Klassenstrijd in Suriname*. Nijmegen: SUN, 1972.

PALMIER, LESLIE H. *Indonesia and the Dutch*. London: Oxford University Press, 1962.

PANDAY, DHANPATI. *The Arya Samaj and Indian Nationalism (1875-1920)*. New Delhi: S. Chand, 1972.

PANDAY, R.M.N. *Agriculture in Surinam 1650-1950: An Enquiry into the Causes of Its Decline.* Amsterdam: H.J. Paris, 1959.

PIERCE, BENJAMIN EDWARD. *Kinship and Residence among the Urban Nengre of Surinam: A Re-evaluation of Concepts and Theories of the Afro-American Family.* New Orleans: Tulane University, Doctoral Dissertation, 1971.

—. "Status Competition and Personal Networks: Informal Social Organisation among the Nengre of Paramaribo," *Man* 8, no. 4 (December 1973): 580-591.

POLL, WILLEM VAN DE. *Suriname.* Paramaribo: Varekamp, 1959.

POST, A.H.C., *et al. De Sittewasie: De Velmekstaking en haar Konsekwenties.* Paramaribo: n.p., 1969.

PREMDAS, RALPH R. *Ethnic Politics in Guyana.* Manuscript, 1974.

PRICE, RICHARD. *Saramaka Social Structure: Analysis of a Maroon Society in Surinam.* Rio Piedras: University of Puerto Rico, 1975.

—, ed. *Maroon Societies: Rebel Slave Communities in the Americas.* New York: Doubleday, 1973.

PRINS, J. "De Islam in Suriname: Een Orientatie," *Nieuwe West-Indische Gids* 41 (1961): 14-37.

PRINSON, N.J., *et al. Nederland en de Zelfstandigheid van Suriname en de Nederlandse Antillen: Een Standpuntbepaling Voorbereid door een Werkgroep van D'66, de PPR en de PvdA.* Amsterdam: 1973.

QUINTUS BOSZ, AKSEL JOHANN. *Drie Eeuwen Grond Politiek in Suriname.* Groningen: Rijksuniversiteit Groningen, 1954.

—. "Misvattingen Omtrent de Staatkundige Ontwikkeling van Suriname," *Nieuwe West-Indische Gids* 40 (1960): 3-16.

—. "De Ontwikkeling van de Rechtspositie van de Vroegere Plantageslaven in Suriname." In *Emancipatie 1863/1963*, ed., Surinaamse Historische Kring. Paramaribo: Lionarons, 1964.

RABUSHKA, ALVIN and SHEPSLE, KENNETH A. *Politics in Plural Societies: A Theory of Democratic Instability.* Columbus: Charles E. Merrill, 1972.

RAE, DOUGLAS. *The Political Consequences of Electoral Laws.* New Haven: Yale University Press, revised edition, 1971.

— and TAYLOR, MICHAEL. *The Analysis of Political Cleavages.* New Haven: Yale University Press, 1970.

RAVALES, ROBIN (pseud. Dobru). *Wan Monki Fri: Bevrijding en Strijd.* Paramaribo: El Dorado, 1969.

Reflektor (Paramaribo Monthly). 1972-1974.

RENSELAAR, H.C. VAN. "De Houding van de Creoolse Bevolkingsgroep in Suriname ten Opzichte van de Andere Bevolkingsgroepen," *Bijdragen tot de Taal-, Land- en Volkenkunde* 119, no. 1 (1963): 93-105.

—. "Het Sociaal-Economisch Vermogen van de Creolen in Suriname," *Tijdschrift van het Koninklijk Nederlandsch Aardrijkskundig Genootschap* 80, no. 4 (October 1963): 474-481.

— and SPECKMANN, J.D. "Social Research on Surinam and the Netherlands Antilles," *Nieuwe West-Indische Gids* 47, no. 1 (1969): 29-59.

RIJK VAN OMMEREN, H.N. "Harry Johan van Ommeren 1879-1923." In *Emancipatie 1863/1963*, ed., Surinaamse Historische Kring, Paramaribo: Lionarons, 1964.

RUBIN, VERA. "Culture, Politics and Race Relations," *Social and Economic Studies* 11, no. 4 (December 1962): 433-455.

RYAN, SELWYN. *Race and Nationalism in Trinidad and Tobago*. Toronto: University of Toronto Press, 1972.

SAMSON, PH.A. "Kiesvereenigingen in Suriname," *De West-Indische Gids* 28 (1947): 161-174.

—. "Parlementair Geschiedkundige Beschouwing." In *Gedenkboek: 100 Jaar Staten van Suriname, 1866-1966*. Paramaribo: Staten van Suriname, December 1966.

SCHERMERHORN, R.A. *Comparative Ethnic Relations: A Framework for Theory and Research*. New York: Random House, 1970.

SEDOC-DAHLBERG, BETTY NELLY. *Surinaamse Studenten in Nederland: Een Onderzoek Rond de Problematiek van de Toekomstige Intellectuele Kadervorming in Suriname*. Amsterdam: University of Amsterdam, 1971.

SEGAL, AARON. *The Politics of Caribbean Economic Integration*. Rio Piedras: University of Puerto Rico, 1968.

SHILS, EDWARD. "The Integration of Society." In *Center and Periphery: Essays in Microsociology*, ed., Edward Shils. Chicago: University of Chicago, 1975.

SIMONS, R.D. "Dr. Herman Daniel Benjamins 1850-1933." In *Emancipatie 1863/1963*, ed., Surinaamse Historische Kring. Paramaribo: Lionarons, 1964.

SINGH, PAUL. *Guyana: Socialism in a Plural Society*. London: Fabian Society, October 1972.

SLUISDOM, E. "De Best Gesproken Taal in Suriname," *K.N.A.C. Geografisch Tijdschrift* 4, no. 4 (1970): 349-353.

SMIT, A.L.R. *Surinaamse Bauxiet Maskerade*. Paramaribo: n.p., July 13, 1947.

SMITH, M.G. "Ethnic and Cultural Pluralism in the British Caribbean." In *Pluralisme Ethnique et Culturel dans les Sociétés Intertropicales*. Bruxelles: INCIDI, 1957.

—. "Institutional and Political Conditions of Pluralism." In *Pluralism in Africa*, eds., Leo Kuper and M.G. Smith. Berkeley: University of California Press, 1971.

—. "Pluralism in Precolonial African Societies." In *Pluralism in Africa*, eds., Leo Kuper and M.G. Smith. Berkeley: University of California Press, 1971.

—. "Social and Cultural Pluralism," *Annals of the New York Academy of Sciences* 83 (1960): 763-777.

—. "Some Developments in the Analytic Framework of Pluralism." In *Pluralism in Africa*, eds., Leo Kuper and M.G. Smith. Berkeley: University of California Press, 1971.

SMITH, RAYMOND T. "Race and Political Conflict in Guyana," *Race* 12, no. 4 (April 1971): 415-427.

SPECKMANN, J.D. "De Houding van de Hindostaanse Bevolkingsgroep in Suriname ten Opzichte van de Creolen," *Bijdragen tot de Taal-, Land- en Volkenkunde* 119, no. 1 (1963): 76-92.

—. "The Indian Group in the Segmented Society of Surinam," *Caribbean Studies* 3, no. 1 (April 1963): 3-17.

—. *Marriage and Kinship Among the Indians in Surinam*. Assen: Van Gorcum, 1965.

—. "De Plurale Surinaamse Samenleving." In *De Plurale Samenleving: Begrip Zonder Toekomst?*, by A.N.J. den Hollander, *et al.* Meppel: J.A. Boom, 1966.

—. "De Positie van de Hindostaanse Bevolkingsgroep in de Sociale en Ekonomische Struktuur van Suriname," *Tijdschrift van het Koninklijk Nederlandsch Aardrijkskundig Genootschap* 80, no. 4 (October 1963): 459-466.

STEDMAN, J.G. *Narrative of a Five Years' Expedition Against the Revolted Negroes of Surinam in Guiana on the Wild Coast of South America from the Years 1772 to 1777....* Amherst: University of Massachusetts Press, 1972.

SUPARLAN, PARSUDI. *The Javanese in Surinam: Ethnicity in an Ethnically Plural Society.* Urbana: University of Illinois, Doctoral Dissertation, 1976.

Surinaams Bauxiet: Een Beschrijving van de Samenwerking in de Ontwikkeling van een Bodemrijkdom. Paramaribo: Surinaamsche Bauxite Maatschappij, 1955.

SURINAAMSE HISTORISCHE KRING, eds. *Emancipatie 1863/1963: Biografieën.* Paramaribo: Lionarons, 1964.

SURINAAMSE STUDENTEN UNIE, *et al. Imperialisme en Klassenstrijd in Suriname.* Leiden: Surinaamse Studenten Unie, 1974.

"Surinam," *Focus* 21 (September 1970).

SURINAME. Algemeen Bureau voor de Statistiek. *Suriname in Cijfers No. 33, Derde Algemene Volkstelling.* Paramaribo: 1967.

—. —. *Voorlopig Resultaat Vierde Algemene Volkstelling, Suriname in Cijfers No. 60.* Paramaribo: 1973.

—. Economic Information Service. *A Statistic Survey of Surinam.* Paramaribo: 1975.

—. Grondwet Commissie. *Ontwerp-Grondwet van Suriname met Bijbehorende Memorie van Toelichting.* Paramaribo: August 1975.

—. *Grondwet voor de Republiek Suriname.* Paramaribo: Gouvernementsblad van Suriname no. 170, 1975.

—. *Staatsregeling van Suriname.* Paramaribo: 1955.

—. Staten van Suriname. *Handelingen,* Selected meetings, 1933-1934, 1936-1937, 1937-1938, 1938-1939, 1940-1941, 1941-1942, 1955-1956, 1956-1957, 1959-1960, 1975-1976.

—. Stichting Planbureau Suriname. *Eerste Schets van de Ontwikkelingsmogelijkheden van Suriname.* Paramaribo: 1951, two volumes.

Suriname (Paramaribo newspaper). 1945-1958.

Suriname-Bulletin (Amsterdam monthly). 1970-1975.

Suriname van Slavernij Naar Onafhankelijkheid: De Geschiedenis van Suriname 1674-1974. Amsterdam: Stichting ter Bevordering van de Studie der Geschiedenis in Nederland, 1975.

De Surinamer (Paramaribo newspaper). 1936-1937.

SUURHOFF, J.G. "De Vakbeweging in Suriname," *El Dorado* 1 (1949): 251-257.

SYPESTEYN, C.A. VAN. *Afschaffing der Slavernij in de Nederlandsche West-Indische Koloniën, uit Officieële Bronnen Samengesteld.* Amsterdam: 1866.

TEMPEL, C.P. VAN DEN. "Suriname's Positie in de Internationale Politiek," *Beleid en Maatschappij* 2, no. 9 (1975): 248-255.

TEYLINGEN, HENK VAN. *Bedek je Schande: Suriname van Binnen Uit.* Amsterdam: Arbeiderspers, 1972.

TRAA, A. VAN. *Suriname van 1900-1940.* Deventer: Van Hoeve, 1946.

TROUWBORST, A.A. "Ethnicity and Culture." Paper presented at Symposium on Interethnic Relations, Meeting of Society for Applied Anthropology, Amsterdam, March 19-23, 1975.

TRUMAN, DAVID. *The Governmental Process.* New York: Alfred A. Knopf, second edition, 1971.

"*25 Juni*" (Paramaribo newspaper). 1960.

UNITED NATIONS INDUSTRIAL DEVELOPMENT ORGANIZATION. *Final Report: A Survey of Industry and Its Potential in Surinam.* N.P., July 24, 1972.

VAN DYKE, VERNON. "The Individual, the State, and Ethnic Communities in Political Theory," *World Politics* 29, no. 3 (April 1977): 343-69.

VATAN HITKARI PARTIJ. *Onze Politiek.* Paramaribo: El Dorado, 1967.

CORLY VERLOOGHEN (pseudonym of Rudy Bedacht). *De Glinsterende Revolutie: Met een Inleiding over het Revolutionnair Proces in Suriname.* Amsterdam: 1970.

Verslag van de Commissie tot Bestudering van Staatkundige Hervormingen in Suriname. The Hague: Staatsdrukkerij, 1948. Two Volumes.

VERTON, PETER. "Emancipation and Decolonization: The May Revolt and Its Aftermath in Curaçao." Paper presented to the Second Annual Conference of the Caribbean Studies Association, St. Lucia, January 9, 1976.

Volksbode (Paramaribo newspaper). 1969-1972.

VOORHOEVE, JAN and LICHTVELD, URSY M., eds. *Creole Drum: An Anthology of Creole Literature in Surinam.* New Haven: Yale University 1975.

VOORHOEVE, JAN and RENSELAAR, H.C. VAN. "Messianism and Nationalism in Surinam," *Bijdragen tot de Taal-, Land- en Volkenkunde* 118, no. 2 (1962): 193-216.

Vrije Stem (Paramaribo newspaper). 1960-1975.

VROON, L.J. "Voorgeschiedenis, Opzet en Resultaten van het Surinaamse Tienjarenplan," *Nieuwe West-Indische Gids* 43 (1962-1963): 25-74.

WAAL MALEFIJT, ANNEMARIE DE. *The Javanese of Surinam: Segment of a Plural Society.* Assen: Van Gorcum, 1963.

—. "Het Sociaal-Economisch Vermogen van de Javanen in Suriname." *Tijdschrift van het Koninklijk Nederlandsch Aardrijkskundig Genootschap* 80, no. 4 (October 1963): 467-473.

WALLE, J. VAN DE. *Een Oog Boven Paramaribo: Herinneringen.* Amsterdam: Em. Querido, 1975.

—. *Suriname (Rapport Uitgebracht door het Hoofd van den Gouvernements Pers Dienst in Suriname).* Paramaribo: July 15, 1945.

— and WIT, H. DE, eds. *Suriname in Stroomlijnen.* Amsterdam: Wereld Bibliotheek, 1958.

De Ware Tijd (Paramaribo newspaper). 1957-1975.

WENGEN, G.D. VAN. *The Cultural Inheritance of the Javanese in Surinam.* Leiden: E.J. Brill, 1975.

—. *De Javanen in de Surinaamse Samenleving.* Leiden: n.p., 1972.

WEST, KATHARINE. "Stratification and Ethnicity in 'Plural' New States," *Race* 13, no. 4 (1972): 487-495.

De West (Paramaribo newspaper). 1936, 1937, 1942-1975.

De West-Indiër (Amsterdam monthly). 1952.

WESTERLOO, GERARD VAN. *Frimangron: Reportages uit een Zuid-Amerikaanse Republiek.* Amsterdam: Arbeiderspers, 1975.

WIJNTUIN, EMILE ET AL. *Weidmann: Priester, Politicus, Vakbondsleider.* Paramaribo: Leo Victor, 1975.

WILGUS, A. CURTIS, ed. *The Caribbean: British, Dutch, French and United States.* Gainesville: University of Florida Press, 1958.

WINTER, JOHANNA MARIA VAN. "De Openbare Mening in Nederland over de Afschaffing der Slavernij," *West-Indische Gids* 34 (1953): 61-90.

WIT, Y.B. "Is Paramaribo te Groot?" *Nieuwe West-Indische Gids* 45 (1966): 77-93.

WOLBERS, J. *Geschiedenis van Suriname*. Amsterdam: H. de Hoogh, 1861; reprinted by S. Emmering, 1970.

WOLF, S.W. *Suriname, Gisteren, Vandaag, Morgen*. Den Haag: Pressag, 1975.

WOODING, C.J. *Winti: Een Afro-Amerikaanse Godsdienst in Suriname: Een Cultureel-Historische Analyse van de Religieuze Verschijnselen in de Para*. Meppel: Krips Repro, 1972.

WOUTERS, A.E. *Suriname: Toeristische en Historische Informatie*. Amsterdam: Albert de Lange, 1972.

YOUNG, CRAWFORD. *The Politics of Cultural Pluralism*. Madison: The University of Wisconsin Press, 1976.

ZIELHUIS L. *Buitenlandse Migratie van Suriname in 1971*. Paramaribo: Ministerie van Sociale Zaken, March 1973.

— and GIRDHARI, D. *Migratie Uit Suriname*. Paramaribo: Ministerie van Sociale Zaken, December 1971.

— and —. *Migratie Uit Suriname*. Paramaribo: Ministerie van Sociale Zaken, June 1973. Two Volumes.

Zwart op Wit: Een Overzicht van het Beleid der Regering der Samenwerkende Partijen in Suriname. Paramaribo: D.A.G., 1963.

INDEX

Abaisa. See Kitty, Ronald
Aboikoni, Granman of the Saramaccaners: 148
abrasa: 47, 193, 209
Actiefront: 133-135, 137, 145, 145n, 146
Actiefront Dihaat: 146, 149
Actie Groep: 126-127, 129, 130-131, 133, 134, 137, 140-143, 145n, 146-154, 207; alliance with *Eenheidsfront* (See *Actiefront*); alliance with NPS, 145, 151-154, 177, 200, 204-205; internal divisions, 154, 156, 157; alliance with VHP and SRI, 157, 160, 205
Actie Groep '73: 168-170, 172
Adhin, J. H.: 75, 171, 191, 192, 196n
Afobaka Dam: 2, 92, 100-101, 117, 132, 137, 148, 157. See also Brokopondo Agreement
Agrarische Partij: 71, 75, 77, 96n
agriculture: 1-4, 15-16, 22-26, 30-32, 34, 51, 138, 164
Agt, A. van: 165, 167
Albina: 12, 114
Alcan Aluminium Limited: 138
Alcoa. See Aluminium Company of America, *Surinaamse Bauxiet Maatschappij*, and Suralco
Al Haq: 60n
Algemeen Handelsblad: 98
Allende, Salvador: 188
alumina: 3, 116-117, 137
aluminum: 2-3, 116-117, 136-137, 181
Aluminum Company of America: 2-3, 103, 116-117, 122, 137-138. See also *Surinaamse Bauxiet Maatschappij* and Suralco
Amerindians: 4-5, 6-7, 21-22, 25; tribes, 5; religions, 9, 11; languages, 11; residence, 13; in politics, 5, 125-126, 133, 174
anti-consociationalism: 205, 208
apartheid: 43, 54, 119, 157
Arichero, Eugene: 174
Arron, Henck: 162, 162n, 163, 175; as Minister-President, 175-178, 180-187, 189-195, 201, 209
Aruba: 186
Arya Dewaker: 10, 28
Arya Pratinidhi Sabha: 10, 60n, 64
Arya Samaj: 10, 28, 63-64, 75, 108
Asian Marriage Laws: 42, 45-47, 83-84, 105, 106, 106n
assimilation: as Dutch policy, 42-44, 46, 199; as Creole policy, 51-52, 54, 58, 139; as Hindustani policy, 106, 139
Australia: 64
autonomy question: 49-50, 54-59, 64-67, 82-83, 97-100, 199; linked to election reform, 58, 66, 72
AVROS: 136-137
Axwijk, S.: 95
Azimullah, Evert: 69n, 112, 164n, 177

'*baas in eigen huis*': 54, 65
balata-bleeding: 34, 39
Balata Compagnie Suriname: 39
Barbados: 21, 138
Barth, Frederik: 198n
bauxite: 2-3, 39, 50, 116, 137, 164, 181
Beatrix, Crown Princess: 196
Belgium: 202
Benjamins, Herman D.: 33-34
Bergen, H. M. C.: 95, 97n, 156
Berghe, Pierre van den: 197-198
Bevrijdings Front: 168
Bharat Oeday: 28
Billiton Bauxiet Maatschappij: 3, 132, 138, 164, 181
Billiton Mineworkers Union: 96n, 103
Biswamitre, C. R.: 45n, 46, 59, 75n, 108, 110, 114-115, 119, 121-122, 124, 152-153, 156n
Black Power Organization: 161, 163, 173, 208

Bosnegers Eenheids Partij (BEP): 169-172
Bos Verschuur, B. W. H.: 53, 55, 55n, 56-57, 66, 77n, 86-87, 104
Brahmans: 27, 28n, 73
Brazil: 1, 22, 178
British Guiana. See Guyana
British West Indies: 23
Brokopondo Agreement: 116-117, 119, 120, 128. See also Afobaka Dam
Brokopondo district: 12-14; electoral district of, 132, 134-135, 145, 147, 149-150, 159, 171-173
Brons, Governor Johannes C.: 57, 58, 66, 67, 70
Bruma, Eddy: 99n, 128, 144n, 170n, 171, 189; and *Wie Eegie Sanie*, 123-124; and PNR, 130, 131n, 144-146, 186, 200; labor activities of, 157-158, 161; and *Bevrijdings Front*, 168; and NPK, 168, 170, 186, 194n; in NPK Cabinet, 180-181
Bruynzeel: 164
budget crisis (1966-1969): 140-141, 151, 154, 156
Buiskool, J. A. E.: 62, 62n, 63, 68, 68n, 70, 84, 90; as Minister-President, 97, 97n, 98-100, 104
Burnham, Forbes: 102, 110
Buschkens, Willem: 17-18
Bush Negroes: 5-6, 25, 124-125, 148, 154; treaties with the Dutch, 6, 23, 194, 194n; tribes, 6; religions, 9, 11; residence, 6, 13; cultural institutions, 18; in politics, 132, 137, 148, 170-171, 174; chiefs (Granmans), 148, 171. See also Maroons

Cabinet crises (1950-1951): 86-92, 203; (1953), 104-106; (1954), 106-107; (1966), 144, 144n
Cabinet-formation: 203-205; (1949) 84; (1951) 97; (1955) 114, 114n; (1958) 122, 139-140; (1963) 135, 140; (1967) 151-153, 207; (interim 1969) 156; (1969) 160; (1973) 176
Cabinet government, established: 68, 82-83
cacao: 2, 34
Cairo, Willy: 163
Canada: 202n
Caribbean Free Trade Area: 138
Carmichael, Stokely: 161
caste (Hindu): 10, 19, 27, 63, 64, 108
Castro, Fidel: 128
Catholic People's Party (Netherlands): 69, 78
Catholics: 5, 8-10, 19, 33, 34, 120; subsidies, 42; and universal suffrage, 49, 57; in politics, 60-61, 75-78, 91, 115, 182-183, 200. See also *Progressieve Surinaamse Volkspartij* (PSV)
Census: (1950) 81; (1964) 5, 9, 11, 13-16, 143, 150-151; (1971) 5, 164-165, 179
Centrale 47 (C-47): 158, 164, 168
Centrale van Landsdienaren Organisaties (CLO): 164, 166, 168
chamars: 10, 27
Chamber of Commerce: 176
Chandieshaw, Persoewan: 154
Chile: 178, 188
Chinese: 7, 24-25, 67, 123; religions, 9; languages, 11; residence, 13; cultural institutions, 18; occupations, 24, 36, 51-52; in politics, 77, 80, 150, 169, 174, 180
Christelijke Sociale Partij (CSP): 70-71, 77-79, 95-96, 111n, 118
civil service jobs: 3, 39, 44-45, 51-52, 53, 57, 133, 140, 151-152, 164, 204-205, 207-208
civil war, fear of: 183
Clarke, Albertina: 180. See also Liesdek-Clarke, Albertina
CLO-Bulletin: 166
Colonial *Staten*. See *Staten* of Surinam
Comins, D. W. D.: 27, 30n, 31n
Coloreds: 6, 22, 32, 35-37, 74. See also Creoles, color-line conflict
color-line conflict among Creoles: 6, 22, 32-39, 40, 42, 47, 74, 76-77, 89, 91, 101-102, 107, 200, 207
Comité Christelijke Kerken: 183
Comité Steun aan het Eenheidsfront: 115
Commewijne district: 7, 12-14, 34; election district of, 72, 76, 79-81, 84, 93-96, 109, 111, 118-119, 132, 134-135, 143, 146-147, 149-150, 159, 169, 171-173, 194
Communism: 39, 40, 99n, 102, 131n, 132, 144, 162n, 170, 170n
Comvalius, R. B. W.: 77, 80, 95
'Concordia' (Masonic Lodge): 37, 58
concubinage: 17-18; among Creoles, 17-18, 34-35; among Hindustanis, 18-19; among Javanese, 29
Congres Partij: 85, 90, 96, 108, 109, 111n, 118
consociationalism: 147, 153, 157, 160, 202-208; defined, 202. See also *verbroedering*
Constitutions. See *Staatsregelingen* (1936-1950), *Staatsregeling* (1950-1975), and *Grondwet* (1975-)
contract labor: 2, 4, 7, 24-31, 34, 44n; debate over policy, 25; termination in India, 29
Coronie district: 12-14, 34; election district of, 72, 78-81, 94-96, 109, 111, 121, 134-135,

145-146, 149-150, 159, 172-173
Creole-Asian relations: 21, 25, 32, 67-68, 71, 71n, 105, 182-183, 199. See also Creole-Chinese, Creole-Hindustani, and Creole-Javanese relations
Creole-Chinese relations: 123
Creole-Hindustani relations: 16, 25, 31-32, 43, 52, 60, 71n, 75, 93, 94, 101, 105-108, 110, 120, 122-123, 144, 151, 160-163, 167, 170n, 174-177, 183, 186, 207. See also *verbroedering*
Creole-Javanse relations: 19, 93, 122-123
Creoles: 5, 8, 19, 32ff, 54, 72, 117; acculturation of, 17-18, 33-34, 38, 42, 199 (See also assimilation); consumption habits, 18, 122-123; family structure, 17-18, 39; history, 21-26, 32-42; internal divisions, 6, 47, 71, 78, 90n, 91, 94, 101, 103, 123, 148, 150, 163, 199, 204 (See also color-line conflict); labor emigrations, 34-35, 39; languages 11-12, 33-34 (See also *Sranantongo*. Dutch); literacy, 38; mixed parentage of, 6-7; occupations, 14-16, 35-36, 52, 107, 140; prostitution, 35; religions, 9-11; residence, 13-14, 34; self-image, 61, 123
crisis of brokerage: 142, 177, 204n
cross-cutting ties: 73, 101, 206
Cuba: 128
cultural borrowing: 17-20, 43
culture of poverty: 18
Curaçao. See Netherlands Antilles
Currie, Governor Archibald: 133

Dames Comité: 77
Dasiman, R.: 190
Defaris, C.: 99n
Demerara. See Guyana
Democratische Eenheids Partij (DEP): 104-106
Democratische Unie Suriname (DUS): 169, 172
Demokratische Volksfront (DVF): 169-170, 172, 200
Depression, effects of: 39
Derby, F.: 192n
Despres, Leo A.: 198n
Dew, Anke: 19
Dew, Edward: 142n, 178n, 203n, 204n
Dobru. See Ravales, Robin
Doedel, Louis: 39
Doelman, Ming: 59
Doelwijt, Thea: 175
Doglas: 7, 169, 176
douane strikes: (1970) 163; (1973) 165-167
Drenthe, Eugene: 168-169
Drielsma, J. A.: 90, 97
Dundas, R.: 146n
Dutch (language): 11, 17-19, 31, 42-43; use in elections, 110, 147-148
Dutch (people): 7, 32, 36, 38, 123, 150; peasant immigrants, 24; school teachers, 155. See also Netherlands
Dutch East Indies. See Indonesia
Dutch Reformed Church: 37, 40
'Dutchification': 33, 42-44, 124

Education: 17, 83-84, 86-87, 163; for Asians, 31, 42, 51-52; for Creoles, 33-34, 36, 38
'*Eendracht maakt Macht*': 53n
Eenheidsfront: 107-122, 129n, 133, 139, 204, 207
election campaigns: (1905) 36; (1947) 66; (1949) 77-78; (1950) 91; (1951) 95; (1955) 109-110; (1958) 120; (1963) 133; (1967) 143-148; (1969) 156; (1973) 168-171
election system: 58, 63, 66, 68, 70-73, 74, 91-93, 93n, 108-110, 113, 131-135, 139, 143-145, 169, 190-195, 199-200, 207
elections: 53; (1930) 75n; (1943) 56; (1946) 58; (1947) 66; (1948) 70; (1949) 74-82, 173; (1950) 90-91, 173; (1951) 93-97; (1953) 104-106; (1954) 107; (1955) 103, 107-111, 207; (1956) 112-113, 207; (1958) 118-122, 173; (1963) 133-135; (1967) 148-151; (1969) 156-160; (1973) 168-176
Eliazer, L.: 88, 96n
Emanuels, S. D.: as Minister-President, 122, 124-125, 128, 130, 139, 140n
emigration to the Netherlands: 158, 164-165, 179-180, 183; 188, 201; Creole, 158, 165, 167, 179, 179n; Hindustani, 179, 179n, 201; Javanese, 179n, 183, 190; motivations for, 164, 179; policy towards, 165, 167, 179, 188; reception in the Netherlands, 165
employment: 3, 14-16, 116
England: 21, 23, 26, 29, 31, 43, 64-65
Enloe, Cynthia: 189n, 199, 206-207
Ensberg, E. M. L: 120
Essed, Frank: 120, 124, 131-132, 136, 146, 158, 164
ethnic fragmentation: 6, 8-20, 71, 73, 88-89, 101, 123, 142, 150, 163, 200, 203, 207. See also color-line conflict, Creole, Hindustani, and Javanese internal divisions
European cultural institutions: 17-18, 42. See also assimilation

European Economic Community (Common Market): 136-137
Evangelische Broeder Gemeenschap (EBG): 10, 33-34, 55, 70, 78, 91, 120, 150
ex-slaves: 2, 6, 21, 24-25, 34-35
extended family: 4, 7, 18, 36, 39

Faverij, A. I.: 114n
Ferrier, J. H. E.: as Minister-President, 114, 118; as Governor, 156, 160, 167, 182, 186; as President, 196
FEHOMA: 155
Findlay, David: 69, 77, 77n, 85-87, 90, 92, 95, 97, 97n, 99, 103-107, 107n, 114-116, 118-122, 134, 150, 151-152, 156, 160, 203
fishing: 15-16, 114-115
Foetoeboi: 69
foreign affairs: 130, 136, 181
foreign investment: 114-117, 124n, 136-138, 148, 164, 181, 191, 193-195. See also Alcoa, Billiton, Schweig, Bruinzeel, ORMET, Reynolds, Alcan, United Fruit, etc.
forestry: 2-3, 5-6, 164
Freeland League for Jeweish Territorial Colonization: 67
French Guiana: 1, 114, 126; disputed borders with, 1n, 180, 189
Fuente, Emile de la: 49, 77n, 89n, 90, 110, 120
Furnivall, J. S.: 23

Gadden, J.: 194
Gandhi, Mahatma: 31, 186
Gastmann, A. L.: 100n
Genderen, Olton van: 162n, 180
general strike (1973): 165-169
Geological Mining Service: 155, 167
Germans: 24
Germany: 47, 50, 53-54, 136-137, 148
Gessel, E. A.: 99n, 167, 178
gold mining: 2, 34
Goslar: 50, 50n
Governor of Surinam: 150, 196; powers of, 45-47, 66, 68, 82-83, 91, 167, 182; Surinamer as, 131, 133
Great Britain. See England
Grondwet (1975-): 180-184, 189-190, 191-196
gross domestic product: 2, 4
Guatemala: 116
Guda, Leonard H.: 120
Guyana: 1, 31n, 102, 108, 110, 114, 131, 138, 148, 191n; disputed borders with, 1n, 180, 189

Hagen, J.: 53, 53n
Hall of Records, destruction of (1975): 184
Hardjo, Salikin M.: 64, 68n
Heidweiller, Henricus F.: 120
Helman, Albert. See Lichtveld, Lou
Helsdingen, W. H. van: 59
Herrenberg, Henk: 201n
Herrnhutters. See *Evangelische Broeder Gemeenschap*
Hindorie, George: 186-188, 194, 194n, 195
Hindostaanse Progressieve Partij (HPP): 168-172, 176, 176n
Hindostans-Javaanse Centrale Raad: 59-60, 63
Hindostans-Javaanse Politieke Partij (H-JPP): 63-64, 66, 68-69, 71, 75, 199-200
Hindus: 8-10, 19, 27, 42, 89, 94, 108-109, 154; weddings, 19, 42, 45-47; subsidies, 42, 46, 89; rivalry with Mohammedans, 88, 92, 94, 101, 106, 108, 203; internal divisions, 10, 28, 63-64, 75, 108
Hindustani-Creole relations. See Creole Hindustani relations
Hindustani-Javanese relations: 93
Hindustanis: 6-8, 16, 26-32, 67, 72; acculturation, 18-19, 42 (See also assimilation); businesses, 52; cultural institutions, 18-19; drive for education, 31, 51, 199; history, 26-28, 30-32, 41, 43-47, 51; internal divisions, 74-75, 88, 94, 101, 103, 110, 112, 126-127, 130-131, 150, 203-204; land hunger, 31; languages, 11-12 (See also *Sarnami Hindostans*); occupations, 7, 14-16, 31, 51-52, 107, 140, 199; organizations, 28, 52; political representation, 45-46, 57; religions, 9-10 (See also Hindus, Mohammedans); residence, 13-14, 51-52, 144
Hirasing, Harry: 145n, 146, 168, 168n
Hof van Justitie: 62
Hohenlohe, Princess Alexandra von: 148
hokjespolitiek: 157
Holi Phagwa: 154n, 160, 183
Hoost, E.: 192, 194
Hotel Lashley, destruction of (1975): 184
Huender, Governor Willem: 70-73, 84
Husain Ali, I.: 91, 96

Idenburg, A. W. F.: 43
Idul Fitr: 154n, 160
Immigration Fund (1878): 26
Independence: 73, 98-99, 99n, 100, 104, 124, 128-132, 152, 158, 162-163, 167, 170, 174-175, 177-196, 201, 204-205, 207-209

India: 26-27, 28n, 29, 31, 94, 127, 202n
Indonesia: 22, 24, 28-30, 36-38, 42-45, 49, 64-65, 76, 83, 89, 93, 141
Interim Orders (1950): 82-84, 86
intermarriage, racial: 6-7, 43, 52, 199
intermarriage, religious: 10, 199
International Bauxite Producers Association: 181
Internationale Werkloze Unie: 77
Islam. See Mohammedans
Ismael, Joseph: 30n

Jagan, Cheddi: 99, 102, 108, 110
Jamaludin, S. M.: 84, 92, 94-95, 96n, 97, 119
Jankie, R. L.: 153
Japan: 64
Jarikaba banana plantation: 157
Java. See Indonesia
Javanese: 6-8, 28-32, 72; acculturation, 18-20, 76; adjustment difficulties, 29-30, 44; cultural institutions, 10-11, 18-20, 30; desire for emigration, 41, 76, 89, 93; family structure, 19, 29; history, 28-32, 41, 44-47, 51; holders of balance of power, 101, 106, 113; internal divisions, 10-11, 19-20, 64, 76, 141, 150, 204; languages, 11-12, 42; manipulation by others, 19, 93; medical care, 29; occupations, 7, 14-16, 51-52, 140; organizations, 30n, 52, 59-64, 76; political representation, 45-46, 93; prostitution, 29, 51; religions, 9-11; residence, 13-14, 51; sex ratio among immigrants, 29
Javanese-Creole relations. See Creole-Javanese relations
Javanese-Hindustani relations. See Hindustani-Javanese relations
Jews: 8, 22-23, 32, 35, 37-38, 57; religious subsidies, 42; proposal for post-War immigration, 67
joint ventures: 116-117, 164
Jong, Andries de: 4
Jongbaw, C. H. H.: 77, 97n
journalism. See press
Juglall, W. E.: 63, 90-91, 95, 97
Juliana: as Crown Princess, 56, 56n; as Queen, 70, 100, 114, 137

Kanhai, K.: 109, 113, 139
Karagjitsing, K.: 112-113
Karamat Ali, A. G.: 147, 169, 176
Karamat Ali, Asgar: 59, 59n, 68n, 75-76, 85, 89
Karamat Ali, M. Ashruf: 76, 84, 97n, 104, 108-109, 113, 114n, 115, 119, 121n, 204
Karg, Cyriel: 161
Kaulesar Sukul, J. P.: 31, 68, 68n, 69
Kaum Tani Persatuan Indonesia (KTPI): 76, 79, 82-85, 88-91, 93-96, 104, 106, 108-109, 111, 113, 118-121, 129, 133-135, 145, 145n, 146, 149-150, 153n, 200, 203-204; internal divisions, 113, 138, 141, 145, 207; in Cabinet, 113, 136, 138, 140n, 204; in PNP-bloc, 157-160, 168; in NPK, 168-173, 208
Keerveld, Humphrey: 162n
Kerngroep: 134n
Kernkamp, W. J. A.: 100
Kielstra, Governor Johannes C.: 32, 42-47, 49, 51-57, 74, 83, 89
Kieskring II. See Suriname district
kiesverenigingen: 53, 53n
Killinger, Frans: 38-39, 67
kinderbijslag: 78
Kingdom Commission (1974): 179-180, 189
Kitty, Ronald ('Abaisa'): 167-168, 209
Klaasesz, Governor Jan: 90-92
Klerk, C. J. M. de: 26-28, 30n
Kletter, G.: 104-106
Kloos, Peter: 4-5
Koenders, J. G. A.: 69, 69n
Kolader, P. A. R.: 95, 114n
Kom, Anton de: 35, 39-42, 44, 76
Koningsverger, J. C.: 43
Kota Gede: 76
Kraan, William: 56, 58, 77
Krikomaka: 161, 163, 173, 208
Kross, Rudi F.: 201n
Kruijer, G. J.: 4, 19, 30n, 51, 201n
Kuiperback, J. G.: 114n

Labor unions: 57, 71, 96n, 103-104, 155, 158, 160-161, 163-168; and constitutional right to strike, 192, 194-195
Lachmon, Jagernath: 84, 88, 89n, 97n, 99-100, 162-163; background, 31, 60, 139; and H-JPP, 63, 69, 69n; and VHP, 75, 85, 92-94, 96n, 109n, 158, 160, 169, 203; and Pengel, 102-108, 111-113, 115, 117-119, 127-128, 135-136, 139-140, 141, 143, 144n, 147, 152-154; and NPK, 170, 170n, 176-179, 182-184, 186-196, 201, 209
Lalla Rookh: 26
Lamur, Humphrey: 8
land policy: 31-32, 44
Lauriers, L. A.: 77n
Lebanese: 7, 52, 150
Lee Kon Fong, Charles: 174, 180, 185-186,

190
Lenoir, J. D.: 194n
Lewis, Oscar: 18
Lichtveld, Lou: 21, 61, 61n, 66, 84, 86-92, 100, 203
Lichtveld, Ursy: 33n
Lier, Rudolf van: 33, 35-38, 40-43, 50-51, 74, 91
Liesdek-Clarke, Albertina: 185-186, 189, 195
Lieuw Kie Song, A. P.: 96n
Lijphart, Arend: 202, 202n, 203n, 205
Lim A Po, F. H. R.: 66, 68n, 77, 79n, 80, 85-87, 92, 95, 97, 97n, 99n, 104-105, 139
Lim A Po, Walter: 118, 120
Linggadjati Agreement (1946): 65
Lobato, M. I.: 114n
Lutheran Church: 37

MacMay, A. J.: 90n, 95
Makka: 90
Malaysia: 202
manumission: 22
Marienburg sugar plantation: 7, 28, 30n, 76, 157, 167
marginal men: 52
Maroons: 22-23. See also Bush Negroes
Marowijne district: 12, 14; by-election (1954), 107; divided in two electoral districts (1963), 132; general elections, 72, 79-81, 94-96, 107, 109, 111, 133-135, 145-147, 149-150, 171-173
marriage. See Hindus, Mohammedans, intermarriage, concubinage, and individual ethnic group headings under family structure
Marxist-Leninist Center: 166
Max Havelaar (by Multatuli): 37
May, Arhtur: 106; as Minister-President, 156
Mazrui, Ali: 197, 206
'Mighty Sparrow': 148
Miranda, J. A. de: 68n, 85, 89
Miranda, Julius Cesar de: as Minister-President, 84, 86, 88, 92, 139, 203
Miranda, V. M. de: 136
miscegenation: 6-7, 19, 22, 176
Mitrasing, F. E. M.: 58, 62, 89, 89n, 95, 97, 100, 109
Moengo: 2, 12, 39, 57n, 80, 103, 167
Moeslim Partij (MP): 59, 68, 71, 75, 85, 199-200
Mohamed Radja, H. W.: 87, 92, 94-95, 97, 111n, 119, 176
Mohammedans: 8-11, 19, 30, 42, 73, 75, 94, 101, 154; conflict with Hindus, 88, 92, 94, 101, 106, 108, 113, 150, 203; internal divisions, 10-11, 119, 141, 147-148, 150; *Moeslim Partij*, 59; subsidies, 42, 46, 89; weddings, 19, 42, 45-47
Moravian Brethren. See *Evangelische Broeder Gemeenschap*
Moslems, See Mohammedans
Multatuli (E. Douwes Dekker): 37
Multi-ethnic alliances: 200. See also consociationalism, verbroedering
Mungra, Alwin: 144n, 170n
Mungra, J. S.: 64, 94, 99-100, 109n, 117, 117n
Muslims. See Mohammedans

Napoleonic Wars: 24, 43
Nationaal Socialistische Beweging (NSB): 55
Nationale Comité Suriname: 99
Nationale Partij Kombinatie (NPK): 168-174, 176, 176n, 177-180, 182, 184-192, 196n, 205, 208; fragmentation, 175, 180-181, 183, 185-186
Nationale Partij Suriname (NPS): 61-64, 66-69, 74-80, 81n, 82-91, 93-99, 115-122, 133-135, 138-139, 147-150, 158-162, 162n, 164-165, 200, 205, 207; and *Unie Suriname*, 62-63; and universal suffrage, 63, 66, 70-73; internal government of, 77, 85-86, 89, 147, 162, 180; divisions within, 76-77, 85-89, 97, 99-101, 103-109, 111, 162n, 162-163, 175, 180-181, 183, 185-186, 203, 207, 208; *verbroedering* with VHP, 102-103, 105-113, 122, 127, 131, 135-136, 139, 141, 204; and PSV, 117-122, 127, 132-133; and nationalism, 123-132; and election reforms (1963) 131-133, (1966) 143-145; end of *verbroedering*, 142-145, 147-148, 151-153, 162-163, 204, 207-208; and AG, 153, 177; effort to become multi-racial, 147, 157, 160, 173-174; and Independence, 162, 167, 177-194; in NPK, 168, 173-174, 180-181, 208
National Hospital: 87-88
nationalism: in Surinam, 66-67, 73, 104, 124-132, 207; among students in the Netherlands, 98-99, 99n, 102, 124. See also Independence
Nationalistische Beweging Suriname (NBS): 124-125, 128-129, 130, 141, 207
nationality issues: 93, 98, 165, 167, 179-180, 196, 196n; double nationality demand, 179-180, 188-189
National People's Party: 146n
Nawa Yuga Oeday: 28

Nazism. See *Nationaal Socialistische Beweging*
Nederlandse Handel Maatschappij: 28
Neger-Engels. See *Sranantongo*
Neger Politieke Partij (NPP): 69, 69n, 70-71, 77-79
Negroes, See Creoles, Bush Negroes
nengre. See *volkscreolen*
Netherlands: 6, 17, 36-38, 47, 49, 50, 53-57, 68, 70-71, 91-93, 204; colonial rule, 22ff; cultural policy, 33-34, 42-47, 51, 199; government-in-exile, 53, 56; decolonization, 59-60, 64-66, 68-70, 82-84, 93, 97-101; armed forces. 91. 97. 100; foreign aid, 92, 100-101, 110, 114, 122, 140-141, 154, 181, 185, 189, 201, 205; threat to curtail Surinamese immigration, 165, 167; labor support to 1973 general strike, 166; and Independence of Surinam, 177-178, 178n, 181, 183-190
Netherlands Antilles: 34, 36, 39, 49, 68, 70, 77, 82, 86, 93, 98, 100, 114, 167, 179
newspapers. See press
Nickerie (city). See Nieuw Nickerie
Nickerie district: 12-14, 72, 113, 145, 194; general elections, 78-81, 95-97, 109, 111, 133-135, 143, 146-150, 159, 171-173
Nickerie Eenheids Partij (NEP): 109, 111n, 113
Nickerie Onafhankelijke Partij (NOP): 118, 120-121, 129-131, 133-134, 141, 145
Nieuw Amsterdam (Commewijne): 57n, 84, 93
Nieuw Nickerie: 12, 19, 57n, 114, 120, 131, 145n, 167
Nieuws, Het: 78
Nooitmeer, Rufus: 189-190
Nordlinger, Eric A.: 202n

Oedayrajsing Varma, R. D.: 109n, 118
Olin-Mathieson. See ORMET
Ommeren, H. C. van: 77, 85-91, 95, 203
Ommeren, H. van: 62, 77
Onverdacht: 3, 80
Onze Gids: 54
Onze Tijd: 126
Ooft, C. D.: 38, 61, 127, 144, 184
Oranje Hindoe Groep: 60
Oranje Politieke Partij: 60n
ORMET: 136, 138, 140n, 144n, 155, 204
Ormskirk, Fred: 63, 76-77, 85
'outbidding': 103, 112, 123, 125, 135, 139, 141-142, 144-145, 160, 206-208; defined, 206
Overbeek, Robert: 137n
Overzeese Gas en Electriciteits Maatschappij (OGEM): 164

Pad van Wanika: 132, 176
Pakistan: 94
Pan-American Union: 83, 86
Panday, R. M. N.: 24, 32
Pandits: 28n, 57n, 112
Para district: 12, 14, 34, 72, 88, 128, 132, 143; general elections, 78-81, 94-96, 109, 111, 134-135, 146, 149-150, 159, 172-173
Paramaribo (city): 12, 18, 22, 24, 34-35, 37, 39-41, 49, 50-52, 57n, 65, 67, 76-77, 90, 107, 110, 114, 165-168, 182
Paramaribo district: 12-14, 72, 118, 143; by-elections, 90-91, 104, 107; general elections, 77-81, 94-96, 109, 111, 133-135, 146, 149-150, 159, 169, 172-173
Paranam: 3, 12, 50, 80, 103, 117, 132, 167
Paranam Mineworkers Union: 96n, 103, 157
Parliament of Surinam: 182, 196. See also *Staten*
Parliament of the Netherlands: 25, 26, 43, 45-47, 68, 70, 82-84, 98; and Surinam's Independence, 185-190
Partij Suriname (PS): 104-106, 108-109
Partij van de Nationalistische Republiek (PNR): 130-134, 137,140-141, 144, 146, 149-150, 157-159, 161, 162n, 164-165, 194, 200, 207; in NPK, 168, 168n, 170, 173-175, 180-181, 186-187, 192, 201, 208
Pengel, Johan Adolf: 97n, 99n, 111, 122, 124n, 127, 132, 134-135, 148, 150, 177, 186, 205, 207; background, 76-77, 138-139; and NPS, 76, 80, 86-87, 120-124, 131, 147, 157-158; and David Findlay, 88, 90-92, 95, 97, 99, 103-107, 107n, 109, 151-152, 203; and Jagernath Lachmon, 89, 102-108, 111-113, 115, 117-119, 128, 135-140, 142-143, 144n, 147, 152-153; fall (1969), 155-156; death (1970), 162
Peoples Progressive Party (Guyana): 102-103, 110
Pergerakan Bangsa Indonesia Suriname (PBIS): 30n, 64, 68-69, 75-76, 79-80, 81n, 82, 84, 90
Persatuan Indonesia: 64, 76. See also *Kaum Tani Persatuan Indonesia*
Philips, Paul A. M. van: 120
plantation system: 2, 4, 6, 22-32, 34-35, 37, 39, 44, 48, 51, 64
Poetoe, Dewnarian: 120, 129, 130
Police: performance in 1973 general strike, 166; racial balance in, 166, 166n, strike

(1970), 163
political parties: 50, 59ff. See also individual parties by name
political socialization: 42, 201. See also 'Dutchification'
Ponit, J. D.: 60, 60n
population: 4ff, 34; growth rate, 5, 8, 154
Pos, R. H.: 59, 68n, 84, 97n
Prade, Hans: 146n, 163, 170
President of Surinam: 182, 191, 193
press: 35, 37, 38-41, 53-54, 56, 62, 65, 78, 110, 161-163, 165-166, 176, 182-183. See also individual papers by name
proportional representation (PR): 60, 63, 70-71, 75, 91, 119, 130-133, 132n, 143-146, 190, 194-195
Progressieve BosNeger Partij (PBP): 157, 170, 170n, 194n
Progressieve Nationale Partij (PNP): 142, 146, 148-150, 153-154, 158, 162-164, 169-170, 170n, 171-172, 200, 207; internal divisions, 163, 205; PNP-bloc (1969), 157, 205, 208
Progressieve Surinaamse Volkspartij (PSV): 60-62, 68, 68n, 69-71, 73, 77-80, 82, 85, 90, 95, 105, 108-109, 114-116, 128, 131-137, 140n, 144-146, 149, 200; alliance with NPS and VHP, 118-122, 127, 132-133, 136, 143, 204; divisions within, 115-116, 118; in PNP-bloc, 157, 160, 168; in NPK, 168, 173, 187, 208
Progressieve Werknemers Organisatie (PWO): 57, 164
Pronk, J.: 184n
prostitution: 29, 35, 51
Protestants: 8-10, 19, 33-34, 37; in politics, 49, 70-71, 75-78, 91, 115, 182-183, 200; subsidies, 42
public works: 39, 106-107, 166, 176
Puerto Rico: 115, 158

Rabushka, Alvin: 191n, 201-202, 206
race relations: in colonial period, 22, 32-42. See also color-line conflict
Radhakishun, H.: 109n, 116n, 118, 165-166, 170
Rae, Douglas: 73
Rakim, G.: 141, 145, 150, 153n
Ramayana: 176
Rambaran Mishre, S.: 59, 92
Ramdjan, Islam: 113, 119, 147, 174
Ramdjan, R.: 134n
Ramlakhan, Maurits: 103n
Ravales, Robin (Dobru): 1, 4n, 124, 128, 209
Redmond, Sophie Monkou: 90-91
religion: 8ff. See also Catholics, Protestants, Hindus, Mohammedans, *Winti*
religious holidays: 42, 154, 154n, 160-161, 183
religious rivalry: 10-11, 28, 30, 61-64, 70, 73, 75-76, 78, 88, 92, 94, 106, 108, 183, 200, 203
Rens, Just: 47n, 95, 105-106, 106n, 108, 111, 120, 132, 136, 144, 144n, 146, 170
Rens, L. L. E.: 114n, 115n
Renselaar, H. C. van: 122-123, 141
Reynolds Metals Company: 164. See also ORMET
Rhodesia: 178
rice: 2, 7, 39, 51, 94, 113, 115
riots: (1891) 37-38; (1931) 50; (1933) 41-42; (1955) 110; (1967) 149-150; (1970) 163; (1973) 165-168; (1975) 184
Roman Catholic Church. See Catholics
Roosevelt, Franklin Delano: 50
Rosevelt, J. F. A. Cateau van: 26
Roundtable Conferences: first (1948), 68-70, 82, 85; second (1952), 97-99, 104, 107n, (1954) 100, 107; third (1961), 129-130, 204
Rusland, Harold: 164
Rutgers, Governor A. A.: 39-40, 43
Ryan, Selwyn: 206

Salimin, A.: 63
Sanatan Dharm: 10, 28, 60n, 63-64, 75, 92, 108, 112
Sanches, Simon: 67-68
Sandvliet, C. S. H.: 121n
Sang A Jang, A.: 114, 122
Saramacca district: 12-14, 34, 67, 72, 108-109, 194; by-election (1956), 112-114, 152; general elections, 79-81, 95-96, 108-109, 111, 146-147, 149-150, 172-173
Sardjoe, R.: 192n, 194n
Sarekat Rakjat Indonesia (SRI): 141, 143, 146, 149-151, 153n, 205, 207; in VHP-bloc, 158-160, 169, 172-173
Sariman, J.: 170n
Sarnami Hindostans: 11-12, 78, 119, 129, 147, 169-170
Sartori, Giovanni: 206n
Savornin Lohman, Governor M. A. de: 37, 191
Schneiders-Howard, G. R.: 53n, 77, 80
school teachers strikes: (1969) 155; (1970) 163-164
Schroeff, G. J. C. van der: 62, 68n, 77n, 84-87, 93, 95, 103-104, 115

Schweig, E. S.: 114-115, 119-120, 124, 129
Second World War: 32, 47, 50-56, 199
Sedney, Jules: 124, 124n, 136, 146, 146, 155; as Minister-President, 160-166, 173
Seljee, H.: 111n
settlement pattern: 12ff, 202
Sewberath Misser, H. F.: 109n, 112-113
Shepsle, Kenneth A.: 191n, 201-202, 206
shifting alliances: 73, 101-102
Shriemisier, H.: 75, 92, 97n, 108, 139
Simons, R. D.: 33
Sitalsing, L. B.: 110, 111n, 113
slave revolts: 22-23
slavery: 4-6, 21-25, 37; Abolition, 24-25, 34-35, 44, 124-125
Smit, A. L. R.: 54, 57n, 77, 80, 97, 97n, 99n, 106-107, 107n
Smit, W. G. H. C. J.: 114n
Smith, M. G.: 17, 198n
'*Sociaal Democratische Vrouwen Bond*': 53n
Social Democratic Unity Party: 146n
Sociografisch Instituut (University of Amsterdam): 12
Soedardjo, S.: 121
Soemita, Iding: 76, 89, 92-93, 106, 109, 113, 115, 118-119, 129-130, 141
Sommelsdijk, Governor Cornelius van Aerssen van: 23n
Somohardjo, Salim: 174, 180, 183, 185, 188, 190
Spain: 188
Speckmann, J. D.: 10, 18-19, 27, 51, 122-123, 141
Sranantongo: 11-12, 18, 19, 31, 33, 43, 49, 69, 69n, 78, 110, 123-128; banned, 33-34; use in elections, 110, 170
Staatsregeling of Surinam (1950-1975): 82-83, 91n; termination of, 192-195
Staatsregelingen of Surinam (1936-1950): 45-47, 53, 66, 68, 82-83
State Supervision Period (after slavery): 24-25, 34
Staten of Surinam: 25-26, 32, 36-37, 49, 57, 66-68, 91-92, 101, 103-106, 108-109, 132-133, 135, 139-140, 142, 150-151, 167, 203; and Governor Kielstra, 44-47, 53-56; structural changes, 45; and autonomy question, 59-60, 65-66, 68-73, 97-101; and election changes, 71-73; and Interim Orders, 82-84; and Lichtveld-van Ommeren crisis, 87-90, 203; and Statute, 99-100; and Schweig question, 114-115; and Brokopondo Agreement, 116-117, 128-129; and shield, flag, and anthem bills, 126-128; election reform (1963), 132-133; enlargement of, 132-133; electoral reform (1966), 145; 1968 budget debates, 154-155; ethnic polarization in, 174-176; Independence question, 177-178, 180, 185-188, 190-196
Statute of the Kingdom of the Netherlands: 66, 83n, 97-100, 107, 114, 124, 127-128, 130, 165, 167, 189, 207; repeal of, 177, 182, 182n, 189, 196
Stedman, John: 23
suffrage issue: 53, 57-63, 66
suffrage requirements: 32-33, 37, 49, 53, 57
sugar: 2, 7, 21-26, 64. See also plantation system and agriculture
Sukarno, Achmed: 64-65
Suparlan, Parsudi: 19-20, 205
Suralco: 117, 128, 132, 136-137, 157, 181
Surinaamsche Arbeiders en Werkers Organisatie: 40
Surinaamsche Bauxiet Maatschappij: 2n, 3, 39, 50, 67, 116-117. See also Aluminum Company of America, Suralco
Surinaamsche Immigranten Vereeniging: 28, 45
Surinaamsche Islamietische Vereeniging: 28
'*Surinaamsche Kiesvereniging*': 53n
Surinaamse Democratische Partij (SDP): 109, 114, 134, 144-146, 148-153, 156n, 169
Surinaamse Hindoe Partij (SHP): 63-64, 68-69, 71, 75, 94
Surinaamse Landbouwers Organisatie (SLO): 76
Surinaamse Volks Partij (SVP): 118
Surinaamse Vrouwen Front: 169, 172
Surinaamse Werknemers 'Moederbond': 103, 164
Surinam Armed Forces: 50, 137; composition under new Constitution (*Grondwet*), 182, 189, 191, 193, 195-196
Surinam coat of arms: 99, 124-126, 207
Surinam flag: (1959), 99, 124-128, 207; (1975), 191, 196, 196n
Surinam national anthem: 99, 124-128, 207
Surinam national holiday: 99, 124-125, 129
Surinam-American Industries Limited (SAIL): 124n. See also Schweig, E. S.
Suriname district: 12-14, 143-144; general elections, 72, 76, 79-81, 95-96, 108-109, 111, 133-135, 146, 149-150, 169, 172-173
Suriname: 53-54, 78, 86, 136, 154
Suriname Aluminum Company. See Suralco
Suriname, De: 53-54, 54n, 57, 58, 78, 86, 112

Surland banana plantation: 164
Switzerland: 202

Telegraaf, De: 38
Tendeloo, C.: 68n
ticket-balancing: 168-169
Tilburg, Governor J. van: 118, 131-132
Torarica Project: 137, 148, 152, 205
Trefosa. See Ziel, Henny de
Trinidad: 31n, 138, 161, 202, 206
25 Juni: 129n

Uganda: 170n
unemployment: 3-4, 39, 44n, 148, 164
Unie Suriname: 53-54, 56-59, 61-64, 73, 75n, 90, 114, 149, 200; ties to NPS, 62-63, 70
United Fruit Company: 116, 164
United Hindustani Party. See *Verenigde Hindostaanse Partij* (VHP)
United Nations: 83, 91, 100, 100n, 114, 193
United States: 3, 50-51, 55-56, 136
Universal Declaration of the Rights of Man: 188
universal suffrage: 49, 57-61, 68-71, 73, 93-94, 101-102, 139, 199-200
Untouchables: 10, 27
urbanization: 32, 34, 44, 51-52, 144
Uyl, Joop den: 178, 183-185, 187-189, 196

Vatan Hitkari Partij: 147. See also *Verenigde Hindostaanse Partij*
Veer, E. J. van de: 114n
Venezuela: 181
verbroedering: 102, 105-106, 108-113, 123, 127-129, 131, 133, 135-136, 139, 141, 147-148, 152, 160, 175, 204
Verenigde Hindoe Partij: 94-97, 99, 109. See also *Verenigde Hindostaanse Partij*
Verenigde Hindostaanse Partij (VHP): 31, 60, 75-80, 82-85, 90, 93, 116-122, 133-135, 149-151, 175, 200; internal government, 106, 154; divisions in, 87-92, 94, 101, 112, 117-118, 126-127, 186-188, 207-208; *verbroedering* with NPS, 102-103, 105-113, 116, 127, 131, 135-136, 139, 141, 204; in Cabinet, 122, 135, 160, 204; and *Actie Groep*, 126-127, 129-131, 141, 153-154; end to *verbroedering*, 142-145, 147-148, 151-153, 162-163, 204, 207-208; alliance with SRI, 143, 157; VHP-bloc, 157-160, 172-173, 176, 205, 208; alliance with PNP-bloc, 160-168, 179; and Independence, 129-131, 162, 169-170, 177-178, 180-194, 196, 196n, 204
Verenigde Indiaanse Partij (VIP): 133, 134n
Verenigde Volkspartij: 169, 172
verzuiling: 200
Vice-President of Surinam: 191, 193, 195
Volkscrediet Bank: 117, 156
volkscreolen: 33-35, 37-38, 42, 69-70, 80, 90n, 101-102, 105, 107, 139; 'latent animosity' of, 35, 38, 40-42, 74, 91, 139
Volkskrant, De: 176
Volksstem, De: 90, 103, 103n, 105
Vondeling, A.: 187
Voorhoeve, Jan: 33n
Vooruitstrevende Hervormings Partij: 168. See also *Verenigde Hindostaanse Partij*
Vooruitstrevende Moslims Partij: 169, 172
voter turnout: (1949) 75; (1951) 95; (1969) 173; (1973) 173
voting behavior: 81-82. See also elections
voting irregularities, allegations of: 149-150, 156, 171
Vreede, S. H. R.: 174
Vries, H. J. de: 117
Vries, H. L. de: 62, 97n; as Governor, 150-151, 153-154
Vries, I. de: 106
Vriesde, E.: 180
Vrije Stem: 165n, 183

Waal Malefijt, Annemarie de: 29
Wageningen rice plantation: 157-158
Walle, J. van de: 38, 44n, 51n, 52n, 54n, 56n, 59n
Ware Tijd, De: 121, 126, 148, 150, 162, 165n, 178-180, 183, 183n, 193
Waterloo sugar plantation: 157
Weidmann, Leonardus Josephus: 57, 60-61, 70-72, 77-78, 115, 200
welfare: 4, 39, 133, 208
Welter, C. J. I. M.: 43-47
Wengen, G. D. van: 19-20, 51
West, De: 38-39, 53-54, 56, 58, 60n, 61, 61n, 67, 69, 75n, 77-78, 84-86, 88, 90, 93-94, 99, 103-105, 110, 112, 125-126, 143, 150, 152, 154, 160, 183
Westindiër, De: 99n
West Indies Federation: 138
West Surinam: bauxite development, 136, 164; separate state proposed, 178
Wie Eegie Sanie: 123-125
Wijngaarde, Johan: 54n, 86
Wijngaarde, Purcy: 62, 65, 74, 77n, 84, 86-87, 136
Wijntuin, Emile: 187, 191, 193

Wij Slaven van Suriname (by Anton de Kom): 40
Wilhelmina, Queen: 49, 53-56, 60, 70, 127
Williams, Eric: 23, 138
Winti: 9, 11, 18-19
Wix, A. R.: 111n
Wolbers, J.: 21-22, 25
women, political role of: 40, 53n, 169
Wong, O.: 77n, 80, 92
Wongso, H.: 113

Young, Crawford: 198-199, 202n, 206-207

Zalmijn, W.: 180
Zanderij (airfield): 2, 50
Ziel, Henny de (Trefosa): 127n